Islamic Marketing and Branding

Islamic Marketing and Branding: Theory and Practice provides a concise mix of theory, primary research findings and practice that will engender confidence in both students and practitioners alike by means of the case study included in each chapter.

Through three main parts (Branding and Corporate Marketing; Religion, Consumption and Culture; and Strategic Global Orientation), this book provides readers, from areas across the spectrum covering marketing, organisational studies, psychology, sociology and communication and strategy, with theoretical and managerial perspectives on Islamic marketing and branding. In particular, it addresses:

- Insights into branding and corporate marketing in the Islamic context.
- An introduction to Islamic consumption and culture, rules and regulations in brands and consumption in Islamic markets.
- An identification of how the strategic global orientation of the Islamic approach is practised and how it works in different Islamic countries such as emerging countries. Readers are introduced to a variety of business and management approaches which, once applied to their business strategies, will increase their chances of successful implementation.

Addressing both theoretical and practical insights, this book is essential reading for marketing and branding scholars and students, as well as CEOs, brand managers and consultants with an interest in this area.

Islamic Marketing and Branding

Theory and Practice

Edited by T. C. Melewar and S. F. Syed Alwi

Routledge
Taylor & Francis Group

LONDON AND NEW YORK

First published 2018
by Routledge

2 Park Square, Milton Park, Abingdon, Oxfordshire OX14 4RN
52 Vanderbilt Avenue, New York, NY 10017

Routledge is an imprint of the Taylor & Francis Group, an informa business

First issued in paperback 2020

British Library Cataloguing-in-Publication Data
A catalogue record for this book is available from the British Library

Library of Congress Cataloging-in-Publication Data
A catalog record for this book has been requested

ISBN: 978-1-4724-4096-9 (hbk)
ISBN: 978-0-367-59367-4 (pbk)

Typeset in Bembo
by Apex CoVantage, LLC

To my grandmother, Esah binti Abdul
T. C. Melewar

To my parents, Salamah and Syed Alwi
S. F. Syed Alwi

Contents

Contributors

Wan Marhaini Wan Ahmad serves as a senior lecturer at the Department of Finance and Banking, Faculty of Business and Accountancy, University of Malaya, Kuala Lumpur, Malaysia. Her interest lies in Islamic economics and finance primarily in Islamic banking, zakat and waqf. She holds a PhD in Islamic finance from the University of Edinburgh, Scotland. Currently she advises a few local financial institutions on Shariah matters.

Ali Al-Makarami (PhD, Brunel University, UK) is a project coordinator at Saudia Airlines. He works on cultural impact on brand-customer relationships and has contributed several papers on the topic with a particular focus on Arabic and religious culture. Relevant papers were published in the proceedings of several marketing conferences in the UK, Switzerland and Malaysia. He recently contributed to EMAC 2013 with a working paper on brand value assessment, while he was a PhD student at Brunel.

S. F. Syed Alwi (BSc, MSc, PhD) received her PhD from Manchester Business School, UK, and is currently a Senior Lecturer of Corporate Brand Management at Brunel Business School, Brunel University London, UK. Formerly, she served as Senior Lecturer in Marketing at the University of Malaya, Malaysia. She has more than 16 years' experience in teaching and research and currently is leading the Applied Corporate Brand Management Program at Brunel University. Her research interests include branding at the product and corporate level and her current work is exploring this concept in the context of higher education, entrepreneurial celebrity within the UK and Malaysia. She taught mainly modules related to corporate brand management and marketing such as strategic corporate brand consulting and principles of marketing. Her work has appeared in several reputable academic journals such as *Journal of Business Research, European Journal of Marketing, Journal of Brand Management, Journal of Product and Brand Management, Industrial Management* and *Data Systems and Corporate Reputation Review*. Recently, she co-authored a book (with Professor T. C. Melewar) entitled *Corporate Brand: Area, Arena and Approaches* (Routledge). She has also completed three major research projects in branding as the lead Principal Investigator and has served as joint guest editor in several special editions of academic journals with branding focus, such as *International Studies of Management & Organizations* (ISMO) in Corporate Branding and Corporate Reputation and *Asia Pacific Journal of Marketing and Logistics* (APJML) in Branding in Asia. Currently she serves as Visiting Professor in Brand Management at University Catholica del Sacro Cuore, Milan, Italy.

Norbani Che-Ha is an Associate Professor in the Department of Marketing, and Director of Services Research and Innovation Centre, Faculty of Business and Accountancy,

University of Malaya, Kuala Lumpur, Malaysia. Her research interests are in marketing capabilities, consumer behaviour and small and medium enterprises. She publishes widely in several journals such as *Journal of Business Research, Journal of Strategic Marketing, Marketing Intelligence and Planning* and many others. She also contributes to several book chapters and has written many books on her own.

Nesrine Eltawy is a researcher at Brunel Business School, Brunel University London, UK. She holds a PhD in supply chain management from Brunel Business School, Brunel University London. She has a research background in logistics and operations management. She is an author of an international journal article and several international conference papers. She is also a peer reviewer for the *International Journal of Operations and Production Management*. Her research interests are in agile supply chain, lean supply chain, qualitative research methods and supply chain management in developing countries.

David Gallear is Professor of Operations Management at Brunel Business School, Brunel University London, UK. His research interests lie in operations, supply chain and quality management/business excellence, with a particular focus on sustainability issues, relationships and corporate responsibility in supply chains. His research typically examines the nature, form and determinants of supply chain purchasing strategy relationships, the supply chain mechanisms and models in manufacturing and service that can leverage sustainability in operations, and sustainability performance. He also has keen interests in knowledge transfer in supply relationships and strategic and operational issues in SMEs. He has published numerous peer reviewed articles in journals such as *International Journal of Operations and Production Management, International Journal of Production Research, Industrial Marketing Management, International Journal of Production Economics* and *OMEGA*, alongside a number of research monographs, edited works and journal special issues.

Balkis Haris received her PhD from Manchester Business School, UK, and currently is a Senior Lecturer of Finance in the Faculty of Business and Management, Universiti Teknologi MARA, Malaysia. She has more than 18 years' experience in teaching and research. Currently, she teaches Issues in Finance, Portfolio Analysis and Islamic Capital Market. Her ongoing research work has appeared in *Research Journal of Finance and Accounting*. Her main research interest is in corporate finance and investment with a focus on market-based research, disclosure and regulation. She is an assistant editor for the *Journal of Islamic Marketing* (JIM) and also served as a guest reviewer for the *Asian Journal of Business and Accounting* (AJBA) and *Journal of Emerging Economies and Islamic Research* (JEEIR), and as a reviewer for several international and national conferences. She is a certified Professional Halal Trainer by HIDC (Halal Industry Development Corporation) since 2013. She served as a member in one big consultancy project for Mass Rapid Transit (MRT) Malaysia in 2014.

Faridah Hassan is Director of iHalal Management and Science (iHALALMAS), Universiti Teknologi MARA Shah Alam, Malaysia. Previously she was a Director, Institute of Business Excellence, Malaysia, heading the research consultancy, training and publication unit. Currently, she is an adjunct professor and external examiner for several local and foreign universities, an active Fellow Member of the professional Chartered Institute of Marketing (UK), Vice Chairman of the Board Council and Regional

Member for the Malaysian Chartered Institute of Marketing, Vice President of the World Academy of Islamic Management and Malaysian Consumer and Family Economics Association. Her appointments were, among others, twice as a dean, an independent board of directors member, as well as a former panel investment advisor for a publicly listed trust fund company. Her 36 years of teaching, supervising, examining, and panel advising involve undergraduate, post-graduate and professional courses. Her research interests are in the areas of Halal marketing and strategic management for small and medium companies, financial institutions and trust funds, public and private education, and tourism and government agencies.

Aliakbar Jafari is a Chartered Fellow of the Chartered Institute of Marketing (FCIM) and a Senior Lecturer in Marketing at the University of Strathclyde, UK. His research falls within the general context of interpretive consumer research and market studies with a focus on consumer culture, theories of globalization, emerging markets, transformative consumer research, and religions/spiritualities. He has published in several academic journals such as *Marketing Theory; Consumption, Markets and Culture; Journal of Marketing Management; Journal of Business Research; The Sociological Review; Iranian Studies; Journal of Islamic Marketing; Iranian Journal of Management Studies; International Journal of Management Concepts and Philosophy*; and *Tourism Management*, as well as in different edited books. He is co-editor of *Islam, Marketing and Consumption: Critical Perspectives on the Intersections* (Routledge, 2016) and the four-volume set *New Directions in Consumer Research* (Sage Publications, 2015).

Erne Suzila Kassim received her degree from Indiana University in Bloomington, USA, majoring in Economics and Sociology. Upon her graduation, she worked as a Quality Engineer and was responsible for managing the Total Airport Management Solutions for the Kuala Lumpur International Airport (KLIA). She then studied for a MSc in Information Technology and also a PhD in Information Technology, mainly specializing in digital innovations. She has been awarded with research grants for projects in e-learning, green IT, e-commerce and IT for micro-enterprises. She has written journal articles and conferences proceedings. Currently, she also serves as a reviewer for multiple international conferences and academic journals. She teaches courses in information systems and IT project management, focusing on pervasive technology, and the risks and quality management of business applications projects. Her research interests include social networking, business intelligence analytics for improving customer equity and big data for halal applications. She is currently a fellow at the Institute of Halal Management and Science, Universiti Teknologi MARA, Malaysia.

Kaouther Kooli is a Lecturer in Marketing at Bournemouth University, UK. She is a member of the Academy of Marketing and Chair of its Business to Business Special Interest Group (B2B SIG). She is a Fellow of the Higher Education Academy. She has published in a number of academic journals including the *Journal of Business and Industrial Marketing*. Her research interests include B2B marketing and also e-marketing.

Jonathan Liu, BSc(Hons), MBA, CMgr, FCMI, MBCS, FHEA, is Professor of Global Business Management at Regent's University London, UK. He is the Business and Management Faculty's Research Leader and is responsible for developing and supporting research initiatives in the field of Business and Management. He teaches and researches in Entrepreneurship and Venture Management. He is the Editor-in-Chief of the *International Journal of Business Performance Management* with Inderscience Publishers. He is on the editorial board of the *Journal of Islamic Marketing* and book review editor of the *Journal of Technology Management* in China. He publishes extensively and has over a hundred articles and ten books published in subject areas relating to Business and Management. He is on the Council of the National Conference of University Professors, a council member of the Universities China Committee in London, a Fellow of the Higher Education Academy and a Chartered Fellow of the Chartered Management Institute. He is a trustee and board member of the Directors of Ming-Ai (London) Institute. He joined Ming-Ai's board in 2010 after having been associated with Ming-Ai as a volunteer resource person since 1996. He volunteers his time to Ming-Ai to support the development of charity and community projects that promote British-Chinese welfare in London and the UK.

T. C. Melewar (BSc, MBA, PhD) is a Professor of Marketing and Strategy at Middlesex University London, UK. He has previous experience at Brunel University London, UK; Zurich University of Applied Sciences, Switzerland; University of Warwick (Warwick Business School), UK; De Montfort University, UK; and MARA Institute of Technology in Malaysia. He teaches Corporate Branding, Strategic Marketing Management and International Marketing for a range of undergraduate, MBA, and executive courses with companies such as Nestlé, Safeway, Corus (now Tata) and Sony. He was a Visiting Professor at Groupe ESC Grenoble, France; Humboldt University, Berlin, Germany; and the University of Malaya, Malaysia. Currently, he is a Visiting Professor at the University of Lincoln, UK. He has taught MBA and Master in International Business programmes in countries such as Germany, Sweden, France, Russia, Georgia, Moldova, Indonesia and Malaysia. His research interests include corporate identity/branding and international marketing strategy. He has published over eighty refereed journal articles in journals such as the *Journal of International Business Studies, International Marketing Review, European Journal of Marketing, Journal of World Business, Industrial Marketing Management, International Marketing Review, Journal of Marketing Communications, International Journal of Market Research* and *International Journal of Advertising* among many others. He was the Joint Editor-in-Chief for the *Journal of Brand Management* and is now the Emeritus Editor of the journal. He is also on the Editorial Advisory Board for the following journals: *Journal of Marketing Communications, Corporate Reputation Review, Marketing Intelligence and Planning, Journal of Marketing Management* and *Corporate Communications: An International Journal*. He has written three books on corporate branding and international marketing.

Rusnah Muhamad received her PhD in Islamic Accounting from the University of Malaya, Malaysia and is an Associate Professor of Accounting at the University of Malaya, Malaysia. Her PhD research was related to financial reporting for the Islamic banking industry. She teaches Financial Accounting and Reporting, Accounting for Business Decision Making and Islamic Banking and Finance for a range of undergraduate, MBA, and executive courses at the University of Malaya. Her research interests, among others, include Islamic banking and finance, financial reporting from an Islamic perspective, Corporate Social Responsibility (CSR), Islamic tourism and Islamic business ethics.

Melewar is one of the world's most influential scholars on corporate branding, reputation and image and Sharifah Alwi has also published widely in the field. Professor Melewar has published in top journals such as *Journal of International Business Studies* and has one of the highest citation rates of any marketing scholar, with nearly 8000 citations on Google Scholar and an h-index of 125. TC is now Professor of Marketing and Strategy and Head of the Department of Marketing, Branding and Tourism at Middlesex University, where we are colleagues again.

Similarly, I have known Dr Alwi for about five years, also from Brunel University, where she is a Senior Lecturer in Corporate Brand Management at Brunel Business School and I know her as an author of excellent research papers in top journals that I have guest-edited. Amongst many other achievements, Dr Alwi has guest-edited many journal special issues, including *Asia Pacific Journal of Marketing and Logistics* and *Journal of Islamic Marketing*. Sharifah also sits in the editorial board of *Asia Journal of Business and Accounting*. Dr Alwi has published in top journals such as *Journal of Business Research* and *European Journal of Marketing*. She has been the Principal Investigator of major projects on marketing in the Islamic world, notably on Islamic Branding and Marketing for Malaysia.

Both of the editors are branding experts, and have published together, for example, the book *Corporate Branding: Arenas, Areas and Approaches* published by Routledge in 2015. And they are co-authors of one of the few papers on Islamic marketing in top marketing journals (with Rusnah Muhamad, author of one of the chapters of this book), 'Segmentation and brand positioning for Islamic financial services', published in the *European Journal of Marketing* in 2012. Both hail originally from Malaysia and as such, have long been steeped in an Islamic marketing culture.

The reader of this book will find a treasure-trove of gems related to Islamic marketing, including marketing strategy; corporate branding and reputation; products, services, halal and certification bodies, financial services; communication strategies; and tourism. Looking at a couple of chapters by way of illustrations, Chapter 5 will help the reader to understand the marketing communications that will help to build brand awareness that can influence both Muslims and non-Muslims to patronise Islamic banking. Importantly, Islamic banking awareness among non-Muslims is becoming increasingly important in Islamic finance sectors. Chapter 10 builds on these foundations to recognize the implications of the great diversity characterizing emerging Muslim-majority markets and the new Muslim middle classes, entrepreneurs and business networks on consumption, competition and global marketing management. Importantly, although there are universal Islamic values and norms, how these are interpreted, negotiated and experienced in the daily lives of Muslim consumers is far from uniform and fixed. The growth of the new Muslim middle classes coincides with the increasingly significant role Islamic business networks and Muslim entrepreneurs play in the global markets.

These brief examples will, I hope confirm the need for this book and whet the reader's appetite for the (halal?) meat that will be found within! The book will have an important place on my own bookshelf and many others in helping doctoral, masters and final year undergraduate students in business and marketing with a comprehensive treatment of the nature of Islamic consumption and cultures, related to marketing and branding strategy globally.

Charles Dennis
Professor of Consumer Behaviour
Middlesex University London
Business School

Foreword

I am delighted to have the opportunity to write the foreword to this exciting book. As a professor of consumer behaviour, I am acutely aware of the need for academic staff, students and courses in marketing to bolster knowledge of Islamic marketing. A few years ago, I enjoyed making a television documentary on Christmas shopping with actor and comedian, Adrian Edmondson (which, along with other appearances including with news presenter Sir Trevor McDonald OBE, earned me the sobriquet 'Professor Shopping'!). The programme was great fun and I have shown it to students many times to illustrate aspects of consumer behaviour in an entertaining way. But can I still use it? When a growing proportion of my students are Muslims and, more importantly, a growing proportion of marketing activity involves satisfying the needs and wants of Muslims? According to US research company Pew Research Centre, Islam has 1.6 billion adherents, or 23 percent of the global population and Muslims make up more than 50 percent of the population in nearly 50 countries. Research by Prof Dr Suhaiza Zailani and colleagues, published in the *Journal of Agribusiness Marketing* in 2010, reports that the halal market is worth $2.3tn (£1.6tn) annually worldwide (of which about 60 percent is food), increasing at $500bn a year.

The massive Islamic market calls for major adjustments in marketing particular products (e.g. halal), distribution (considerations of credit and interest payments) and promotion (e.g. restrictions on portrayals of the female body). Yet western marketers are only just starting to wake up to the opportunities of Islamic marketing. Speaking at the second *Muslim Lifestyle Expo* in London in 2016, Shelina Janmohamed, vice-president of Ogilvy Noor, an Islamic branding agency, pointed out that "A huge opportunity is being missed by corporate brands . . .", albeit many smaller businesses are taking advantage and growing fast.

A spot check of 100 of the most downloaded articles in top marketing journals on both sides of the Atlantic reveals none on Islamic marketing (only two are cross-country/culture and neither of those concern countries that are predominantly Muslim). The implication is that the basis of academic marketing is overwhelmingly founded in Western cultures.

In this context, this book is significant and timely. And these authors are ideally qualified to produce it. I am proud to have known Professor TC Melewar for over a decade from when we became colleagues at Brunel University. Since that time we have worked together on many projects such as joint-editing and conference organising, and I have always valued his support and mentoring. Enabled by that support, I have supervised numerous research students from predominantly-Muslim countries, gaining a useful viewpoint on the material of this book. I am grateful to Professor Melewar for opening up many potential publishing opportunities, including, for example a chapter in his book *Asia Branding*, (in which Dr Sharifah Faridah Syed Alwi also has a chapter). Professor

Melbourne, Australia. Additionally, he is also on the committee board of the Malaysian Finance Association.

Sarah Turnbull is a Fellow of The Chartered Institute of Marketing and a Senior Lecturer at the University of Portsmouth, UK. She spent 15 years working as a practitioner in advertising agencies both in London and Dubai. Her Middle East experience includes managing a number of prestigious government accounts including Emirates. Her main research interest is in advertising and the advertising creative development process in particular. She has published a number of studies on the advertising industry in the UK and the Middle East in international journals. Additionally, she has contributed to industry publications and has a number of book contributions on advertising and brand communication.

Jonathan A. J. Wilson is Associate Professor and Associate Dean of Richmond American University in London, UK. His career began over twenty years ago in industry before he moved into academia and consulting, tackling the ABCDs of Business and Culture: Advertising, Branding, Communications, and Digital. He has spoken at conferences across the globe on over 100 occasions, and published over 200 pieces of work in, amongst others: *Harvard Business Review, Journal of Marketing Management, The Guardian, Huffington Post*, and *Thomson Reuters*. He is a Halal Tourism Officer in the Ministry of Tourism for the Republic of Indonesia; an Executive Trainer for Al Jazeera Media Network; and Editor-in-Chief for the *Journal of Islamic Marketing*. Islamica 500 lists him in the Top 50 Global Thought Leaders for his work in Islamic Economics, Halal Branding, and Muslim Millennials.

Mazia Yassim is a Lecturer in Marketing at the University of Greenwich, UK, and also holds a Research Associateship in the charity sector. Her research interest is in consumer behaviour, Islamic marketing, culture, sports and arts marketing, and social marketing. She has published widely and also acts as a reviewer for academic journals.

Dorothy Yen (PhD, University of Leeds, UK) is a Senior Lecturer in Marketing at Brunel Business School, Brunel University, UK. She has several years of experience of working in advertising and market research firms and is currently teaching the modules of 'marketing communications' and 'consumer behaviour' to postgraduate students at Brunel. She works on cross-cultural inter-firm business relationships with a particular focus on Anglo-Chinese interactions and the Chinese notion of *guanxi*. She has published in the *Journal of Business Research, Industrial Marketing Management, Journal of Marketing Management, The Marketing Review, Journal of General Management, Higher Education Studies*, and *Total Quality Management*.

Cedomir Nestorovic is Professor of International Marketing and Geopolitics at ESSEC Business School, Singapore, and the Director of the ESSEC Executive MBA Asia-Pacific programme. He holds a PhD from the Institute of Political Sciences in Paris. He has taught geopolitics and international marketing at the ESSEC Business School for more than 20 years, with a specific focus on Islamic Business and Management. His latest book is *Islamic Marketing: Understanding the Socio-Economic, Cultural and Politico-Legal Environment*, which was published by Springer in 2016. Based at the ESSEC Asia Pacific campus in Singapore, he is the academic co-director of the MBA programme at the Arabian Gulf University in Manama, Bahrain. He participates regularly in meetings dealing with Islamic Business, such as the World Halal Forum in Kuala Lumpur, and the Kuala Lumpur Islamic Finance Forum. He is also one of the initiators and keynote speakers of the academic conferences devoted to Islamic Marketing and Branding, such as the International Conference on Islamic Marketing and Branding in Kuala Lumpur and London, and the Global Islamic Marketing Conference in Dubai and Abu Dhabi. Appearing frequently in print and electronic media, he works closely with companies on issues pending with Islamic markets. He has been awarded the title of "Professor of the Week" by *The Financial Times* in 2012 for his contribution to Lexicon on Islamic finance.

Ismah Osman is a Senior Lecturer in the Arshad Ayub Graduate Business School, Faculty of Business and Management, Universiti Teknologi MARA Shah Alam, Malaysia. She teaches Introduction to Fiqh Muamalat, Advanced Fiqh Muamalat and Islamic Asset and Wealth Management at postgraduate levels. Her research focuses on Islamic and halal marketing, and consumer behaviour in Islamic banking contexts. She has been with Universiti Teknologi MARA since 2000. She holds a PhD from the International Islamic University, Malaysia, in Islamic Banking and Finance, and a masters degree in Business Management from Keele University, UK. She is currently an Assistant Editor of the *Journal of Islamic Marketing* and a Fellow of the Institute of Halal Management and Science at Universiti Teknologi MARA.

Saad Mohd Said is a Senior Lecturer in the Department of Economics, Faculty of Economics and Administration, University of Malaya, Kuala Lumpur, Malaysia. His research interests are in small and medium enterprises, macroeconomics performance and policy, labour productivity and the services industry. He has published several books related to his areas of interest. He is actively involved in research and consultancy work for various private and public institutions in and outside Malaysia.

Özlem Sandıkcı is a Professor of Marketing at the School of Management and Administrative Sciences, Istanbul Şehir University, Turkey. Her research addresses sociocultural dimensions of consumption and focuses on the relationship between globalization, marketing, and culture. Her work is published in various journals including the *Journal of Marketing, Journal of Consumer Research, Journal of Business Research, Marketing Theory, Business History Review*, and *Fashion Theory*, and several books. She is the co-editor of the *Handbook of Islamic Marketing* (Edward Elgar, 2011) and *Islam, Marketing and Consumption: Critical Perspectives on the Intersections* (Routledge, 2016).

Mohd Edil Abd Sukor lectures on finance and Islamic finance for both undergraduate and postgraduate programmes in the Faculty of Business and Accountancy, University of Malaya, Malaysia. His research interests include stock market seasonalities, Islamic banking and Islamic capital market. He holds a PhD in finance from the University of

Acknowledgements

We would like to mention that preparation of this book has been very stimulating yet challenging for us. We believe we have brought a vital and unique collection of thoughts from academics and practitioners who pursue their enthusiasm on advancing Islamic Marketing and branding issues in different contexts globally. Islamic marketing and branding theories are still in their very early development stage. It is not a simple task to gather the topic and case studies. We hope that papers and case studies compiled in this book advance the readers' knowledge and provide clarity in the understanding of Islamic marketing theoretically and empirically around the globe.

We would like to express our deepest gratitude to all our esteemed colleagues who have contributed chapters to this book from around the world. Lastly, special thanks to Kristina Abbot for her strong support, as well as the team at Routledge, whose encouragements have helped us in producing this book.

Introduction

S. F. Syed Alwi and T. C. Melewar

Islamic marketing and branding is a new marketing subject that sits within the wider Marketing discipline, close to the topic of ethnic marketing. The attention paid by scholars, students and practitioners to the subject has increased over the last fifteen years and several major and reputable universities in Islamic and Western countries are now offering related programmes within their marketing curriculum. In particular, two journals are dedicated to publishing Islamic marketing and branding papers to advance our knowledge within this field: one, *Journal of Islamic Marketing*, was launched by Emerald in 2010, and the other, the *International Journal of Islamic Marketing and Branding*, was introduced by Inderscience Publishers in 2015. We are also witnessing an increase in the number of Religion and Marketing/Islamic Marketing scholars and practitioners adding their contribution to the earlier studies undertaken in this area (e.g. Usunier and Stolz, 2016; Nestorvic, 2016; Sandıkcı and Rice, 2011; Al-serhan, 2011). In addition, many Islamic marketing and branding conferences have been held around the globe dedicated to advancing our knowledge of theory and practice.

In terms of business practice, we are witnessing the spreading availability of halal products and services across the spectrum. These are now prevalent in both Muslim and non-Muslim countries and cater to the growing demand fostered by Muslim markets. Other products and services that are growing include cosmetics, pharmaceuticals, apparels, hospitality, banking and insurance, all demanded by this segment of the market in one form or another. This is reflected in the increased awareness shown by multinational corporations in formulating their marketing strategies to cater for the needs of Muslim consumers. In particular, more and more brands are sold and differentiated using the Islamic marketing approach. For example, clearance has to be obtained worldwide from the Islamic accreditation body to permit using 'halal' logo/labelling before selling 'halal' food, cosmetics and pharmaceutical related products to Muslim markets. However, the Islamic marketing approach is not necessarily limited to applying 'halal' alone. Researchers need to go beyond religion, products, industries, context and geographic region to understand the consumer buying behaviour and decision-making process of Muslim consumers across Islamic countries and the wider world.

Nevertheless, the growth of Islamic marketing could be explained by the changing environment. Examples include the growing Muslim consumer population, their increased purchasing power and the choices available to them to make decisions based not just on religious grounds but also on other factors such as globalisation and its effect on the Muslim world. (Nestrovic, 2016). Today there are more educated Muslims around the globe than ever and their incomes are rising, which has led to an increase in their purchasing power. One obvious example is women and education. Whilst women in certain

Islamic countries were often not allowed to seek higher education in the past, this trend is rapidly changing because of globalisation (Nestrovic, 2016). Muslim females are now amongst the largest populations in the higher education sector (Nestrovic, 2016). With the increase in education and employment among women, there is a corresponding increase in the contribution they make, and they play an important role in boosting the Islamic economy (Nestrovic, 2016). Furthermore, as reported by Dinar Standard in Global State Economy Report 2015, the total population of Muslim countries is 1.47 billion, and this number constitutes 22.8 percent of total world population. From this total (22.8 percent), the total GDPs of their countries come to US$5.7 trillion, which equals 8.3 percent of World GDP (Dinar Standard, 2015). The two largest sectors where expenditure occurs are food and lifestyle (with $1.8 trillion, expected to increase to $2.6 trillion in 2020) and Islamic banking assets (with $1.35 trillion in 2014, projected to reach $2.6 trillion in 2020), (Dinar Standard, 2015).

In terms of the service sector, there is already a growing interest in understanding Islamic segmentation in this context. For example, a study by Muhamad, Melewar and Syed Alwi (2012) identifies that the possible market segmentation for Islamic banking can be divided into the following: (1) values (psychographic segmentation) which constitute opinions and attitudes, activities and lifestyles, and (2) benefit sought from product or product attributes. Specifically, a service brand in the Islamic Financial Service (IFS) is positioned on the basis of values vis-à-vis religious conviction, such as: (a) religious conviction, (b) economic rationality, (c) ethical observance and economic rationality and (d) product attributes such as pricing-interest rates, service quality, reputation and image. However, due to limited research in this area, there are few segmentation and positioning insights available to guide academics and marketers on how to formulate targeting and marketing strategies.

The key challenge for Islamic marketing and branding is that, being relatively new in the area, there are more questions raised than answers: What is Islamic marketing and the Islamic brand? What is the significance of understanding this topic? How does it differ from that of conventional marketing? Theoretically, could we use the conventional marketing paradigm in the subject or do we need a new one? Who are these consumers? How do we segment and target them? Where are they located? And more importantly, what does the future hold for the topic as research and in the business world?

Several scholars argue that Islamic marketing is not only about the 'halal' product and logo, rather it is about a way of life (Alserhan, 2011) and since religion determines the culture of a country, it remains a question as to how practitioners adapt this to their marketing strategy. As stated (Nestrovic, 2016), in business, religion can be a constraint. However, it can also offer much in the way of opportunity. Naturally it is necessary for companies to adapt their marketing practices in line with the religion of the country they are operating in because they are not in a position to change it. Hence, there is a pressing need to advance knowledge and fully understand the best way forward for companies wishing to market their products and services to Muslim consumers.

Therefore, we see our book *Islamic Marketing and Branding: Theory and Practice* as an essential guide for marketing and branding scholars. In particular, it will inform scholars whose researchers are based around ethnic marketing within the Muslim market. The book is also relevant for practitioners, including CEOs and marketing and brand managers whose businesses are involved in selling ethnic product brands, of which halal products are a prime example. This book is unique in offering short case studies to assist a practical understanding. The use of case studies previously within this topic has been limited, not least because of the difficulty in compiling them given the newness of the area. However, with the emergence of Islamic marketing, branding scholars from across the globe are advancing our practical understanding of the subject and our book brings together some of that knowledge in a user-friendly way; scholars representing different segment groups and markets have joined forces to provide a short case study at the end of each chapter of the book. The book, in combining theory and practice, will not only support the work of scholars and practitioners but also benefit undergraduate and postgraduate research students.

In particular, our book addresses the following targets:

1   The increasing interest of marketing and branding scholars and research students in the area.
2   Ethnic marketing scholars and students.
3   CEOs, brand and advertising managers and brand consultants who would be able to draw comparisons across different arenas (or industries) and different locations (or areas) on how to brand position their companies, corporations and products, as well as learning how to address the cultural issues which arise.
4   Finally, all stakeholders would be able to advance their knowledge of the methodological and research design approaches in focusing on how best to carry out such research in this new area.

Our book objectives and content

Our book introduces the concept of Islamic marketing and offers insight into how this concept applies throughout the marketing mix for several products and services. The book also discusses how brand is differentiated within this context by, for example, the notions/concepts of *Shariah*, logo (e.g., halal) and corporate brand and institution (e.g., certification bodies). By relating these concepts, wherever appropriate, to consumption and culture, comparison is made with other target segments such as the conventional or, as it is more commonly referred to, the non-Muslim market. The book concludes by applying the Islamic marketing concept to the international or global marketing context and discusses the global challenges ahead.

The book addresses the following objectives:

*   Readers will gain insight into branding and corporate marketing in the Islamic context. The book enables readers to compare, contrast and appreciate how corporate brand and reputation works throughout.
*   Readers will be introduced to Islamic consumption and culture in the discussion and analysis of *Shariah* rules and regulations and, as appropriate, in the relationship between brands and consumption in Islamic markets.
*   Readers will also be in a position to identify how the strategic global orientation of the Islamic approach is practised and how it works in different Islamic countries, emerging countries included. In particular, the book will provide an insight into Islamic communication and distribution strategies, and a specific mode of entry into Islamic markets will be analysed and discussed. Readers are introduced to a variety of business and management approaches which, once applied to their business strategies, will increase their chances of successful implementation.

Because of the newness of the area, the concept is still emerging, making the book vital to help advance our understanding of the concept and offer guidance in terms of how to apply the concept within current business practice. The text provides a concise mix of theory, primary research findings and practice that will engender confidence in both students and practitioners alike by means of the case study included in each chapter. In particular, through three main parts, our book provides readers from areas across the spectrum covering marketing, organisational studies, psychology, sociology and communication and strategy with theoretical and managerial perspectives on Islamic marketing and branding. The three main parts are:

Part I   Branding and Corporate Marketing
Part II   Religion, Consumption and Culture
Part III   Strategic Global Orientation

The first part covers branding and corporate marketing and consists of three chapters: Corporate brands and marketing strategy (Chapter 1), Islamic products and services: the concept of halal and certification bodies (Chapter 2) and Islam and the reputational landscape (Chapter 3). Part I underlines the importance of enhancing trustworthiness among stakeholders by addressing transparency across the whole corporate brand process and by highlighting the substantial impact it has on designing marketing strategy to Muslim markets and on buying decision. Addressing in detail halal branding as a process and the question of who is behind the brand (the awarding or certification bodies) is vital to consumers and to stakeholders in general as it greatly influences consumers' buying decision making.

The second part highlights religion, consumption and culture by means of four chapters focusing upon the relationship between religiosity, consumption, values and culture within different contexts and covers industries such as banking and tourism in Malaysia and Saudi Arabia.

The final part, strategic global orientation, provides a brief description of the various global markets within Islamic marketing countries and highlights marketing strategy, brand communication and supply chain management practices across Muslim markets.

An overview of all the chapters and their contributors is given below.

Part I of the book

Our opening chapter, contributed by **Jonathan A. J. Wilson and Jonathan Liu,** focuses on the importance of recognising that marketing can be differentiated at both product and corporate level within the Islamic context. Within the context of the economies of large Muslim populations, they address the key areas and critical success factors surrounding Islamic corporate branding and marketing. Corporate branding within the Islamic context can be applied through 'spiritual entity'. This is a concept that has been applied in the past to donors only. In this chapter it is argued that this concept has validity for both consumers and multiple stakeholders as no distinction should be drawn between them in the context of Islam needs clarification. They further suggest that brand traits have a part to play in communicating brand message. Brand traits, e.g. the halal concept, should be at the heart or at the foundation of economics and corporate identity formation not just at the level of brand consumption. The authors conclude by promoting the recognition that sees brand as human; aligning their stance with current thinking on brand as a person with human personality traits.

Chapter 2, contributed by **Kaouther Kooli**, provides an understanding of how 'brand' is applied within the context of the Muslim consumer. Kaouther proposes the existence of three levels of Muslim consumer behaviour by focusing firstly on the way Muslims relate to their own identity in order to choose, buy and consume products and services, secondly, on the way consumers investigate the characteristics of Islamic products and services and thirdly, on the classification of Islamic products and services (which relates to Islamic product consumption). The author emphasises that Islamic brand attributes comprise tangible/functional and intangible and spiritual/holistic attributes and offers the reader an opportunity to reconsider brand equity within the Islamic context whilst finding a balance between maximising brand values (prestigious) and encouraging worship at the same time.

Aliakbar Jafari contributes Chapter 3, which focuses on the reputational landscape within an institution (the corporate brand). This chapter presents an analysis of the prevailing debates on what constitutes 'Islamicness' in contemporary market space. According to the author, 'Islamicness' is a fluid concept, constantly (re)shaped by multiple factors and ideologies in the contemporary spaces of the market. In order to build and sustain reputation in highly politicised and symbolised global socioeconomic systems, organisations need to avoid transient identity anxieties and adopt a long-term strategic approach. Brand building should be based on a long-term corporate vision that considers the changing landscape of religious perceptions and orientations. The author concludes that scholars should revisit the idea of positioning the organisation as a 'holistically Islamic' enterprise and avoid making huge claims of association with the 'Islamic'. The author stresses that only if the organisation is capable of following the principles of Islam should it make claims of Islamicness; otherwise, the organisation should ethically follow market rules without associating itself with Islam and the Islamic.

Part II of the book

Part II consists of four chapters. In Chapter 4, **Ismah Osman, Faridah Hassan, Balkis Haris and Erne Suzila Kassim** discuss the importance of religion and consumption effect on products and services. They propose that halal offers great business potential in the local and global marketplace within different segmentations, segmentations that vary across sectors of the halal industry according to degree of religiosity, lifestyle and culture and level of education and sophistication. Sectors include food and beverage, fashion, media and recreation, travel and hospitality, pharmaceutical and cosmetics and Islamic banking and finance. The authors remind that marketing strategy implementation within the Islamic context should not only be based on a person's level of religiosity. Interestingly, the non-Muslims are also embracing halal for the fact that the halal concept emphasises safety, hygiene and wholesomeness of products and services. The authors have also emphasised the need to have a sound understanding of what Islam and *Shariah* mean, their legal framework and how they impact upon consumption and business in general.

Chapter 5, contributed by **Norbani Che-Ha, Wan Marhaini Wan Ahmad, Mohd Edil Abd Sukor and Saad Mohd Said**, uncovers the differences between non-Muslim views on Islamic banking and that of Muslims with specific emphasis on Islamic banking in Malaysia, and takes into account the perceptions, level of understanding, knowledge and Islamic brand awareness of non-Muslims. Whilst the majority of Islamic countries do not need to do this since most of their bank customers are Muslim, most customers of Islamic banking in Malaysia are by contrast non-Muslims, and the system of banking has been in place since 1983. Their study offers quantitative findings collected from both Muslim and non-Muslim consumers from a number of banks within Malaysia.

In Chapter 6, **Ali Al-Makrami and Dorothy Yen** extend the concept of brand values within the Muslim market. This chapter discusses the capabilities and strengths of the Islamic branding framework in creating and sustaining strong brands. This is done through a deliberate process of designing and delivering superior value to target Muslim customers. The authors emphasise that brand manufacturers should carefully examine the depth of their cultural understanding in order to avoid an over-hasty entry into Islamic markets. This is necessary because the lack of a thorough appreciation of the religious and cultural motivations and reasons behind Muslim consumer behaviour could hinder or even block completely the existence of a brand in desirable markets. They argue that despite the trends that indicate a growing market for brands globally, there is as yet no clear consensus on how best to advocate enduring value for Muslim consumers, which would be achievable only by means of a sound understanding of Islamic value systems. Therefore, the authors offer a framework with the objective of assisting global brands in overcoming the barriers that can prevail in Islamic markets all the way from the introductory stage through to the operational stage to that later stage of building a relationship with Muslim consumers, this by means of a concept known as value maximisation.

Part II concludes with Chapter 7 by **Rusnah Muhamad** on consumption and cultures. This chapter concerns itself with the topic of Islamic tourism, a subject which is emerging as an increasingly popular new sub-sector within the travel and holiday industry. Over recent years Muslims worldwide have become increasingly affluent and are travelling with their families and friends, presenting huge opportunities for the tourism industry players to develop innovative ways of using Islamic tourism products and services to cater for the needs of this largely untapped but lucrative niche market. Hence, the chapter stresses the need for the market (Muslim travellers) and their religious requirements to be understood in order to help Islamic tourism products and services successfully compete within this target market. In particular, marketers could address two core consumer factors when designing products and services and when communicating the Islamic tourism message i.e. the availability of halal products and facilities for Muslim travellers performing daily prayers.

Part III of the book

In Part III, readers will be introduced to strategic global orientation and to marketing mix in the context of the Muslim market across the different geographic regions of the world.

Cedomir Nestorovic provides the opening for this part (Chapter 8) by investigating the similarities and differences between the economic dimensions of the Islamic world and by examining how the differences between countries might influence a differentiated marketing approach. Since the Islamic religion influences all aspects of Muslim consumer behaviour, public life, private life and family life, Islam will, from a marketing standpoint, define what is prescribed, what is forbidden or what is permissible, with the result that the marketing offer has to be in tune with the tenets of Islam. The chapter suggests that despite the general misconception among non-Muslims that Muslim behaviour is the same the world over, the Muslim world is in fact diverse, with differences based on interpretations of Islam on one side and economic realities on the other. The author concludes that, for this reason, it is difficult to have one unique homogenized Islamic market.

In Chapter 9, **Sarah Turnbull** provides an understanding of how communication strategies are employed by Islamic brands and how they target Muslim consumers. The author explains that this is an emerging area of academic and practitioner study, and the chapter considers current theoretical and contemporary perspectives within the marketing communications industry. In particular, the need for a sound understanding of Islamic ethics and Muslim culture by brand owners should be recognised to ensure successful brand communication. That is, communicating 'fair' and 'truthful', 'appreciation of women's role in society' and 'to respect elders' are among the important values to be incorporated into communication strategies as proposed by the author. This could help create an emotional bond and subsequently provide a sustainable competitive advantage for brands in generating long-term brand loyalty.

Chapter 10, contributed by **Özlem Sandıkcı**, discusses the marketing strategy and implications of emerging Muslim-majority markets and provides an analysis of the key dynamics involved, placing particular emphasis on the need to adopt a socio-culturally situated approach to the Islamic marketplace as necessitated by the multiplicities and complexities of Muslim markets around the world. Instead of focusing on a narrow conceptualization of halal, marketing scholars and practitioners are encouraged to expand their work by paying attention to how Islamic norms and principles play out more widely in the daily lives of Muslims. Thus marketers will gain enhanced insight into the conceptualizations of religion–market interaction and, in creating a deeper level of communication between themselves and Muslim consumers, be at the cutting edge in helping brands to achieve a sustainable and profitable position in the newly emerging markets of Muslim-majority countries.

In Chapter 11, **Nesrine Eltawy and David Gallear** discuss ways in which companies and businesses might enhance their supply chain performance when conducting business in Middle Eastern Islamic areas. First and foremost, they emphasise the need to clarify the definition of and to enhance understanding of the Islamic context. In doing so, the authors are challenging the conventional approach that has informed the work of previous researchers. In particular, they argue that building supply chain relationships and partnerships for companies working within Middle Eastern business environments is of extreme importance if companies are to succeed in enhancing business supply chain performance.

Finally, **Mazia Yassim** concludes the book (in Chapter 12) by providing a critical analysis of how Islamic marketing and branding can, as a topic, be moved forward, and the challenges it faces. Mazia Yassim explains the extent to which Islamic marketing has made strides since its formal conception and has managed to establish itself as a distinct discipline. Critical discourse and the nature of current research within the discipline are discussed and calls made for an examination into how the discipline might evolve in the future. However, there is a need for researchers to expand the contexts in which they conduct further studies, and for more variety and insight to be introduced into their approaches. The greatest challenge Islamic scholars and marketers face is in being more critical and insightful especially when discussing their own research implications. Lack of critical aspect hinders the advancement of this discipline. The author argues that whilst Islamic consumers share the same religious beliefs, they do not necessarily share the same values, and for one strategy to fit all Muslim target markets and all Islamic countries is impossible. The chapter concludes by considering how researchers might go about questioning why they are engaged in this discipline and whether they are prepared to become fully immersed in this complex debate, thereby committing themselves to shaping the future of the discipline.

We are truly grateful to our contributors, all of whom are well known in this area, in coming together to contribute the submissions which make up this book. All the submissions have been grouped according to the type of perspective under consideration, making it easy for students and practitioners to access information on trends, theory and practice in Islamic marketing and on branding in the international arena.

Due to the newness of the field of Islamic marketing and branding, it has been a challenging task for the editors to include every possible relevant topic in one book. We apologise in advance to readers who may feel that some topics have been overlooked. The book does not attempt to cover all issues, rather to initiate the application of marketing and branding concepts, in the Islamic sense, into practice. It fosters enthusiasm by encouraging original thought and by the stimulation of ideas surrounding topics, industries, contexts and approaches critical to this field. Contributors have duly tried to address the conceptual debate on how to enhance and advance our understanding of the ways in which Islamic marketing and branding are different from and similar to conventional marketing practices, and they have provided insight into the design of the marketing mix and marketing practices within Muslim target markets. Within this same religion, a one-size-fits-all strategy is impossible to implement due to the different pillars across Islamic countries. It is for this reason that marketers cannot treat all groups as similar or apply standardised marketing and branding strategies. Rather, a unique approach is required, and to balance that approach with conventional practices is still very important if Muslim consumer behaviour is to be properly understood and brand equity built to fit in with it.

Finally, we would like to thank again all those who have contributed to make this project a reality. Any success in this regard is to be credited to the authors. Thanks to the stimulating and contemporary topics provided, we are certain that this dynamic field of study and practice will continue to develop in the future. We welcome feedback and suggestions, which may be sent to S F Syed Alwi at Brunel University, sharifah.alwi@brunel.ac.uk.

References

Al-Serhan, B. (2011), *Principles of Islamic Marketing*, London, UK: Gower Publishing Limited.

Dinar Standard. (2015), *Global State Economy Report 2015 Growth, Strategy, Research and Advisory*. www. dinarstandard.com/state-of-the-global-islamic-economy-report-2015/ (accessed 18 December 2016).

Muhamad, R., Melewar, T. C., and Alwi, S. (2012), "Segmentation and Brand Positioning for Islamic Financial Services", *European Journal of Marketing*, Vol. 46, No. 7/8, 900–921.

Nestorović, Č. (2016), *Islamic Marketing: Understanding the Socio-Economic, Cultural, and Politico-Legal Environment*, New York: Springer.

Sandıkcı, Ö. and Rice, G. (Eds.). (2011). *Handbook of Islamic Marketing*. Cheltenham, UK: Edward Elgar Publishing.

Usunier, J. C. and Stolz, J. (2016), *Religions as Brands: New Perspectives on the Marketization of Religion and Spirituality*, London: Routledge.

Part I

Branding and corporate marketing

1 Corporate brands and marketing strategies

Jonathan A. J. Wilson and Jonathan Liu

Learning outcomes

At the end of this chapter, the reader should be able to:

1 Understand brand theory from several perspectives, or schools of thought
2 Map the relationship and significance of brands according to varying stakeholder perspectives
3 Identify marketing strategies within a hierarchy of Islamic compliance, Muslim cultures, and ethnocentrism
4 Reflect upon the impact of macro and micro factors on the theory and practice of Muslim consumption patterns and economic transactions

Key points

1 The Muslim economic landscape.
2 The argument for viewing brands and branding as entities linked to spirituality and animism.
3 What are the nascent schools of Branding thought and practice?
4 What is the role of the Corporate Branding amongst stakeholders?
5 What renders something Islamic and/or Halal?
6 How should Islamic brands and marketing deliver emotive, compelling and competitive propositions?

Introduction

A prima facie case can be made for Islamic Branding and Marketing being understood simply as the permissibility and compatibility of practices and offerings according to the teachings of Islam. However, the call to atomise, evaluate and certify all activities formally and subsequently label them cogently under legally branded corporate architectures has given rise to a new cultural phenomenon – and this is on the rise, inside and outside of Muslim geographies across the globe. Globalisation, change at scale, economic, technological, Hertzberg's hygiene and control factors are also transferring the domain of Islam more and more to a vanguard of businesses and branded consumption – as opposed to being just a religious imperative driven by the clergy. This chapter addresses the key areas and critical success factors necessary to deliver strategic approaches to Islamic Corporate Branding and Marketing.

Muslim geographies and economic factors

One quarter of the world's population are Muslim, with well over half of Muslims today under the age of 25 – which prompted Miles Young, global CEO of Ogilvy, to assert that Muslims are the "third one billion", following interest in Indian and Chinese billions, in terms of market opportunities (Ogilvy Noor, 2010, 2011). Furthermore, Muslims are expected to increase by over 35 percent in the next 20 years.

When considering the acronyms for the emerging economies to watch: in 2001 it was BRIC (Brazil, Russia, India and China); and more recently in 2013 MINT (Mexico, Indonesia, Nigeria, Turkey), and CIVETS (Columbia, Indonesia, Vietnam, Egypt, Turkey and South Africa) – then it is apparent that economies with large Muslim populations are growing in importance (Wilson, 2014a).

In addition, this is a trend on the increase in the West. The 2011 Census in the United Kingdom has the Muslim population at 2.7 million, which is 4.8 percent of the total population. Of those, around 100,000 are converts to Islam, about two thirds of whom are female. There were an estimated 5,200 conversions to Islam in 2011, making it the fastest growing religion in the UK between 2001 and 2009 – with Muslims increasing at a rate that is almost 10 times faster than the non-Muslim population. The French city of Marseilles is approximately one third Muslim, with predictions suggesting that it will soon become the first Muslim majority city in Europe (Wilson, 2014a; National Geographic, 2012; BBC, 2012).

Three arguments are usually presented to justify the imperative for operationalising Islam-centric business models, which are as follows:

1   Economic argument:

    Relies on deductive findings, based upon data presented to demonstrate the market potential through financial value, geographies and future sustainability through growing population figures.

2   Consumer-based perspective:

    Posits that beyond market value and size, there exists a consumer-based religious obligation to develop the sector, also inherent in their faith. There are growing needs and wants, with desires to align these with Islam and varying Muslim identities, regardless of temporal gains.

3   Geopolitical imperative:

    Commerce linked with Islam is influenced by geopolitics, and is held to be crucial when building international relations, political stability, and unique, yet collaborative and co-dependent national brand equities.

However, these perhaps are not reflective enough of the true nature of what is Islamic and Halal [which will be defined and discussed later], or embody the full range of their potential critical success factors. Furthermore, it is questionable whether we are witnessing developments in Islamic markets (as is posited) or Muslim markets (Wilson et al., 2013).

Pragmatically, it could be argued that what we have are Muslim markets and economies, with the aspiration of creating an Islamic system, through the sum total of Muslim
economies galvanizing themselves under a banner of 'Brand Islam' (Wilson, 2014a). Or
alternatively, this may be about Muslim geographies drawing from Islamic frames of reference and schools of thought collaboratively. On first reading, these two perspectives may
appear to be saying the same thing. However, the order in which this process happens will
yield differing consequences. The first is a bottom-up approach, and the second top-down
(Wilson, 2014b).

Branding as a spiritual entity

Brands with duplicitous transient and transcendent attributes push analysis towards more
figurative, tacit and implicit states, demanding more of marketers than simple financial
calculations based on purely economic value drivers. The following chapter takes a broad
view of corporate branding, in the interests of focussing attention on the cognitive affective and behavioural traits of external stakeholders – in line with more consumer-centric
brand approaches and the increase in two-way media communication channels, which are
creating new patterns of consumption.

Recent geopolitical events, trade and commerce in the Middle East and North Africa
(MEANA) and Asia Pacific regions, the heartlands of the Muslim world, emphatically
point to religious observance remaining a fundamental component, which impacts on
corporate and individual value systems (Liu and Wilson, 2011; Wilson and Hollensen,
2013). Anecdotally, Islamic Finance, *Halal* and *Kosher* certified products and services are
witnessing recession resistance and growth, beyond their core audience of faithful followers, supported by empirical evidence from BrandFinance® observing that "the Middle
East has seen a 78% growth in brand value, based on high demand for Islamic banking
products and services" (Wilson and Liu, 2010).

At the very heart of the matter, when societies try to understand and ultimately control
religion, frequently wider discussions split thought into two basic camps and philosophical
mind-sets, namely: either proving or refuting if there is such a thing as a divine being (if
not many). And similarly, if there is such a thing as an afterlife, and what impact does this
have on our conceptual understanding of transcendence? (Wilson and Hollensen, 2013).
The argument being that rational proof and evidence offers easier anchors for control.
Polemically it is argued that the fact that the majority individuals live believing that an
afterlife is present means that from a business and economics perspective of supply and
demand, these concepts should be viewed as, rather than needing an answer, instead being
served and evaluated. Furthermore, established proof and evidence of human thoughts,
feelings and actions suggest that from a business perspective a sufficient platform for
advancement already exists. Therefore, what remains key is a refinement of understanding
towards practical day-to-day affairs and their impact, rather than an over-arching philosophical debate.

Currently, many definitions of religion within business and management are often
restrictive and literalist. The argument here is in favour of scanning and examining a wide
spread of human activities – such as sport, music, fashion and food. The view is that each
has the propensity to evoke a form of fanaticism, ritualism and spirituality, demonstrable
of a common ground – which is arguably religious (Wilson and Liu, 2009). This identified religious fervour, which stretches beyond conventional definitions of religion to more
post-modern pluralism and consumption, we have termed *Neo-spiritualism*.

Furthermore, religious and spiritual value systems appear to:

1   Govern critical aspects of decision making
2   Blend cognitive, affective and conative routed processes
3   Draw from diverse viewpoints but arrive at similar conceptual destinations
4   Encourage vertical and horizontal relationship building
5   Oscillate between esoteric and exoteric interpretations
6   Involve storytelling, linked to consumption and rituals
7   Be situation specific
8   Set clear boundaries supported by psychological contracts
9   Create didactic polarisation of systems
10 Help emotionally mediate and mitigate individual losses

Brands are created with the intention by their owners of encouraging consumption, patronage and the formation of a relationship, which it could be argued ultimately craves their worship – so much so that with their increase in importance, some brands have both individually and collectively managed to attain 'god-like' statuses. Driving this movement has been a trend of drawing from, aligning and blending religious language, rituals, mythology, symbolism and meanings – in order to gain deeper significance and competitive advantage. This has been embedded within the brand itself and/or been supported by marketing communications messages.

Even within monotheistic doctrines, there is the suggestion that humans have a propensity towards comparable polytheistic practices, whilst however being discouraged. In the Abrahamic monotheistic faiths, worshipers are commanded to worship one deity. Maltby et al. (2002) state that "the word 'gods' is usually interpreted broadly to include not just other religious deities, but non-religious concepts and persons as well" (p. 1160). Muslims are reminded on numerous occasions within the Qur'an and supporting religious texts, such as *ahadith*, of the ease by which they may in fact behave as polytheists.

Maltby et al. (2002), however, go on to assert that

> it could be hypothesised that attitudes toward celebrities would be unrelated to religiosity. The concept of compartmentalisation might be invoked in support of this hypothesis. We compartmentalise when we take beliefs and mentally separate them from their unpleasant consequences. This allows us to maintain positive feelings about ourselves by detaching ourselves from the unpleasant consequences. Thus, Christians can believe in the story of the Good Samaritan, but detach themselves from the responsibility of behaving like the Good Samaritan.
>
> (p. 1160)

The symbiotic phenomenon of corporate branding and religion appears to be applicable in a comparable fashion to elite celebrities, who seek to craft their identities into corporate brands – able to offer further brand extension opportunities. It can also be argued reciprocally that corporate brands seek to emulate the emotive and human qualities of celebrities (Wilson and Liu, 2009). Whilst Maltby et al. (2002) largely comment on and obtain data from Christians, these traits can be extended to include worshippers from other faiths, such as Islam.

In addition, atheists and agnostics, as part of a polemical discourse, are often described by their religious counterparts as in fact creating their own rituals and objects of desire;, which could be comparably interpreted as being a form of religion, as observed by Jindra

(2004). Examples lie in politics, sport, music and celebrities, amongst others. Notable examples are present when studying the reverence shown by fans of such individuals as Elvis Presley, Michael Jackson, Bob Marley, Tupac Shakur and David Beckham. Jindra (2004) also talks of Star Trek fans organising, recruiting and holding ceremonies/conventions, with fan bases that resemble religions. Furthermore this appears to stretch to inanimate objects, where consumers have queued up overnight to purchase the latest Apple handset or sports jersey, despite already being able to fulfil many of the functions, through existing product offerings.

Giles (2002) argues that fame can be interpreted as a quest to preserve a unique part of life for eternity – which applies the concept of a belief in the hereafter. Giles (2000) extends this to liken celebrity worship to religious worship. Evidence of this lies in the illicit acts of some celebrities being ignored, mentally deleted, mitigated or even forgiven (Wilson and Morgan, 2011). Furthermore, according to Giles (2002) the similarities between religion and celebrity worship in their psychological and physical demonstration of obsessive compulsion appear apparent. These are manifest in surrounding rituals and day-dreaming.

Nascent schools of branding thought and practice

Following a taxonomy undertaken by Heding, Knudtzen and Bjerre (2009), representative of a systematic analysis of 300+ brand management research articles, spanning the period of 1985–2006, it is suggested that these various approaches can be categorised within seven groups:

1   Economic
2   Identity
3   Consumer-based
4   Personality
5   Relational
6   Community
7   Cultural

"These seven 'schools of thought' represent fundamentally different perceptions of the brand, the nature of the brand-consumer exchange, and how brand equity is created and managed" (Heding, Knudtzen and Bjerre, 2009, p. 3). Through their analysis, Heding, Knudtzen and Bjerre (2009) also sought to highlight key terms which have come into existence.

This chapter focuses on the following identified terms: Brand Community, Brand Culture, Brand Loyalty and Brand Relation as a basis for further discussions. The rationale is that they appear to be of most relevance when investigating the nature of various brand interactions. Groups 2–7 as identified by Heding, Knudtzen and Bjerre (2009) are reflective of a movement towards the defining tacit and figurative aspects of a brand, which suggest that emotion plays a significant role – and in doing so human characteristics are projected onto a brand, termed the *Pinocchio effect* by Wilson and Liu (2009).

Following this, the practice of reciprocity is driving forward the concept that brands interact with consumers beyond the surface assumption of economic gains being the only critical success factor. Furthermore, Bourdieu (1977) discusses the concept of symbolic capital and its accumulation, which is manifest in prestige, status and reputation. Following this, Pitt et al. (2006) suggest that organisations and individuals that give more away, contribute to community or provide more services "are held in higher regard and reputation" (p. 124).

With regard to the cultural approach, the assertion is that it is a by-product of a phenomenon where "the brand is subjected to social and cultural changes completely outside the brand manager's control . . . this means that the marketer is not the only author behind the brand meanings" (Heding, Knudtzen and Bjerre, 2009, p. 211). A cornerstone of the cultural approach lies in the assertion that a brand is perceived as a cultural artefact. Holt (2002) asserts that in the cultural approach, "A 'bottom-up' interpretation of data is applied; the informants are not expected to express idiosyncratic meanings, but rather to be acting as mouthpieces of the surrounding culture" (p. 73). From this we assert that brands attempt to do just this – by embedding themselves within more and more experiential communities.

Aaker (1991), de Chernatony and McDonald (2003), Czellar (2003), Franzen and Bowman (2001), Keller (1993) and Lindstrom (2005) state that brands are best understood from a consumer perspective. As consumers interact and are subjected to the influence of non-consumers outside of their brand community, their understanding is examined with respect to those 'others' that they choose to engage with, and hence will have a bearing on their stake.

Building on Holt's (2002) position articulated in 'Why Do Brands Cause Trouble?', this chapter presents an adjunct position, which focuses on the effects of Islamic branding. Holt (2002) asserts that brands dictate tastes, through becoming cultural products. In doing so, brands afford companies the opportunity to dodge civic obligations. Furthermore, in response to this phenomenon, the anti-branding movement seeks to address this trend – and here is where the battleground lies.

The dynamics within the Islam-centric practices demonstrate a similar pattern of events – however, they differ in the manner in which the battle is being fought. Ingredient branding plays a central role in the Muslim psyche, as a means by which authenticity and heritage are evaluated. Most visibly this can be seen with single-issue politics groups calling for a boycott of certain brands and the emergence of subsequent copy-cat boycott brands, such as Mecca Cola, Qibla Cola, Zam Zam Cola and Evoca Cola. Therefore, it would appear that being *Islamic* is something that is both an ingredient and a core brand proposition itself, whereby such duplicity and oscillations have the potential to cause trouble. Furthermore, Islam, Halal and Islamic memes may be explicit, implicit or tacit.

Corporate stakeholder analysis

Brand theory reflects tensions that exist when trying to position stakeholders according to their role, influence, motivations and gains. From a corporate perspective, the idea of *Homo sociologicus* is apparent in the formalisation of Corporate Altruism, and Corporate and Social Responsibility (CSR) functions. Branding is used in many of these cases as a means by which activities can be linked back to the organisation – using Public Relations frameworks. In doing so, organisations are operating under an idea of reciprocity and delayed gratification. Branding plays a supporting role to integrated Marketing Communications in these activities. However, through adopting this role there is also a reciprocal value enjoyed by the brand, which helps to build its efficacy. Furthermore, with management theory suggesting that employees should be viewed as being internal customers, the idea that a brand is an external function and marketing tool appears outdated.

Freeman (1984) defines a stakeholder as being "any group or individual who can affect or is affected by the achievement of an organisation's objectives" (p. 46).

It is worth noting that brands with duplicitous transient and transcendent attributes push stakeholder analysis towards more figurative, tacit and implicit states, demanding the inclusion of additional parties – due to their influence. Furthermore, brands require analysis that reflects this departure from purely economic value drivers.

Following Freeman's (1984) definition, Mitchell, Agle and Wood (1997) state that stakeholders can be identified as being

> primary or secondary stakeholders; as owners and nonowners of the firm; as owners of capital or owners of less tangible assets; as actors or those acted upon; as those existing in a voluntary or an involuntary relationship with the firm; as rights-holders, contractors, or moral claimants; as resource providers to or dependents of the firm; as risk-takers or influencers; and as legal principals to whom agent-managers bear a fiduciary duty.
>
> (pp. 853–854)

Within the extensive list of identifying factors provided by Mitchell, Agle and Wood (1997) appears a construct that seeks to classify parties according to a scale of:

1 Ownership of associated assets
2 Participatory positive/neutral/negative relationships
3 Propensity to influence positively/negatively
4 Reciprocal duty, trust and confidence.

Broad versus narrow view of stakeholder analysis

Broad: "companies can indeed be vitally affected by, or they can vitally affect almost anyone" (Mitchell et al., 1997, p. 857)
Narrow: focussing on those whom an organisation is dependent upon "for its continued survival" (Freeman and Reed, 1983, p. 91)

Windsor (1992) highlights that broad or narrow views of the stakeholders' universe affect the way in which they are defined and subsequently classified. The Freeman (1984) definition takes a broad view and suggests that "companies can indeed be vitally affected by, or they can vitally affect almost anyone" (Mitchell, Agle and Wood, 1997, p. 857) whilst that expressed by Freeman and Reed (1983) in parallel is narrower, focussing on those whom an organisation is dependent on "for its continued survival" (p. 91).

Clarkson (1995) suggests that "corporations manage relationships with stakeholder groups rather than society as a whole" (p. 92) and that stakeholders' interests may be towards past, present or future corporate activities (p. 106). He also asserts that the term "*stakeholder* is not synonymous with *shareholder*" (p. 112). Following this, Clarkson (1995) classifies stakeholders into *primary* and *secondary* groups. Primary stakeholders are defined as those "without whose continuing participation the corporation cannot survive as a going concern" (Clarkson, 1995, p. 106). Clarkson (1995) states that they "typically are comprised of shareholders and investors, employees, customers, and suppliers, together with what is defined as the public stakeholder group" (p. 106). Secondary stakeholders according to Clarkson (1995)

> are defined as those who influence or affect, or are influenced by, the corporation, but they are not engaged in transactions with the corporation and are not essential for its survival. . . . They have the capacity to mobilize public opinion in favor of, or in opposition to, a corporation's performance.
>
> (p. 107)

Brand architecture and positioning

Beyond the physical market positioning and architecture of brands, their spatial relationship in the mind of consumers is of significance, according to ownership and alignment with consumers' value systems (Ries and Trout, 1982; Marsden, 2002). As an extension of associative network mapping of the human memory (Galton, 1880; Freud, 1924; Deese, 1965; Anderson and Bower, 1973) and drawing from Zipf (1965) and Dawkins (1976), Marsden (2002) ascribes the science of culture and creativity to a process of positioning *memetics* (genes of meaning).

Within this process, corporate brands aim to offer a transparent paper trail of heritage antecedents, which both attract and guide consumers on a path of assimilation. From this, a brand's essence housed within a cultural context and sustained by stakeholders maintains its strategic value (Holt, 2002, 2004, 2005; de Chernatony, 2001). Brands rely on stakeholders to their ascribe meaning and value. However it can also be argued that corporate brands are the glue that binds stakeholders together – and therefore a relationship of symbiosis and reciprocity exists.

Research undertaken by Fiedler and Kirchgeorg (2007) supports the view that stakeholder groups can be identified and "the attributes differ substantially among customers, employees, shareholders and journalists" (p. 183). This correlates with Jones (2005) view, where he seeks to arrange internal and external stakeholder groups around a brand centred "daisy wheel" (p. 18); which is also termed as a hub-and-spoke model by other sources. In contrast, Bhattacharya and Korschun (2008) assert:

> Much of the current thinking in stakeholder theory is still tied to the classic hub-and-spoke model, in which stakeholders are distinct and mutually exclusive. However there is a growing consensus that a firm's constituents are actually embedded in interconnected networks of relationships through which the actions of the firm reverberate with both direct and indirect consequences.
>
> (p. 113)

Therefore they suggest that "one urgent need involves frameworks that identify key stakeholders and describe their motivations for collaborating with the firm" (p. 116). From this it can be taken that branding attempts to do just this – embedding itself within more and more communities. In doing so brands draw in more stakeholders, ultimately sacrificing power from the hands of the corporate brand owner, knowingly or not – but as a necessary evil to ensure its success. Brands require the oxygen of communication to survive and therefore depend on their stakeholders to breathe life into them. It therefore follows that the more stakeholders that exist and discuss a brand's existence – warts and all, the positive and negative, the longer their life and potentially the more health they will enjoy. Following these discussions, this chapter presents two approaches to brand stakeholder analysis: a *Broad-based Macro View* and a *Narrow-based Micro* view.

Having reviewed the theoretical relationship between brands and their various stakeholders, the following section now attempts to position stakeholders according to their involvement (as exhibited in Figure 1.1). In the interests of attempting to take a broad-based view of involvement, or *stake*, parties will be mapped according to their level of interest, demonstrated through communication. From this, stakeholders are investigated, according to ownership and non-ownership of the brand. In doing so, the focus is shifted

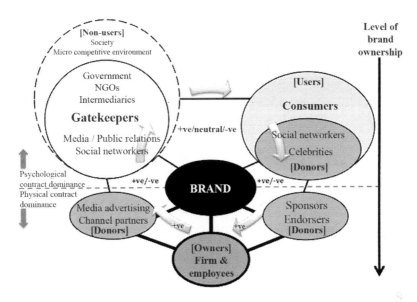

Figure 1.1 Brand stakeholder model – through communication mapping

Source: Wilson, 2011a

towards values rooted in opinion. The strategic value to corporate brand management is that participation and inter-connected opinions and states are communicated – converging towards the brand. In keeping with Mitchell, Agle and Wood (1997), a coefficient of time is also introduced, which preserves dynamism in relationships and stakes.

Stakeholders are positioned according to:

1   Ownership/non-Ownership/temporary Ownership, *Donorship*
2   Usage/non-Usage
3   Communication
4   Stake – qualified according to: bargaining power/interest/impact

Each of these states is seen to have a positive, negative or neutral effect on the brand in question.

The dotted line represents a notion of contractual obligations: which are actual, in a physical format, or implied and psychological. For example, when looking at the media, advertising channel partners are bound by formal written agreements, whilst journalists who act as public relations gatekeepers have no obligation to support or champion a brand. From this it can also be seen that those who share a psychological contract pose a greater potential threat to brands, due to a lack of control over their communications and ability to influence brand meanings and perceptions.

Notes:

A broad view of stakeholders is taken – at a macro/mezzo level, drawing from the cultural approach to branding, along with Freeman's (1984) definition, and the attributes listed by Mitchell et al. (1997). This presents stakeholder roles as *interconnected* and *dynamic* states, which are subject to time-specific communication, influence and self-defined legitimacy. Here, intangible and figurative aspects of branding are taken into consideration, which also suggest that

- Roles can and will shift.
- Interest groups may oscillate between homogeneity and heterogeneity.
- Individuals occupy *states* which are subject to variance and are a culmination of collective interactions.

Diamond et al. (2009) talk of the *brand gestalt* which best explains brand power through "a combination of elements, and the reciprocal influences among them". In this, they assert that powerful brands may not be those

> with the greatest number of positive associations or those with the most compelling myths or the largest and most interactive communities or those with the largest and most interactive communities or those that provide spectacular retail environments with the most opportunities for emplaced coercion. They may instead be brands whose components evidence the greatest degree of synergy and whose constituent parts best complement and enhance one another.
>
> (Diamond et al., 2009, p. 131)

Guiding principles of Islamic branding and marketing

Classical definitions of Halal

Halal[1] is an Arabic word that can be found in the Qur'an, which can be translated simply as meaning permissible, according to the teachings of Islam. The Qur'an (literally meaning 'The Recitation' in Arabic) is considered to be word of Allah (Arabic for the monotheistic God), as revealed to the Prophet Muhammad, by the Angel Gabriel (Jibra'il in Arabic). The Qur'an presents a framework that blends interconnected narratives, references to nature, historical events and the future, polemical arguments, interrogatives, analogies, allegories and rhetoric, signs and symbolism – all of which are designed to offer guidance to the faithful. The Arabic used and verses are held to be of the highest written and spoken calibre.

Following the revelations, scholars undertook a systematic and scientific mapping of the Qur'an to the sayings and practices of the Prophet Muhammad and his closest companions, in order to derive an understanding of how the teachings should be interpreted and implemented. These form the foundations of Shari'ah law. The term 'law' perhaps fails to communicate what the shari'ah is and is designed for. A more correct translation of the Arabic word shar'iah would be 'well trodden path', as it has a wider remit, covering crime, politics, economics, business, science, family relations, hygiene, diet, moral conduct, etiquette and worship.

An example of the depth of knowledge available can be seen when looking at a Tafsir (Arabic for Qur'anic exergesis) by Al-Qurtubi, who is one of many scholars to write one. Aisha Bewley has translated the Tafsir Al-Qurtubi into English, covering the first two chapters of the Qur'an (out of 114), and this runs over 782 pages. Tafsir Al-Qurtubi is of particular interest as it analyses the Qur'an from the perspective of the inhabitants of

Muslim Spain. Therefore, when reviewing the role of Islam in the West, as is often debated, in fact precedents have already been set centuries ago (Wilson, (2012b).

An example of methods for interpreting texts for legal and linguistic rulings identified by Ramic (2003) is listed as follows:

- The General Meaning (*al-'Amm*)
- The Specific (*al-Khass*)
- The Specification of Meaning (*al-Takhsis*)
- The Apparent (*al-Zahir*)
- The Explained (*al-Muhkam*)
- The Alluded Meaning (*Isharat al-Nass*)
- The Inferred Meaning (*Dalalat al-Nas*)

Here, similarities can be seen with more modern methods of grounded theory coding, hermeneutics, critical discourse and content analysis.

A further example of interest hails from al-Qayrawani (1999), who examines the classical Islamic scholar and founder of the Maliki school of thought, Imam Malik. Imam Malik is also the first person to record and write a collection of *ahadith* (Arabic for sayings and practices of the Prophet Muhammad). Subsequently, there have been several other books of *ahadith* from different scholars. Central to Malik's approach was giving consideration to and presenting a coherent narrative of guidelines to every facet of human existence and daily living. Therefore, when considering the Halal landscape today, I argue that books such as Malik's are of use when considering fields like Muslim consumer behaviour. Furthermore, the very fact that there are chapters devoted to hospitality means that the text lends itself to being a pragmatic and accessible source of reference.

Furthermore, whilst there are immutable and specific rules and guidelines, within these the shari'ah is intended also to accommodate evolutionary thought, practice and progression. The fundamental principle underpinning these activities is that individuals have the correct intention, and their decisions are derived from evidence. The word *Muslim* is derived from the Arabic, meaning one who consciously submits to Allah, in accordance with Islam. However, it is also worth mentioning that consciousness is judged according to free will and the ability to reason. So for example, children, those with certain mental disabilities, and even nature are considered to have such a relationship with their creator, without having to declare their faith.

A basic acceptance and understanding of what is Halal is central to every Muslim's belief – falling under the umbrella of what is considered to be information that is known by necessity. The opposite of this word in Arabic is *Haram*.[2] A general rule of Islamic jurisprudence holds everything as Halal, unless stated otherwise, with the exception of meat.[3] Therefore a Muslim (follower of Islam) who has a sound grounding in Islam should be able to identify what is Halal and what is not.

Halal as a new cultural phenomenon

It would be easy to dismiss this simply as being the commercialisation and commodification of religion by industry; however, there are strong indications that this is also being driven by consumers.

There are two key influencing factors that are encouraging consumer engagement:

9/11: Firstly, we are seeing Muslims searching for a way to reach out and harness the spirit of spirituality in a post 9/11 era, in an attempt to re-claim their religion and challenge wider negative perceptions. Similar patterns of behaviour can be found historically, following social and geopolitical events affecting post-war Germany, Japan and the African-American civil rights movement. Parallels can also be drawn with sentiments expressed during the Industrial Revolution, which are largely attributed to Christian entrepreneurs: of wealth and value creation being moral acts – and acts of worship intended to pave the roads of paradise for the faithful on earth and in the hereafter. The sentiments are very much that:

- Religion does have a place in business, offering an additional or revised set of guiding principles and moral compass.
- Religious beliefs are a key segmentation criterion and trait.
- Business can be a vehicle for transformational social change linked to religion.
- An Islamic economy offers a new unit of analysis, in addition to national and geographical, which redefines boundaries and tends towards a more cultural frame of reference.
- Islamic economics is a contemporary and grounded approach to challenging some counterproductive current worldviews of Islam, which often pose Islam as being a construct that is de-coupled from the West, or capitalism – through focussing on social interaction and transactions in the widest sense.

Social media: Secondly, social media affords consumers the ability to engage with each other across geographies, and with economic and business issues much more. This has expanded the net of stakeholder engagement further away from narrow-based perspectives of stakeholders being defined as people on whom a business relies for survival, towards broad-based views where a stakeholder is someone who has an interest and a voice. More so than ever, consumers have a voice on various platforms, which give them power, legitimacy and urgency. Furthermore, there has been a democratisation of information that allows individuals and collectives the opportunity to debate, mediate, collaborate, create and adjudicate.

Classifying and categorising Islamic marketing

In connection with Halal and Islamic finance, currently there are debates that question what "Islamic Marketing" actually means. For example, does it only consider how marketers should communicate with Muslims? Or is being a Muslim an essential element needed to execute Islamic Marketing? A fundamental development is that now the field is more than simply marketing a religion, or marketing to the faithful. Furthermore, if Islamic Marketing is posited as a subset of religion, as argued by Wilson and Grant (2013), it runs the risk of being a fad.

If Islamic Finance and Marketing are to cement their legitimacy and unique attributes over the long term, then these factors have to be considered. Also, like other niche areas that have crossed over to being viewed as mass transnational markets, they will evolve. In light of these observations, Wilson (2012a) proposes the following working definition of Islamic Marketing, which sees it existing on three interdependent levels (see Figure 1.2):

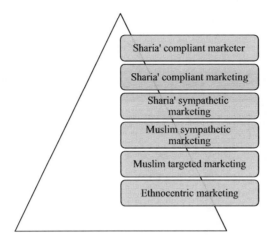

Figure 1.2 Hierarchy of Islamic marketing approaches

Source: Wilson, 2012a

1   The acknowledgement of a God-conscious approach to marketing: from a marketer's and/or consumer's perspective, which draws from the drivers or traits associated with Islam.
2   A progressive school of thought, which has a moral compass that tends towards the ethical norms and values of Islam and how Muslims interpret these, from their varying cultural lenses.
3   A multi-layered, dynamic and contextual gestalt phenomenon of Muslim and non-Muslim stakeholder engagement, which considers the creation and preservation of explicit, implicit and tacit signalling associated with Islam. These cues, triggers and networks are embodied by objects and experiences – which give rise to reciprocal cultural artefacts that are facilitated by marketing.

Therefore, the suggestion here is that the bedrock of marketing products and services successfully should rely upon an approach that is predominantly ethnocentric. Marketers often highlight shari'ah compliance and target predominantly those partners and consumers who seek compliance – rendering the product offering as niche and rational, which does not necessarily achieve full penetration. Instead, the argument is that moving down the pyramid from top to bottom could be a strategic corporate objective, but equally there is no reason why the same objectives could not be attempted in tandem, instead of in a sequential hierarchy.

Following the same train of thought, marketing communications should contain a depth of encoded messages that appeals to a selection of homogenous segments. Shared culture and ethnocentrism are held to be unifying factors that can mediate heterogeneity.

The Islamic Brand paradigm

Central to an Islamic Brand paradigm are two positions: firstly, any brand has the potential to engage with Muslim consumers; and secondly, if a brand craves treatment and consideration as a living entity, in what was termed previously the *Pinocchio effect* (Wilson and Liu, 2009), should it not instead be classified conceptually as *Muslim* within Islamic Brand

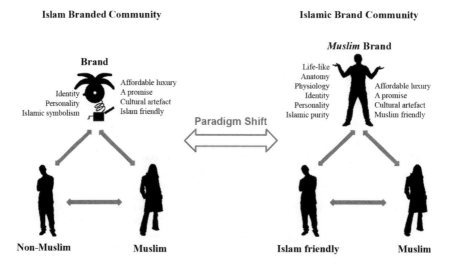

Figure 1.3 Creating Islamic Brand communities

Source: Wilson and Liu, 2011

theory? The reason is that within current literature descriptions of brands, *ceteris paribus*,[4] they are rendered as emotional complex organisms. Furthermore, a brand has no free will – like animals who are also considered Muslims, *de facto*[5] *et de jure*.[6]

Finally, a question which still remains contentious is what makes something an Islamic Brand? The following positions are reflective of differing perspectives:

- Positive assertion by the organisation, through the brand
- The nature of the product or service offering
- Country of origin
- Destination of the brand
- The faith of the corporate owner(s)
- Halal ingredient certification
- The share of Muslim and Muslim/Islam-friendly consumer base
- The share of Muslim employees
- Positive citation of Muslim friendly consumer and employee policies/practices
- Islamic- or Islam-inspired symbolism and messages (see illustration as shown in Figure 1.3)

Furthermore, Wilson and Liu (2010) suggest that *Halal* will always be an enigma: "What is deemed halal is ultimately governed by the heavens and subsequently therefore can never remain in its entirety within materialist branding frameworks" – and as such, a literal and pre-scriptive definition of an Islamic Brand, will remain elusive" (Wilson and Liu, 2010, p. 108).

Pragmatically it does not transpire that all Islamic corporate brands necessarily are Halal, or completely Halal – especially where there are an extensive number of branded product or service offerings. The following four product examples housed within non-Islamic/ Halal corporate brands illustrate this point, even where these named offerings are in fact permissible:

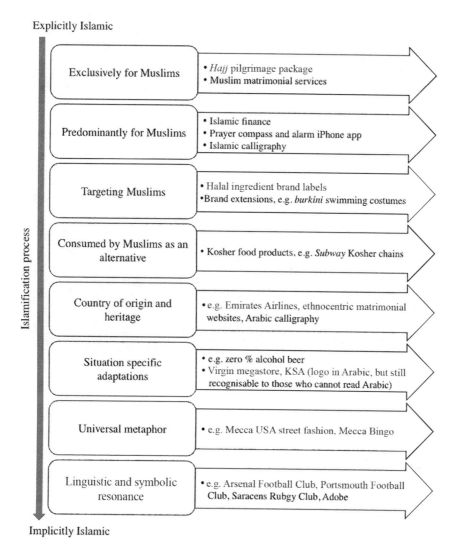

Explicitly Islamic

Islamification process

Exclusively for Muslims	• *Hajj* pilgrimage package • Muslim matrimonial services
Predominantly for Muslims	• Islamic finance • Prayer compass and alarm iPhone app • Islamic calligraphy
Targeting Muslims	• Halal ingredient brand labels • Brand extensions, e.g. *burkini* swimming costumes
Consumed by Muslims as an alternative	• Kosher food products, e.g. *Subway* Kosher chains
Country of origin and heritage	• e.g. Emirates Airlines, ethnocentric matrimonial websites, Arabic calligraphy
Situation specific adaptations	• e.g. zero % alcohol beer • Virgin megastore, KSA (logo in Arabic, but still recognisable to those who cannot read Arabic)
Universal metaphor	• e.g. Mecca USA street fashion, Mecca Bingo
Linguistic and symbolic resonance	• e.g. Arsenal Football Club, Portsmouth Football Club, Saracens Rubgy Club, Adobe

Implicitly Islamic

Figure 1.4 Hierarchy of Islamic Branding perspectives and interpretations
Source: Wilson and Liu, 2011

1 Cobra Zero beer is Halal, consumed by Muslims and well received, but not Islamic in the classical sense, nor does it profess to be.

2 Mecca Bingo and Mecca USA (clothing companies) carry brand names which are clearly inspired by Islam, and the holiest of Islamic places. Furthermore, they seek to inspire consumers through these associations, in the same manner of unrivalled devotion exhibited by Muslims. However, neither brand professes to be *Islamic*. Also, with such weak associations, this has the potential to cause these brands trouble. Having stated this, it is possible that Muslim consumers may in fact gravitate towards Mecca USA clothing – purely and simply because it does reaffirm and enhance an Islamic identity when worn by a Muslim. In contrast, this phenomenon is far less likely to be the case with Bingo.

Figure 1.5 Outside the mall containing the Virgin Megastore, Jeddah, KSA

Source: Wilson, J.A.J.

3   The Virgin Megastore in Jeddah, Saudi Arabia (KSA), along with a Virgin café in the same mall, provides a Halal environment for consumers. The shops and products are deemed to be compatible with Islam – albeit at times perhaps tenuous, with some of the music CDs containing material that some more conservative quarters would find offensive. Virgin also adapted its logo into Arabic whilst being able to preserve its symbolism – ensuring that it is still recognisable to non-Arabic speakers (see Figure 1.5).

   Arabic is the language of Islam. Arabic calligraphy is held in high esteem, not only for this reason, but also as it is considered to be Islam's outlet for creative and artistic expression – in a way comparable to Christian iconography.

4   Emirates Airlines also uses Islamic calligraphy and Arab symbolism. They cater to a Muslim audience by providing Halal offerings and fly to destinations which are largely Muslim countries. Yet, they adopt a more pluralistic position in serving the wider community with alcohol and enforcing a uniform for female cabin crew that has 'half-a-*hijab*[7]' – worn only on one side of the head.

Furthermore, brand theory puts forward the proposition that a brand can be separated from the product and service in that: name, personality, identity, relationship, etc. can be created separately from the offering – and in doing so this expands the collective meaning, purpose and consumption of the tangible and intangible entity. For example, following basic Pavlovian and inductive principles: irreverence, seduction and desire can be the attributes of a brand, which are then grafted onto the functionality of a product or service – resulting in the creation of an irreverent and seductive object of desire. Within the Halal industry, it is

Islam and more specifically Halal which assumes this position conceptually, rather than any corporate or product brand. Therefore, it is Halal instead of branding which becomes the paradigm (see these interpretations further as exhibited in Figure 1.4).

The challenge of mass production and globalisation

In the initial stages of Halal development, it could be argued that the reasons for its inception were that it was a reaction in Muslim-minority or narrow-majority populations for a need to provide assurances that food was fit for Muslim consumption, and it presented an opportunity for Muslim economic and business growth.

However, now further down the line, another reason for the Halal phenomenon continuing to gain traction, in a similar way to organic, fair trade and other initiatives, is driven by the need to identify, regulate, control, track and communicate far more processes and activities. This is expanding the remit and definition of Halal in such a way that it is encapsulating more of the classical interpretations as to what Halal is and is for. In a nuanced, transnational, multicultural and pluralist global landscape, with interconnected supply chains and trade agreements, there is now an understanding that a Halal paradigm has to play a central role in Islamic economics.

Changing consumption patterns

Being a Muslim is not necessarily a defining factor as to whether these propositions are appealing to businesses or consumers. This is very much about mind-sharing and developing an alternative business model and value proposition which crosses over. Niche is becoming mainstream.

Secondly, as I mentioned earlier, the majority view is that Halal is the norm and Haram, or non-Halal, is the exception. Whilst I concur with this construct as a general principle, it appears that the recent phenomenon of creating Halal logos and branding strategies has created both opportunities and challenges, which are changing classical interpretations and understanding of what Halal is.

The drivers for this are a type of hyper-sensitivity and hyper-interactivity which are encouraged by:

- The commodification of entities through branding and national boundary ownership
- Hyper-information exchanges and education, which bring constituent components under scrutiny
- The mass manufacture of bulk commodities
- Technological and genetic engineering advancements
- Challenges by single-issue politics and anti-branding movements

This is especially interesting, as the phenomenon of branding products as Halal is also being practiced in countries, such as Saudi Arabia, with almost exclusive Muslim majorities. Whilst some may see this as a positive movement encouraging Muslim commerce and consumption, underpinned by Islam, it is also possible that a by-product may be the repositioning of Halal labelling as a hygiene factor, whose absence could encourage greater perceived consumer risk.

Whilst the intention has been to create an Islamic approach to human existence, in many ways the emergence of Islamic Finance and Halal has been reactionary – and therefore about purification and risk reduction. The potential impact that this has on businesses and Muslim consumers is that a sense of caution, fear or suspicion could increase – everything needs to be branded as Halal, and nothing seems Halal enough. Therefore, whilst everything is Halal unless stated otherwise according to religious texts, this is in many ways being reversed today according to consumer behaviour and business practices – everything appears not to be Halal, unless stated as such. The long-term effect is that Halal will continue to be used as a niche and reactionary strategy, generating 'me too' or Islamic versions of existing offerings. In doing so, agenda setting and true innovation, rather than just adaptation strategies, can never occur.

Thirdly, Islamic Finance and Halal are still finding their way as to how these offerings can be promoted and communicated. What claims can be made reasonably, ethically and in a compelling way without falling into the trap of some previous marketing approaches? Also, should there be stricter constraints on consumerism? Or for example, how do we reconcile essential marketing activities where models in adverts and celebrities are selected according to criteria of physical attractiveness, allure and their ability to enact opulence, amongst other things?

Conclusions

Especially as they are rooted in dynamic, transnational and emerging markets, Halal, Islam and Muslims will always present market opportunities whilst also causing brand academics and practitioners nuanced challenges. But in many ways these problems are no different than those posed by other consumer segments balancing macro and micro factors, where niche offerings attempt to cross over.

However, what is acute to the relationship between marketers and Muslims is the fact that many Brand theories have been developed in isolation from, or at their worst as part of, a foreign hegemony – which all parties are seeking to overturn (Wilson and Liu., 2010). Furthermore, the number of Muslims is growing and growing in proportion to other segments (Wilson, 2014a, 2014b, Ogilvy, 2010).

Whilst conceptually and culturally brands and branding have always existed, brand theory as defined in business academic writing has largely hailed from the West, until recently. Just as the Ancient Greeks and Romans, Arabs, Indians and Chinese have collectively laid down many of the fundamentals of mathematics, we argue that marketers are in a middle passage of learning – which necessitates the same cross-fertilisation of concepts. Branding in particular, due to its ethereal qualities, will pose even bigger problems when trying to understand what brands can do and how they manage to do it.

If Islamic Brands are to take centre stage as a global force across segments and beyond to non-Muslims, they cannot be neutered and sanitised when considering their emotional brand anatomy and physiology. We suggest therefore that these traits could be preserved when rendering a brand analogous to a Muslim, rather than Islam. This aligns thinking with current schools of mainstream brand thought, which frame brands as being like humans, as a form of animism.

Muslim consumer behaviour and corporate practices point towards perspectives which reframe Halal – rendering it a modern construct existing within boundaries rooted in economics, identity formation and branded consumption. The challenge faced by marketers from an academic, Islamic and ethical perspective is to identify, understand and respond to this phenomenon; which is a dynamic and cyclical process, whose final verdict is finite and perishable – due to hyper-sensitivity, hyper-interactivity and environmental factors influencing Muslim perceptions of what is Halal.

Moving forward, a key area for discussion therefore is what emotional elements are acceptable within Islamic and Halal paradigms: how can they be evoked, and to what degree can they be deployed? As stated by Wilson and Liu (2010), few Islamic corporate brands appear yet to be able to satiate both the rational and the emotional beyond mere functional and materialistic interpretations. For example, emotions such as seduction and humour appear to be contentious topics when discussed in connection with Islamic Brands (Wilson and Hollensen, 2011). If overtly Islamic and Halal brands are to take centre stage, within the psyche of the Muslim consumer and beyond to a wider global audience, they cannot be neutered and sanitised.

Issues for further discussion

1 The role of Islamic faith in business, management, consumption and consumerism.
2 The challenges of implementing branding strategies, which as a by-product may be commercialising the Islamic faith, with positive and negative implications.
3 The relevance and appropriateness of using Islamic faith as a homogenous and generalisable unit of analysis.
4 Appraising whether principles grounded in Islam in fact generate new approaches that no longer conform with conventional perspectives on corporate branding and marketing.

Case study

Challenges facing Islamic branding and marketing

Read the following passage and reflect upon the impact on how corporate Islamic brands and Islamic marketing can be executed in the marketplace, for a brand of your choice, in a specific industry sector. There is no one right answer, and therefore you should attempt to produce several solutions. What you should consider is that this exercise is designed to increase both your information and knowledge base.

Halal is an Arabic word which means 'permissible' or 'lawful' and is used in the Qur'an to indicate what actions and consumption are permissible. In Chapter 5, Surah Al-Ma'idah – 'The Table Spread', several verses outline what animals can be eaten and who would make a suitable spouse. What is deemed to be Halal also covers food from Jews and Christians, classifying them both as "people of the book". Technically, according to the Shari'ah, everything is permissible unless stated otherwise. This means that for example, Kosher meat and food is also in fact Halal too.

Whilst Halal has always existed, interestingly, Halal labelling is a new cultural phenomenon, only several decades old. Halal logos and Islamic labels are constructs that were created to label a minority of product and service offerings in response to concerns about Muslim consumers being able to identify and establish whether goods were in fact fit for consumption according to their religious values and laws. This has also led to further restrictions being imposed where Halal certification in some quarters has only been granted to Muslim owned, run or staffed businesses, in particular concerning the slaughter of animals.

In many ways its inspiration comes from the American Jewish community's decision over one hundred years ago to investigate and certify products and practices formally and then subsequently label them.

Islamic Finance and Halal in the current marketplace are demonstrating tendencies towards a reliance on being product driven. Here, product quality and compliance first and foremost means atomizing and judging ingredients.

Furthermore, Islamic Finance could alternatively be viewed as Halal finance – as Halal means permissibility according to the teachings of Islam. Halal commodities, such as food, beverages, pharmaceuticals and cosmetics, which are branded with a Halal logo, have to be 100 percent Halal, otherwise they are not Halal. However, whilst Islamic Finance is Halal, in many instances it falls short of being 100 percent Halal according to the same benchmarked rules applied to Halal labelled commodities. And within this paradigm lies a paradox.

As Islamic Finance progresses, flourishes and gains more leverage, it will invariably become more "Halal". However, as Halal certification or branded labelling is applied to more commodities, services and experiences, such as tourism and entertainment, then the pendulum could swing the other way, as they will face additional challenges when attempting to maintain their status as being things that are entirely Halal. This is because there will be more critical factors of influence being appraised, and especially those that are difficult to control.

The multi-trillion dollar Halal industry is growing rapidly. The Australian and New Zealand economies in particular have benefitted from Halal exports, with government involvement. Beyond Halal animal slaughter, there is also a growing trend of processed fruit and vegetables also carrying Halal labelling, in response to concerns of food contamination, in light of the mainstream industry UK horsemeat scandal of 2013.

One statistic that is rarely discussed is a trend where it is not only Muslims that consume Halal – there are a growing number of Muslim restaurants, especially serving Indian and Indian subcontinent food, such as curry, that serve all of their diners the same Halal food, as do airline companies and tourist destinations from the Muslim world.

In addition, some global Western companies have taken advantage of Halal markets too, but in some ways have treated this as a "not in my backyard" arm to their operations. Donna Karan launched a Ramadan collection on the catwalk in the UAE in 2014 but missed the opportunity to serve a market of educated affluent Muslim females on US home soil.

In the technology and social media sectors, there has been an increase in Muslim smartphone apps, user-generated content message forums, and review websites. Zilzar and Halal Trip have received mainstream media attention, whilst there have also been attempts to develop other alternative social media platforms to ones like Facebook, and dating and matrimonial websites, which have tighter controls on content, enabling them to more explicitly celebrate Islamic values.

In the shadow of European and North American socio-political debates in connection with community cohesion and national identity, there is evidence to suggest that these are stifling wider involvement and association with Halal industries. Because of this, discussions about security have become less about ensuring food security and transparency along Halal supply chains, and more about national security and the suggestion that Halal consumption could be a catalyst and indicator of religious extremism.

At the beginning of 2015, a new European commission counter-terror plan was proposed, which requires the blanket collection and storage of personal data records, for up to five years, of all passengers flying in and out of Europe. The UK House of Lords said that the 42 separate pieces of information collected will enable the police and security services to deduce aspects of passengers' history, conduct and behaviour. Notably, two variables that have sparked debates are the analysis of whether someone books a one-way ticket (as a possible indicator of someone being a jihadi fighter or suicide bomber), or orders a Halal meal (suggesting that he or she exhibits traits of a form of non-violent extremism, which makes that passenger sympathetic to acts of terrorism and inciting religious hatred, or even considers future involvement in violent terrorist activities).

Other non-Muslim members of the public historically have been investigated according to their diet, postcode, level of education and career, in order to deduce social mobility and health prospects. But this is a sensitive issue, where a degree of caution has always been exercised, for fear of bringing on a scenario similar to that presented in the Hollywood movie *Minority Report*. The fear is that if Halal is viewed in the way that is being inferred, then effectively findings and subsequent views run the risk of criminalising not only Muslims, but also their diet.

Case questions for discussion

1   What are the additional future challenges faced by Islamic and Halal brands, and how can they be remedied?

2   Literature and industry practice often focuses on the creation of Shari'ah compliant products and services. In line with post-industrialist thought and growing knowledge economies, should Islamic and Halal markets be more people-driven and people-centric – in terms of corporate brand identities and the potential for consumers to influence product and service offerings? What steps need to be taken?

3   Should the terms *Islamic* and *Halal* be marks which indicate a commitment towards ethics, values and best practice? or should they remain almost as lowest common denominators of functional compliance? Beyond this, consider whether there is scope to develop additional levels of classifications, as part of a brand portfolio approach – yielding niche, bastion, value and premium sub-brands with nuanced and extra aspects of the more intangible elements of what are traditionally held to be Halal? Therefore, does this mean that there should be an expansion or further constrictions made on the use of terms like *Halal*, in line with Islamic teachings?

Notes

1 Halal (حلال): Halal is the most common spelling used in the English/Basic Modern Latin alphabet; although it is also sometimes written as *Halaal*, or *Helal* – due to the differences in regional accents and difficulties with creating a transliteration; which accurately represents its correct pronunciation. This however should not be confused with the word *Hilal*, which refers to a crescent moon. The classical Arabic pronunciation is most correctly achieved by the spelling *halaal;* with a stress being placed on the last syllable. Similarly the word Islam (اسلام) follows the same pattern and is pronounced *Islaam*. The word Halal is used universally by all Muslims, regardless of their level of understanding of the Arabic language. It is a word that is considered part of the basic vocabulary of those who choose to follow the Islamic faith and hence its meaning should be understood.
2 Confusingly for non Arabic speakers, *Haram* (حرام) [pronounced *Haraam*] is written using the same English/Basic Modern Latin alphabet as *Haram* (حرم) [pronounced *Haram*]. The second version has a completely different meaning; referring to the holy sites of Mecca, Medina and Jerusalem.
3 Meat becomes purified (halal) through following correct slaughtering procedures and spiritual practices. In contrast, milk for example is considered pure, unless contaminated with impure substances. These rulings are derived by scholars from the Qur'an (A book which is said to be the word of God/ Allah – transmitted by the Angel Gabriel/Jibril, to the Prophet Muhammad) and Hadiths/Ahadith (Documented sayings and practices from the Prophet Muhammad and his close companions). These basic principles and frameworks are sufficiently flexible to be able to derive rulings, for any new phenomena – for example the burden of risk and accountability between a buyer and seller, when making an internet transaction.
4 *ceteris paribus*: Latin phrase used to assert the formulation of a specific and predictive causal relationship, meaning: 'all other things being held equal, or constant'.
5 *de facto*: Latin expression used to denote and connote 'in practice and concerning fact'.
6 *de jure*: Latin expression used to denote and connote 'in principle and concerning the law'.
7 *hijab* is Arabic for screen in its general definition, and is also used to describe a headscarf used to cover and conceal a female's chest area and all of the hair on her head.

References

Aaker, D. A. (1991), *Managing Brand Equity: Capitalizing on the Value of a Brand* Name, New York: Free Press.
al-Qayrawani, I. A. Z. [d.386 AH] (1999), *A Madinan View on the Sunnah, Courtesy, Wisdom, Battles and History*, Trans. by Abdassamad Clarke, London: Ta-Ha Publishers.
Anderson, J. R. and Bower, G. H. (1973), *Human Associative Memory*, Washington, DC: Winston & Sons.
Bhattacharya, C.B. and Korschun, D. (2008), "Stakeholder Marketing: Beyond the Four Ps and the Customer", *Journal of Public Policy and Marketing*, Vol. 27, No. 1, Spring, pp. 113–116.
BBC (2012), "Heart and Soul – Marseille: France's Muslim City", *BBC World Service*. www.bbc.co.uk/mediacentre/proginfo/2012/23/ws-heartandsoul-marseille.html

Bewley, A. (2003), *Tafsir Al-Qurtubi – Classical Commentary of the Holy Qur'an*, London: Dar Al-Taqwa.

Bourdieu, P. (1977), *Outline of a Theory of Practice*. Cambridge, UK: Cambridge University Press.

Clarkson, M. B. E. (1995), "A Stakeholder Framework for Analysing and Evaluating Corporate Social Performance", *Academy of Management Review*, Vol. 20, No. 1, pp. 92–117.

Czellar, S. (2003), "Consumer Attitude Toward Brand Extensions: An Integrative Model and Research Propositions", *International Journal of Research in Marketing*, 20, p. 97.

Dawkins, R. (1976), *The Selfish Gene*, Buckingham: Open University Press.

de Chernatony, L. and McDonald, M. (2003), *Creating Powerful Brands*, 3rd ed., Heinemann: Elsevier Butterworth.

Deese, J. (1965), *The Structure of Associations in Language and Thought*, Baltimore, MD: John Hopkins Press.

Diamond, N. et al. (2009), "American Girl and the Brand Gestalt: Closing the Loop on Sociocultural Branding Research", *Journal of Marketing*, Vol. 73, May, pp. 118–134.

Dutton, Y. (2002), *The Origins of Islamic Law: The Qur'an, the Muwatta and Madinan 'Amal*, London: Routledge Curzon.

Fiedler, L. and Kirchgeorg, M. (2007), "The Role Concept in Corporate Branding and Stakeholder Management Reconsidered: Are Stakeholder Groups Really Different?", *Corporate Reputation Review*, Vol. 10, No. 3, pp. 177–188.

Franzen, G. and Bowman, M. (2001), *The Mental World of Brands – Mind, Memory and Brand Success*, NTC Publications.

Freeman, R. E. (1984), *Strategic Management: A Stakeholder Approach*, Boston: Pitman.

Freeman, R. E. and Reed, D. L. (1983), "Stockholders and Stakeholders: A New Perspective on Corporate Governance", *California Management Review*, Vol. 25, No. 3, pp. 93–94.

Freud, S. (1924), *Collected Papers*, London: Hogarth.

Galton, F. (1880), "Psychometric Experiments", *Brain*, Vol. 2, pp. 149–162.

Giles, D. (2000), *Illusions of Immortality: A Psychology of Fame and Celebrity*, London: Palgrave Macmillan.

Heding, T., Knudtzen, C. F. and Bjerre, M. (2009), *Brand Management – Research, Theory and Practice*, New York: Routledge.

Herzberg, F. I. (1959), *The Motivation to Work*, New York: John Wiley and Sons.

Holt, D. B. (2002), "Why Do Brands Cause Trouble? A Dialectical Theory of Consumer Culture and Branding", *Journal of Consumer Research*, Vol. 29, June, 70–90.

Holt, D. B. (2004), *How Brands Become Icons: The Principles of Cultural Branding*, Brighton, MA: Harvard Business School Press.

Holt, D. B. (2005), "How Societies Desire Brands: Using Cultural Theory to Explain Brand Symbolism", in Mick, D. and Ratneshwar, S. (Ed.), *Inside Consumption*, London: Routledge.

Jindra, M. (2004), "Star Trek Fandom as a Religious Phenomenon", *Sociology of Religion*, Vol. 55, No. 1, pp. 27–51.

Jones, R. (2005), "Finding Sources of Brand Value: Developing a Stakeholder Model of Brand Equity", *Brand Management*, Vol. 13, No. 1, October, pp. 10–32.

Keller, K. L. (1993), "Conceptualizing, Measuring, and Managing Customer-Based Brand Equity", *Journal of Marketing*, Vol. 57, No. 1, pp. 1–22.

Lindstrom, M. (2005), *Brand Sense: How to Build Powerful Through Touch, Taste, Smell, Sight and Sound*, London and Sterling, VA: Kogan Page.

Liu, J. and Wilson, J. A. J. (2011), "The Impact of Culture and Religion on Leadership and Management Training: A Comparison of Three Continents", *Journal Pengurusan*, Vol. 33, pp. 29–36.

Maltby, J. et al. (2002), "Thou Shalt Worship No Other Gods – Unless They Are Celebrities: The Relationship Between Celebrity Worship and Religious Orientation", *Personality and Individual Differences*, Vol. 32, pp. 1157–1172.

Marsden, P. (2002), "Brand Positioning: Meme's the Word", *Marketing Intelligence and Planning*, Vol. 20, No. 5, pp. 307–312.

Mitchell, R. K., Agle, B. R. and Wood, D. J. (1997), "Toward a Theory of Stakeholder Identification and Salience: Defining the Principle of Who and What Really Counts", *Academy of Management Review*, Vol. 22, No. 4, pp. 853–886.

National Geographic. (2012), "Marseille's Melting Pot". http://ngm.nationalgeographic.com/2012/03/marseille/dickey-text/1

Ogilvy, N. (2010), "Brands and Muslim consumers", Keynote transcript address by Miles Young, CEO, Ogilvy & Mather Worldwide, *Oxford Global Islamic Branding and Marketing Forum*, 26–27 July, Saïd Business School, University of Oxford, Oxford.

Ogilvy, N. (2011), "Branding Halal – The Rise of the Young Muslim Consumer", Shelina Janmohamed and Nazia Du Bois, *Sparksheet*, (Online), 4 October. http://sparksheet.com/branding-halal-the-rise-of-the-young-muslim-consumer/

Pitt, L. F., Watson, R. T., Berthon, P. and Zinkhan, D. W. G. (2006), "The Penguin's Window: Corporate Brands From an Open-Source Perspective", *Journal of the Academy of Marketing Science*, Vol. 34, No. 2, pp. 115–127.

Ramic, S. H. (2003), *Language and the Interpretation of Islamic Law*, Cambridge, UK: The Islamic Texts Society.

Ries, A. and Trout, J. (1982), *Positioning: The Battle for Your Mind*, New York: Warner Books.

Wilson, J. A. J. (2011a), "The Brand Stakeholder Approach – Broad and Narrow-Based Views to Managing Consumer-Centric Brands", in Kapoor, A. and Kulshrestha, C. (Eds.), *Branding and Sustainable Competitive Advantage: Building Virtual Presence*, Hershey, PA: IGI Global.

Wilson, J. A. J. (2011b), "New-School Brand Creation and Creativity – Lessons From Hip-Hop and the Global Branded Generation", *Journal of Brand Management*, Vol. 19, No. 2, October/November, pp. 91–111.

Wilson, J. A. J. (2012a), "Islamic Leadership: Bedouins in the Boardroom and Profiting From Prophethood – Lessons From John Adair", *TMC Academic Journal*, Vol. 6, No. 2, pp. 48–62.

Wilson, J. A. J. (2012b), "The New Wave of Transformational Islamic Marketing – Reflections and Definitions", *Journal of Islamic Marketing*, Vol. 3, No. 1, pp. 5–11.

Wilson, J. A. J. (2013a), "Boris Discusses Smart Cities and Economies of the Future", *Huffington Post*, 31 October. www.huffingtonpost.co.uk/jonathan-aj-wilson/boris-discusses-smart-cities-future-economies_b_4180077.html

Wilson, J. A. J. (2013b), "Global Islamic Economy Summit and World Exp 2020 boost Dubai's Halal credentials", *Huffington Post*, 2 December. www.huffingtonpost.co.uk/jonathan-aj-wilson/global-islamic-economy_b_4366436.html

Wilson, J. A. J. (2013c), "The Halal Value System", *Changing World, New Relationships* [report] 9th World Islamic Economic Forum (WIEF), October, PricewaterhouseCoopers (PwC) Malaysia, http://read.pwc.com/i/190845/68 pp. 68–72.

Wilson, J. A. J. (2013d), "Londonistan Opens for Business With the Muslim World: Shari'ah Student Loans and Sukuk (Bonds) to Come", *Huffington Post*, 30 October. www.huffingtonpost.co.uk/jonathan-aj-wilson/world-islamic-economic-forum_b_4176094.html

Wilson, J. A. J. (2013e), "Ninth World Islamic Economic Forum Comes to a Close – Roundup and Future Prospects", *Huffington Post*, 4 November. www.huffingtonpost.co.uk/jonathan-aj-wilson/9th-world-islamic-economi_b_4206758.html

Wilson, J. A. J. (2014a), "Brand Islam Is Fast Becoming the New Black in Marketing Terms", 18 February, *The Guardian*, Guardian Media Network, www.theguardian.com/media-network/media-network-blog/2014/feb/18/islamic-economy-marketing-branding

Wilson, J. A. J. (2014b), "Islamic Economics 2.0 – Creating a Halal Wealth and Knowledge Economy", [whitepaper], *Thomson Reuters*, 7 May. www.zawya.com/story/Islamic_Finance_Gateway_Islamic_Economics_20__Creating_a_Halal_Wealth_and_Knowledge_Economy__By_Dr_Jonathan_AJ_Wilson_070514-pdf_080514073608/

Wilson, J. A. J. (2014c), "Islamic Economy: Leap of Faith", *Vision – Fresh Perspectives From Dubai*, [magazine] January, http://vision.ae/en/business/articles/islamic_economy_leap_of_faith

Wilson, J. A. J. (2014d), "Konichiwa Halal: Japan Opens Its Arms to Muslim Diners", *Aquila Style*, 11 July. www.aquila-style.com/focus-points/global-snapshots/konichiwa-halal/72161/

Wilson, J. A. J. (2014e), "Revisiting the Philosophical Arguments Underpinning Islamic Finance and Halal", [whitepaper] *Thomson Reuters*, 10 March. www.zawya.com/story/Islamic_Finance_

Gateway_Revisiting_the_philosophical_arguments_underpinning_Islamic_finance_and_Halal__By_
Dr_Jonathan_Wilson-pdf_060314122451/

Wilson, J. A. J. (2014f), "Where Hip-Hop Culture and Arabic Calligraphy Collide", *Aquila Style*, 4 April.
www.aquila-style.com/focus-points/muslimlifestyle/hip-hop-calligraphy-collide/62500/

Wilson, J. A. J., Belk, R. W., Bamossy, G. J., Sandikci, O., Kartajaya, H., Sobh, R., Liu, J., and Scott, L.
(2013), "Crescent Marketing, Muslim Geographies and Brand Islam: Reflections From the JIMA Senior Advisory Board", *Journal of Islamic Marketing*, Vol. 4, No. 1, pp. 22–50.

Wilson, J. A. J., and Grant, J. (2013), "Islamic Marketing – a Challenger to the Classical Marketing
Canon?", *Journal of Islamic Marketing*, Vol. 4, No. 1, pp. 7–21.

Wilson, J. A. J. and Hollensen, S. (2013), "Assessing the Implications on Performance When Aligning Customer Lifetime Value Calculations With Religious Faith Groups and *After* Lifetime Values – a Socratic
Elenchus Approach", *International Journal of Business Performance Management*, Vol. 14, No. 1, pp. 67–94.

Wilson, J. A. J. and Liu, J. (2009), "'The Pinocchio Effect' – When Managing the Brand Creation Process,
Across Cultures", *TMC Academic Journal*, Vol. 4, No. 1, pp. 45–58.

Wilson, J. A. J. and Liu, J. (2010), "Shaping the Halal Into a Brand?", *Journal of Islamic Marketing*, Vol. 1,
No. 2, pp. 107–123.

Wilson, J. A. J. and Liu, J. (2011), "The Challenges of Islamic Branding: Navigating Emotions and Halal",
Journal of Islamic Marketing, Vol. 2, No. 1, pp. 28–42.

Wilson, J. A. J. and Liu, J. (2012), "Surrogate Brands – the Pull to Adopt and Create Hybrid Identities –
via Sports Merchandise", *International Journal of Sport Management and Marketing*, Vol. 11, No. 3/4,
pp. 172–192.

Wilson, J. A. J. and Morgan, J. E. (2011), "Friends or Freeloaders? Encouraging Brand Conscience and
Introducing the Concept of Emotion-Based Consumer Loss Mitigation", *Journal of Brand Management*,
Vol. 18, No. 9, August, pp. 659–676.

Windsor, D. (1992), "Stakeholder Management in Multinational Enterprises", in S. N. Brenner and
S. A. Waddock (Eds.), *Proceedings of the Third Annual Meeting of the International Association for Business and
Society*, Belgium: Leuven, pp. 121–128.

Zipf, G. K. (1965), *Psychology of Languages*, Cambridge, MA: MIT Press.

2 Islamic products and services

The concept of Halal and certification bodies

Kaouther Kooli

Learning outcomes

At the end of this chapter, the reader should be able to:

1 Understand how Muslim identity determines their behaviour
2 Define Islamic product and services
3 Discuss characteristics of Islamic products and services
4 Understand the certification process for Islamic products and services
5 Understand Islamic branding

Key points

1 Islamic products and services becoming very important due to the massive worldwide Muslim market.
2 Muslim identity and consumption.
3 Islamic products and services and the notion of Halal, the role of Halal certifying bodies.
4 The notion of Halal products and services generating three ways to approaching Islamic Branding: Islamic branding by compliance, Islamic brands by origin and Islamic brands by customer.

Introduction

Religion has a deep influence and effect on society and human behaviour. Religion, as an important cultural factor, profoundly impacts consumption activities and the lifestyle of its followers. Religious beliefs and teachings influence consumer choices. Understanding the consumer behaviour in the context of religion can help both the academic researchers to advance the theories of consumer behaviour and practitioners to succeed in their marketing efforts.

Religion is an important cultural factor to study because it is one of the most universal and influential social institutions that has significant influence on people's attitudes, values and behaviors at both the individual and societal levels. There has been a great focus on the culture and sub-cultural factors in relation to consumer behaviour research. There is, however, very limited research on the role of region as an element of culture.

Islam is the fastest growing religion in the world. Muslim population has been increasing at a fast pace through birth rate as well as high rate of conversion from other religions.

Muslim population represented 28.26 percent of the world population and 7.6 percent of the population in Europe in 2014 (Muslimpopulation.com, 2015). In the UK, from 2001 to 2011, the number of Muslims increased by almost 75 percent (Cooper, 2015) to reach to 2,787,000 (TheGuardian.com).

As per the report published in Dawn.com, Halal goods business is worth an estimated USD 580 billion, and it is growing at a very fast pace in all parts of the world. For example, during the past eight years, the number of Halal-certified businesses in Singapore has grown from 530 to 2000.

Several studies have predicted the rise of the number of Muslims in the UK and worldwide (Tieman, 2015; Kuran, 1997), which emphasises the importance of the Muslim community in the UK and their impact in relation to consumer spending. According to the research conducted by the Muslim Council of Britain (2015), the Muslim community contribute significantly to the UK economy. Wright (2015) claimed that "Britain is slowly waking up to the idea of a 'Muslim consumer'. In 2013, The Muslim Council of Britain (MCB) estimated the spending power of British Muslims as £20.5 billion, with the contribution of £31 billion to the UK economy.

However, the literature about Muslim consumption is still at its infancy, and tells little about the way Muslims relate to their identity when choosing, buying and consuming Halal products and services. According to a research study conducted by Amin H. (2014), existing literature does not adequately address the factors that influence Halal marketing, and conventional consumer behaviour theories fail to capture or accommodate the Islamic perspectives of consumer behaviour.

Additionally, little scholarly work has been done to understand the characteristics of Islamic products and services and very few attempts have been made to provide a classification of Halal goods.

The purpose of this chapter is:

Firstly, to discuss how Muslims relate to their identity to choose, buy and consume products and services
Secondly, to investigate the characteristics of Islamic products and services
Thirdly, to suggest a classification of Islamic products and services
Fourthly, to provide a specimen of Islamic product consumption

About Muslim identity and consumption

Influence of identity on consumer behaviour has been widely discussed in the literature. Identity plays a central role in the context of consumption (Jansson-Boyd, 2010). Reed et al. (2012, p. 310), define identity as "any category label with which a consumer self-associates that is amenable to a clear picture of what a person in that category looks like, thinks, feels and does". Vignoles et al. (2006), portrayed identity as the subjective concept of oneself as a person constructed through a complex interplay of cognitive, affective, and social interaction processes, occurring within particular cultural and local contexts (Greenwald, 1980; Markova´, 1987; Reicher, 2000; Swann, 1983).

Previous literature has emphasised the role of religion in identity formation (Ebstyne King, 2003; Damon, 1983; Erikson, 1968). Ebstyne King (2003) suggests that religion potentially offers an ideologically, sociologically and spiritually rich context for identity formation. In addition, once an individual has decided about his religious identity, he or she will feel the need to express and communicate this choice (Cosgel and Minkler, 2004).

This can happen through consumption behaviour where individuals relate to their own religious identity as well as to other individuals' religious norms, beliefs and perceptions to choose the goods they purchase and consume (Cosgel and Minkler, 2004). It has been demonstrated that members of different religious groups base their purchase decisions on their religious identity (Schiffman and Kanuk, 1997).

In the current transnational context and the vast immigration movement throughout the current and the last century, Muslim consumption has become an up-to-date subject that goes beyond its religious aspect and involves businesses and trade all over the world (Lada et al., 2009). Muslim consumption is generating a big market that significantly changed the way businesses, in both Muslim and non-Muslim countries, relate to their markets (Hanzaee and Ramezani, 2011). It is important for businesses to design branding strategies that take into account "information obtained from the Islamic market, including customers, competitors and the business environment" (Alserhan, 2010, p. 36).

The Islamic concept of utility is based on Islamic jurisprudence (shariah). Islamic Shariah is a system of guidance which is developed based on the instructions from the Quran, quotes of the prophet, and rulings of the authentic Muslim scholars. Contrary to the conventional economics concept of utility, the Muslim consumption, according to the Shariah, does not encourage maximization of utility without limit. It rather encourages consumption following strict practice of moderation.

Religious beliefs along with cultural values shape consumers' choices and influence their buying behaviour. A Muslim consumer is required to determine lawfulness and non-lawfulness of the goods prior to consumption to ensure that they are in compliance with the principals of Shariah, and is also expected to demonstrate modesty and condemnation of extravagance in consumption.

It is, therefore, important to bring insight to what can be considered as Islamic goods and why some goods are allowed and others are not. Hence, the purpose of this chapter is to provide a discussion of what Islamic goods are and to propose a classification of these goods based on existing literature.

What is an Islamic product?

According to conventional economic, goods that satisfy consumers' needs and can be exchanged in the market are considered having economic utility. Islamic economics offers a different perspective; it does not limit definition of goods and their utility to their economic value alone. The Islamic framework for consumption is based on cleanliness and purity of goods in addition to their exchangeability in the market.

Islam encourages charity and advocates simplicity, moderation and balanced pattern of consumption and spending. Muslims' consumption behaviour is derived with different Halal Certification Agency sources. The first supreme source is the Quran followed by sayings of Prophet Muhammad (Hadith), his tradition (Sunnah) and in Fiqh (interpretation) of the Islamic jurists. Interpretation is considered when the texts in the two main sources do not give a specific answer to a specific problem in the society. According to Lada et al. (2009, p. 68), "which foods are Halal or which foods are haram, is decided according to the Holy Quran and the Glorious Shari'ah". Most Muslims use these sources to make decisions about their everyday consumption. Only these sources can be used to attest that some goods are allowed for Muslim consumption, thus "Halal", and some others are not Halal or forbidden. Halal consumption is therefore an important issue for Muslims. It has been widely discussed in the literature about Islamic products and services.

There are several factors that determine the Halal status of a particular product or service. Amongst others, it is largely dependent on its nature, and how it was made. The concept of Halal applies not just to food, but also drink, clothing, medicine, cosmetics, finance, business ethics, human relations, manufacturing and production methods.

For products and services, Muslims refer to set principals that address general issues subject to interpretations. Jurists and scholars play a major role in providing guidance on the specific issues.

Islam teachings encourage Muslims to consume Halal and steer clear of haram. Consumer products can become Halal if the raw materials used in producing them are Halal and the production process is compatible with Islamic way.

According to Islamic Council of Victoria, Australia (ICV), in general every food is considered Halal in Islam unless it is specially prohibited by the Qur'an or the Hadith. By official definition, Halal foods are those that are:

a   Free from any component that Muslims are prohibited from consuming according to Islamic law (Shariah).
b   Processed, made, produced, manufactured and/or stored using utensils, equipment and/or machinery that have been cleansed according to Islamic law.

Another example is pharmaceuticals and cosmetics. Cosmetics and pharmaceutical products may contain animal-derived ingredients; in order for them to be Halal, they have to be produced in accordance with the process and procedures recommended by Shariah. Shariah compliant means ensuring that production and logistics are also compliant, that the business is financed with permissible funds and that safety and hygiene meet religious and ethical standards.

From the business and economic point of view, it is evident that production of Halal goods benefits not only Muslims, but also the producers as the acceptance of their products and services increase due to this additional feature (Thomas and Selimovic, 2015). In some non-Muslim countries, Nestlé has seen in this Halal issue an opportunity and has consequently created a Halal committee that ensures that the company is offering Halal products to its Muslim customers (Alserhan, 2010a).

Concept of 'Halal'

Several definitions of the word "Halal" have been suggested in the literature. Halal is an Arabic word which means "permissible; licit; lawful" (almaany.com dictionary) according to Islamic law. According to Canada, the word 'Halal' literarily means permissible or lawful in Islam. Opposite to Halal is haram, which means unlawful or forbidden. Rajagopal et al. (2011) stated that "Halal literally means "permissible" – and in translation it refers to "lawful" according to followers of Islam religion, Tieman (2011, p. 187) explained that "Halal is a Quranic term that means permitted, allowed, lawful or legal . . . and a Halal product is a product fit to consume for Muslims". Hanzaee and Ramizani (2011, p. 3) consider that "Halal products are those that are Shariah compliant, i.e. do not involve the use of haram (prohibited) ingredients, exploitation of labour or environment, and are not harmful or intended for harmful use". Kamali (2003) claimed that Halal is anything permissible under Islamic law.

The word Halal is frequently used as an attribute for food (Lada et al., 2009; Kamali, 2003) or financial services (Abedifar et al., 2015).

The life of the Muslim revolves around the concept of Halal, which is not only limited to food; rather it is a universal term that applies to all facets of life.

The concept of Halal in Islam has very specific motives:

a   To preserve the purity of religion
b   To safeguard the Islamic mentality
c   To preserve Life
d   To safeguard property
e   To safeguard future generations
f   To maintain self-respect and integrity

Classifying Halal products and services

Previous literature has considered several types of Halal goods separately. Very little attempt has been done to classify Halal goods. In this section, a synthesis and categorisation of goods is provided.

Alserhan (2010b) suggested the following categories of Halal goods: (1) food, (2) lifestyle, (3) services, including finance, hospitality and logistics, among others.

Halal food

The Quran clearly states foods that are prohibited, hence not Halal. "He has forbidden you only dead animals, and blood, and the swine, and that which is slaughtered as a sacrifice for other than God" (Quran 2:173). In the Quran, reasons have been given for forbidding some categories of food e.g. swine flesh and not for others: "for that surely is impure" (Quran 6: 145).

ICV Australia interprets from the Shariah that all foods are considered Halal except the following (which are haram):

- Alcoholic drinks and intoxicants
- Non-Halal animal fat
- Enzymes* (microbial enzymes are permissible)
- Gelatine* – from non-Halal source (fish gelatine is Halal)
- L-cysteine (if from human hair)
- Lard
- Lipase* (only animal lipase need be avoided)
- Non-Halal animal shortening
- Pork, bacon/ham and anything from pigs
- Unspecified meat broth
- Rennet* (all forms should be avoided except for plant/microbial/
- synthetic – rennet obtained from Halal slaughtered animal is
- permissible)
- Stock (a blend of mix species broth or meat stock)
- Tallow (non-Halal species)
- Carnivorous animals, birds of prey and certain other animals
- Foods contaminated with any of the above products

Garbade et al. (2013) emphasised the need for a Halal integrity network support for Halal food which consists in: (1) Halal logistics, (2) Halal network, and (3) Halal certification bodies (Tieman, 2015).

Halal lifestyle

Bin and Dowlatabadi (2005, p. 198) defined lifestyle as "a way of living that influences and is reflected by one's consumption behaviour". According to Kucukemiroglu (1999, p. 473), it refers to "(1) the way people spend their time, (2) what interests they have and what importance they place on their immediate surroundings (3) their view of themselves and the world around them and (4) some of their basic demographics characteristics".

According to Muslimlifestyle.co.uk (2015), for Muslims across the world, the preference to buy in accordance to their faith and Islamic values has grown considerably in the last 10 years. With Halal food and Islamic Finance leading the way, the modern discerning Muslim consumer seeks select products and services that are socially conscious, ethically fair and fit their way of life.

Since Islam is a code of life, it requires its followers to lead their lives according to its teachings and guidelines. From social affairs to travel to entertainment, a set code of conduct is to be followed when availing a service or buying a product. There are Muslim consumer groups and Islamic councils that provide guidance in this regard. They generally list the products and services, both food and non-food products, on their website with the explanation as to why they are not Halal or if they are doubtful (Mashbooh). Muslim consumers can obtain information and seek guidance from these councils from personal care products to medicines. In Muslim countries, Ministries of Religious Affairs provide such services.

Services

The Quran refers also to economic and financial issues where trade is regulated according Shariah, e.g. trade of forbidden products is not permissible e.g. pork and alcohol as well as the contract concerning the supply of these good (The Islamic Financial Services in the United Kingdom). The following financial goods are enumerated: personal accounts, personal finance, home finance, Islamic insurance or Takful, investment and wealth management, Islamic bond or Sukuk and business finance.

Halal certification, how do Muslims know that the goods they purchase are Halal?

Certification of Halal tangible products

Muslims are cautious about consuming Halal food. There are number of professional governmental bodies which are authorised to provide Halal certification to the food products. In Muslim countries, it is carried out by the Ministry of Religious Affairs, whereas in non-Muslim countries, it is done by government authorised Islamic councils and certification agencies. There are a number of approved certification bodies in non-Muslim countries; an example of a list of approved Halal certification bodies for cattle slaughtering is provided on www.Halalmui.org/images/stories/pdf/LSH/LSHLN-LPPOM%20MUI.pdf.

Certification of Halal financial services

The certification and approval of banks' products and services is supervised by a Shari'ah Supervisory Board, also known as a "religious board". Islamic Banking has attracted particular attention in efforts to appeal to the Muslim consumer. This sector is primarily influenced by the requirement of Shariah, which maintains three major prohibitions: usury (the payment and collection of interest), trading in financial risk, and investing in businesses considered haram (Kearney, 2006).

The religious boards have both supervisory and consultative functions. According to the Institute of Islamic Banking and Insurance (islamic-banking.com), Islamic financial institutions that offer products and services conforming to Islamic principles must, therefore, be governed by a religious board that acts as an independent Shariah Supervisory Board comprising at least three Shariah scholars with specialised knowledge of the Islamic laws for transacting, in addition to knowledge of modern business, finance and economics.

Raphie et al. (2013) provide a list of the most influential certification bodies for financial services e.g. in the Bahrain Accounting and Auditing Organization for Islamic Financial Institutions and the Malaysian Islamic Financial Services Board, which issue standards on interpretation of Islamic law focusing on accounting and auditing and on risk management and corporate governance.

Islamic branding

Aaker and Biel (2013 p. 33) defines a brand as a "name that refers to the product of a particular manufacturer in a particular product category" that lives in consumers' minds (Keller and Lehmann, 2006). A brand is a unique story that associates products to consumers' personal stories, personalities, what the firm promises to solve and its position relative to its competitors (Busche, 2014). It includes (1) tangible features e.g. its physical appearance, performance data, package, guarantees or warrantees that are attached to it; and (2) other aspects related to consumer attitude toward the company that produces the product or toward the brand itself and belief about the brand in relation to self and others (Aaker and Biel, 2013)

A brand is built on the product in order to (1) enable a firm to differentiate its offering from its competitors' offerings (2) assist customers in choosing amongst products and services and (3) guarantee a particular quality level, reduce risk and/or engender trust (Aaker and Biel, 2013, Keller and Lehmann, 2006).

Brand equity is the value a brand adds to the firm's offering (Farquhar, 1989). Based on previous studies, the concept of brand equity can be discussed from three perspectives:

Firstly, the cognitive psychology or customer based perspective, which explains brand equity as the differing response of consumer in terms of a brand's marketing mix (Aaker, 1991; Keller, 1993). With respect to this perspective, brand equity is the outcome of the consumer response in terms of marketing activities (Berry, 2000; Yoo and Donthu, 2001; Netemeyer et al., 2004; Christodoulides et al., 2006; Tolba and Hassan, 2009; Buil et al., 2013).

Secondly, the information economic perspective of brand equity based on the signalling theory (Erdem et al., 2006) considers brand equity as the increase in the utility that is achieved through a brand name that a product is attached to (Erdem and Swait, 1998). Moreover, the brand name works as a signal to the consumers that the product holds a specific quality (Erdem et al., 2006). Also, Erdem and Swait (2004), Damodaran (2006) and Keller (2009) mentioned that, based on the signalling theory, the brand plays an important role in mitigating the risk perceived by consumers, reducing the information cost and increasing utility through its role as a signal of the product or service quality.

Finally, the financial-based perspective explains brand equity in financial terms and considers brand equity as a measurement of a firm's value in the market, after subtracting the tangible value of the assets (Simon and Sullivan, 1993). In this perspective, brand equity is a name that represents a firm's asset that holds value due to its future use in monetary terms (Haigh, 1999; Ambler, 2003; Atilgan et al., 2005; Shankar et al., 2008).

Based on previous conceptualisations of brand equity (Christodoulides and de Chernatony, 2010), two main perspectives can be identified: the cognitive perspective or the customer-based perspective and the firm-based or the financial-based perspective.

It is vital for Islamic brands to be successful to consider issues such as brand equity, which in turn raises the importance of branding, defined by Jones and Bonevac (2013) as the defining general category the brand will be placed in to indicate how this brand differs from others.

Questions related to Islamic brand equity and branding are becoming of big interest, and many global companies have already considered these issues in their branding strategies. In addition, Islamic branding has recently emerged as a distinctive body of knowledge (Alserhan, 2010a, 2010b; Wilson and Liu, 2011). However, for businesses, designing Islamic branding remains puzzling (Fitriati, 2012, Botts, 2012) and, although there is abundant literature on the subject, Islamic branding remains "contentious" (Wilson and Liu, 2011, p. 33). Alserhan (2010b) stressed the conflictual debate around the relationship between the notion of Halal and Islamic branding and consequently emphasised three different ways to define Islamic branding:

1 Islamic branding by compliance, portraying faith based brands, applied mainly in the food and finance industries. Businesses base their branding on Shariah compliance.
2 Islamic brands by origin: good examples can be found in the airline and telecom industries in Muslim some countries, such as Egypt and Turkey. According to Alserhan (2010b, p. 38), these brands "acquire" the description "Islamic" simply because they originate from Islamic countries. These brands can offer not permissible products such as alcohol, so not designed specifically to Muslim needs. In addition, Muslim countries can be producers of non-Islamic products and so the origin of non-Islamic brand e.g. Tunisia and Turkey produce wine.
3 Islamic brands by customer: multinational companies owned by non-Muslims promote brands that include in their target Muslim consumers. Nestlé Halal list (2014) provides an annual Halal brands list that can be used by Muslim consumers. These brands have not been only designed for Muslim consumers. They also suit all Nestlé potential consumers.

Based on Wilson and Liu (2009, 2010) and Koshy (2010), Wilson and Liu (2011, p. 32) added that "brands and Islam, both collectively and independently, encourage worship and present a promise to consumers − as an affordable luxury, which is reaffirmed and offers perceived mass prestige". Brands have to assimilate religious concerns (Aoun and Tournois, 2015), as a result, issues of brand equity and maximising brand values have to be reconsidered.

Aoun and Tournois (2015) suggested a framework explaining how brands integrate religious concerns into their strategies through Halal branding. They claimed that holistic branding offer insight into a spiritual dimension which goes beyond the mainstream literature on branding.

Islamic brand attributes

Aoun and Tournois (2015) rely on the claim that brand attributes go beyond the functional and emotional attributes. They provide a model that identifies three types of attributes:

1   Tangible functional attributes
2   Intangible brand attributes
3   Spiritual/holistic attributes which give the brand a worldview and contribute to holistic branding: spiritual ethos and belief system, sustainable and eco-ethical philosophy, wholesomeness and inclusiveness (Figure 2.1)

Conclusion

The Muslim community is one of the fastest rising consumer markets in the world and, hence, represents a major growth opportunity for businesses around the world. Throughout

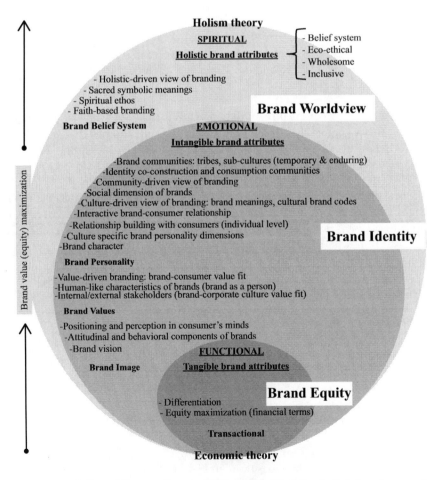

Figure 2.1 Aoun Isabelle and Tournois Laurent (2015, p. 123), "Building holistic brands: an exploratory study of Halal cosmetics", *Journal of Islamic Marketing*, Vol. 6 Iss. 1 pp. 109–132.

the world, Muslims are becoming increasingly active as consumers, investors and manufacturers, bankers and traders, competitors and suppliers, and are becoming real partners in a global economic system.

There is a need to know more about how Muslims refer to their religion and to its sources of law in order to choose Islamic brands and products. Most importantly it is vital for businesses that are targeting Muslims to understand how their identity is shaped by the religion. Halal certification institutions play a major role in guiding Muslim consumption of products and services. Islamic branding is challenged by specific external factors e.g. institutional environment and intrinsic and personal factors e.g. identity. Including the holy aspect to a brand is particularly challenging for businesses that are targeting Muslims in Muslim countries and particularly in non-Muslim countries.

Issues for further discussion

1   The Islamic products and services market is expanding in Western countries. This will call for further investigation towards how in these countries, non-Muslims perceive Islamic products and services.
2   Challenges facing managers of Islamic branding in Muslim countries and non-Muslim countries.
3   Halal vs Islamic brand attributes similarities and differences.
4   Spiritual and holistic brand attributes in Muslim countries and non-Muslim countries.

Case study

Social media and the portrayal of Tunisian women post-civil uprising

Dr Amna Khan and Dr Kaouther Kooli

The Hijab and women's status and role in the society constitute one of the prevalent debates that have been nurturing the Muslim countries for centuries. In Tunisia, recent civil uprising increased these debates alongside other debates i.e. cultural, political, social and economic changes. There is no doubt that Tunisian women live an identity crisis led by a very controversial environment. Tunisian women were favoured by the Maliki School of interpretation, which gives women a relatively better position in a very patriarchal Muslim society where law and rules are set by men. The independence in the 1950s brought stronger rights to Tunisian women led essentially by a political willingness to modernise Tunisian society, which was previously tribe led. Modernising Tunisian society cannot be achieved without women's emancipation and thus without the abolition of any slavery symbol.

The Tunisian uprising in December 2010 reignited the debate on Hijab. Technology has been playing an important role, allowing people to share their views and perceptions of Hijab and the role of Tunisian women in the society. Information and communication technology has deeply transformed the world and societies.

Tunisia, alike many other Arab countries, has witnessed the consequences of the Internet. Social media has been a key driver of the social uprising. Tunisian people have been experiencing social media as a means of socialising with others, sharing information, expressing views which are difficult to do because of political repression and taboos in the society.

Facebook posts made by Tunisian around the issues of women attire in Tunisia were observed from November 2011 to January 2012.

The posts that presented information on the political system and religion challenged the notion of a rationale for an Islamic state.

"There have never been in the history of Arab countries Islamic states, it is impossible, the so-called Islamic States based on Sharia are only iconic and used to cover and conceal the nature of some despotic and tyrannical sovereign or other."

The respondent bases his/her opinions of an Islamic state on historical events, and according to the respondents a state based on Islamic principles is not achievable. The implementation of an Islamic state is perceived negatively as a disguise to oppress citizens of that nation. The use of such language to express perceptions of what an Islamic state would represent indicates that this respondent feels that an Islamic state would result in citizens having less freedom to make decisions about how they would like to practice their faith. This is supported by the following statement by one of the respondents:

> secularism the separation between religion and politics . . . then why are you interfering with religion . . . if you do not want to apply the command of God let other people practice their religion as they wish . . .

An Islamic state and policies that are consequentially developed to implement Islamic laws are perceived to result in a withdrawal of choice of behavioural and consumption decisions, particularly relevant to the consumption of faith and wearing the Hijab. These consumption activities are considered important in reflecting the role of women in society and their identities.

Another category identified in the analysis was the use of verses and teaching of the Prophet (PBUH) to validate or provide credibility to statements. On several occasions posters make reference to the Quran to indicate the importance of observing the veil. Two examples are presented below:

> The prophet said: 'when a young woman reach puberty, she must only show her face and her hands till the wrists'

and,

> Hijab is a rule without any doubt and the argument is in Quran, anybody denying this can go back to Quran.

The Quran for Muslim is the word of God and therefore cannot be disputed or questioned. Using verses of the Quran to legitimise their statements suggests that the posters are not willing to consider other opinions, which suggests that adoption of the Hijab is a matter of personal choice. Therefore, this implies that women's identity which is voiced through the consumption of fashion is not a matter of choice but rather pre-determined and prescribed in such society through observing religion, more particularly through the interpretation of Islamic law. This gives an idea about how Tunisian people consider the sources of Islamic law. The first supreme source is Quran followed by the Sunnah, based on the prophet Hadith or talks. The other sources are people's interpretation of Quran and Hadith. Interpretation is considered when the texts in the two main sources do not give a specific answer to a specific problem in the society. The posts highlight the ranking people give to these sources and the attitudes towards them.

Case questions for discussion

1   Based on the Facebook posts cited in the text, how does the society shape Tunisian women's attire consumption?
2   Based on the information in the text, how do Tunisians rank Islamic law and use it to make decisions?
3   How do the different sources of law shape Muslim women's identity and consumption in general? Compare Tunisia to other Muslim countries.

References

Aaker, D. (1991), *Building Strong Brands*, New York: The Free Press.

Aaker, D. A. and Biel, A. (2013), *Brand Equity and Advertising: Advertising's Role in Building Strong Brands*, London and New York: Psychology Press, Taylor and Francis Group.

Abedifar, P., Ebrahim, S. M., Molyneux, P. and Tarazi, A. (2015), "Islamic Banking and Finance: Recent Empirical Literature and Directions for Future Research", *Journal of Economic Surveys*, Vol. 0, No. 0, pp. 1–34.

Alserhan, B. A. (2010a), "Islamic Branding: A Conceptualization of Related Terms", *Brand Management*, Vol. 18, No. 1, pp. 34–49.

Alserhan. B.A. (2010b) "On Islamic Branding: Brands as Good Deeds", *Journal of Islamic Marketing*, Vol. 1, No. 2, pp.101–106.

Ambler, T. (2003). *Marketing and the Bottom Line: Creating the Measures of Success*, 2nd ed. London: Financial Times/Prentice Hall.

Atilgan, E., Aksoy, S. and Akinci, S. (2005), "Determinants of the Brand Equity: A Verification Approach in the Beverage Industry in Turkey", *Marketing Intelligence and Planning*, Vol. 23, No. 3, pp. 237–248.

Aoun, I. and Tournois, L. (2015), "Building Holistic Brands: An Exploratory Study of Halal Cosmetics", *Journal of Islamic Marketing*, Vol. 6, No. 1, pp. 109–132.

Berry, L. (2000), "Cultivating Service Brand Equity", *Journal of the Academy of Marketing Science*, Vol. 28, No. 1, pp. 128–137.

Bin, S. and Dowlatabadi, H. (2005), "Consumer Lifestyle Approach to US Energy Use and the Related CO_2 Emissions", *Energy Policy*, Vol. 33, pp. 197–208.

Botts, M. (2012), "Islamic Branding and Marketing: Creating a Global Islamic Business", *Journal of Islamic Marketing*, Vol. 3, No. 3, pp. 286–287.

Buil, I., Martinez, E. and de Chernatony, L. (2013), "The Influence of Brand Equity on Consumer Responses", *Journal of Consumer Marketing*, Vol. 30, No. 1, pp. 62–74.

Busche, L. (2014), *Lean Branding*. [online]. O'Reilly Media. www.myilibrary.com?ID=689052 (accessed 8 January 2016).

Cooper, V. (2015), "UK Muslim Population of 26 Million by 2051?", *The Commentator*. www.thecommentator.com/article/5632/uk_muslim_population_of_26_million_by_2051 (accessed 1 September 2015).

Christodoulides, G. and de Chernatony, L., 2010. Consumer-based brand equity conceptualization and measurement: A literature review. *International Journal of Market Research*, Vol. 52, No. 1, pp.43–66.

Cosgel Metin, M. and Minkler, L. (2004), "Religious Identity and Consumption", *Review of Social Economy*, Vol. LXII, No. 3, pp. 339–350.

Damodaran, A. (2006), *Dealing With intangibles: Valuing Brand Names, Flexibility and Patents*. Working paper, New York University, New York.

Damon, W. (1983), *Social and Personality Development*. New York: Norton.

Erdem, T. and Swait, J. (1998), "Brand Equity as a Signaling Phenomenon", *Journal of Consumer Psychology*, Vol. 7, No. 2, pp. 131–157.

Erdem, T. and Swait, J. (2004), "Brand Credibility and Its Role in Brand Choice and Consideration", *Journal of Consumer Research*, Vol. 31, No. 1, pp. 191–199.

Erdem, T., Swait, J. and Valenzuela, A. (2006), "Brand as Signals: A Cross-Country Validation Study", *Journal of Marketing*, Vol. 70, No. 1, pp. 34–49.

Erikson, E. H. (1968), *Identity: Youth and Crisis*. New York: Norton.

Ebstyne, K. P. (2003), "Religion and Identity: The Role of Ideological, Social, and Spiritual Contexts", *Applied and Developmental Science*. www.researchgate.net/profile/Pamela_King5/publication/240519158_Religion_and_Identity_The_Role_of_Ideological_Social_and_Spiritual_Contexts/links/551182780cf24e9311ce8081.pdf (accessed 15 September 2015).

Farquhar, P. H. (1989), "Managing Brand Equity", *Marketing Research*, Vol. 1, pp. 24–33.

Fitriati, A. R. (2012), "Islamic Branding and Marketing: Creating a Global Islamic Business", *Journal of Islamic Marketing*, Vol. 3, No. 3, pp. 283–285.

Greenwald, A.G. (1980), "The totalitarian ego: Fabrication and revision of personal history", American Psychologist, Vol. 35, No. 7, pp. 603–618.

Heidarzadeh Hanzaee, K. and Ramezani, M. R. (2011), "Intention to Halal Products in the World Markets", *Interdisciplinary Journal of Research in Business*, Vol. 1, No. 5, pp. 01–07.

Garbade, P. J., Fortuin, F.T. and Omta, O. (2013), "Coordinating Clusters: A Cross Sectoral Study of Cluster Organization Functions in the Netherlands", *International Journal on Food System Dynamics*, Vol. 3, No. 3, pp. 243–257.

Hanzaee Kambiz, H. and Ramezani, M. R. (2011), "Intention to Halal Products in the World Markets", *Interdisciplinary Journal of Research in Business*, Vol. 1, No. 5, pp. 01–07.

Haigh, D. (1999), *Understanding the Financial Value of Brands*. London: Institute of Practitioners in Advertising.

Jansson-Boyd, C.V. (2010). *Consumer Psychology*, Maidenhead: Open University Press.

Jones, C. and Bonevac, D. (2013), "An Evolved Definition of the Term "brand": Why Branding Has a Branding Problem", *Journal of Brand Strategy*, Vol. 2, No. 2, pp. 112–120.

Kamali, M. H. (2003), *Principles of Islamic Jurisprudence, Islamic Texts* 3rd ed. Cambridge, England: The Islamic Texts Society.

Kearney, 2006, Addressing the Muslim Market, Can You Affort It or Not? [Online] Available: http://imaratconsultants.com/wp-content/uploads/2012/10/Addressing-Muslim-Market.pdf (March, 2016).

Keller, K. (1993), "Conceptualizing, Measuring, and Managing Customer-Based Brand Equity", *Journal of Marketing*, Vol. 57, No. 1, pp. 1–22.

Keller, K. L. and Lehmann, D. R. (2006), "Brands and Branding: Research Findings and Future Priorities", *Marketing Science*, Vol. 25, No. 6, pp. 740–759.

Koshy, A. (2010), Keynote speech, The ICBM 2010 Second International Conference on Brand Management, Institute of Management Technology (IMT), Ghaziabad, 8–9 January.

Kucukemiroglu, O. (1999), "Market Segmentation by Using Consumer Lifestyle Dimensions and Ethno-centrism: An Empirical Study", *European Journal of Marketing*, Vol. 33, No. 5/6, pp. 470–487.

Kuran, T. (1997), "The Genesis of Islamic Economics: A Chapter in the Politics of Muslim Identity", *Social Research*, Vol. 64, No. 2, pp. 301–338.

Lada, S., Tanakinjal, G. H. and Amin, H. (2009), "Predicting intention to choose halal products using theory of reasoned action", International Journal of Islamic and Middle Eastern Finance and Management, Vol. 2 No. 1, pp. 66–76.

Markova´, I. (1987), "Knowledge of the self through interaction", In K. Yardley, & T. Honess (Eds.), Self and identity: psychosocial perspectives (pp. 65–80). New York: Wiley.

Muslimpopulation.com (2015), "Muslim Population in the World". www.muslimpopulation.com/World/ (accessed 1 September 2015).

The Muslim Council of Britain (2015), "British Muslims in Numbers, a Demographic, Socio-economic and Health Profile of Muslims in Britain Drawing on the 2011 Census". www.mcb.org.uk/wp-content/uploads/2015/02/MCBCensusReport_2015.pdf (accessed 15 September 2015).

Nestle Halal List (2014), https://deenandthedunya.wordpress.com/2014/07/23/nestle-halal-list-2014/ (accessed on 1/10/2015).

Netemeyer, R. G., Krishnan, B., Pullig, C., Wang, G., Yagci, M., Dean, D., Ricks, F. and Wirth, F. (2004), "Developing and Validating Measures of Facets of Customer Based Brand Equity", *Journal of Business Research*, Vol. 57, 209–224.

Raphie, H., Frank, D. B. and Udo, K. (2013), "Halal Certification for Financial Products: A Transaction Cost Perspective", *Journal of Business Ethics*, Vol. 117, pp. 601–613. doi: 10.1007/s10551-012-1534-9

Reed, A., Forehandb, M. R., Puntonic, S. and Warlo, L. (2012, December), "Identity-Based Consumer Behaviour", *International Journal of Research in Marketing*, Special Issue on Consumer Identities, Vol. 29, No. 4, pp. 310–321.

Reicher, S. D. (2000), 'Against methodolatry', British Journal of Clinical Psychology, 39, pp. 1–6.

Schiffman, L. G., and Kanuk, L. L. (1997), *Consumer Behavior*, 9th ed. Upper Saddle River, NJ: Prentice Hall, p. 446.

Shankar, V., Azar, P. and Fuller, M. (2008), "Brand Equity: A Multicategory Brand Equity Model and Its Application at Allstate", *Marketing Science*, Vol. 27, No. 4, pp. 567–584.

Simon, C. and Sullivan, M. (1993), "The Measurement and Determinants of Brand Equity: A Financial Approach", *Marketing Science*, Vol. 12, No. 1, pp. 28–52.

Swann, W. B., Jr (1983), Self-verification: bringing social reality into harmony with the self. In J. Suls & A. G. Greenwald, Eds., Psychological Perspectives on the Self, Vol. 2. Hillsdale, NJ: Lawrence Erlbaum, pp. 33–66

Thomas, P. and Selimovic, A. (2015), "'Sharia on a Plate?' A Critical Discourse Analysis of Halal Food in Two Norwegian Newspapers", *Journal of Islamic Marketing*, Vol. 6, No. 3, pp. 331–353.

Tieman, M. (2011). The Application of Halal in Supply Chain Management: In-Depth Interviews. *Journal of Islamic Marketing*, Vol. 2, No. 2, pp.186–195.

Tolba, A. and Hassan, S. (2009), "Linking Customer Based Brand Equity With Brand Market Performance: A Managerial Approach", *Journal of Product and Brand Management*, Vol. 18, No. 5, pp. 356–366.

Vignoles Vivian, L., Regalia, C., Manzi, C., Golledge, J. and Scabini, E. (2006), "Beyond Self-Esteem: Influence of Multiple Motives on Identity Construction", *Journal of Personality and Social Psychology*, Vol. 90, No. 2, pp. 308–333.

Keller, K.L., (2009). Managing the growth tradeoff: Challenges and opportunities in luxury branding. Journal of Brand Management, 16(5-6), pp.290-301.

Wright, H. (2015), "YBMs: Religious Identity and Consumption Among Young British Muslims", *International Journal of Market Research*, Vol. 57, No. 1, pp.151–163.

Wilson, J. A. J. and Liu, J. (2009), "The Polytheism of Branding: Evaluating Brands Through Their Worship", in Nafees, L., Krishnan, O. and Gore, T. (Eds), *Brand Research*, New Delhi: Palgrave Macmillan, pp. 207–229.

Wilson, J.A. and Liu, J., 2010. Shaping the halal into a brand?. Journal of Islamic Marketing, 1(2), pp.107-123.

Yoo, B. and Donthu, N. (2001), "Developing and Validating a Multi-Dimensional Consumer-Based Brand Equity Scale", *Journal of Business Research*, Vol. 52, No. 1, pp. 1–14.

3 Islam and the reputational landscape

Aliakbar Jafari

Learning outcomes

At the end of this chapter, the reader should be able to:

1 Critically discuss that 'Islamicness' is a fluid concept, constantly (re)shaped by multiple actors and ideologies in contemporary spaces of markets
2 Recognise that in order to build and sustain global reputation, corporations should avoid short-term engagements with market-generated fads that are often the outcome of transient identity anxieties
3 Acknowledge that brand building should be based on a long-term corporate vision that considers the changing landscape of religious perceptions and orientations
4 Critically evaluate the risks involved in the organisation's unwarranted claims to Islamicness

Key points

1 Reputation is socially constructed and is evaluated based on the organisation's expected behaviours.
2 'Islamicness' is a fluid concept, constantly (re)shaped by multiple actors and ideologies in contemporary spaces of markets.
3 To build and sustain global reputation, corporations should avoid short-term engagements with market-generated fads that are often the outcome of transient identity anxieties.
4 Brand building should be based on a long-term corporate vision that considers the changing landscape of religious perceptions and orientations.
5 If and only if the organisation is capable of following the principles of Islam should it make claims of Islamicness; otherwise, the organisation should ethically follow market rules without associating itself with Islam and the Islamic.

Introduction

This chapter presents an analysis of the prevailing debates on what constitutes 'Islamicness' in contemporary spaces of markets. It argues that in order to build and sustain reputation in highly politicised and symbolised global socioeconomic systems, organisations need to avoid transient identity anxieties and adopt a long-term strategic approach.

Reputation and branding

Reputation, as the term indicates, is all about recognition. And in the social reality of life, recognition is not a self-given status; rather, it is an earned position of being respected and valued by different stakeholders in a given context for an organisations' outstanding value proposition or contributions. As Askari et al. (2009) contend, corporate reputation is socially constructed by different agents. That is, consumers, customers, business partners, regulatory bodies, media, activist groups (e.g., environmentalists), business analysts, internal employees, and the like determine the reputation of the organisation. These agents can positively or negatively influence corporate reputation. In other words, if the corporation is consistently committed to observing a series of criteria common to these agents' checklist, then the organisation will be seen as a business entity with high reputation. Otherwise, lack of commitment to such criteria will result in poor perceptions amongst the agents, and the end result will be the destruction of brand or corporate reputation. In the landscape of religion, corporate reputation is influenced by the same agents; yet, the key problem is that religion may not be understood in the same way by the above-mentioned agents, especially if these agents come from different sociocultural backgrounds and have various interpretations of the religion. These issues raise a series of questions that need to be critically thought of.

This chapter therefore is meant to arouse critical thinking amongst students in the general field of business and also practitioners interested in developing sustainable reputation for their organisations. The chapter does not intend to provide crystal-clear answers mainly because the question of strategic reputation and brand building in relation to Islam is not a simple one. The basic formula for building successful brands and reputation is not complicated: make your promise clear, communicate it clearly with your stakeholders/audience, and deliver it thoroughly and perfectly (Askari et al., 2009). This is a rule that applies to any brand and organisation. Therefore, generally speaking, in terms of branding and corporate identity and reputation building, nothing new can be said. Any good book/article about strategic branding and building corporate identity can provide very useful insights. Yet, when branding and corporate identity are brought into sensitive and complicated domains such as religions, they become seriously problematic. This is because, unlike other topics such as sports, arts, education, computing, foods and beverages, or automotive industries, religion is not just another context in which branding and corporate reputation can be practised based on generally accepted norms and ethical marketing rules. Religion is a multifaceted phenomenon. It is not simply about a set of values and beliefs in a specific creed and its sacred pillars and symbols. Religion is highly intertwined with geopolitics, economics, and ideologies of identity, power relations, and issues of socioeconomic inclusion/exclusion. Tapping on these issues, this essay is an attempt to demonstrate some of the complexities that underlie bridging business and religion (in this case, Islam), particularly in this point in time when there is so much confusion about Islamicness.

Confusion about Islamicness

Recently, 'Islam' and 'Islamic' have become buzzwords in the realm of business and management studies. They are used without precision. Students, practitioners, and scholars keep talking about many combinations such as Islamic products/services, Islamic business, Islamic consumers, Islamic markets, Islamic brands, etc. without making clear distinctions between different terms. Obviously, there is confusion amongst people as what each of these terms mean. Do they mean Sharia-compliant practices, Sharia-compliant products/ services, or consumers/customers who are highly committed to Sharia and as a result of their commitment to Islam seek such products/services? A short statement by Miles Young (2008), the CEO of Ogilvy Noor, clearly captures this existing confusion about what is generally known as 'Islamic brands' in contemporary debates on Islamic branding and business:

> A strong sense of community and welfare underpins all activity, informing business ethics. Islam has little space for imagery and heavy reliance on verbal communication. In varying degrees, Sharia compliance recognizes these requirements, and to some degree, perhaps unsurprisingly, 'Sharia compliant' has become a synonym for 'Islamic brand'. But Islamic branding is actually more complex than this, and exists at three levels. At the most exclusive level, overtly Islamic brands place their appeal strictly on Sharia principles. These are especially concentrated in the finance and food sectors. Beyond that, there are brands created by Islamic-rooted organizations informed by Islamic belief but which are pluralist in their appeal (airlines or telcos would be an example). And, further still, there are brands which emanate from Islamic countries but which are not specifically religious in character; many Turkish brands fall into this category. Confusingly, the distinction is not often made: but what all three should have is a common purpose, which is to re-balance the importer-exporter relationships between the Islamic and non-Islamic world.

Young is absolutely right by saying that Islamic brands and Sharia-compliant products/ services are mistakenly used interchangeably. Yet he himself is not clear about 'Islamicness'. His examples of airlines or telcos (telecommunication companies) are not really manifestations of Islamic beliefs; rather, they are examples of organisations emerging from Muslim geographies with mixed Islamic and un-Islamic practices. This is a common mistake in contemporary debates on the Islamic that associates everything related to Muslim geographies to the Islamic. Simply because a brand/organisation originates from a geographical location in which Islam is a major religion does not mean that we are talking about Islam and the Islamic. This is like saying that Virgin Atlantic, Apple, Coca Cola, Chelsea, Bayern Munich, and many other brands are Christian because they originate from contexts in which Christianity has traditionally been a major religion. The examples Young refers to as "created by Islamic-rooted organizations informed by Islamic belief" cannot and should not be analysed with an Islamic lens. For example, Emirates Airlines and Etihad Airways (both originating from the UAE), Qatar Airways, Turkish Airlines, and Malaysia Airlines simultaneously serve Halal food and alcohol on board. Similarly one could argue that since British Airways, Air France, KLM, and others serve Halal food as well have Islamic tendencies. Or since major European airports (such as Heathrow, Amsterdam, Charles de Gaulle) have multi-faith prayer rooms, they have religious tendencies. These options and facilities are there only in order to better serve customers in an inclusive manner. Surprisingly, despite strong religious tendencies in the servicescapes of Muslim majority contexts (such as airports), multi-faith prayer rooms are either non-existent or rare.

However, Young is totally right when he says that Islamicness should not jeopardise business relationships and the import-export balance between Muslim and non-Muslim geographies. Currently, there is a growing tendency in the so-called 'Islamic' business and management studies and practice that is unfortunately widening the chasm between Islamic and non-Islamic worlds. This is an historical *déjà vu* which is rooted in Orientalist and essentialist classifications of the world (Sandıkcı, 2011; Jafari, 2012; Jafari and Sandıkcı, 2015, 2016). There are serious socioeconomic risks in the essentialist discourses that separate the Islamic from the non-Islamic in the realm of business practice. These discourses may eventually result in the sacralisation of self (what is known as 'Islamic business') and demonisation of the other (the non-Islamic business). Therefore, underneath Young's statement there are many implications and cautions for businesses that are somehow related to Islam and Muslim geographies. If claims of Islamicness are made public, they should not be uttered as lip-service and theoretically; they should be delivered comprehensively in practice based on the authentic and cosmopolitan values of Islam.

Two strategic choices

Over the past two decades, much has been written on the nexus of Islam, business, and markets. Here I do not intend to provide a literature review simply because the extant literature cannot be deservedly analysed and critiqued in a short space. What I intend to do instead is to set forth a critical line of argument towards understanding the challenges of building and sustaining corporate reputation in relation to Islam. To be more specific, I will demonstrate that in order to achieve a sustainable reputation, corporations need to primarily determine their strategic vision very clearly and *honestly* for themselves before embarking on operationalising their business agendas. Options are not abundant; indeed, they are limited to two major strategic paths: (1) to thoroughly follow Islamic principles in theory and practice and position the organisation as a 'holistically Islamic' oriented business enterprise; and (2) to ethically follow market principles without making big claims of association with Islam and Islamic principles. This proposition applies to all organisations, regardless of their country of origin (whether they originate from Muslim or non-Muslim geographies), and across different industry sectors around the world.

There are two main reasons for this rather radical proposition: Firstly, any precarious claims of association with Islam and the 'Islamic' may eventually lead to the organisation's downturn in the long term. This is because reputation is closely related to 'expected behaviour' (Askari et al., 2009). It means that once a claim is made, the claimer is expected to behave in line with the claim made. For example, if an organisation claims that they are Islamic in essence (e.g., corporate philosophy), their internal and external activities should all be based on the principles of Islam. Otherwise, by making such a claim without exercising or with partial practice of Islam, the organisation will only destroy their corporate reputation. Second, a host of complex and interconnected changes are happening in today's global socioeconomic and political landscapes, which make reputation a relative concept for businesses. These macro dynamics influence business practices at a micro level. Due to their deeper impact, these issues are discussed under separate sub-headings below.

Awareness about the Islamic

There is unprecedentedly increasing awareness about 'the Islamic' around the world. This awareness is changing people's perceptions and expectations of 'Islamicness' in different ways (Sandıkcı and Jafari, 2013). Yet, perceptions of the 'Islamic' are not ubiquitously positive as there are also negative and sceptical perceptions towards the 'Islamic'. For example, in the post-9/11 world we have seen an upsurge of anti-Islamic sentiments (particularly in the West). For example, during 2009–10 Domino's Pizza 'Halal menu only' raised criticisms and caused offence to those who did not want to eat Halal food and wanted their pepperoni back (Wilkes, 2009; The Telegraph, 2010). In the end, the company had to reduce Halal-ness only to slaughtering chickens in a Halal way, maintaining pre-slaughter stunning as their responsibility to animal welfare protocols. Parallel to this, brutal terrorist activities that are taking place in the name of Islam in different parts of the world (e.g., Iraq, Syria, Nigeria, Afghanistan, Sudan) are hurting Muslims themselves and making Muslim populations be more aware of what is at stake with Islamicness. On the other hand, expectations of the 'Islamic' are not thoroughly clear, as there are varying needs to be fulfilled by Islamic agendas. As a result of disparate religious orientations and socio-economic backgrounds of Muslim populations, people have different interpretations of what the 'Islamic' should mean and should do. For example, whilst for some consumers, Islamicness might be confined to the presence of Sharia-compliant products/services, others may see Islamicness in corporations' attempts geared towards local socioeconomic developments. The decision to be seen as Islamic or otherwise then is left at the discretion of the organisation and its social settings because its reputation will depend on what its stakeholders expect of it.

Competitive Islamicness

Second, in the intensively competitive landscape of political economy, nation-states are engaged in multi-level rivalries (regional, international, and global) in order to gain national advantage over other countries, and in the midst of such competitions Islam is being increasingly instrumentalised (Jafari, 2012; Süerdem, 2013). For example, states in Muslim geographies (e.g., Malaysia, Saudi Arabia, UAE, Turkey) compete over political/economic hegemonies in Muslim geographies by utilising market capacities. The emergence of Halal economy and national competitions over regulating the Halal are good indicators of these rivalries. However, given the increasing political literacy of people around the world, individuals understand the instances of instrumentalisation of the religion. In Eickelman's (2000, p. 125) words, "mass education and mass communications . . . profoundly influence how people think about the language of religious and political authority throughout the Muslim world." Political literacy of the stakeholders will, in the long term, leave little room for organisations to build their reputation based on opportunistic behaviours and religious instrumentalisation.

Religious discrepancies

Third, the world we are living in today is wrought with cultural misunderstandings, identity conflicts, inter/intra-religious tensions, socioeconomic injustice, and ethno-religious hybridities (Jafari et al., 2014). For example, there are internal tensions between different Muslim groups in Iraq, Sudan, Yemen, Syria, Nigeria, Afghanistan, Pakistan, and so forth. Amongst many other reasons (e.g., political authority, socioeconomic marginalisation), religious discrepancies are the main source of conflict amongst communities. On the other hand, as a result of Islamophobia, Muslims living in multi-ethnic/cultural societies are not capable of freely practising and communicating their religious identity. They may feel issues of stigma and social exclusion. In such instances, whilst some may use Islamic-related products/services to resist their dominant environments, others may refrain from associating themselves with such market contents and use alternative non-Islamic products/services and lifestyles (Jafari and Goulding, 2008). Therefore, these situations make religious associations a problematic site in which religiosity becomes a fluid concept that shifts between different political and ideological identity systems. Likewise, people's association with brands and market contents will be transient and dependent on the conditions of the contexts in which they temporarily (e.g., as sojourners) or permanently reside. Research also indicates that in their everyday life situations, people perform religiosity not simply as a set of cultural practices but also as a means of creating and communicating distinctions of identity through ethnocentric preferences for products/services of certain countries (Kaynak and Kara, 2002; Ganideh and Al Taee, 2012) or lifestyle choices (Wong, 2007; Jafari and Süerdem, 2012). These identity dynamics mean that corporations' reputations strongly depend on liquid identity shifts of consumers/customers as major stakeholders.

Alternative religiosities

The rapid progress of neoliberalism and consumerism has facilitated the emergence of alternative religiosities (Gauthier and Martikainen, 2013) that offer both opportunities and challenges for enacting religious orientations and associations in the realm of markets and consumption (Jafari and Visconti, 2014). This means that the traditional boundaries between religions are becoming more opaque. Therefore, individuals can abandon associations with religious labels to freelance in the horizons of cosmopolitan religiosities (e.g., identifying oneself as spiritual instead of religious). Since markets are increasingly seen as producers of cultural signs and symbols in a sign economy (Slater, 1997), businesses should be aware of the complicated semiotic systems of the markets in which they perform. Alternative religiosities and spiritualities are more concerned with practicalities of life. As Gauthier and Martikainen (2013) stress, people interested in such alternatives are more concerned with salvation in this world, in the here and now. They are less bothered with traditional forms of belief in creeds with their symbolic systems. The more symbolic meanings businesses attach to themselves, the less likely they might be in winning these groups of people. Although alternative religiosities and spiritualities are just emerging, businesses should be aware of their own practices and the contributions they make to the market sign systems. This is particularly important for businesses that pursue long-term strategies of building corporate reputation.

Anti-religious movements

Parallel to the resurgence of religion, anti-religious movements are also proactively disrupting the religious landscape globally as well as in local contexts (Jafari, 2015). This means that anti-religious movements attempt to counteract promotions of religion-related business practices and market activities. Anti-religious movements, in Kitcher's (2011) words, are classified as militant atheism, an ideology that fights manifestations of religion and religiosity in social life. A quick look at the discourse of militant atheists (see for example, Boycott Halal, 2014) demonstrates the depth and breadth of a systematic attack on the foundations of religion and religious practices in society. Markets in particular are sites where religious, un-religious, and anti-religious symbolism is used through consumption-scapes and servicescapes in order to show differences and similarities between disparate groups (Jafari et al., 2014; Jafari, 2015). As such, corporate reputation strategies should keep an eye on how the organisation may respond to various opposing voices that attack religious manifestations.

All of these points indicate that consumers and businesses alike can face myriad dilemmas and challenges in their day-to-day interactions with one another and with other market making institutions such as states, sociocultural traditions, religious authorities, media, and social movements in diverse sociocultural contexts. Understanding these inter-connectivities is vital for businesses' sustainable development and reputation building. In light of this discussion, I will explain even more complexities that surround the current status of 'Islamic' business and the prevalent assumptions in this domain.

Some prevalent assumptions about 'Islamic' business and markets

Quite often, when 'Islamicness' is discussed in different areas of business studies, certain assumptions seem to be taken for granted: (1) Muslims seek Sharia-compliant consumer goods/services and business practices; (2) 'Islamic' markets are large in size (estimated 2 billion people) and lucrative in financial worth (estimated trillions of dollars), hence there are great opportunities for organisations to target these markets; (3) 'Islamic' business practices are healthy for the welfare of society at large, therefore they should be opera-tionalised in full capacity in business practices; (4) closely related to the previous point, there are global opportunities for Islamic brands to penetrate in 'non-Islamic' contexts too. These assumptions which prevail in the extant literature (Alserhan, 2010, 2011; El-Bassiouny, 2014, 2016; Temporal, 2011; Wilson and Liu, 2010, 2011; Wilson and Grant, 2013) are sometimes treated as holistically true. Indeed, they are not. These statements are only *partially* true; therefore, corporations should not capitalise on these assumptions hast-ily. The reality is more complex than it seems to be on the surface.

Muslim consumers

It is true that there are Muslims who are in search of Sharia-compliant market offer-ings. The rise of the concept of Halal is a good indicator of this trend. The Halal is now becoming a global phenomenon. Yet, an historical analysis of markets and consumption in Muslim geographies indicates that Halal was not a prominent term in the past. In Muslim geographies everything was perceived to be Halal by default. The Halal, in its mundane and practical meaning, would apply mainly to foods and beverages. Meat, for example, was perceived to be completely prepared in a Halal way. The typical meat consumed in Muslim geographies did not contain pork or pig related substances. There was no debate on pre-slaughter stunning either. Any alcohol-free beverage was also regarded as Halal by default. However, nowadays, Halal is no longer a simple label. It encompasses a series of complicated requirements for 'holistic Halal' (Ambali and Bakar, 2014), a thorough Sha-ria-compliant process starting from an early point in the supply chain all the way through to the point of disposition (of goods and services).

An important point to bear in mind is that awareness about Halal is not unidirectional. That is, it is not always sought after by consumers only; Halal is a discourse which is also being enforced, from a top to bottom manner, by states and regulatory bodies. Fischer (2008, 2011), for example, demonstrates how the Malaysian state uses the Halal discourse to hegemonise Muslim Malays over other ethnic minorities (i.e., the Chinese and Indi-ans) and pre-empt potential ethnic conflicts in the country. The Malaysian case explicitly depicts that the dynamics of ethnic identities have a great influence on the growth and acceptability of Halal brands in a given sociocultural context. Fischer explains that in pursuit of political, economic, and sociocultural goals, the Malaysian state has naturalised/nationalised Islam in the post-colonial Malaysia. The state has used market development and consumerism as effective means of enhancing its citizens' education, living standards, skills, and business entrepreneurial spirit. As such, Islam has been leveraged to erase the colonial history of Malaysia and project the country as a sophisticated self-sufficient nation. Therefore, awareness of Halal and the 'Islamic' is a multifaceted phenomenon which cannot be analysed from a consumer perspective (bottom to top, or pull strategy) only.

Apart from states, businesses also play an important role in creating awareness about the 'Islamic'. As such, businesses may use segmentation criteria and branding to promote and sell certain products and services in the name of the 'Islamic'. Examples are abundant. Tekbir, a Turkish hejab apparel company, has established itself as an Islamic fashion retailer in the clothing industry with branches in countries such as Turkey, Chechnya, Egypt, Tunisia, Azerbaijan, Bosnia Herzegovina, and Macedonia. Mecca Cola, first launched in France in 2002, has now become a well-known brand around the world, specifically targeting pro-Muslim consumers. The number of Muslim dating websites is also increasing in virtual spaces. Such websites seem to have emerged with a view to facilitating marriage amongst single Muslims who do not want to follow traditional ways of marriage usually initiated by families or those who do not want to follow un-Islamic socialisation traditions amongst opposite sexes. Besides, nowadays there are Islamic hospitality online platforms and offline agencies that promote Islamic holiday resorts and travelling services.

These examples obviously demonstrate that these companies serve certain market segments; yet, they are not criticism-free. For example, Süerdem (2013) argues that much of the debate on Islamic brands and business practice is rooted in the instrumentalisation of Islam in search of economic gains. Süerdem's account is critical in the sense that it highlights the fact that aesthetic surgeries of brands at a label level (i.e., branding) does not make any business practice Islamic. Corporations that instrumentalise Islam in their promotion and segmentation criteria are not truly Islamic in nature; they engage in opportunistic behaviours to take advantage of people's varying emotional and pragmatic interests in Islam. Such corporations which unintentionally contribute to stereotypical representations of Muslims (through market segmentation) may neglect the major pillar of Islam which is devotion to social justice and enhancing people's quality of life at large.

'Islamic' markets

'Islamic' markets are indeed considerably large in size and attractive in financial value. Yet, this should not be simplistically tempting for businesses. From human and socioeconomic development perspectives, Muslim geographies consist of some of the poorest and most underdeveloped societies in the world (Rice, 1999; Jafari, 2012). The implication is that in such contexts there are people who are struggling, on a day-to-day basis, with the basic needs of life, such as clean drinking water, shelter, medical services, social security, and so forth. These people have different expectations from the 'Islamic' and their aspirations are different from those of (relatively) affluent individuals. The less affluent people from less socioeconomic backgrounds are more concerned with the deeper promises of Islam to establish 'social justice' in human society (Qutb, 2000/1953) than superficial surgeries of brand names and Islamic-looking business practices. They may also reject brands and businesses (both Western and local) not because they manifest Western values, but because they are perceived to be associated with socioeconomic inequalities in society that underpin these people's everyday life situations in spaces of markets and consumption (Izberk-Bilgin, 2012). Acknowledging socioeconomic underdevelopments in Muslim geographies means that corporations need to go beyond the surface level to address a variety of issues (e.g., price sensitivity, product availability, service innovations, job creations) specific to the local contexts. Czinkota and Ronkainen (2003) have already argued that global companies can win people's hearts in less affluent contexts by addressing such values. Whether branded as Islamic or non-Islamic, businesses that deliver such values will be more acceptable to people in these localities.

'Islamic' business practices

There is no doubt that 'Islamic' business practices are healthy for the welfare of society at large. Research (Beekun, 1996; Rice, 1999; Saeed et al., 2001) has already argued that business ethics from an Islamic perspective offers a unique value proposition towards enhancing quality of life for all stakeholders. The uniqueness of Islamic business ethics lies in the fact that whilst it promotes market activities and profit maximisation, it defines a clear framework within which these activities should take place. The optimum value of business practice from an Islamic perspective is social welfare and justice. That is, businesses are seen as means (and not ends) to achieve salvation not only in the life hereafter but also in this very worldly life. The implementation of Islamic business ethics, however, is a major challenge because there are many institutional obstacles that influence its performativity. Rice (1999) tactfully argues that the biggest hurdle before the implementation of Islamic principles in business is the political structures that instrumentalise Islam for economic and political gains. Jafari (2012) also raises concerns over such structural problems that render Islamic business ethics theoretical. In practice, cronyism, corruption, and opportunism in Muslim geographies nourish underdevelopments through business activities. In other words, business opportunities actually work against the principles of Islam.

Global opportunities

It is true that there are global opportunities for brands from Muslim geographies to penetrate 'non-Islamic' contexts. Ogilvy Noor's Miles Young (2008) posits:

> Meanwhile, in the West, recent research (by JWT) amongst Muslim consumers has highlighted their importance as an attractive market segment. Already in the US, they are being described as the 'new Hispanics'. While recognition of this new 'target' for primarily Western marketers is timely, simply leaving it there is probably not enough. There is a bigger angle; what is the role of Islam in the growing multi-literalism of the global economy itself? The pure arithmetic, of course, is persuasive at one level, and all the more so outside of the UK and the US. There are 1.6 billion Muslims worldwide, rising fast. Of these, only 20 per cent belong to the Arab world, the majority being located in south and east Asia. The rub, however, is that the Islamic world still only accounts for 5 per cent of the world's GDP. The issues of the Islamic world tend, therefore, to be those of the developing world. Brands which compete in the global market place are the necessary weapons for avoiding long term economic marginalization. It is as simple as that.

Young rightly identifies the importance of international expansion of brands from Muslim geographies to development discourses. Businesses are powerful means of resolving underdevelopments in local contexts (Czinkota and Ronkainen, 2003). They can not only represent their home countries in their foreign host markets and enhance their country of origin's image overseas, but also pave the way for other businesses (especially SMEs) for internationalisation. They can also immensely contribute to the quality of life in their local contexts by creating jobs, enhancing business and life standards, impacting social policy, strengthening technological infrastructures, accelerating modernisation of industries, and improving market regulations and governance. These activities which have strong policy and development implications can, in the long term, contribute to the success of brands and corporations emerging from Muslim geographies.

As mentioned earlier, Mecca Cola has achieved success in many countries across the world. Yet, it should also be observed that in order to achieve global success, corporations do not need to necessarily carry the label of 'Islamic'. Mecca Cola's success lends itself to the political and humanitarian cause of supporting Palestinians who were caught up in difficult life conditions imposed by Israel. The Iraq and Afghanistan wars also intensified anti-Western sentiments amongst pro-Muslim consumers who wanted to cry out their opinion through consumer activism. Not many companies may gain success in this way. Due to its political cause, Mecca Cola did attract many consumers; yet it certainly repelled some other consumers who would not buy into the brand's activist agenda. There are always two sides to the coin. Corporations seeking expansion into markets outside their geopolitical borders need to be aware of all possibilities of acceptability or rejection.

There are many brands originating from Muslim geographies that have succeeded in global markets without following a political cause or leveraging Islamicness. The Turkish Arçelik company has become a global supplier of white goods and home appliances not because it has emerged from a Muslim country, but because it has delivered value to consumers. High-quality products, excellent aftersales service, efficient distribution systems, and fair pricing strategies are the key strengths of the company. Similarly, what makes Aljazeera a global player in the multimedia industry sector is its capabilities and understanding of the needs of its audiences. Emirates Airlines, Turkish Airlines, Ülker (Turkey), Aida (Iran), 1&1 (Iran), and many other brands have the same story. Of course, country of origin always remains a critical factor in the acceptability of brands to markets; yet, generally speaking, businesses should know that in order to succeed in global markets, they do not need to associate themselves with Islam and the Islamic, especially if this association happens to be a superficial one. From another angle, it could also be argued that Adidas, Puma, Coca Cola, BMW, Sony, Samsung, Apple, Singapore Airlines, and hundreds of global brands that have penetrated Muslim geographies for a long time have no claims of association with the 'Islamic'. What matters most is what value the brand delivers to people and how stakeholders evaluate the brand.

Revisiting the two options: positioning the organisation as a 'holistically Islamic' enterprise or making no big claims of association with the 'Islamic'

These are the two choices I suggested earlier in the beginning of this chapter. In order to be 'holistically Islamic', the organisation ought to follow Islamic principles thoroughly, both theoretically and practically. Having an Arabic name, a green and crescent-related logo, including the term 'Islamic' in the company's name, offering Sharia-compliant products/services, producing Sharia-compliant promotional materials, recruiting Muslim (looking) employees, or following a political cause related to Muslims does not make an enterprise truly Islamic. Islamicness of a business enterprise lies in its vision towards value creation, not just in an economistic way on the surface, but as an all-encompassing business philosophy deeply rooted in the principles of Islam. This can be achieved if and only if the concept of value in Islam is understood.

Soroush's (2000) analysis can shed some light on what value means in Islam. According to Soroush, there are two types of values: guiding values and serving values. Guiding values – "those for the sake of which we live" (e.g., spirituality and morality) – need material realisation through serving values – "those that exist for the sake of living" (e.g., sociality and productivity) (p. 39). In Islam, temporal and secular affairs (such as business activities) are regarded as the most immediate and available means of serving values to help humankind to embrace eternal guiding values that would transcend the worldly life. Amongst a large number of guiding and serving values, the key ones that are immediately related to the discussion in this chapter are the concepts of faith and wealth respectively. The relationship between these two could be best explained in Imam Ali's (the first Imam of the Shiites) words: "Poverty makes one's faith imperfect, perplexes his reason and is a cause of animosity" (Dashti, 2005, p. 505). This is the same notion that Qutb (2000/1953) emphasised in his thesis of social justice in Islam. That is why in Islamic teachings and practices maximum emphasis is put on economic self-sufficiency of humankind because poverty is seen as the root of all evil (e.g., lack of human dignity, fraud, theft). Interestingly, socioeconomic justice – which is a means and not an end in itself – is not what Islam seeks to establish only for Muslims but for all members of human society. Socioeconomic justice fertilizes the seeds of peace, wellbeing, stability, and serenity in society. Any business with Islamic agendas should leverage such a perspective.

Islamicness for organisations means looking at the business as a means of contributing to the welfare of community at large. It also means aversion from ethnocentrism. Islamic-oriented businesses should not arouse ethno-religious sensitivities and tensions. They should follow a social justice philosophy throughout their activities, from the gestation of the organisation all the way through different business operations (e.g., financing, supply, production, networking, promotion, distribution, aftersales services, human resource management, customer management, Corporate Social Responsibility, database marketing). Social justice in this scenario means ensuring that all these activities are transparent and all internal and external stakeholders are treated fairly and with respect to human dignity. An Islamic-oriented organisation would also engage in market competition in just manners. It would formally and informally avoid cronyism, corruption, and lobbying, which are sometimes politically justified in the name of networking. Islam in no way approves of such corruptive acts.

Islam also emphatically promotes honesty, even if honesty causes loss to the teller of truth. As such, from an Islamic perspective, any deceptive act is un-Islamic. Businesses with an Islamic agenda should meticulously monitor all their activities to ensure that honesty rules. Consumers and customers of such businesses must feel assured that they are not prey to the games of economic profit-making systems that instrumentalise Islam in the name of Sharia-compliant products/services. Deceptive advertising and promotion should therefore be completely avoided. The brand should stand for the values guided by Islam and not by markets. Markets, as I mentioned earlier, are means, not ends. To implement such values, human capital is the key driver. Organisations should develop a human resource strategy that encourages understanding and genuine faith in these values so that employees can deliver the values on a day-to-day basis. In business networks, workplace, and servicescapes personal attitudes (e.g., ethnocentrism) and behaviours (e.g., responsiveness to others' needs) influence the way corporate values are manifested and performed.

These examples are not exhaustive. They are only meant to draw an overall picture of what a holistically Islamic business enterprise should be like. The image depicted above is of course the ideal situation and a framework for businesses to operate in. But this is not an impossible situation. The above-mentioned features were all practised in the past. Dost (2008) demonstrates that Islamic values resembled markets and business practices in early Islamic periods. In small-scale businesses, these features prevail in many societies as well. Small businesses are often easier to manage in the sense that in day-to-day activities, business owners' deep religious values obviously influence business practices. However, at a corporate level, it is really difficult to identify an organisation that is holistically Islamic. My failure to identify one might also be related to my limited knowledge.

Alternatively, if the organisation is not capable of following a holistically Islamic path or is not willing to take the plunge to do so, the best option is then to avoid making big claims to the Islamic. Research (Gait and Worthington, 2008) reveals that even if the organisation is associated with Islam (e.g., Islamic banking and finance), in the presence of religious conviction, still consumers consider corporate, service quality, and pricing as their main criteria for their customs with the business enterprise. Those organisations whose business requires them to offer Sharia-compliant products and services (e.g., foods and beverages or financial products/services) should ensure that their products/services are fully Sharia compliant but simultaneously should avoid building their reputation on claims of being (or being perceived as) holistically Islamic enterprises. In other business sectors where Sharia compliance is not a determinant criterion (e.g., home appliances, fashion, automotive, telecommunications), organisations should carefully follow business ethics frameworks in their entirety without associating themselves with the Islamic. Failure to deliver on claims will not only damage the corporate image but also seriously damage the image of Islam in the eyes of those who are not familiar with Islam in depth. Opportunistic behaviours should therefore be totally avoided by businesses.

Conclusion

The aim of this chapter was to prompt critical thinking about what constitutes Islamicness in the realm of branding and corporate reputation. It was discussed that reputation is socially constructed and is evaluated by different stakeholders based on the organisation's expected behaviours. It was also argued that 'Islamicness' is a fluid concept, which is constantly (re)shaped by multiple actors and ideologies in contemporary spaces of markets. Therefore, in order to build and sustain global reputation, corporations should avoid short-term engagements with market-generated fads that are often the outcome of transient identity anxieties. This means that brand building should be based on a long-term corporate vision that considers the changing landscape of religious perceptions and orientations. In conclusion, it was highlighted that if and only if the organisation is capable of following the principles of Islam should it make claims of Islamicness; otherwise, the organisation should ethically follow market rules without associating itself with Islam and the Islamic.

Issues for further discussion

1   To what extent do you (dis)agree with the proposed strategies in this chapter?
2   Given the existing Islamophobia, what are the challenges businesses emerging from Muslim geographies face in building reputation in international markets?
3   Do you know of any corporation that is holistically Islamic? How would you evaluate their reputation?
4   In your view, what are the characteristics of an Islamic-oriented business?

Case study

OnePure and MYPURE

The following two short case studies are developed based on the online analysis of two companies' websites and activities: (1) OnePure (Halal Beauty), a producer and distributor of Halal beauty products such as eye crème, anti-aging crème cleanser, target serum: acne solution, and the like; and (2) MYPURE (Natural Beauty), distributor of the world's top organic body care products. Both of these companies are in the health and beauty sector. Whilst the former focuses on Sharia-compliant products and manufacturing procedures, the latter stresses the naturalness of its products. These two cases are presented briefly; yet, further information needs to be collected about these two companies (from their websites and other sources such as YouTube and business reports) to develop in-depth discussions on the issues raised earlier in this chapter.

OnePure Halal Beauty

The company was founded in 2006 by Layla Mandi, a Canadian-born, Dubai-based entrepreneur who also runs her own business consultancy (LaylaMandi.com). The company distributes its products through a series of leading stores, including French department store Galeries Lafayette and on Saudi Arabian Airlines. Layla Mandi successfully created and sustained the brand OnePure proactively. She has been publicising the brand through her interviews with media such as BBC, CBC, GEO, Astro Awani, AFP, and other TV channels and newspapers. She also continuously participates in international exhibitions and conferences (e.g., Beauty World Middle East, the World Halal Forum in Malaysia, the 2nd Annual Halal Congress in Sharjah, the Global Islamic Branding and Marketing Forum at The Said Business School, University of Oxford) to promote her brands (Layla Mandi, as the entrepreneur and consultant, and also OnePure, as the beauty company). OnePure was also nominated at the 2013 Global Islamic Economy Summit in Dubai for the Islamic Economy Award in Cosmetics.

OnePure emphasises that its products are Sharia compliant: "The Islamic authority (Imam) inspects the production facilities and factories to make sure there are no haram products or alcohol (including fluids used to clean the equipment) used in the manufacturing process. Testing is done on the individual products and ingredients to make sure there are no pork or animal by-products. It is a time-intensive process. . . . [F]inally the certificate is issued for each and every product if all requirements are met to become Certified Halal." However, simultaneously, the company emphatically highlights the high quality of its products and their price competitiveness, hence assuring its consumers of the value of OnePure products. Apart from the Sharia compliance of its manufacturing processes, as the company uses the word "Halal" in its logo, and that OnePure products deliver value to Muslim consumers, there is no claim made to Islamicness in the company's operations (e.g., finance, human resource management, promotion, distribution). In other words, the company does not claim that it is Islamic; rather, the claim is that its Sharia-compliant products suit those (Muslim) consumers who seek such products.

The company has built its reputation most successfully in regions such as the Persian Gulf Arab countries and Malaysia. The brand's success is mainly due to Layla Mandi's strategically less costly public engagement through interviews with media and conferences/forums in which business analysts spread the word about the brand. This reputation seems to be most obvious amongst Muslim consumers.

MYPURE Natural Beauty

MYPURE was founded in 2004 by Simon Golding and started out in a small cabin at the end of the garden. Soon the company grew in the number of employees and is now located in a converted barn on an old farm in Kent, UK. The company is determined to continue to remain inspired by natural beauty products and the latest developments in natural ingredients. The company is also one of the UK's first online distributors of purely natural and organic beauty products. The company has a wide range of products for women and men and presents itself as a family products brand.

MYPURE is not in any way associated with the 'Islamic', as the company sees itself inclusively dedicated to all those consumers who seek after purely organic products: "We believe that cosmetics, toiletries and home cleaning products made from natural and organic ingredients are easier on our bodies and less likely to cause problems like allergic reactions and skin sensitivity. Products made from natural ingredients are less polluting during manufacture and they biodegrade quickly after use. Great for you, even better for earth. . . . Of course, it goes without saying, but we'll say it anyway, NONE of the products stocked at MYPURE have been tested on animals. . . . We have a lot of fun testing these products so you can be sure they are free from nasty chemicals and that they work well too. We hope MYPURE is your first port of call for all your organic beauty needs."

The company has used a multi-brands strategy in the sense that each product made of a natural ingredient is branded in order to represent that particular natural ingredient. Now the company distributes around 40 brands. The company's online and offline activities are all focused on naturalness of their products and that these products are healthy for consumers. A key brand augmentation strategy of the company is also the active blog they are using on the website in order to inform consumers of the latest news and generate buzz about MYPURE.

Case questions for discussion

1   In terms of product positioning, what are the key differences between the two companies? Do you see these companies in direct rivalry? With regard to product positioning, what are the advantages and disadvantages of each company?

2   Which company has more inclusive target markets? Which company has more opportunities for building international reputation? What are each company's challenges in doing so?

3   Given the fact that OnePure's focus is on Sharia-compliant products, is there any need for the company to move towards a holistically Islamic enterprise in the future?

References

Al Ganideh, S. F. and Al Taee, H. (2012), "Examining Consumer Ethnocentrism Amongst Jordanians From an Ethnic Group Perspective", *International Journal of Marketing Studies*, Vol. 4, No. 1, pp. 48–57.

Alserhan, B. A. (2010), "On Islamic Branding: Brands as Good Deeds", *Journal of Islamic Marketing*, Vol. 1, No. 2, pp. 101–106.

Alserhan, B. A. (2011), *The Principles of Islamic Marketing*, Surrey: Gower Publishing Limited.

Ambali, A. R. and Bakar, A. N. (2014), "People's Awareness on Halal Foods and Products: Potential Issues for Policy-Makers", *Procedia – Social and Behavioral Sciences*, vol. 121, March, pp. 3–25.

Askari, H., Iqbal, Z. and Mirakhor, A. (2009), *New Issues in Islamic Finance and Economics: Progress and Challenges*, Singapore: John Wiley & Sons.

Beekun, R. I. (1996), *Islamic Business Ethics (Human Development)*, Herndon, VA: International Institute of Islamic Thought.

Boycott Halal. (2014), www.boycottHalal.com/ (accessed 20 May 2014).

Czinkota, M. R. and Ronkainen, I. A. (2003), "An International Marketing Manifesto", *Journal of International Marketing*, Vol. 11, No. 1, pp. 13–27.

Dashti, M. (trans.) (2005), *Nahjolbalaghe*. Qom: Amir-Almo'menin Research Cultural Institute.

Dost, S. (2008), *The Idea of Free Market in Islam*. http://atlasnetwork.org/wp-content/uploads/2009/03/suleyman-dost-essay_new.pdf (accessed 10 May 2014).

Eickelman, D. F. (2000), "Islam and the Language of Modernity", *Daedalus*, Vol. 129, No. 1, pp. 119–136.

El-Bassiouny, N. (2014), "The one-billion-plus marginalization: Toward a scholarly understanding of Islamic consumers". *Journal of Business Research*, Vol. 67, pp. 42–49.

El-Bassiouny, N. (2016), "Where is 'Islamic marketing' heading? A commentary on Jafari and Sandikci's (2015) 'Islamic' consumers, markets, and marketing". *Journal of Business Research*, Vol. 69, No. 2, pp. 569–578.

Fischer, J. (2008), *Proper Islamic Consumption: Shopping Among the Malays in Modern Malaysia*. Copenhagen: NIAS Press.

Fischer, J. (2011), *The Halal Frontier: Muslim Consumers in a Globalized Market*, London: Palgrave Macmillan.

Gait, A. and Worthington, A. (2008), "An Empirical Survey of Individual Consumer, Business Firm and Financial Institution Attitudes Towards Islamic Methods of Finance", *International Journal of Social Economics*, Vol. 35, No. 11, pp. 783–808.

Gauthier, F. and Martikainen, T. (eds.) (2013), *Religion in Consumer Society: Brands, Consumer and Markets*, Farnham, UK: Ashgate Publishing Limited.

Izberk-Bilgin, E. (2012), "Infidel Brands: Unveiling Alternative Meanings of Global Brands at the Nexus of Globalization, Consumer Culture, and Islamism", *Journal of Consumer Research*, Vol. 39, No. 4, pp. 663–687.

Jafari, A. (2012), "Islamic Marketing: Insights From a Critical Perspective", *Journal of Islamic Marketing*, Vol. 3, No. 1, pp. 22–34.

Jafari, A. (2015), "Towards an Understanding of Religion-Related Vulnerability in Consumer Society", in Hamilton, K., Dunnett, S. and Piacentini, M. (Eds.), *Vulnerable Consumers: Conditions, Contexts and Characteristics*. London: Routledge, pp. 173–184.

Jafari, A., Özhan Dedeoğlu, A., Üstündağli, E., Regany, F. and Batat, W. (2014), "Rethinking Religion in the Context of Ethnicity and Wellbeing", *Marketing Theory* Vol. 15, No. 2, pp. 287–295.

Jafari, A. and Goulding, C. (2008), "'We Are Not Terrorists!' UK Based Iranians, Consumption, and the 'Torn Self'", *Consumption, Markets, and Culture*, Vol. 11, No. 2, pp. 73–93.

Jafari, A. and Sandıkcı, Ö. (2015), "Islamic' Consumers, Markets, and Marketing: A Critique of El-Bassiouny's (2014) 'The one-billion-plus marginalization'". *Journal of Business Research*, Vol. 68, No. 12, pp. 2676–2682.

Jafari, A. and Sandıkcı, Ö. (2016), "The Ontological Pitfalls of Islamic Exceptionalism: A Re-Inquiry on El-Bassiouny's (2014, 2015) Conceptualization of 'Islamic Marketing'". *Journal of Business Research*, Vol. 69 No. 3 pp. 1175–1181.

Jafari, A. and Süerdem, A. (2012), "An Analysis of Material Consumption Culture in the Muslim World", *Marketing Theory*, Vol. 12, No. 1, pp. 59–77.

Jafari, A. and Visconti, L. (2014), "New Directions in Ethnicity Research From a Wellbeing Perspective", *Marketing Theory*, Vol. 15, No. 2, pp. 265–270.

Kaynak, E. and Kara, A. (2002), "Consumer Perceptions of Foreign Products: An Analysis of Product-Country Images and Ethnocentrism", *European Journal of Marketing*, Vol. 36, No. 7/8, pp. 928–949.

Kitcher, P. (2011), "Militant Modern Atheism", *Journal of Applied Philosophy*, Vol. 28, No. 1, pp. 1–13.

Qutb, S. (2000/1953), *Social Justice in Islam*. J. B. Hardie and H. Algar (trans.). New York: Islamic Publications International.

Rice, G. (1999), "Islamic Ethics and the Implications for Business", *Journal of Business Ethics*, Vol. 18, No. 4, pp. 345–358.

Saeed, M., Ahmed, Z. U., and Mukhtar, S. M. (2001), "International Marketing Ethics From an Islamic Perspective: A Value-Maximization Approach", *Journal of Business Ethics*, Vol. 32, No. 2, pp. 127–142.

Sandıkcı, Ö. (2011), "Researching Islamic Marketing: Past and Future Perspectives", *Journal of Islamic Marketing*, Vol. 2, No. 3, pp. 246–258.

Sandıkcı, Ö. and Jafari, A. (2013), "Islamic Encounters in Consumption and Marketing", *Marketing Theory*, Vol. 13, No. 4, pp. 411–420.

Slater, D. (1997), *Consumer Culture and Modernity*. Cambridge: Polity Press.

Soroush, A. (2000), *Reason, Freedom, and Democracy in Islam*. M. Sadri and A. Sadri (Eds.). Oxford: Oxford University Press.

Süerdem, A. (2013), "Yes My Name Is Ahmet, But Please Don't Target Me. Islamic Marketing: Marketing Islam™?" *Marketing Theory*, Vol. 13, No. 4, pp. 285–295.

Temporal, P. (2011), *Islamic Branding and Marketing: Creating a Global Islamic Business*, Singapore: John Wiley & Sons.

The Telegraph (2010), "Domino's Pizza Scraps Halal Menu". www.telegraph.co.uk/foodanddrink/foodanddrinknews/7946771/Dominos-Pizza-scraps-Halal-menu.html (accessed 11 May 2014).

Wilkes, D. (2009), "The Domino's Branch Where You Can't Get a Pepperoni Pizza – Because They Only Do Halal". www.dailymail.co.uk/news/article-1142022/The-Dominos-branch-pepperoni-pizza – Halal.html (accessed 11 May 2014).

Wilson, J. A. J. and Grant, J. (2013), "Islamic Marketing – a Challenger to the Classical Marketing Canon?", *Journal of Islamic Marketing*, Vol. 4, No. 1, pp. 7–21.

Wilson, J. A. J. and Liu, J. (2010), "Shaping the Halal Into a Brand?", *Journal of Islamic Marketing*, Vol. 1, No. 2, pp. 107–123.

Wilson, J. A. J. and Liu, J. (2011), "The Challenges of Islamic Branding: Navigating Emotions and Halal", *Journal of Islamic Marketing*, Vol. 2, No. 1, pp. 28–42.

Wong, L. (2007), "Market Cultures, the Middle Classes and Islam: Consuming the Market?", *Consumption, Markets and Culture*, Vol. 10, No. 4, pp. 451–80.

Young, M. (2008), "Islamic Branding: The Next Big Thing?" www.wpp.com/wpp/marketing/branding/islamic-branding/ (accessed 20 May 2014).

Part II

Religion, consumption and culture

4 Religion and Halal consumption

*Ismah Osman, Faridah Hassan, Balkis Haris
and Erne Suzila Kassim*

Learning outcomes

At the end of this chapter, readers should be able to:

1 Recognize the importance of religion towards consumption
2 Understand the key features *of Maqasid Shari'ah* of consumption in Islam
3 Acknowledge the impact of consumption and consumerism in the essence of *Maqasid Shari'ah*
4 Acquire the ability to apply the concept of consumption from Islamic perspectives
5 Differentiate between Muslim and non-Muslim consumers pertaining to Halal consumption
6 Appreciate the development of Muslim consumption of goods and services through various segmentations

Key points

1 Religion has a very significant influence on consumer behaviour.
2 The importance of *Shari'ah* (Islamic Law) and its association to consumption is indeed relevant towards consumer behavior.
3 The understanding of *Maqasid Shari'ah* towards developing theoretical framework on consumption is pertinent, from the viewpoint of Islam.
4 There are dissimilarities between Muslims and non-Muslims pertaining to Halal consumption.
5 Segmentations can be developed in relation to the Muslim consumption of goods and services.

Introduction

There is indeed a plethora of studies pertaining to religion and its effects on the consumption of products and services. More importantly, Islam currently being the second largest religion of the world is expected to expand and will probably exceed the world's largest religious population, which is Christianity (Lipka and Hackett, 2015). It is important to note that almost all consumer products and services are embedded within the foundation of Islamic faith in which they embrace; from the banking and insurance products, Halal food and beverages, telecommunication, logistic, hospitality and tourism, media and advertising, cosmetics and toiletries, pharmaceuticals, education system, to name a few. Islam propagates quality and wholesomeness for all the goods and services we consume, as mentioned in the Holy Qur'an Allah says, { . . . He allows them as lawful what is good (and pure) and prohibits them from what is bad (and impure)} (Holy al-Quran 7 : 157). Significantly, the concept of *Halal* and *tayyib* is not only prescribed to the Muslims, but even the non-Muslims may advocate to the same paradigm.

Hence, the development of Islamic marketing and consumerism is extremely rapid for both Muslims and non-Muslims, as this is one of the elements that initiate market segments. Marketers frequently create products and marketing programs designed to meet the consumers' requirements. They need to cater to the principles of Islam, particularly at the early stage of its product development. More importantly, the whole process of its production needs to be monitored and greatest thoughts need to be acquired and exploited in order to achieve conformity towards *Halal* for all products and services. A dedicated Muslim indeed needs to adopt the entire religion of Islam, as a way of life, in all matters and circumstances, including the consumption of goods and services in his daily living.

The non-Muslims, on the other hand, are also embracing Halal for the fact that the Halal concept emphasises safety, hygiene and wholesomeness of products and services. The word Halal is synonymous with food, but it goes beyond food or slaughtering of animals. Nevertheless, Halal is not just a mere religious obligation for the Muslims, but a universal standard, deemed to be appropriate especially when associated with consumerism. Temporal (2011) has highlighted the prospective of the Islamic brands to inter-connect with non-Muslims globally. Firstly, it is important to view those products or services as embracing mutually established common principles concerning "purity, health and wellness" (p. 11). Secondly, there is a growing demand on the quality values pertaining to Islamic products and services, and finally, the accessibility of Islamic products and services in relation to non-Muslim population. More importantly, there is significant attention of the international brands to drive its business to the Muslim majority and minority countries.

The issues of religion and consumption in Islam are the focus of this chapter, specifically with regard to its objectives relating to Islamic law and consumerism in Islam. We will then further establish the concept of *Halal in Islam*, and consumption from Islamic perspective. Subsequently, the discussion of the objectives of *Shari'ah* and its relationship to consumption is further elaborated. Significantly, a theoretical framework is developed to illustrate Halal consumption from the non-Muslim perspectives, as well as the Muslims.

Religious values and consumption of Halal

Religion is indeed one of the important factors where Muslims in particular need to decide and live according to the Islamic rulings, in which they have to adhere to the principles of permissibility (Halal) and prohibition (haram) in all forms of social interactions. More importantly, religion guides people in their lifestyle, image and identity (Cosgel and Minkler, 2004). According to Kahf (n.d.), consumption in Islam is built within two elements; firstly the needs towards consumption of products and services, and secondly, the relationship between consumption and success in the Hereafter. Consecutively, Zarqa (Siddique, 1981: 56) views consumption in Islam to be very much related to rewards within *Shari'ah* perspectives, and it is basically bounded by three conditions. Firstly, consumption is associated with good intention towards the Creator, due to the fulfilment of needs, in accordance to its level of consumption – *dharuriyyat, hajjiyat* and *tahsinniyat*. Secondly, soundness and sense of balance, as well as moderation towards consumption is undoubtedly pertinent and needs to prevail at all times. Thirdly, consumption in Islamic perspectives is concentrated upon the fulfilment of spiritual needs, rather than material or physiological needs.

The study on the role of religious values particularly, with the intention to choose Halal products, by Mukhtar and Butt (2012) found that Muslims living in multi-religious societies are considered more conscious about permissibility of products and this apparently has serious implications for international companies operating in food, cosmetics, pharmaceutical products and other products and services. Using the theory of reasoned action (TRA) the study established that intra-personal religiosity positively influences attitudes towards Halal products and their intention to purchase them. Another study that took place in the Sydney metropolitan area conducted by Razzaque and Chaudhry (2013) empirically investigated the impact of religious commitment of Muslim consumers in a non-Muslim country, on their purchase decision-making process, with the aim of identifying the sources of information that Muslim consumers perceive to be the most important element. The study concluded that food and personal hygiene products are important to religious Muslims. Product labelling emerged as the antecedent to Muslim consumers' involvement in brand decision making.

Delenar (1990) investigated the significant relationship between religious factors on perceived risk in purchase decision. It is argued that a person's religious orientation may influence the buying behaviour "across a broad spectrum of product classes". The samples were from affluent Catholic and Jewish households residing in the Northeast USA with the sampling frame of 1,500 households. The findings of the study suggested that religion and religious orientation should be viewed as important variables and have potential influence on marketing and consumption. On the other hand, the impact of different religiosity dimensions on the attitude of Muslim youth towards fashion studied by Farrag and Hassan (2015) suggested that a negative relationship exists with religious values and attitudes of youth towards fashion. Although the study has several limitations which might hinder the generalisability of the findings, especially on the use of students as samples, the findings are important to remind entrepreneurs and marketers that generally they cannot neglect the element of religion in their marketing activities.

According to Jamal and Sharifuddin (2015), religiosity predicts a significant amount of variance in purchase intentions, especially on Halal-labelled products. The study used British Muslim consumers as samples and data collection from 10 in-depth interviews and 303 self-administered questionnaires. The objective of this study is to investigate the motivations in searching for information and assessing the suitability of brands for consumption according to Islamic principles. The study showed that British Muslims with vertical collectivist orientations and high levels of religiosity are most likely to buy Halal-labelled products and support stores that sell such products. Consumption of Halal-labelled foods is a basic qualifying condition for developing, maintaining and reinforcing an overall Islamic lifestyle and identity (Sandikci and Ger, 2011). Indeed, the British Muslims' identity in the context of the global consumer culture (Cleveland and Laroche, 2007) creates numerous acculturation outcomes (Penaloza, 1994) and culture-swapping (Jamal and Sharifuddin, 2015).

The consumption of Halal cosmetic products is currently becoming more popular. Abd Rahman, Asrarhaghighi and Ab Rahman (2015) performed a study on knowledge and religiosity on the attitudes towards Halal cosmetic products and the attitudes on the intention to buy them. The results of the study provide some implications of firms competing in the cosmetic industry. Religiosity is one of the main factors that should be taken into account when promoting cosmetic products. Eventually, as the relationship between attitude and intention to choose Halal cosmetics is similar to the relationship for Halal foods, marketers may try similar approaches to promote both products. However, there is a low penetration among consumers towards Halal cosmetics, compared to the consumption of Halal foods.

In conclusion, all investigations mentioned above show that religious values and consumption are two common related factors that have been taken seriously by consumers nowadays. Hence, the producers, marketers and retailers need to apply the *Halal* concept comprehensively in all of its marketing activities.

The principles of *Shari'ah* and Muslim consumption

Shari'ah literally denotes the road to the watering place or the straight path to be followed (Lahsasna, 2013). Conceptually, it means the sum total of Islamic teaching and system, which was revealed to the Prophet Muhammad (peace be upon him) and recorded in the Holy Book of Al-Quran, as well as deducible from the Prophet's divinely guided lifestyle, called the Sunnah, in which it contains a comprehensive set of legal and ethical doctrines and obligations (Laldin, 2006). Hence, it comprehends the commandments of Allah and the way of life as prescribed by Allah to mankind. *Shari'ah* indicates "commands, prohibitions, guidance and principles that Allah has addressed to mankind pertaining to their conduct in this world and salvation in the next" (Lahsasna, 2013, p. 5). Allah says: {So judge between them by which Allah has revealed, and follow not their desires away from the truth which has come unto thee. For each We have appointed a divine law and a traced-out way} (Holy Quran, 5:48).

Laldin (2006) stated that Imam al-Shatibi has mentioned that *maslahah* (benefit) to mankind is the main factor for the establishment of Islamic law by Allah. More importantly, he pointed out that the establishment of Islamic law or *Shari'ah* is for the betterment of human beings in this world and the Hereafter. Similarly, *mafsadah* (preventing from harm) is equally important in *Shari'ah*, in which it eradicates those harmful elements from the society. In other words, *maslahah* is conveying the *manafi'* (advantages) and eliminating the *mafasid* (evils).

However, Laldin (2006) further elaborated that a certain *maslahah* can only be decided by the mind (*'aql*) or the Shari'ah. Nevertheless, if its deliberation is assigned only to the *'aql* or human intellect, then people will be incapable of delineating the exact *maslahah*. This is based on the fact that man has limited understanding of the things that are happening around him. Consequently, he would not be able to decide what is of *maslahah* to him, as he himself has trouble comprehending whether some issues are considered *manafi'* (benefit) or *mafsadah* (evil). It is only the Creator of man who understands the real substance of man, thus, man will gain benefits through the belief of *Shari'ah* and its application in his daily life as mentioned by Allah: {And whoever is grateful, truly, his gratitude for (the good of) his ownself, and whoever is ungrateful; Certainly! My Lord is Rich (Free of all wants), Bountiful.} (Holy Quran, al-Naml: 40).

Maqasid al-Shari'ah and its significance to consumption

The establishment of *Maqasid al-Shari'ah* (objectives of Shariáh) can be achieved by promoting three important components, namely; necessities (*Daruriyyat*), complements or needs (*Hajiyyat*) and embellishment or luxuries (*Tahsiniyyat*) (Lahsasna, 2013). According to Auda (2008), necessities (*Daruriyyat*) are the basic elements of a good life, and protecting them constitutes the goals of *Maqasid Shari'ah*. Necessities (*Daruriyyat*) can be categorised as safeguarding faith (*ad-din*), life (*an-nafs*), intellect (*al-'aql*), posterity (*an-nasl*), and wealth (*al-māl*) (Chapra, 2008).

Necessities (*Daruriyyat*)

Daruriyyat (necessities) refers to "the necessities and the essentials that people depend on, and without them the whole society will be in total disaster, disorder and disruption. As a result of that, it will end in total collapse" (Lahsasna, 2013). Ibn 'Ashur (2006) defined *Daruriyyat* as "things whose realisation is essential for the community both collectively and individually. The social entity of the community will not function properly if there is any defect in these things". According to Majid, Mahmud and Aziz (2012), Imam Al-Ghazali mentioned that all economic activities are related to providing basic human needs – food, clothing and shelter. These basic human needs are consistent with *Shari'ah*, thus, Al Ghazali tries to deliver information from his economic inquiry of various material matters that relate to providing better human conditions, as part of the idea of Islamic social welfare.

Conveniences (*Hajiyah*)

Conveniences comprise all activities and things that are not vital to the preservation of the above mentioned five foundations but are required to relieve or remove impediments and difficulties of life. Eventually, conveniences promote and complement necessities (*daruriyyah*), and their irrelevance leads to hardship, but not to the total disruption of normal life.

Refinements (*Tahsiniyah*)

This category includes those goods and services that go beyond the limits of conveniences. It includes things that complement or make life easier or more comfortable. It also refers to activities and things that go beyond the limits of complementary (*Hajiyyat*) and whose realisation leads to refinement and attainment of human life, and somehow reflects worldly accomplishment. For example, a car may be considered a luxury item for a common man, but it may be essential for a marketing executive. Furthermore, the things that beautify life also fall under this category, such as eating delicious food or wearing nice clothes.

Consumerism in Islam is subject to the doctrines of *Maqasid al-Shari'ah*, specifically the upholding of the principles of *Halal and haram*, the incorporation of *Shari'ah* and the realization of moral and ethical values. In addition, the concept of permissibility (*Halal*) established in Islam denotes those elements in which Allah has created, in which individuals may gain benefit from them. Therefore, nothing is haram except what is prohibited by a sound and explicit *nas* or evidence. This can be reflected upon the two main sources of Islamic law; the Quranic verses or the explicit Sunnah (practice or saying of the Prophet Muhammad [pbuh]).

Al-Qardhawi (1997) has defined permissibility (Halal) and prohibitions (haram) as:

Al-Halal (the lawful): That which is permitted, with respect to which no restriction exists, and the doing of which the Law–Giver, Allah, has allowed.

Al-Haram (the prohibited or unlawful): That which the Law–Giver has absolutely prohibited; anyone who engages in it is liable to incur the punishment of Allah in the Hereafter, as well as a legal punishment in this world.

Al-Makruh (the detested): That which is disapproved by the Law-Giver but not very strongly. The makruh is less in degree than the haram, and the punishment for *makruh* acts is less than for those that are haram, except when done too excessively and in a manner which leads an individual towards what is haram.

The world Halal population

The *Islamic Finance Today* (May 2016) has stated that the global Halal segment is promptly establishing further in the world economy, exclusively propelled by a number of demand and supply aspects. From the demand side, a fast expanding Muslim population combined with growing wealth in the Muslim-dominated economies are the main growth drivers, spearheading the increased demand for *Shari'ah*-compliant products and services.

As per the latest statistics from Pew Research Centre (www.pewresearch.org/), Muslims are forecast to rise up to 26.4 percent of the world's total projected population of 8.3 billion by 2030. The 56 mostly Muslim countries of the world represented a GDP of about USD 6.7 trillion in 2013 and is expected to grow to twice the rate of the global population (Thomson Reuters, 2014). Alongside the population growth, the real GDP growth rates are in the regions of the Middle East and North Africa (MENA), Asia and sub-Saharan Africa, which are home to large Muslim populations, and they are expected to range between 4.5 percent and 6.7 percent during 2014 and 2015 (Malaysian International Finance Centre (MIFC Report, 2014).

According to the report by the Pew Research Centre (2015), as of 2010, Christianity was by far the world's largest religion, with an estimated of 2.2 billion adherents, nearly a third (31 percent) of all 6.9 billion people on Earth. Islam was second, with 1.6 billion adherents, or 23 percent of the global population. If the current demographic trends tend to continue, eventually Islam will nearly catch up to their figure, by the middle of the twenty-first century. Between 2010 and 2050, the world's total population is expected to rise to 9.3 billion, which caused a 35 percent increase. Over that same period of time, Muslims – a comparatively youthful population with high fertility rates – are projected to increase by 73 percent. The number of Christians is also projected to rise, but more slowly at about the same rate (35 percent) as the overall global population. As a result, according to Pew Research Centre projections, by 2050 there will be near parity between Muslims (2.8 billion, or 30 percent of the population) and Christians (2.9 billion, or 31 percent), possibly for the first time in history.

Apparently, Thomson Reuters, in collaboration with Dinar Standard (2015) has also reported that the global Muslim spending on food and beverages (F&B), travel, Islamic finance, fashion, recreation and media, as well as pharmaceutical and cosmetics, is indeed on the rise. This is illustrated in the table below, highlighting the seven key sectors of the Halal industry, while focusing on the global Muslim spending for the year 2014. The percentage of global expenditures, and the growth of those sectors by 2020 is further illustrated. Eventually, the Halal economy can be driven through Muslim demographic entities; the participation of global multinationals like Nestle, KFC, McDonalds; the developed economies seeking growth markets; the growing global Islamic economies; as well as Islamic ethos-values and Intra–Organisation of Islamic Cooperation (OIC) trade growth (Malaysian International Finance Centre, 2015). Consequently, there is a tremendous potential for growth in the Halal economy, with the anticipation that Islamic finance would lead the squad, particularly towards providing financing for the industry. Table 4.1 explains the Halal consumption of goods and services worldwide.

Table 4.1 Muslim global spending on goods and services

	Food and beverages	Travel	Islamic finance	Fashion	Media and recreation	Pharmaceutical	Cosmetics
Global Muslim spending (2014)	1,128 billion USD	142 billion USD	1.8 trillion USD (in assets)	230 billion USD	179 billion USD	75 billion USD	54 billion USD
Percentage of global expenditure	16.7%	11%	24%	11%	5%	7%	7%
Percentage of increase (in 2013)	4.3% (1081 billion USD)	6.3% (134 billion USD)	10–12% (1.66 trillion USD)	2% (226 billion USD)	18% (151 billion)	4% (72 billion)	17% (46 billion)
Growth by 2020	1,585 billion USD	233 billion USD	3.25 trillion USD (assets)	327 billion USD	247 billion USD	106 billion USD	80 billion USD

Source: Islamic Finance Today (May 2016)

Muslim segmentation on consumption of goods and services

It is important to take note that Muslim consumers can be segregated into two major characteristics; firstly, they are those who are very devoted to the religion and pre-scribed to its teachings, and secondly, those who are quite liberal. Hence, religiosity plays a crucial role in determining the level of Halal consumption among Muslims and it is very important to take into consideration the similarities and differences across global Muslim markets in terms of religiosity, as well as culture and lifestyle (Tempo-ral, 2011). Table 4.2 illustrates the comparisons pertaining to Muslim consumption of goods and services. Considerably, there are studies that were conducted to identify con-sumer behaviour, particularly the Muslim consumers with regard to Halal consump-tion. Among them were the JWT Research and Ogilvy studies, focusing on market segmentation. They were conducted on a large scale and the concentration of those studies is very much applied to market segmentation, in order for this heterogeneous market to be divided into smaller segments. This helps to assist efficiency and effec-tiveness of the products and services, by corresponding to the customers' exceptional needs and wants.

Market segmentation: studies by J. Walter Thomson

According to Temporal (2011),J. Walter Thomson has carried out three studies involving Muslim population in the United Kingdom, the United States of America and the coun-tries within the Eastern Hemisphere. Hence, Temporal (2011) stated that from the study, the segmentation of Muslim consumers needs to be divided by dimensions focusing on the following elements:

a Self-view and mind-set → dreams, aspirations and personal choices
b Practices → traditions and culture influencing Muslims
c World view → attitudes toward media and advertising
d Relationships → attitudes toward men and women, family and friends, and generational differences

The four elements of the above dimensions were then translated to identify the segment across the markets in the Eastern Hemisphere, as they are the main Muslim–majority countries (Temporal, 2011). The countries under study were Algeria, Egypt, Saudi Arabia,

Table 4.2 The similarities and differences of Muslim consumption of goods and services

Similarities	Differences
• Common faith, values and identity as Muslims	• Diverse locations
• Similar dietary requirements (Halal)	• Multiple language and dialects
• Similar lifestyle requirements (finance, education, entertainment, tourism)	• Various cultural and lifestyle differences
• Strong sense of community and welfare	• Varying degrees of Islamic adherence
	• Varying degrees of education, affluence and market sophistication

Source: Temporal (2011, p. 52)

United Arab Emirates, Jordan, Iran, Turkey, Pakistan, Malaysia and Indonesia (Temporal, 2011). Basically, he stated that the findings of the research consider that there are five categories of segmentation pertaining to Muslim consumers and they are as follows.

1   Religious conservatives (composed 17 percent of the respondents) (Temporal, 2011)

- Extremely religious individuals
- Extremely conservative
- Do not approve of gender interaction
- Expect others to follow religious practices
- Anti-media and information averse
- Not brand conscious as consumers
- Would override their personal choices for religious beliefs
- Muslims living in Egypt, Algeria and Jordan

2   Pragmatic strivers (composed 24 percent of the respondents) (Temporal, 2011)

- Non-traditional
- Ambitious
- Open-minded
- Willing to compromise religious values in order to get ahead in life
- Muslims living in Turkey, Iran and Pakistan

3   Extreme liberals (composed 21 percent of the respondents) (Temporal, 2011)

- Very liberal, independent and assertive
- Not very particular about traditional and religious practices
- Pragmatic individuals who like to explore different possibilities although they do not conform to religious/societal norms
- Muslims living in Indonesia, and some Malaysian Muslims

4   New Age Muslim (composed 19 percent of the respondents) (Temporal, 2011)

- Somewhat traditional and embrace religious values
- Do not expect others to follow religious practices
- Religious by nature
- Believe in female empowerment and gender equality
- Pro-media and realize the potential advantages of the internet
- Muslims living in Saudi Arabia, United Arab Emirates, Pakistan and Malaysia

5   Social conformists (composed 19 percent of the respondents) (Temporal, 2011)

- Believe that social norms should be adhered to, even if it means overriding personal choice
- Do not approve the reason-based approach of "Generation Next"
- Lack self-confidence and depend on others to make decisions
- Not particularly religious and positively disposed toward Western values
- Muslims living in Algeria, Saudi Arabia and Iran

Indeed, the study can assist marketers in understanding the attitude, culture and lifestyle when it comes to the consumption of Halal products among Muslims. Although there are differences in the understanding of Halal among Muslims, what is more important, the consumption of products needs to address those issues of whether those products are deemed permissible (*Halal*) or prohibited (*haram*) (Hassan, 2013). Hence, the process involving Halal should always be addressed at all times, without contemplating the level of religiosity. Therefore, this need to be transformed within the system of beliefs and practices, in which those groups of people interpret and respond to what they feel as supernatural and sacred (Johnstone, 1975); in addition to culture and lifestyle.

In relation to this, Muhamad (2011) carried out a study pertaining to market segmentation in Islamic banks in Malaysia. She concluded that market segmentation can be based on the value dimensions; firstly, religious conviction where customers patronize certain Islamic banks due to their compliance to Islamic principles (*Shari'ah*). Secondly, a combination of both religious conviction and economic rationality that indicates customers who emphasise religious commitment, as well as pricing and return, reputation of the bank, service quality and innovation. Lastly, ethical values where customers may opt for Islamic banks due to their ethical entities of finance.

Although marketers need to address the different segmentations revolving around the Halal market, they are required to abide by the general rules and principles that have been set by the Creator and His messenger, the Prophet Muhammad (pbuh), at all times.

Market segmentation: studies by Ogilvy on traditionalists and futurists

In addition, Ogilvy and Mather have conducted a study where they believed that there are six segments (Young, 2010) which can be broadly segmented into two consumer groups: "futurists" and "traditionalists".

"Traditionalists" are generally more conservative in nature, more comfortable with what is already familiar to them, which reinforces their focus and sense of social harmony, culture and belonging. This group is therefore less likely to adopt change easily, making them more difficult to penetrate as potential consumers. Some characteristics of traditionalist are as follows (Young, 2010):

- They have an extreme desire for harmony and belonging
- They are collectivists, seeking a sense of belonging
- They tend to be more strongly aligned with the *Shari'ah* values of tolerance and compassion
- They are proud of their faith, in a quiet way
- Larger proportion of Muslims: 60 percent of total consumers
- Older generation than futurists: 35 years+
- Fall along the more collectivist side seeking belonging and social harmony
- More rooted to traditions
- Need for safety environment

Temporal (2011) explained that the "traditionalists" are composed of the following elements:

1   'Connected': They are those who see themselves as part of the web-like network of the Ummah (and who, therefore, tend to view technology as a positive enabler).

Compassion ranks highly as a value with them. They would say, 'religion connects me' (27 percent of the sample).

2 'Grounded': Islam is their anchor; religion and culture are inseparable. They were 23 percent of the sample. They seek peace in all their thoughts by being close to Allah. They would say 'religion centres me'.

3 'Immaculates': They seek disciplined perfection in religion, and many consistently reject the impure. They would declare 'religion purifies me'.

On the other hand, the "futurists" are generally defined as consumers who believe in both faith and modernity (Temporal, 2011). Some characteristics of the futurists are as follows (Young, 2010):

- They are more fiercely proud.
- They see themselves as steadfast followers of Islam in a modern world.
- They are driven by a purpose, a purpose very different from their peers.
- They are more individualistic.
- Their religion is their own choice, not just imposed on them.
- Their pride is intense, regardless of the extent to which they would be categorised as "devout".
- They believe in "struggle" – the struggle to remain true to their faith while carving out success in life.
- They believe in education, and with it, the right to ask questions – typically deeper and more probing about the intentions of businesses than the traditionalists.
- They want to get ahead as activists and they see Islam as an enabler.
- They seek to integrate a more globalised lifestyle with their own culture, but such actions are done without fundamental compromise.
- They value creativity.
- They are global.
- They feel strong responsibility to an Islam to help change things for the better, for example, the words of a famous Islamic T-shirt, 'Keep smiling, it's Sunnah'.
- They believe in both faith and modernity.
- They are young and well-educated: Generation Y and Generation Z.
- They are global and seek to integrate a more globalised lifestyle; fully engaged in the world; well-travelled with international exposure.
- They are proud of who they are: wear Islam with pride; strong reliance on faith and ethical values of Islam.
- They are tech-savvy: Generation C that signifies "Connected Generation".
- They are unafraid to challenge: prone to question the details behind what they buy; believes in education as drivers of change.
- They thirst for information, transparency and accountability thus, it is "important not to follow blindly".

Correspondingly, Deloitte and Noortel (2015) stated that the futurists consists of the following elements.

1 "Identifiers": Islam is a uniform they wear with pride – "religion identifies me". They want to see it strengthened and defended. They represent 27 percent of the sample.

2   "Movers": successful change agents. For them, religion is what you do with it: "religion enables me". They are internet-savvy, for instance. They represent 6 percent of the sample.
3   "Synthesizers" represent 6 percent of the sample. They are pragmatic, and adapt religious practice to their needs. As one said, "travelling by camel is Sunnah but we need to travel by plane". They would say "religion individuates me".

One of the implications of the futurists is their attitude to Halal, especially to the majority of the Muslim markets. The futurists are increasingly prone to question the details behind what they buy. It is a fact that *Shari'ah* compliance is an important entity, especially for all Halal products and services. Therefore, any insensitive behaviour, fault or mistakes towards these products will be very much under scrutiny, and these regrettably would not be accepted by the futurists. Global marketers need to be acutely aware of this, and more importantly, they need to observe the ground rules that are becoming more demanding. The scepticism of futurists in particular means that a simple Halal logo is no longer enough (Young, 2010). One of the respondents stated that indeed the Halal logo is important, but at the same time, the producers need to ensure that the ingredients, as well as the utensils used to cook those foods, are certified as Halal and *tayyib*.

Although "traditionalists" are the larger of the two Muslim consumer groups at 60 percent of those surveyed, the "futurists" at 40 percent of those surveyed still represent a significant pool of potential users. Consequently, they represent the consumer segment that is most likely going to shape the Muslims' consumer markets. Figure 4.1 illustrates the division of Muslims' segmentation into two categories; the first row depicts the futurists, while the second line illustrates the traditionalists.

The next section discusses the six pillars of the Halal industry; which include food and beverage, travel and hospitality, Islamic banking and finance, media and communication, pharmaceuticals and cosmetics and modest fashion, in particular. They provide the general Halal requirements, its industrial development, as well as the challenges and opportunities posed by the environment; the internal and external threats for the global Halal market to move forward, locally and internationally.

The Identifiers (27%) • Wear Islam with pride • Want religion to be strengthened and defended *'Religion Identifies Me'*	The Movers (6%) • Internet savvy • Act as change agents *'Religion Enables Me'*	The Synthesizers (6%) • Pragmatic • Adapt religious practice to their needs *'Religion Individuates Me'*	THE FUTURISTS
The Immaculates (11%) • Seek discipline and perfection *'Religion Purifies Me'*	The Grounded (23%) • Religion and culture are inseparable *'Religion Centres Me'*	The Connected (27%) • Technology is positive, and compassion ranks highly *'Religion Connects Me'*	THE TRADITIONALISTS

Figure 4.1 The futurists and the traditionalists
Source: Deloitte and Noortel (2015)

The pillars of the Halal industry

Food and beverage

Driven by the growing demands, the Halal food market continues to build its momentum across the global food supply chain. This report estimates that global Muslim spending on F&B has increased 4.3 percent to reach $1,128 billion in 2014. This takes the potential core Halal food market to be 16.7 percent of global expenditure in 2014 (Thomson Reuters and Dinar Standard, 2015).

From Asia to America, the Halal food sector is becoming a major source of growth in both the Islamic and the wider global economy. Of course, there are challenges as well. There is a continuing struggle for Halal food standards and accreditation, with more education of such topics required in OIC countries. The recent ban on Halal and Kosher slaughter in Denmark along with scary stories about Halal food in the media reflect a current attitude established in Europe. Engaging and overcoming these challenges will be pivotal to the future success of the Halal food sector. However, a testament to this sector's strength is that the success of the Halal food market remains constant across different cultures and continents.

Food and beverages are rendered Halal except for the following elements (Toronto Public Health, 2004):

- animals improperly slaughtered, or dead animals, carnivorous animals and other components that are clearly prohibited
- intoxicants or alcohol or any elements that are intoxicant (drugs)
- pork and its by-products e.g. gelatine, lipase, pepsin
- meat from animals not slaughtered according to the Islamic dietary law
- alcohol and foods prepared with alcohol e.g. candies and cakes that include alcohol such as rum cake
- food containing blood and blood by-products e.g. blood pudding
- food made with any of the following: whey prepared with non–microbial enzyme, rennet, animal shortening, monoglycerides and diglycerides from an animal source, sodium stearoyllactylate, L–cysteine

Some examples that have taken place in the development of the Halal food market are as follows (Thomson Reuters and Dinar Standards, 2015):

- Scandinavian company HKScan created the Aafiyah range of Halal poultry products launched in UK in Sainsbury's nationwide in April 2015. HKScan is one of the leading meat producers in Northern Europe, with net sales of approximately $2.2 billion. Their Halal food emerged when they saw a gap in the UK market with second generation Muslims requiring readily prepared Halal meals.
- KQF launches UK's first HMC-certified 'Halal Macon Rashers' – strips of smoked beef or chicken that can be used in exactly the same way as bacon. The product is sold in large UK retailers and is also exported to EU countries. KQF also launched new German-inspired Halal Hot Dogs, after aligning with a German specialist in sausage manufacturing.
- There is a speculation that Turkey's sugar beet processor giant, Konya Şeker's well-known brand Torku, is preparing to enter the cola market, to compete with Coca-Cola and Pepsi. A few years ago, Pepsi, Coca-Cola or one of the other foreign cola firm applied to TSE for Halal certification, but TSE declined the application as they

didn't want to give their formula. Experts say Torku Cola would easily get Halal certification from TSE as they provide their formula.

• In Malaysia, Nestle Malaysia and its Halal Centre of Excellence have become the
biggest producers of Halal products in the world. In the United States of America,
Saffron Road with its Halal and organic produce has become the model of success for
both Muslim and non-Muslim aspiring entrepreneurs.

The challenges and opportunities are as follows (Thomson Reuters and Dinar Standard,
2015):

Table 4.3 Challenges and opportunities

Challenges	Opportunities
There is ongoing confusion surrounding Halal standards, primarily because they are being produced by so many different government-linked organizations; private organizations and independent Halal certification bodies (HCBs).	Leading standardization bodies are taking steps to harmonize Halal Standards within.
The absence of any viable international schemes to accredit Halal certification bodies (HCBs) has long been a problem for the Halal industry.	Despite the uncertainties in the regulatory framework, the Halal food sector remains vibrant.
Difficulty in obtaining *Shariáh*-compliant funding.	Online technologies enable global market access to be a viable reality even for small start-ups.
The lack of harmonisation in standards which is considered as trade barriers, thus, making it difficult for exporters to reach out to the global Halal market.	OIC countries that have expertise in Halal food processes have an opportunity to develop partnerships with non-OIC countries eager to strengthen their Halal capabilities.
The variety of standards and the corresponding Halal logos has resulted in confusion among consumers, manufacturers and distributors. On a larger scale, the disunity in standards has also effectively affected import regulations and created artificial shortages of raw materials (Yong, 2014).	An opportunity to develop tracking technology.
There is no Muslim country included in the list of Halal meat exporters.	An increased demand for hormone-free meat.
A Muslim consumer, like its global counterpart, lives in a modern world and is characterised by a younger and more affluent crowd. This group of people have a greater awareness of health and are reading labels not just to check if the product is rightfully Halal, but also assessing its nutritional value (Yong, 2014).	Halal food has the opportunity to be the global standard for safe, wholesome, humane food.
	Develop premium organic product lines. There is an increased global demand for organic and natural food.
	Development of strong brands.
	Investment opportunities in Halal food value chain integration.
	Opportunity for meat producers to enter the Turkish market because of high profit margins in the industry.

Source: State of the Global Islamic Economy Report 2015/16 (2015)

Travel and hospitality

Travelling is indeed encouraged in Islam as a means to ponder the wonders of Allah's creations and to enjoy the beauty of this great universe. By travelling, the human soul will develop a strong faith in the oneness of the Creator. Travelling can also help one to fulfil the obligations of life. Relaxation is essential to enable one to strive hard after hours of working. It should be of no surprise that today, the Muslim-friendly travel has transcended the paradigm of the Islamic economy to become a major sector within the wider global economy itself.

It is estimated that the global Muslim spending on travel (outbound) was $142 billion in 2014 (excluding Hajj and Umrah), making the Muslim travel market 11 percent of the global expenditure. This is a 6.3 percent increase from last year (Thomson Reuters and Dinar Standard, 2015).

Some requirements of Halal in the tourism sector may include certain elements including (Razak, 2013):

- The hotels should not sell and serve alcohol.
- Has separate gym and pool hours for men and women.
- The hotels should not serve any pork-based products and by-products.
- The hotels should enable Muslims to perform daily Islamic rituals.
- Entertainment available is appropriate to the moral values of Muslims.

Subsequently, some landmark progress in Halal tourism and hospitality are as follows (Thomson Reuters and Dinar Standard, 2015):

- Tourism Australia signed a five-year, $22.5 million marketing deal with Etihad Airways to promote Australia to leisure and business travellers in key overseas markets. The new Memorandum of Understanding signed in June 2015 extends an existing three-year deal worth $9 million that expires this year. The primary focus of the deal will be promoting Australia to international leisure and business travellers within Europe – specifically the launching of new tourism campaigns in the United Kingdom, Germany, France and Italy. The agreement will also cover targeted support for Tourism Australia's trade and business events program.
- Tourism Australia partnered with HalalTrip to produce a Muslim visitors' guide to Australia. The guide provides information on "the best places to visit, shop, dine and pray" in the eight regions of Australia. There are sections in the booklet listing Halal food outlets and mosques in each of the regions. The guidebook was released as a printed booklet as well as a downloadable eBook optimized for tablets and iPads. The eBook also provides links to more information on the HalalTrip site.
- Japan is actively seeking to become more Muslim-friendly to attract Muslim travellers especially from neighbouring Malaysia and Indonesia. Japan has been working with Crescent Rating, an accreditation body related to tourism that conducts workshops, as well as research studies, to build its capabilities towards the Muslim market.
- HalalBooking.com, a travel search and booking website for Halal-conscious travellers has achieved tremendous success, with their bookings for their Turkey based hotels amounting to millions per resort. Yamsafer, a hotel booking start-up from Palestine, raised a $3.5 million from Global Founders Capital. Certainly, there are some challenges, especially to cater the needs to both Muslims and non-Muslims at the same time, and being able to appeal to the Muslim traveller without alienating the non-Muslims.

- Top world hotel chains are investing heavily in Turkey; Accor, Best Western, Hyatt, Intercontinental, Starwood, Ramada Hilton, Marriott and Wyndham have opened new hotels in 2014. The Turkish Standards Institute (TSI) started providing Halal Hotel Certification in June 2014. The first hotel to acquire a Halal certification is Bera Hotel in Antalya city.

The challenges and opportunities of the Halal tourism and hospitality are as follows (Thomson Reuters and Dinar Standard, 2015):

Table 4.4 The challenges and opportunities of the Halal tourism and hospitality

Challenges	Opportunities
Accommodating both Muslims and non-Muslims at the same destination	Hotels may possibly focus on banqueting in order to increase revenue since they are not allowed to offer liquor
Marketing to Muslim travellers without alienating non-Muslims	Convergence with other travel sub-sectors or other Islamic economy sectors
The issues on financing	An opportunity to develop Muslim-friendly resorts
Being Muslim-friendly/Halal means different things to different people	An opportunity to target the rising middle class, especially in South East Asia
	Opportunity to focus on themes such as volunteerism, eco-tourism, ethical tourism and experiential travel
	Opportunity to offer peripheral travel services such as travel insurance

Source: State of the Global Islamic Economy Report 2015/16 (2015)

Islamic banking and finance

One of the most visible components of the Islamic economy, the Islamic finance sector follows the trend and continues to grow from previous years. Islamic finance assets are estimated at $1.81 trillion in 2014, compared to $1.65 trillion in 2013. The breakdown by category is as follows: $1,346 billion for commercial banking, $33.4 billion for Takaful (insurance), $295 billion for Sukuk (bonds) outstanding, $56 billion in funds, and $84 billion for others. Banking and Takaful assets led growth year-on-year with 12 percent and 10 percent growth respectively, while Sukuk and Funds experienced a more modest growth of 6 percent and 7 percent respectively (Thomson Reuters and Dinars Standard, 2015).

Further growth can be seen through having new markets, which are very much in abundance around the world. Several African countries are launching debut sovereign Sukuk, whilst Islamic banking windows in Africa are increasing as well. East Asian countries are working further towards adapting their regulatory frameworks to enable their domestic markets to tap Islamic financing. Central Asian sovereigns (such as Kazakhstan and Azerbaijan) and European banks (in Russia and Germany) are also tying up with Islamic finance through debut sovereign Sukuk and Islamic banking windows respectively (Thomson Reuters and Dinar Standard, 2015).

Some of the requirements of Islamic principles pertaining to Islamic banking and finance are:

- In Islamic teachings, an individual should not get hold of property through courses that have been prohibited (*haram*) by Allah, by means of *riba* (taking and giving out interest or usury), hoarding, bribery and corruption (*rashwah*), monopoly, uncertainty and deceit (*gharar*), gambling, greed, excessive risk and other measures of forbidden deeds.

- Islamic financial system is based on contributing towards the fulfilment of socio-economic objectives and the creation of a fair and just society (Siddique, 1981).

Some major success in the Halal banking and finance are (Thomson Reuters and Dinar Standard, 2015):

- Noor Bank closed AED 1.2 billion Islamic Syndicated Facility for Stanford Marine Group: Noor Bank successfully closed an AED 1.2 billion Islamic Syndicated Structured Finance Facility for offshore vessel Stanford Asia Holding Company ('Stanford'), a subsidiary of Stanford Marine Group (SNG).
- Tunisia's Banque Zitouna raised capital via stake sale to IDB: Tunisia's Banque Zitouna completed a capital raising of 18.5 million dinars ($9.7 million) by issuing common shares to the Islamic Development Bank (IDB), injecting much-needed cash for the bank's expansion strategy.
- Russia appears to replace conventional loans with Islamic finance. Russian banks are already showing interest in this alternative form of credit. Islamic finance will help Russian companies make up for their credit shortage, which was in large part caused by the cooling of relations between Russia and the West.
- In April Saudi Arabia's Islamic investment firm, Sidra Capital, broke into the US market with a SAR350 million (US$93.28 million), to purchase South Carolina property towards its future US acquisition plans. UK *Shari'ah* compliant real estate specialist, 90 North, closed a US$123 million acquisition of Saint Gobain's North American headquarters outside of Philadelphia. More recently, Soho Properties raised US$219 million in *Shari'ah*-compliant funding from financiers in Malaysia, Kuwait and Saudi Arabia to finance the construction of its Tribeca condominium tower in Manhattan (*Islamic Finance News*, 23 June 2016).

Nevertheless, there are challenges, as well as opportunities towards the progress of Halal banking and finance and they are as follows (Thomson Reuters and Dinar Standard, 2015):

Table 4.5 Challenges and opportunities towards the progress of Halal banking and finance

Challenges	Opportunities
High level of unemployment and mediocre growth. Likely impact on Islamic finance: Low growth rates are symptomatic of wider problems for developing economies, such as national structural imbalances and regional geopolitical risk. OIC countries are particularly vulnerable to these weaknesses, and this situation could have a negative impact on how fast the Islamic finance sector continues to expand. Also, several OIC countries are still suffering from high levels of unemployment, and will undoubtedly feel much pressure to combat this negative trend by creating many more jobs. In this regard, Islamic finance	The rise of new markets for Islamic finance in Africa and East Asia. Islamic finance is increasingly realising some of the long-neglected aspirations of core Islamic Economic principles, through the growth of socially responsible *Shariáh*-compliant investments. Some of these include Khazanah's social impact Sukuk in the education sector, asset-based CMBS Sukuk, and innovative new forms of *Shariáh*-compliant finance such as crowdsourced finance for start-ups in Indonesia and a vaccine fund for immunisations.

(*Continued*)

Table 4.5 (Continued)

Challenges	Opportunities
instruments, such as Sukuk, could potentially be of much use: these instruments could boost job creation efforts by acting as a lightning rod that channels greater investment into real economic growth for OIC economies in sectors such as infrastructure and Halal food.	
Lower oil pricing.	Super-abundance of capital: Sovereign Sukuk remains in demand, indicating that there is still much capital chasing with lower but more stable return.
Monetary policy and interest rate.	Strong focus on the real economy.
The issues on the different schools of mazhab (Hanafi, Shafie, Hambali and Maliki) also hinder product development in Islamic banking, capital market and Islamic insurance.	Liquidity Management the Basel III Reforms continues to come into effect, GCC and SE Asia based banks continue to shore up their capital adequacy through issues of Tier-1 Sukuk.

Source: State of the Global Islamic Economy Report 2015/16 (2015)

Islamic fashion

Modest fashion is in trend. The wider fashion industry is facing financial pressures due to the global recession. Yet, in contrast, the modest fashion sector continues to grow, with Muslim consumer clothing market representing the core potential universe for it. This report estimates global Muslim consumer spending on clothing to be $230 billion in 2014, making the Muslim clothing market 11 percent of the global expenditure, with a growth rate of 3.8 percent compared to last year (Thomson Reuters and Dinar Standard, 2015).

The sheer size of the market is demanding attention and investment from across the world. Major mainstream fashion players from Uniqlo, Mango to Tommy Hilfiger have followed DKNY in investing in this sector, while Muslim fashion companies also continue to grow and thrive. E-commerce platforms such as Hijup, Modanisa are receiving investments to grow their user base, while online store Aabhas progressed to move into a brick and mortar place (Thomson Reuters and Dinar Standard, 2015).

Stacey (2013) stated that some of the requirements of Islamic principles pertaining to modest fashion for ladies include the following elements:

- The hijab (covering) must conceal the entire body except the face and the hands.
- It should not be translucent or tight. Tight clothes, even if they conceal the colour of the skin, still describe the size and shape of the body or part of it, and create vivid images.
- It should not attract the attention of the opposite gender; thus it should not be extravagant or excessively opulent. Nor should jewellery and makeup be on display.
- It should not be a garment worn because of vanity or to gain popularity or fame. The female companions were known to wear black and other dark colours, but other colours are permissible; however, a woman must not wear colourful clothes because of vanity.
- It should not be perfumed. This prohibition applies to both the body and the clothes.

For men, on the other hand, the attire they wear should appropriately consist of the following components (Stacey, 2013):

- The attire covers the part of the body from the naval to the knees.
- The attire should not resemble the clothing that is specific to the non-Muslims or Western attire.
- Men should not wear clothing that resemble those worn by women.
- The attire should not be tight or see-through.
- A man is not permitted to wear garments made of silk, or jewellery made of gold.
- Two types of adornment are forbidden to men but permitted for women. These are gold and clothing made of pure silk.

Tremendous progress has been made pertaining to the modest fashion industry and they include (Thomson Reuters and Dinar Standard, 2015):

- Clothing retailer Uniqlo has teamed up with fashion blogger and designer Hana Tajima to create a casual modest wear line. The collection was launched in selected Uniqlo stores across Southeast Asia (Malaysia, Singapore, Indonesia and Thailand) and online just in time for Ramadan 2015.
- Spanish fashion label Mango, as well as American brand Tommy Hilfinger, have launched a special collection for Ramadan 2015 in all Arab countries where the brand is established. The collection is unveiled under the theme "The Perfect Guest" and consists mainly of evening wear.
- Zalora, one of the largest fashion e-commerce sites in Southeast Asia, continues to invest in its modest fashion offerings. Zalora joined forces with designers from Indonesia, like Jenahara Nasution, Ria Miranda and Restu Anggraeni, to create an exclusive Spring/ Summer 2015 collection. In Malaysia, Zalora is collaborating with designer Rizalman to create an exclusive traditional baju kurung (Malay attire) collection for Eid.
- Nealofar Hijab, one of the biggest Muslim fashion brands in Malaysia, aspires to expand the market to New York and the Middle East, having successful years of selling through online orders and boutiques. The scarf and Muslim fashion, usually marketed locally, are now exporting to more than 30 countries, including Singapore, Brunei, the UK, Australia, the Netherlands and the USA (www.therakyatpost.com).

The challenges and opportunities in modest fashion may include as follows (Thomson Reuters and Dinar Standard (2015):

Table 4.6 The challenges and opportunities in modest fashion

Challenges	Opportunities
The Muslim fashion industry is increasingly facing criticism for its seeming over-commercialization of a religious mandate.	Mainstream proposition for modest fashion.
Lack of funding leads to lack of vertical integration and slow adaptability.	Vertical specializations. There is plenty of room for growth to develop new labels in a number of largely untapped verticals such as sports apparel, menswear, maternity wear, clothing for teenagers and tweens, work attires and plus size fashion.

(Continued)

Table 4.6 (Continued)

Challenges	Opportunities
Payment, customs and logistics issues hamper the growth of digital commerce. Online channels are the ideal platform for stakeholders in a fragmented market such as the Islamic fashion space to connect and trade with players from all corners of the globe. However, this opportunity is hampered by lack of unified payment platforms, varying customs rules and logistics issues that vary from one country to another.	Versatile clothing for modern Muslim lifestyle.
Increasing competition. The Muslim fashion space is generating interest from non-Muslims as well as global brands such as DKNY, Tommy Hilfiger and Mango.	Fusing traditional elements with modern design.
Fragmented market. Muslim consumers are a very heterogeneous market in terms of socio-economic class and fashion preference. Scaling from one geographic area to another requires various adaptations to existing product offerings and business processes, which may be challenging for small scale players.	By implementing Islamic values throughout the industry value chain, Muslim fashion industry players have the opportunity – and responsibility – to be leaders in the area of ethical fashion to truly reflect the term "Islamic fashion".
An increasing reservation about the over commercialization of what is essentially meant to be a religious mandate.	Eco-friendly clothing.
Non-Muslim global companies are increasing competition in this market to the extent that smaller Muslim fashion companies may suffer.	Empowerment of marginal communities.

Source: State of the Global Islamic Economy Report 2015/16 (2015)

Media and recreation

Thomson Reuters and Dinar Standard (2015) reported that Muslim populations across the universe spent a total of $179 billion on recreation and culture in 2014. This expenditure is expected to reach $247 billion by 2020 (5.8 percent of global expenditure). Global spending on recreation and culture was expected to be US$3.5 trillion in 2014. While this does not represent actual Islamic-themed media segment size, it does represent the potential opportunity of core Muslim consumers. Top countries with Muslim consumers' recreation consumption (based on 2014 data) are Turkey ($20.4 billion), United States ($19 billion), Russia ($10.7 billion), Saudi Arabia ($9.5 billion) and United Kingdom ($9.2 billion). A significant size of the Muslim media and recreation market also exists in countries where Muslims are minorities – especially from Western markets. Muslims in Western Europe (Germany, France, UK) plus North America (US, Canada) collectively spent an estimated $49.21 billion on media and recreation in 2014.

The requirements of Islamic principles pertaining to media and recreation include (Qardawi, 1997)

- The content of the song should not be against the morals and teachings of Islam or be accompanied by other forbidden things in Islam like alcohol.
- The way of singing should be within the confines of Islam, that is, it should not be accompanied by inappropriate movements.

- Exaggeration is deemed to be inappropriate in Islam, and the person who knows that entertainment easily excites him or her should keep away from it.

Some trends and development pertaining to media and recreation are as follows (Thomson Reuters and Dinar Standards, 2015):

- A one million dollar community funded studio for the One Path Network was established in Australia. A range of prominent Muslims, including the grand mufti of Australia, Dr Ibrahim Abu Mohamed, and Associate Professor Mohamad Abdalla from Griffith University, have endorsed the project, established to provide a counterview to the mainstream media coverage of the community.
- British Muslim Radio, the first Muslim oriented radio station is to be launched in the UK. The radio station is part of the license awarded to Sound Digital to broadcast 14 stations nationally from mid-2016. The station will broadcast programming in English, Urdu, Punjabi, Gujarati and Bengali, targeting the multicultural Muslim community.
- A National Film Grant has been established by Islamic Scholarship Fund USA specifically aiming to facilitate and support Muslims entering the world of film, to create artistic, engaging and positive stories about Muslims. The award includes a grant, and also mentorship/networking support from industry professionals to assist the media industry.
- Fortress Film Clinic, a joint venture company, has been set up to help promote the film industry in the Middle East. The new company is taking root at a time when Dubai and UAE are emerging as premier movie production destinations for locals.
- Islamic dramas locally known as Sinetron Religi, which offers Muslims religious guidance in dealing with life's trials and tribulations, are gaining prime time broadcasts in Indonesia. In an attempt to gain as broad a Muslim audience and advertising from heterogeneous Muslim Indonesians, these tele-movies relating to Islam do not have single dominant narrative, blurring the division between "traditionalist", "modernist", "conservative" and "liberal" interpretations of Islamic doctrines. Notable successes have been *Rahasia Ilahi* (God's Secret).
- The Islam Channel has launched a spin-off to its English channel with the launch of the Islam Urdu channel in the UK. The channel aims to target over a million Urdu-speaking south Asian audiences through its new platform, through the engagement of informative e-content which reflects the ever-growing and diverse cultural backgrounds.

The challenges and opportunities in the media and communication may include as follows (Thomson Reuters and Dinar Standard (2015):

Table 4.7 The challenges and opportunities in the media and communication

Challenges	Opportunities
Investors and public perception: public perception and understanding to the format of Islamic content is widely skewed towards a "religious" only educational perspective, thus	The English language unifies varying markets.

(Continued)

Table 4.7 (Continued)

Challenges	Opportunities
limiting funding opportunities for other categories and areas. For content to qualify as Islamic, it need not be restricted to media creating awareness and understanding about the faith alone. The genre can very well encompass mainstream entertainment typologies such as lifestyle; infotainment, etc. through "value based" content creation that is in harmony with universal values in as much complying with ethical codes of the faith.	
Censorship: Although promising, the Islamic-themed genres are highly sensitive with regards to the multicultural global audiences' expectations and reactions, with some of the best work produced being delayed in controversies, from music to movies.	Digital Islamic platform growth driver: Digital revolution through social media, mobile and broadband technologies, smartphones have catalysed the digital Islamic media space. The new media wave has resulted in immense rise and popularity of Digital Islamic Media platforms such as Islamic lifestyle magazines, Islamic travel sites, Islamic Fashion blogs, and Islam.
Bad press: The other challenge pertains to the negative global perceptions relating to geopolitics and Islam. This is affecting acceptance of Islam-inspired global media beyond the Muslim world.	Growing demand for value based content In the games industry. Saudi Arabia recently introduced rating systems for the video game industry recognizing the widely influencing entertainment platform which mostly targets young impressionable minds. The games rating will certify content for restricting games that feature anti-Islamic messages, violence, sex, etc.
Financing remains a major hurdle for Islamic media initiatives.	Attractive demographics: Muslims are today close to 23 percent of the world's population. The fact that the Muslim population is on average younger with a median age of 23 years across all regions, compared to a global average of around 28, makes them extremely attractive for advertisers. The younger "futurist" Muslim market in lucrative markets such GCC are expected to be avid consumers and growth drivers for both online and offline Islamic media content.
	Emerging markets: the fastest media market growth is taking place in major Islamic markets such as Indonesia, MENA, Pakistan, Turkey, India and Malaysia, all with an estimated growth of around 10–15 percent CAGR, more than double the global rate in many cases. This suggests a strong base and potential for Islamic Media penetration and consumption.
	Islamic arts: the heightened and continued interest in Islamic arts, whether outside the Muslim world or within, promises a revival and provides opportunities in this area.

Source: State of the Global Islamic Economy Report 2015/16 (2015)

Pharmaceutical and cosmetics

The State of the Global Islamic Economy Report (2015) estimates global Muslim spending on pharmaceuticals to be $75 billion in 2014, which is 7 percent of global expenditure. Total global spending on pharmaceuticals was estimated to be $1,111 billion in 2014. The potential Muslim pharmaceuticals expenditure is expected to reach $106 billion by 2020. This equates to a 2014–20 CAGR growth rate of 5.9 percent. Top countries with Muslim pharmaceutical consumers are Turkey ($8.8 billion), Saudi Arabia ($6 billion), United States ($5.9 billion), Indonesia ($4.8 billion) and Algeria ($3.56 billion) based on 2014 data. Muslim minority countries such as the United States ($6 billion), France ($2.39 billion), Germany ($2.19 billion), Italy ($0.7 billion) and the United Kingdom ($1.4 billion) account for a total expenditure of $12.6 billion.

Halal pharmaceuticals are products that contain ingredients permitted under the *Shari'ah* law and fulfil the following conditions (Department of Malaysian Standard, 2010):

- Does not contain any parts or products of animals that are non-Halal by *Shari'ah* law or any parts or products of animals which are not slaughtered according to *Shari'ah* law.
- Does not contain *najs* according to *Shari'ah* law.
- Safe for consumption, non-poisonous, non-intoxicating or non-hazardous to health.
- Does not prepare, process or manufacture using equipment contaminated with *najs* according to *Shari'ah* law.
- Does not contain any human parts or derivatives that are not permitted by *Shari'ah* law.
- During its preparation, processing, handling, packaging and distribution, the food is physically separated from any other food that does not meet the requirements stated previously or any other things that have been decreed as *najs* by *Shari'ah* law.

Some trends and development on the development of pharmaceutical and cosmetics within the Halal market are as follows (Thomson Reuters and Dinar Standard, 2015):

- Malaysia plans to produce the world's first Halal vaccine in collaboration with a Saudi company. The Halal Industry Development Corporation (HDC) is providing the facilities and infrastructure for Halal vaccine production for the Saudi firm AJ Biologics, a subsidiary of AJ Pharma Holding, at Enstek Halal Park, Negri Sembilan. The Saudi company has started investments towards developing the plant under its third phase at a cost of RM300 million. There are currently no vaccine producers throughout the world with a Halal certification. Some of the vaccines produced by the company will be plant based and will be labelled as such.
- CCM Duopharma Biotech Bhd (CCMD) recently acquired six pharmaceutical units from parent company Chemical Company of Malaysia Bhd (CCM) and is focusing on growing its bio-therapy pipeline by exploring new niche therapeutic areas, specifically erythropoietin (EPO) and insulin, targeting for it to contribute 30 percent of CCMD's revenue base by 2020. On its Halal pharmaceutical segment, CCMD will continue to leverage its position as a pioneer in the Halal segment and through active involvement in Halal initiatives and collaborations with leading Halal advocates, locally and abroad.
- Tanamera Tropical Spa Products was awarded the National Mark of Malaysian Brand, which indicates quality, excellence and distinction of products and services. Tanamera is currently planning expansion into Kuwait, Qatar, Canada, Bangladesh and Australia.

With a new children's range of products for babies already recently launched, at the end of 2015, they will be launching a new lifestyle range of products, including a natural aromatherapy anti-bacterial spray.

- Iba, India's first Halal certified cosmetics brand, launched several stores throughout India. The products were launched in 2014, followed by establishing their Halal Cosmetics stores. In addition to being Halal, the products are organic and free of animal-derived products. They are also free of any harsh chemicals and animal cruelty.
- A Brazilian company introduces Halal certified diabetic cosmeceuticals. It is revolutionising the diabetes care market with ApoemaR Diabetes Pro Care Halal Certified product line, scientifically created for the prevention and treatment of diabetes-related issues. These products are expected to have an enormous positive social impact, and subsequently lower government health-care spending, in countries with a high concentration of diabetic sufferers.
- Nails Inc, a UK company specializing in nail polish, has produced a limited edition wash-off nail polish range called H2GO. Developed using water, it was especially created to be Halal friendly and can be easily washed off before prayer. The six-piece range was launched on the eve of Ramadan in 2015. Previously, BCI marketed the nail polish line "H", the first to receive Halal certification in the Middle East.
- The focus of Cosmoprof Worldwide Bologna 2016, a leading international beauty industry for forums and exhibition, would be on Halal cosmetics. The exhibition area would be partly dedicated to natural cosmetics, from Halal certified cosmetic companies. This initiative has been developed in partnership with the Italian Halal certification body, WHAD – World Halal Development. Cosmoprof Worldwide Bologna 2016's interest in highlighting Halal cosmetics is due to the fact that according to WHAD, 80 percent of the beauty products sold in the GCC are produced in Europe, specifically in Italy and France. In addition, there is a high demand for Halal cosmetics in South East Asia.
- A small company named Talent Cosmetic from Korea set a milestone in 2014 by becoming the first home-grown cosmetics maker to obtain Halal certification for 141 of its products from Malaysia's state-led Halal certification agency, JAKIM. The firm stated that it is currently working to get more products certified. In addition, the manufacturing facilities of the Indonesian branch of Korean cosmetics manufacturer Cosmax secured the Halal certification from Indonesia, and it is Majelis Ulama Indonesia (MUI) (Halal Focus, 2014).

Challenges and opportunities in relation to the Halal pharmaceuticals and cosmetics industry are as follows (Thomson Reuters and Dinar Standard, 2015):

Table 4.8 Challenges and opportunities in relation to the Halal pharmaceuticals and cosmetics industry

Challenges	Opportunities
Identifying the source of medicines.	Animal derived ingredients in pharmaceuticals are increasingly being replaced by synthetics.
Rapid developments in synthetic biology in the future are causing concern.	Opportunity for the production of Halal vaccines.

Challenges	Opportunities
Many Muslim auditors are not trained in Good Manufacturing Practices (GMP) guidelines, which are important for maintaining quality.	There are many opportunities to educate both consumers and producers in Muslim countries about the transdermal (skin penetrating) nature of some types of cosmetics.
GMP regulations for pharmaceuticals and cosmetics require that companies normalize reproduction for quality control, which has resulted in a shift to synthetic resources, as an alternative to natural ingredients.	Opportunity to market Halal cosmetics to non-Muslim consumers.
Alcohol which is used in various forms.	Opportunity to resolve the issue of the scarcity of Halal gelatine.
The use of ingredients in cosmetics that are dangerous to human beings.	There is a need to develop and publish a Halal Pharmacopoeia and other references for industry players to supplement Halal pharmaceutical standards.
Challenge to get funding for research and development.	To develop inter-Islamic country fast track registration of pharmaceutical products.
Legal guidelines to be developed to protect the intellectual property of the product, particularly the pharmaceutical industry.	

Source: State of The Global Islamic Economy Report 2015/16 (2015)

The framework of Halal

The understanding of Halal should be first encountered by the Halal producers and marketers. There are various documents that provide practical guidance to producers in meeting the Halal requirements. For example, the Department of Standards Malaysia (2004) has developed a Halal standard for foods, the MS1500:2004. It listed seven requirements on the preparation and handling of Halal food and they include:

- Sources of Halal food and drink which include animals (land and aquatic), plants, mushrooms and microorganism, natural minerals and chemicals, drinks and genetically modified food (GMF)
- Slaughtering requirements and process guidelines
- Product processing, handling and distribution
- Product storage, display and servings
- Hygiene, sanitation and food safety
- Packaging and labelling
- Legal requirements pertaining to compliance

In the second revision, the MS1500:2009 (Department of Standard Malaysia, 2009) was developed. Three new requirements are related to management responsibilities and they are:

- The management shall appoint Muslim Halal executive officers or establish a committee which consists of Muslim personnel who are responsible for the implementation of internal Halal control system.

- The management must ensure that the personnel are trained based on the Halal principles and its applications.
- The management shall ensure that sufficient resources (for instance, manpower, facility, financial and infrastructure) are provided for internal Halal control system.

Indeed, there are many other standards that have been created to cater to the implementation of Halal in the market, including Halal supply chain, Muslim friendly hospitality services, quality management system, Halal consumer goods and others. More importantly, global brands should not see consumers through their eyes of being Westerners, but they should understand and be aware of the needs of Muslims and non-Muslims, regardless of the level of religiosity, lifestyle or culture and their heritage. It needs to provide the standardization throughout the whole process, particularly on the basis of the application of *Shari'ah* in all industries, especially for food and beverages.

Accordingly, the theory of planned behaviour is somewhat relevant to the adoption of Halal in the market place. According to Ajzen (1991), the theory of planned behaviour is an extension of theory of reasoned actions that relates to the factor of an individual's intention to perform a given behaviour. There are three variables involved in this theory: firstly, the attitude towards behaviour, which refers to the degree to which a person has favourable or unfavourable evaluation or appraisal of the behaviour, and its relationship to intentions and actions (Ajzen, 1988; Ajzen, 1991); secondly, subjective norms or the social pressure that affects such behaviour; thirdly, perceived behavioural control, which refers to the perceived ease or difficulty of performing the behaviour, and it is assumed to reflect past experience, as well as anticipated impediments and obstacles (Ajzen, 1988).

Halal consumption can be divided into two main components, focusing on the Muslims and the non-Muslims. Using the theory of planned behaviour by Ajzen (1991), Jaafar and Musa (2014) believed that there are salient beliefs that consist of awareness, religious obligations and reputation. However, product quality and Halal certification are two other elements which may have an impact on Halal consumption, based on Aziz and Chok (2013). Awareness denotes showing realization, perception or knowledge of a situation or fact (Jaafar and Musa, 2014). On the other hand, knowledge is defined as the fact or condition of knowing something with familiarity gained through experience or education (Wirtz and Matilla, 2003). Religious obligation refers to the role of religion in affecting an individual's choice or activity (Amin et al.,2011). Figure 4.2 illustrates the conceptual framework for Halal consumption of Muslim consumers based on the study of Jaafar and Musa (2014).

The non-Muslims, on the other hand, may identify different factors pertaining to the adoption of Halal products and services. Aziz and Chok (2013) proposed five factors that determine the purchase of Halal goods. Firstly, Halal awareness, and this is related to the level of knowledge and understanding of Halal. Secondly, Halal certification, in which it is a recognition given by an authorised institution that the products are permissible under Islamic law, and these products, consequently, are consumable by mainly Muslims. Thirdly, product quality denotes "its ability to fulfil the customer's needs and expectations" (Guyana National Bureau of Standards). Fourth, marketing promotional strategy which is essentially pertinent to communicate to the target audience on the benefits of the Halal goods and services. Lastly, branding represents the product name, identity and reputation of a particular good or service in the consumers' mind-sets (Kotler and Armstrong, 2012). Figure 4.3 denotes the model of Halal consumption for non-Muslims based on the study by Aziz and Chok (2013).

Salient belief factors

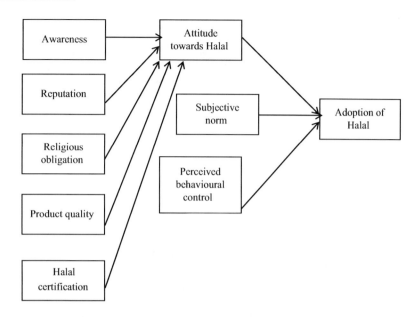

Figure 4.2 Conceptual framework for Halal consumption of Muslim consumers

Source: Jaffar and Musa (2014)

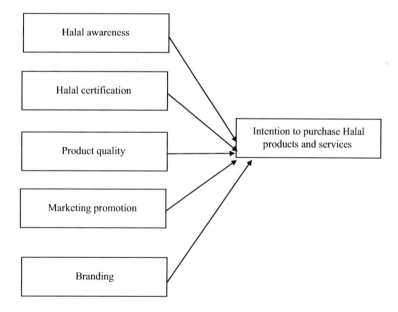

Figure 4.3 Conceptual framework for Halal consumption of non-Muslim consumers

Source: Aziz and Chok (2013)

Conclusion

- There are a lot of potentials for business on Halal to grow in the market, both locally and globally.
- Islamic law or *Shari'ah* principles need to be observed with regard to the legal and Halal framework.
- There are different segmentations to the Muslim markets based on the level of religiosity, lifestyle and culture, level of education and sophistication.
- Segmentations need to also cater to the non–Muslims, particularly with regard to their lifestyle, product quality and Halal awareness.
- There are many challenges and opportunities associated with the sectors of Halal industry, including food and beverage, fashion, media and recreation, travel and hospitality, pharmaceutical and cosmetics and Islamic banking and finance.
- However, the level of religiosity should not be the basis of segmentation, since Islam emphasises the implementation of Halal accordingly.

Issues for further discussion

1   The importance of Halal education and training among employees, as well as consumers, in order to ensure the quality of products and services offered is constantly preserved.
2   It is essential to enhance greater understanding of the numerous facets of Halal certification, specifically in upholding conformity and compliance, towards the development of Halal standards universally.
3   Innovation and creativity need to be encouraged in the offering of all Halal products and services, to further advance the Halal industry towards greater heights.
4   The whole Halal ecosystem requires a systematic and reliable approach, thus, continuous studies need to be further developed in conforming to the ever–changing preferences, values, and demands of consumers across the globe.

Case study

The Halal development in Malaysia

The majority of Malaysia's population are Muslims, up to 60.4 percent, and globally Malaysia is the leader in developing the Halal industry. In 1994, Halal endorsement was given in the form of a certificate with a Halal logo by the Department of Islamic Development Malaysia (JAKIM) (Khalek and Mokhtar, 2016). The Malaysian Halal International Showcase (MIHAS) is the pioneer international food trade fair which, since 2004, has gathered the largest annual gathering of Halal consumers, such as traders, investors, importers and exporters, trade associations and governments with the aim of sourcing and selling quality Halal products on a global level. As the world's largest Halal trade fair and Malaysia's largest food and beverage exhibition, MIHAS is jointly organised by the Ministry of International Trade and Industry (MITI), the Ministry of Entrepreneurial and Cooperative Development

(MECD), Malaysia External Trade Development Corporation (MATRADE) and the Islamic Dakwah Foundation Malaysia (YADIM).

Malaysian Halal brands

Indeed, the establishment of Malaysian brands that are produced by local companies in Malaysia, which represent the taste and preferences of Malaysian best food experience at the international level, is of great importance. The Department of Islamic Development Malaysia (JAKIM) can only present the certification of Halal if the food is processed and prepared in accordance to *Shari'ah* compliance, together with the adherence to JAKIM procedures.

Brahim produces a range of 'Meals Ready to Eat' products featuring favourite dishes that capture the exotic flavours of Malaysia. One can enjoy delicious, wholesome Asian meals in just minutes, reducing meal preparation time by up to 90 percent. These products contain only boneless, skinless lean meat, giving consumers great value at only RM7.25 per pack. They offer varieties of ready to eat rice, meals as well as ready to use cooking sauces. By exporting these products, it introduced the Malaysian taste to the world.

Kart Food Industries Sdn Bhd is the first Malaysian company to have gone into the manufacturing, distribution and sales of Halal Asian ethnic frozen food for the retail, institutional, food service and export markets. The products include Roti Canai, Roti Paratha, Pau, Pizza, Donuts and Murtabak, symbolizing Malaysian food in terms of taste and preference, and introducing Malaysian food to the world.

MAMEE-Double Decker (M) Sdn Bhd was founded in 1971, and has since established itself as a household name for food and beverage serving over 50 products, including favorites such as MAMEE Monster snack, Mister Potato Chips, and MAMEE Chef. MAMEE-Double Decker has set up its manufacturing facilities in Myanmar and Indonesia, in addition to their production location here in Malaysia. All facilities have been awarded ISO 9000s, HACCP and Halal certifications. Their products are currently exported to over 100 countries around the globe, which includes Indonesia, Singapore, France, Australia and Saudi Arabia. It has always been their desire to share one of the most trusted snack brands in Malaysia with the rest of the world. (www.mamee.com/aboutus.html)

Halal Industry Development Corporation (HDC)

The Halal Industry Development Corporation (HDC), established on 18 September 2006, is Malaysia's response for better quality products and services as consumers gain confidence in the Halal process. It helps to coordinate the overall development of the Halal industry in Malaysia. The HDC promotes participation and facilitates the growth of Malaysian companies in the global Halal market where it focuses on the development of Halal standards, audit and certification, plus capacity building for Halal products and services.

Malaysia's major exports were ingredients/condiments and food and beverage to China, the United States, Singapore, Netherlands and Japan. Ingredients include food and non-food ingredients such as fats, additives, salts, emulsifiers and colourings. On the other hand, food and beverages that are exported consist of processed foods, cocoa, margarine, beverages, meat, seafood and other edible products.

Malaysian Halal Park

Halal Park is one of the infrastructures that manufactures and provides support services for Halal in a one-step centre from raw materials until it becomes finished goods. Halal parks have become a success in Malaysia by attracting foreign companies, particularly multi-national corporations, to invest in the Halal parks located across the country, in places such as Penang, Sarawak and Melaka. Various incentives were given to the Halal Park operators, Halal companies operating within the Halal Park, and Halal Logistic Operators such as 100 percent tax exemption for several years and exemption of duty import. This will attract various investors, either domestically or internationally, so that Malaysia can become the central trading hub for Halal products. Malaysia must also intelligently market itself and achieve the Halal hub's main objective of providing a credible platform in connecting a global Halal supply chain and certification for Halal Assurance.

(Source: Hassan, 2013)

Case questions for discussion

1   Analyze the segmentation of Halal food industry in Malaysia.
2   How does the consumption of Halal food appeal to non-Muslims in other parts of the world?
3   Discuss the fundamental elements relating to product positioning for Halal certification, specifically for the food industry.
4   How can the Malaysian Halal brands differentiate themselves competitively from other countries that are also producing Halal products and services?
5   What unique steps does Malaysia need to take in order to position itself as a global Halal hub, especially in the food industry?

References

Ajzen, I. (1988), *Attitudes, Personality and Behavior*, Buckingham: Open University Press.
Ajzen, I. (1991), "The Theory of Planned Behavior", *Organizational Behavior and Human Decision Processes*, 50(2), 179–211.
Al-Qardawi, Y. (1997). "The Lawful and the Prohibited in Islam", Kuala Lumpur, Islamic Book Trust.
Ali, A. Y. (1992). *The Meaning of the Holy Qur'an: New Edition With Revised Translation and Commentary*. Beltsville, MD: Amana Corporation.

Abd Rahman, A., Asrarhaghighi, E. and Ab Rahman, S. (2015), "Consumers and Halal Cosmetic Products: Knowledge, Religiosity, Attitude and Intention", *Journal of Islamic Marketing*, Vol. 6, No. 1, pp. 148–163.

Amin, H., Abdul Rahman, A. R., Sondoh Jr, S. L. and Chooi Hwa, A. M. (2011), "Determinants of Customers' Intention to Use Islamic Personal Financing", *Journal of Islamic Accounting and Business Research*, Vol. 2, No. 1, pp. 22–42.

Auda, J. (2008), *Maqasid Al-Shariáh: A Beginner s Guide*, London: IIIT.

Aziz, Y. A. and Chok, N. V. (2013), "The Role of Halal Awareness, Halal Certification and Marketing Components in Determining Halal Purchase Intention Among Non-Muslims in Malaysia: A Structural Equation Modeling Approach", *Journal of International Food & Agribusiness Marketing* Vol. 25, No. 1

Cleveland, M. and Laroche, M. (2007), "Acculturation to the Global Consumer Culture: Scale Development and Research Paradigm", *The Journal of Business Research*, Vol. 60, No. 3, pp. 249–259.

Chapra, M. U. (2008), *The Islamic Vision of Development in the Light of the Maqasid al-Shariáh,* Jeddah, Kingdom of Saudi Arabia, *Islamic Research and Training Institute*, Jeddah, Kingdom of Saudi Arabia: Islamic Development Bank.

Cosgel, M. M. and Minkler, L. (2004), "Religious Identity and Consumption", *Review of Social Economy*, Vol. 62, No. 3, pp. 339–350.

Delener, N. (1990), "The Effects of Religious Factors on Perceived Risk in Durable Goods Purchase Decisions", *Journal of Consumer Marketing*, Vol. 7, No. 3, pp. 27–38.

Deloitte and Noortel (2015). The Digital Islamic Services landscape: Uncovering the Digital Islamic Services opportunity for the Middle East and the World. Available: http://www2.deloitte.com/content/dam/Deloitte/xe/Documents/financial services/me_Islamic-

Department of Standards Malaysia. (2009), MS 1500:2009 – Halal Food – Production, Preparation, Handling and Storage – General Guidelines (Second Revision), Shah Alam, Sirim Berhad.

Department of Standards Malaysia. (2004). MS 1500:2004 – Halal Food – Production, Preparation, Handling and Storage – General Guidelines (First Revision), Shah Alam, SirimBerhad.

Department of Standards Malaysia. (2010). MS 2424:2010 (P). (2010b). Requirements of Halal Pharmaceuticals – General Guidelines, Shah Alam, Selangor.

Farrag, D. A. and Hassan, M. (2015), "The Influence of Religiosity on Egyptian Muslim Youths' Attitude Towards Fashion", *Journal of Islamic Marketing*, Vol. 6, No. 1, pp. 95–108.

Halal Focus (2014). Gee-Hyun, S. Korea: Talent Cosmetics attains Halal certification. Available: http://halalfocus.net/korea-talent-cosmetics-attains-halal-certification/ [Date retrieved 2016, June 28].

Hassan, F. (2013), *Professional Lecture : Halal Food Marketing – Dare to Win,* Shah Alam, Selangor: Universiti Teknologi MARA Press.

Ibn Ashour, M. A. T. (2006), *Ibn Ashur: Treatise on Maqasid Al-Shariáh.* Trans. by Tahir el-Mesawi, Virginia: International Institute of Islamic Thought (IIIT).

Jamal, A. and Sharifuddin, J. (2015), "Perceived Value and Perceived Usefulness of Halal Labeling: The Role of Religion and Culture." *Journal of Business Research*, Vol. 68, No. 5, pp. 933–941.

Johnstone, R. L. (1975). *Religion and Society in Interaction: Sociology of Religion*, Englewood Cliffs, NJ : Prentice Hall.

Jaafar, M. A. and Musa, R. (2014), "Determinants of Attitude Towards Islamic Financing Among Halal Certified Micro and SMEs: A Preliminary Investigation", *Procedia – Social and Behavioral Sciences*, Vol. 130, pp. 135–144.

Kahf, M. (n.d.). *The Demand Side or Consumer Behavior: an Islamic Perspective*, http://monzer.kahf.com/papers/english/ demand_side_or_consumer_behavior.pdf Digital-Services.pdf (accessed 22 June 2016).

Khalek, A. A. and Mokhtar, R. A. B. (2016). With or without Halal logo? A descriptive analysis of the generation Y perceptions on the National Halal Certification Malaysia. Third Asia Pacific Conference on Advanced Research (APCAR, Melbourne, July). www.apiar.org.au)

Kotler, P. T. and Armstrong, G. (2012). Principles of Marketing, (14th Edition), Essex : Pearson Education Limited.

Lahsasna, A. (2013), *Maqasid Al-Shari'ah in Islamic Finance*. Kuala Lumpur: IBFIM.

Laldin, M. A. (2006), *Islamic Law: An Introduction*. Kuala Lumpur: IIUM Press.

Lipka, M. and Hackett, C. (2015). *Why Muslims Are the World's Fastest-Growing Religious Group*, Pew Research Centre, Washington. www.pewresearch.org/fact-tank/2017/04/06/why-muslims-are-the-worlds-fastest-growing-religious-group/ (accessed 22 June 2016).

Majid, M. Z. A., Mahmud, M. W. and Aziz, A. A. (2012), *Maqasid al-Shari'ah*. Kuala Lumpur: IIUM Press.

Malaysian International Finance Centre (2014). The halal economy: huge potential for Islamic finance. www.mifc.com/index.php?ch=28&pg=72&ac=90&bb=uploadpdf (accessed 15 June 2016).

Malaysian International Finance Centre (2015). Halal ecosystem: Prospects for global growth, 23 September 2015. http://mifc.com/index.php?ch=28&pg=72 & ac=142&bb=uploadpdf. (accessed 30 May 2016).

Mukhtar, A. and Butt, M. M. (2012). "Intention to Choose Halal Products: The Role of Religiosity." *Journal of Islamic Marketing*, Vol. 3, No. 2, pp. 108–120.

Muhamad, R. (2011), Market segmentation and the Shari'ah compliancy process in Islamic banking institutions. International Shari'ah Research Academy for Islamic Finance (ISRA), Research Paper 21/2011.

Osman, I. (2016). "Islamic Financing for Halal Economy", *Islamic Finance Today*, Pioneer Publications Ltd, Sri Lanka, May. www.iftmagazine.com/mag_flip_images/1150/index.php (accessed 25 June 2016).

Penaloza, L. (1994). "AtravensandoFronteras/Border Crossings: A Critical Ethnographic Exploration of the Consumer Acculturation of Mexican Immigrants", *Journal of Consumer Research*, Vol. 21, pp. 32–54.

Pew Research Centre (2015). Muslims and Islam: Key findings in the U.S. and around the world. Available: www.pewresearch.org/fact-tank/2015/12/07/muslims-and-islam-key-findings-in-the-u-s-and-around-the-world/. (accessed 12 June 2016).

Razak, N. H. A. (2013), "Attributes of Shariáh Compliance Hotel", in Marzuki, S. Z. S. and Yahya, W. K. (Eds.), *The Emergence of Global Halal, Shah Alam*: UniversitiTeknologi MARA Press.

Razzaque, M. A. and Chaudhry, S. N. (2013), 'Religiosity and Muslim Consumers' Decision-Making Process in a Non-Muslim Society', *Journal of Islamic Marketing*, Vol. 4, No. 2, pp. 198–217.

Sandikci, Ö. and Ger, G. (2011), "Islam, Consumption and Marketing: Going Beyond the Essentialist Approaches", in Sandıkcı, Ö. and Rice, G. (Eds.), *Handbook of Islamic Marketing*, Cheltenham, UK: Edward Elgar Publishing, pp. 484–501.

Stacey, A. (2013), *Dress Code of Muslim Women*. http://islam.ru/en/content/story/dress-code-muslim-women (accessed 24 June 2016).

Temporal, P. (2011), *Islamic Branding and Marketing: Creating a Global Islamic Business*. Singapore: John Wiley and Sons (Asia) Pte Ltd.

Thomson Reuters and Dinar Standard (2014). State of the Global Islamic Economy Report 2014/2015. http://halalfocus.net/wp-content/uploads/2015/01/SGIE-Report-2014.pdf. (accessed 31 January 2017).

Toronto Public Health (2004). Guide to understand halal food. http://needsinc.ca/asset_library/page/yktt/GuidetoHalalFoods.pdf (accessed 27 June 2016).

Siddique, M. N. (1981), "Muslim Economic Thinking: A Survey of Contemporary Literature", in Ahmad, K. (Ed.), *Studies in Islamic Economics*, Leicester, UK: The Islamic Foundation.

Wirtz, J. and Mattila, A. (2003), "The Effects of Consumer Expertise on Evoked Set and Service Loyalty", *Journal of Services Marketing*, Vol. 17, No. 7, pp. 649–665.

Young, M. (2010), "Muslim Futurism and Islamic Branding Speech by Miles Young", Worldwide CEO of Ogilvy & Mather, at the Inaugural Oxford Global Islamic Branding and Marketing Forum, July 26, 2010. http://thinkethnic.com/wp-content/uploads/2012/02/Miles%20Young%20%20Muslim%20Futurism%20and%20Islamic%20Branding.pdf (accessed on 27 June 2016).

Yong, S. (2014). *Halal the Label of Trust*. www.apfoodonline.com/index.php/features/item/333-halal-the-label-of-trust (accessed 25 June 2016).

Websites

Deloitte and Noortel (2015). The Digital Islamic Services landscape: Uncovering the Digital Islamic Services opportunity for the Middle East and the World. Available: http://www2.deloitte.com/content/dam/Deloitte/xe/Documents/financial services/me_Islamic-

Guyana National Bureau of Standards. Understanding product quality. Available: www.gnbsgy.org/index. php/standards-corner/96-understanding-product-quality. [Data retrieved 2016, June 28]

Halal Focus (2014). Gee-Hyun, S. Korea: Talent Cosmetics attains Halal certification. Available: http:// halalfocus.net/korea-talent-cosmetics-attains-halal-certification/ [Date retrieved 2016, June 28]

Malaysian International Finance Centre (2014). The halal economy: huge potential for Islamic finance. Available: www.mifc.com/index.php?ch=28&pg=72&ac=90&bb=uploadpdf [Date retrieved 2016, June 15]

Malaysian International Finance Centre (2015). Halal ecosystem: Prospects for global growth, 23 September 2015. Available: http://mifc.com/index.php?ch=28&pg=72 & ac=142&bb=uploadpdf. [Date retrieved 2016, May, 30]

Pew Research Centre (2012). The global religious landscape. Available: www.pewforum.org/2012/12/18/ global-religious-landscape-muslim/ [Date retrieved 2016, June 20]

Pew Research Centre (2015). Muslims and Islam: Key findings in the U.S. and around the world. Available: www.pewresearch.org/fact-tank/2015/12/07/muslims-and-islam-key-findings-in-the-u-s-and-around-the-world/. [Date retrieved 2016, June 12]

Toronto Public Health (2004). Guide to understand halal food. Available: http://needsinc.ca/asset_library/page/yktt/GuidetoHalalFoods.pdf. [Date retrieved 2016, June 27]

Thomson Reuters and Dinar Standard (2015). State of the Global Islamic Economy Report 2015/2016. Available: www.dinarstandard.com/state-of-the-global-islamic-economy-report-2015/. [Date retrieved 2016, May 28]

Thomson Reuters and Dinar Standard (2014). State of the Global Islamic Economy Report 2014/2015. Available: http://halalfocus.net/wp-content/uploads/2015/01/SGIE-Report-2014.pdf. [Date retrieved January 31 2017).

The Rakyat Post (2016). Naelofar Hijab to make foray into New York. Available: www.therakyatpost. com/news/2016/02/20/naelofar-hijab-make-foray-new-york/. [Date retrieved 2016, June 27]

5 Exploring the incongruent

Islamic banking and non-Muslim consumers

Norbani Che-Ha, Wan Marhaini Wan Ahmad,
Mohd Edil Abd Sukor and Saad Mohd Said

Learning outcomes

At the end of this chapter, the reader should be able to:

1   Explain the perceptions, knowledge and understanding of non-Muslims regarding Islamic banking
2   Discuss the Islamic brand awareness that induces non-Muslims to patronise Islamic banking
3   Understand the role that promotional tools play in creating awareness and improving the perception of Islamic banking
4   Describe the factors that can be used to create awareness among Islamic banking consumers

Key points

1   Islamic banking awareness among non-Muslims is becoming increasingly important in Islamic finance sectors.
2   It is critical for Islamic banking to focus on the right promotional tools while creating awareness among Islamic banking consumers.
3   Different levels of understanding prevail among different types of Islamic banking consumer groups.
4   Product branding/rebranding should be meaningful, easy to remember and the pull factor that attracts customers, especially non-Muslims, to Islamic banking.

Introduction

Islamic banking has experienced double-digit growth globally since 2006 (Malaysia International Islamic Financial Centre [MIFC], 2014; Ernst and Young, 2016). The potential for growth is significant, considering there are about 1.5 billion Muslims worldwide (about 25 percent of the world's population). However, in 2012, Hong Kong and Shanghai Bank (HSBC) discontinued offering Islamic retail banking products in the United Kingdom and Singapore markets where most customers are non-Muslims. This is consistent with the view indicating that the cost of operating Islamic banking where non-Muslims are the majority is not commensurate to the return (Jenkins and Hall, 2012). Factors such as lack of understanding and product differentiation, complexity of product structure and standardisation and attitude towards Islamic banking are also reasons for the reluctance to participate (Ainley, 1997; Hassan, 2008; Gait and Worthington, 2008; Nienhaus, 2010).

In contrast, in regions with sizable Muslim populations, Islamic banking is growing at a substantial rate. In 2012, Islamic banking accounted for assets valued at US$1.3 trillion, with US$307.2 billion contributed by Middle Eastern countries such as Saudi Arabia, Qatar, Oman, Bahrain and United Arab Emirates, with recorded growth of 16.5 percent. This growth is contributed by the Muslim population and its changing demography (KFH Research, 2013). According to market consensus, the Muslim population is expected to increase by approximately 35 percent in the next 17 years, rising from 1.6 billion in 2010 to 2.2 billion by 2030 (Pew Research Centre, 2011). The young consumers in these countries are increasingly sophisticated about financial services, which has led to significant demand for sophisticated and competitive Shariah-compliant products and services (Loo, 2010). The substantial growth in asset value is also accompanied by expansion of traditional banking into *takaful* (Islamic insurance) and *sukuk* (Islamic fixed-income instruments), as well as fund management services. Thus, the growth of Islamic banking in these countries is expected to be substantial.

Similar exponential growth is recorded in Muslim countries in the Asia Pacific region, particularly Malaysia. Malaysia is a multi-racial country where more than 60 percent of the 27 million population are Malay and the rest are Chinese, Indians and other minorities. Even if Islam is the official religion given that the majority of the population (i.e. the Malays) is typically Muslim, Malaysia is a multi-religion country. Buddhism, Hinduism, Christianity and other religions are also practiced. Compared to other Muslim-dominated countries, the multi-ethnicity and religiosity of the Malaysian population has moulded a different form of growth of Islamic banking in the country.

The growth of Islamic banking in Malaysia is due not only to Muslims' faith in their religion but also to the participation and patronage of non-Muslim Malaysians. For instance, Bank Islam Malaysia Berhad (BIMB) indicates that 70–80 percent of the bank's trade and corporate financing are with non-Muslim customers (Ngui, 2004). PricewaterhouseCoopers reports than more than 50 percent of Islamic banking customers in the country are non-Muslims (PwC, 2008). Chinese consumers at Hong Leong Islamic Bank, Overseas-Chinese Banking Corporation (OCBC) and Bank Rakyat represent 70 percent of their Islamic banking products' clientele (Husin, 2008).

This scenario is in complete contrast to the popular belief that non-Muslims, as discussed previously, are skeptical of Islamic banking and choose not to participate. The question is: Why do Malaysian non-Muslims react differently to Islamic banking products? Has a four-decade exposure to Islamic banking overcome their skepticism of Islamic banking? Has it improved their understanding of the Shariah concepts underlying the products offered, thus differentiating their perceptions vis-à-vis the non-Muslims in the West? Or does the Malaysian financial setup which promotes Islamic banking and creates soundness and versatility of the Islamic banking system in the country change local non-Muslims' perception of Islamic banking and set them apart from non-Muslims in Western countries?

For that matter, the objectives of this study are:

1 To investigate the perceptions, knowledge and understanding of non-Muslims regarding Islamic banking
2 To examine the Islamic brand awareness that induces non-Muslims to patronise Islamic banking

To discuss the above issues, this paper leverages Malaysia as a context. The discussion is organised as follows. This paper proceeds with a review of the literature on Islamic banking in Malaysia and a description of the methodology used in the study. This is followed by analysis and results of the study and implications of the study.

Literature review

Islamic banking in Malaysia

According to the Malaysian Islamic Financial Services Act 2013 an Islamic bank is a company licensed to carry on Islamic banking business with products and operations in compliance with Shariah. Thus, an Islamic bank accepts Islamic deposits on current accounts, deposit accounts, savings accounts and other accounts, with or without the business of paying or collecting cheques drawn by or paid in by customers, accepts money under an investment account and provides finance or any banking business whose aims and operations do not contradict Shariah law.

Islamic banking in Malaysia began in 1983 with the establishment of Bank Islam Malaysia Berhad (BIMB), the first Islamic commercial bank. The bank was established to meet the needs of Malay Muslims for Shariah-compliant banking. This is reflected in the paid up capital which is from local Malay institutions and several government agencies (Bovens et al., 2001). It operates under a tight regulatory system in which it must conform to existing conventional banking guidelines and specific regulations mandated for an Islamic bank by the Islamic Banking Act 1983.

BIMB was allowed to operate without any competition for nearly 10 years. Only in the 1990s did several conventional banks start to offer Islamic banking products and services at their premises under an interest-free scheme (now known as an Islamic banking scheme, or IBS). The scheme allows conventional banking institutions to offer Islamic banking products and services within the existing infrastructure, including staff and branches and also their brand name. The Islamic banking products are promoted by the banks' existing staffs, Muslims and non-Muslims, to all prospective clients – Muslims and non-Muslims alike. Several counters which look like windows are dedicated to selling these products, which prompts the currently popular term *Islamic windows*.

Even though the participation of banking institutions in the scheme is voluntary, by the end of 2012, 16 Islamic banks and 5 international Islamic banks were listed as Islamic and international Islamic banks in Malaysia (BNM, 2014). Remarkably, several of these Islamic banks are owned by non-Muslim Chinese families and foreign shareholders like Hong Leong Islamic Bank Berhad, Public Islamic Bank Berhad, Alliance Islamic Bank Berhad, OCBC Al-Amin Bank Berhad, HSCB Amanah (M) Berhad and Standard Chartered Saadiq Berhad.

At the end of February 2014, the Malaysian Islamic banking industry had expanded to RM423 billion, accounting for 21 percent of the country's banking system's assets. The assets have almost doubled in the last five years and are projected to expand to 25 percent of the total banking assets by 2017 (Ratings Agency Malaysia, 2014).

Due to the prohibition of interest in money lending, Islamic banks differ from conventional banks in terms of the structure and operations of the banking products offered. Functionally, Islamic banks act like conventional banks which mobilise money from the surplus units of the economy to those units that are in need of money and capital. The methods by which Islamic banks mobilise the money, however, differ significantly from their counterparts. Contracts of sale, hire, safe custody, partnerships and agency among others are adopted in addition to the usual loans that are prevalent in the conventional banking system. For deposits, Islamic banks offer safe custody (*wadiah*), agency (*wakalah*) and investment (*mudarabah*) services. For financing services that are interest free, Islamic banks offer debt (either sale-based like *murabahah, bai' bithaman ajil, tawarruq* and *'inah* or fee-based like *ijarah* or *wakalah*) and equity-based financing (*mudarabah, musharakah mutanaqisah*).

Utilising a multitude of Shariah concepts as above enables Malaysian Islamic banks to offer a vast diversity of Islamic banking products that emulate the banking services offered by conventional banks and may sometimes result in a unique competitive edge (Nienhaus, 2010).

Leveraging the uniqueness and versatility of Islamic banking products are the comprehensive Shariah governance and legislative frameworks overseeing the Islamic banking industry. These infrastructural frameworks not only ensure the effective functioning of Shariah-compliant banking products and services but also provide another layer of governance and comfort for customers and investors (BNM, 2013).

Islamic banking brand awareness

With wide participation from local and international banks in Islamic banking, the efforts are expected to help create awareness among Malaysians about their options in banking. Awareness has always being associated with the ability of customers to recall and recognise the brand and match the products/services that are offered by the brand (e.g. Keller, 1993). Awareness can strengthen the brand in the mind of consumers. In this case, the brand is Islamic banking; it is presumed that with all the effort and initiatives put forward by the Malaysian government and the banking sector people are receptive to the brand.

Berry (2000) identifies factors that can be used to create awareness among consumers, such as brand name, advertising, word of mouth and public relations. According to the American Marketing Association, brand is a 'name, term, sign, symbol or design or a combination of them, intended to identify the goods and services of one seller or group of sellers and to differentiate them from those of competitors." Great brand awareness can be capitalised on in creating organisations' competitive advantage. Awareness, on the other hand, can be developed via advertising. Advertising is a tool that can be used not only to reach potential customers but also to influence their awareness, judgments and feelings and consumption behaviour (e.g. Ayanwale et al., 2005; Keller, 2007). It is regarded as a competitive tool for organisations to communicate their functional and emotional values (de Chernatony, 2010). Among the tools of advertising are radio, television, newspapers, billboards, the web and social media.

In addition to advertising, word of mouth (WOM) and public relations are other tools for promotion that can be used by organisations to enhance their presence among consumers. WOM refers to the extent to which consumers share information about a product with their friends, family members and colleagues (Anderson, 1998). WOM is a powerful tool since most consumers trust recommendations from their friends over another promotional medium (Sweeney et al., 2012). Public relations, moreover, is a "form of communication management that seeks to make use of publicity and other nonpaid forms of promotion and information to influence the feelings, opinions, or beliefs about the company, its products or services, or about the value of the product or service or the activities of the organisation to buyers, prospects, or other stakeholders" (American Marketing Association). Public relations activities are crucial in delivering information to consumers and act as tools that can be leveraged in creating and sustaining organisations' reputation among consumers (Bristow et al., 2002).

Understanding Islamic banking and non-Muslims customers

Islam acknowledges the rights of each person, whether Muslim or non-Muslim. These rights become a matter of public policy that a Muslim government must acknowledge and protect. Islam considers religious diversity as a concomitant of God's bestowal of free will and choice on human beings. Islam respects the rights of non-Muslims to hold their religious faith and accommodates their needs to practice their religious rituals. Islam does not prevent Muslims from having good relations with the followers of other religions. The Quran explicitly states that each human has a right to perform economic activities that are pertinent to sustain their lives. There is no compulsion for humans to become Muslim to enable them to live (Al-Quran, 2: 256, 6: 108).

In Islam, the freedom to enter into a contract goes beyond determining the choice of partners in a commercial transaction without coercion. One is allowed to establish an economic transaction of choice as long as it does not contradict Quranic teachings. Thus, from an Islamic point of view in economic transactions that do not violate Shariah law, Muslims may deal and interact with non-Muslims without limitations on volume or value.

Similarly, Islamic banking is not banking that is exclusively for those who believe in Islamic teachings. Islamic banking products and services are offered to both Muslims and non-Muslims. In fact, non-Muslims also are allowed to join the Islamic banking work force.

Non-Muslim customers

Studies on non-Muslims' engagement with Islamic banking can be traced to the 1990s during the introduction of Islamic banking. At that time, non-Muslims had very little knowledge of Islamic banking products (Gerrard and Cunningham, 1997). Most were aware of Islamic banking but could not identify the differences between Islamic and conventional banking (Haron et al., 1994; Abdul Hamid and Nordin, 2001).

This was expected as the market was not accustomed to Islamic banking products. However, the issue persists until the present day; for example, when investigating the determinants of Islamic banking acceptance in Kuala Lumpur, Marimuthu et al. (2010) found that Malaysian, Muslims and non-Muslims alike, have limited knowledge of Islamic banking. Less than 10 percent of the respondents were able to differentiate Islamic banking products. In others studies, such as Amin and Isa (2008), Mahamad and Tahir (2011) and Abdullah et al. (2012), non-Muslim customers possessed a moderate understanding of Islamic banking concepts. They indicated that some of the respondents could correctly define the meaning of Islamic banking, particularly the younger generation and those with higher academic qualifications.

Terminology for products offered

The Arabic terms and terminology used to label products and services might hinder much of the non-Arabic-speaking population in trying to comprehend the products offered in Islamic banking (Bley and Kuehn, 2004). This is in contrast to Jordanians, who are native Arabic speakers who are able to understand the Islamic banking terminology of Murabahah, Mudarabah and Musharakah (Naser et al., 1999). Table 5.1 shows the Arabic terms that are used to classify Shariah-compliant products offered in Islamic banking and their description.

Table 5.1 Shariah compliant products and description

Products	Description
Al Wadiah	It refers to safekeeping or saving with guarantee. It is a contract between the owner and custodian (bank) of the goods (assets, money, valuables, documents, etc) to protect and to ensure safe custody of the goods. It is generally applied in saving and current account.
Al Mudharabah	It refers to profit sharing. It is a contract between the owner (depositor) of the capital and the entrepreneur (bank) for the purpose of participating in the profits made from utilisation of the fund. The profit made will be shared according to the agreed profit distribution ratio between the owner and entrepreneur. However, in the event of loss, the customer will bear all the losses. It is generally applied in project financing, Mudharabah Investment account and saving account.
Al Musyarakah	It refers to joint venture. It is a general partnership between two or more parties into a contract to jointly exploit their capital and to share the profits and losses of the partnership. It is generally applied in project financing.
Al Bai' Bithaman Ajil	It refers to deferred payment sale. It is the sale of goods on a deferred payment basis at a price inclusive of profit margin agreed by both parties. It is generally applied in home financing and land financing.
Al Ijarah	It refers to lease or rent. It is a contract to lease the benefit (use or service) of an asset for an agreed rental. It is generally applied in vehicle leasing and equipment leasing.
Bai Al Salam	It refers to deferred delivery sale. It is a forward contract whereby advance payment is made for the goods to be delivered in the future. It is generally applied in agriculture and project financing.
Bai Al Murabahah	It refers to cost plus mark-up sale. It is a contract whereby the bank finances the purchase of an asset on behalf of a customer and the customer will need to settle the payment for the asset on an installment basis. It is the most widely used product and generally applied in working capital requirement and goods financing.
Bai Al Inah	It is a contract whereby a financier sells an asset to the customer on a deferred payment and then the financier immediately repurchases the asset for cash at discount. It is generally applied in cash line facility and personal financing.

Source: Bank Negara Malaysia (BNM)

The discussion above highlights the background of Islamic banking and issues facing the sector in general. This study acknowledges that a number of studies have been carried out in Malaysia on the subject but most of them are on technical aspects of financial accounting in Islamic banking. Some studies are also based on consumers' perceptions, mostly carried out in the early 2000s. This study extends previous studies; in fact, this paper leverages past studies to benchmark the development and progress of the sector. Also, to our best knowledge, no study has focused on non–Muslims' perceptions, understanding, knowledge and brand awareness of Islamic banking in Malaysia.

Methodology

In trying to fulfil the objectives of the study, a quantitative approach using a survey questionnaire was adopted. Convenience and snowball sampling methods were used to gather data from undergraduate and postgraduate non–Muslim respondents at the University of Malaya.

Students are commonly used as study samples in banking institutions; for example, O'Cass and Grace (2004) used students in studying these institutions. Kent and Allen (1994) and Arora and Stoner (1996) also used students as samples in their consumer research studies.

The questionnaire consists of nine pages inclusive of a cover page that explains the objectives of the study and provides contact details and assurance of the confidentiality of the information provided. This study is part of a bigger research project. The questionnaire comprises six main sections that capture respondents' demographic profile, awareness of Islamic banking products and perspectives on Islamic banking, among other items. A Likert scale ranging from 1 (strongly disagree) to 6 (strongly agree) was employed to test the perspectives on Islamic banking and Islamic brand awareness, whereas a categorical scale was used to measure knowledge and understanding of Islamic banking products.

To minimise measurement error, pre-testing was conducted. Oppenheim (2004) indicated that questionnaires have to be developed, tested and improved several times before being distributed. The questionnaires were distributed to five lecturers and ten students. The respondents indicated favourable feedback on the questions, structure and design of the questionnaire.

A total of 1,000 self-administered survey questionnaires were distributed and 817 questionnaires were returned. After data screening, no response was discarded from the 817 returned questionnaires, but for the purpose of this study only 686 responses were used for analysis.

Instruments of measurement and data analysis procedures

The measurements used for perspectives of Islamic banking and Islamic brand awareness came from established scales. All 30 items on perspectives of Islamic banking were adopted from Bley and Kuehn (2004), Ahmad and Haron (2002), Gerrard and Cunningham (1997), Haron et al. (1994) and Loo (2010). The twenty-one items used to measure Islamic brand awareness were adapted from O'Cass and Grace (2004) and Grace and O'Cass (2005). BNM reports, on the other hand, were used to elaborate knowledge on Shariah-compliant products.

The data collected were analysed using Statistical Package for the Social Sciences (SPSS) version 20. Factor analysis, which is meant to reduce the data and to recap information of the study, was deployed to summarise the structure of the variables (Coakes et al., 2010). Exploratory factor analysis (EFA) with principal components analysis (PCA) with varimax rotation was conducted. The KMO value and Bartlett's test of sphericity were checked to ensure the appropriateness of factor analysis (Pallant, 2010).

Appropriateness was achieved with results showing KMO of 0.857, Bartlett's 5342, df 435 and Bartlett's Sig 0.00 for perspectives on Islamic banking and KMO of 0.91, df 351 and Bartlett's Sig 0.00 for Islamic brand awareness. Tables 5.2 and 5.3 show the results of EFA from perspectives on both Islamic banking and Islamic brand awareness.

Results from the EFA for perspectives on Islamic banking (Table 5.2) show that 24 of 30 items proposed were loaded into five dimensions: prospect of Islamic banking (IB), understanding of IB systems, willingness/preferences for IB, knowledge of IB and advantages of IB. For Islamic brand awareness (Table 5.3), 3 out of 21 items were dropped as they fell below the coefficient of 0.5.

Table 5.2 Results from EFA on perspectives on Islamic banking

	F1	F2	F3	F4	F5
Prospect of Islamic banking (IB)					
IB will be the dominant form of banking in Malaysia.	.73				
IB will give more benefits than CB.	.71				
IB will make Malaysia a role model.	.68				
I knew IB from promotional campaign.	.64				
IB has a bright future.	.62				
IB pay *zakat** on behalf of me.	.62				
Understanding of IB systems					
Transactions in IB are according to Shariah.		.78			
IB is based on Islamic principles.		.71			
IB imposed a fully Islamic concept.		.65			
IB applies profit-loss sharing between bank and customers.		.53			
Return of IB is based on risk sharing.		.50			
Be involved in Shariah-compliance bank is good.		.50			
Willingness/preferences for IB					
Uninterested in IB because I have a/c with CB.			.69		
IB is meant for Muslims only.			.63		
IB is not competitive as other banks.			.52		
I prefer conventional bank.			.50		
Knowledge of IB					
My knowledge of IB is very limited.				.76	
Info on IB is lacking.				.74	
I am not familiar with IB.				.71	
Advantages of IB					
IB facilities are fair to both customers and bank.					.56
IB charge low fees.					.53
IB is low risk due to its fixed instalments.					.52

**zakat* = an obligatory payment made annually under Islamic law on certain kinds of property and used for charitable and religious purposes.

Table 5.3 Results from EFA on Islamic brand awareness

	F1	F2	F3	F4
Advertising	.69			
I like the advertising.				
The advertising is relevant to me.	.73			
The advertising makes me believe that the bank is helpful and friendly.	.69			
The advertising helps me in my decision making.	.72			
The Islamic brand				
I use the services because of the brand.		.56		
The brand means a lot to me.		.63		
The brand tells me what to expect in the banks service outcome.		.76		
The brand is different from conventional banks.		.75		
The brand is relevant to the bank.		.74		
The brand is important in service brand development.		.69		
Word of mouth				
I care about what people say about the bank.			.75	
Word of mouth influences my attitude towards the bank.			.66	
Word of mouth provides me good ideas about the bank.			.82	
Word of mouth helps in my decision making to use the bank services.			.61	
Word of mouth is important in service brand development.			.72	
Public relations			.75	
I trust the public relations of the bank.				.67
Public relations have improved the credibility of the bank.				.71
Public relations are important in service brand development.				65

Table 5.4 Scale reliability

	Items	Cronbach's Alpha
Perspectives on Islamic banking		
Willingness/preference	4	.76
Understanding of IB	5	.72
Knowledge of IB	3	.81
Influence	3	.78
Prospect	3	.82
Islamic brand awareness		
Advertising	4	.74
Islamic brand	5	.85
Word of mouth	5	.76
Public relations	3	.64

The internal consistency of measurement was measured via Cronbach's coefficient alpha (Pallant, 2010). All items showed a value above 0.60, which is acceptable (Hair et al., 2010). The reliability for each dimension is shown in Table 5.4.

Results

Most respondents (77 percent) are aged between 16 and 25 years. This group is followed by those between 26 and 35 years old. More than 90 percent are Malaysian Chinese (95 percent) who are Buddhist (77 percent). Most of them (63 percent) have a bachelor's degree and most (46 percent) have an account with an Islamic bank. Table 5.5 shows the details of the study respondents.

Mean scores are used to gauge the importance of each item of Islamic banking. A mean score of 3.5 and above is considered agreeable and 3.5 and below not agreeable. Table 5.6 shows the result on perceptions of Islamic banking. Items such as 'My knowledge of IB is very limited' (mean 4.31), 'Info on IB is lacking' (mean 4.23) and 'I am not familiar with Islamic banking' (mean 4.31) indicate that many respondents have little knowledge of Islamic banking. This result is consistent with previous studies such Haron et al. (1994) and Ahmad and Haron (2002) indicating that the general public lacks knowledge of Islamic banking.

'Willingness or preferences for Islamic Banking', on the other hand, scored the second highest mean of 3.88. It is interesting to note that most of the respondents disagreed with the statement that 'Islamic banking is only meant for Muslims' (mean = 3.09). However, also important to note is that most of the respondents preferred conventional banking (mean = 4.29) as Islamic banking is regarded as not competitive (mean = 3.91). On understanding Islamic banking systems, respondents' scores are beyond 3.5 and respondents are in agreement on most items of the dimension, such as 'Transactions in IB are according to Shariah' (mean 3.82), 'IB is based on Islamic principles' (mean 4.12), 'IB imposes a fully Islamic concept' (mean 3.92) and 'IB applies PLS [profit-loss sharing] between bank and customers' (mean 3.81); however, they disagree with 'Being involved in a Shariah-compliant bank is good' (3.38).

Knowledge and understanding of available Islamic banking products are obtained via descriptive statistics (i.e. frequencies) as the data collected are in categorical form. Table 5.7 shows that most respondents do not know the Islamic banking products offered. More than 90 percent of respondents does not know products such as Bai'Al Inah (98 percent),

Table 5.5 Profile of respondents

Characteristics	No.	Percent
Age		
16–25 years old	529	77.1
26–35	73	10.6
36–45	42	6.1
46–55	34	5.0
Above 55	8	1.2
Ethnic group		
Chinese	655	95.5
Indian	26	3.8
Others	5	0.7
Religion		
Christian	117	17.0
Buddhist	531	77.4
Hindu	17	2.5
Others	21	3.1
Education		
Diploma	218	31.8
Bachelor's degree	431	63.0
Postgraduate	10	1.5
Others	25	3.7

Table 5.6 Perspectives on Islamic banking

	Mean	SD
Prospect of Islamic banking (3.21)		
IB will be dominant banking in Malaysia.	3.17	1.15
IB will give more benefits than CB.	3.24	1.05
IB will make Malaysia a role model.	3.24	1.19
I knew IB from promotional campaign.	2.91	1.31
IB has a bright future.	3.50	1.13
IB pay *zakat*★ on behalf of me.	3.20	1.27
Understanding of IB systems (3.79)		
Transactions in IB are according to Shariah.	3.82	1.12
IB is based on Islamic principles.	4.12	1.21
IB imposed a fully Islamic concept.	3.92	1.21
IB applies profit-loss sharing between bank and customers.	3.81	1.15
Return of IB is based on risk sharing.	3.66	1.09
Be involved in Shariah-compliance bank is good.	3.38	1.10
Willingness/preferences for IB (3.88)		
Uninterested in IB because I have a/c with CB.	4.04	1.31
IB is meant for Muslims only.	3.26	1.54
IB is not competitive as other banks.	3.91	1.90
I prefer conventional bank.	4.29	1.22
Knowledge of IB (4.31)		
My knowledge of IB is very limited.	4.38	1.27
Info on IB is lacking.	4.23	1.24
I am not familiar with IB.	4.31	1.49
Advantages of IB (3.72)		
IB facilities are fair to both customers and bank.	4.08	8.40
IB charge low fees.	3.42	1.05
IB is low risk due to its fixed instalments.	3.65	1.22

Likert scales from 1 (strongly disagree) to 6 (strongly agree).

★*zakat* = an obligatory payment made annually under Islamic law on certain kinds of property and used for charitable and religious purposes.

Table 5.7 Knowledge and understanding of Islamic banking

I know what is:	Yes	No
Al-Wadiah	155 (23%)	530 (77%)
AL-Mudarabah	146 (21%)	540 (79%)
Al-Musyarakah	135 (20%)	551 (80%)
Al-Bi' Bhitaman Ajil	44 (6%)	642 (94%)
Al-Ijarah	50 (7%)	636 (93%)
Bai' Al Salam	18 (3%)	668 (97%)
Bai' Al Murabahah	65 (9%)	621 (91%)
Bai' Al Inah	14 (2%)	672 (98%)

Bai' Al Salam (97 percent), Al-Bi' Bhitaman Ajil (94 percent), Al-Ijarah (93 percent) and Bai' Al Murabahah (91 percent). These results are in line with studies indicating low knowledge of Islamic Banking products using Arabic terminology (Hamid and Nordin, 2001; Bley and Kuehn, 2004; Gerrard and Cunningham, 1997; Ahmad and Haron, 2002).

In addition to analysing the positive and negative responses received regarding issues of Islamic banking, analysis was also carried out to determine Islamic brand awareness that might lead non-Muslims to patronise Islamic banking. Table 5.8 shows the mean score for awareness of the Islamic brand.

Results show that all factors except advertising score above the aggregate of 3.5 points with Islamic brand having a mean score of 3.49. Word of mouth and public relations score the highest means of 3.78 and 3.79, respectively. Many agree that WOM and public relations contribute to Islamic bank awareness. For instance, 'WOM influences my attitude

Table 5.8 Awareness on Islamic brand

	Mean	SD
Advertising (3.31)		
I like the advertising.	3.29	1.15
The advertising is relevant to me.	3.27	1.05
The advertising makes me believe that the bank is helpful and friendly.	3.36	1.15
The advertising helps me in my decision making.	3.30	1.13
The 'Islamic' brand (3.49)		
I use the services because of the brand.	3.31	1.27
The brand means a lot to me.	3.39	1.26
The brand tells me what to expect in the banks service outcome.	3.43	1.26
The brand is different from conventional banks.	3.59	1.20
The brand is important in service brand development.	3.76	1.21
Word of mouth (WOM) (3.78)		
I care about what people say about the bank.	3.82	1.66
WOM influences my attitude towards the bank.	3.81	1.68
WOM provides me good ideas about the bank.	3.73	1.14
WOM helps in my decision making to use the bank services.	3.73	1.86
WOM is important in service brand development.	3.86	1.24
Public relation (3.79)		
I trust the public relation relates to the bank.	3.65	1.07
The public relation has improved the credibility of the bank.	3.78	1.27
The public relation is important in service brand development.	3.95	1.98

Likert scales from 1 (strongly disagree) to 6 (strongly agree).

towards Islamic banking' (3.81), 'I care about what people say about the bank (Islamic banking)' (3.82), 'WOM helps in my decision making to use the bank services' (3.73) and 'public relations has improved the credibility of the bank' (3.78).

Conclusion

This paper explores non-Muslim views on Islamic banking, including non-Muslims' perceptions, understanding and knowledge and Islamic brand awareness. The two objectives are put forward in the context of Malaysia based on contradictory research issues discussed in the literature on Islamic banking. Many Muslim-minority countries do not aggressively pursue Islamic banking even though the reported growth opportunity of the sector is very promising. This is due to product complexity, lack of understanding of Islamic products and expenditure incommensurate to its return. In contrast to Malaysia, most customers of Islamic banking are non-Muslims, and the system of banking has been in place since 1983. This study can be considered a timely check of Islamic banking activities.

The study respondents are chosen with convenience sampling from undergraduate and postgraduate students. It turns out that 46% of the respondents have an account with an Islamic bank and 52% have an account with a conventional bank. Many agree that they have limited knowledge of Islamic banking and information on Islamic banking is lacking. They also do not see good prospects for Islamic banking. However, they understand that Islamic banking is based on Islamic principles and the transactions are consistent with Shariah, but they are not sure of the benefits to being involved with a Shariah-compliant bank. Most of the respondents also do not know the Islamic terms used to explain the products offered by Islamic banks. In terms of Islamic brand awareness, many indicate that WOM, public relations and the Islamic brand itself play a big role in creating and sustaining the brand building in Islamic banking.

The results of the study clearly indicate the need for a better understanding of Islamic banking. The thrust is to explain what differentiates Islamic banking vis-à-vis conventional banking in terms of how transactions and operations in Islamic banking are handled. Most importantly, customers must be able to realise the benefits they receive as Islamic banking customers. In addition, the terms used for products offered must be easy for all to understand. The product branding/rebranding should be meaningful, easy to remember and the pull factor that attracts customers, especially non-Muslims, to Islamic banking.

In addition to advertising, WOM and public relations are two popular tools respondents used to get information on Islamic banking. Personal interaction is the key term in bridging the gap between customers and Islamic banks. The right medium is needed to deliver the message to the target markets; for instance, with young educated adults, social media should be leveraged to disseminate information to consumers. Opinion leaders and social engagement programs also can be leveraged to reach these segments.

The Islamic brand itself also plays a role in creating awareness of the sector, but its advantages and differences versus conventional banking need to be strengthened. The brand definitely must be associated with product simplicity, benefits and superiority.

Issues for further discussion

1   With most banks in Malaysia starting to add Islamic banking at their premises, Islamic banking must develop a strategy to differentiate its operations vis-à-vis convention banking.

2   Terminology used in Islamic banking is a major issue that needs to be taken seriously. What are the best possible ways to resolve the issue?
3   The reliance on mobile technology and high dependence on social media are among the new challenges for Islamic banking. What are the banks' choices for strategic action?

Case study

Consumers' awareness and perceptions of Islamic banking in Malaysia

Passage of the Islamic Financial Services Act 2013 (IFSA) has brought increased economic and legal attention to the practices of the Islamic banking industry in Malaysia. IFSA has amalgamated several separate laws into a single legislative framework and repealed the Islamic Banking Act 1983, the Takaful Act 1984, the Payment System Act 2003 and the Exchange Control Act 1953. The main objective of IFSA is to promote financial stability and compliance with Shariah principles (Nelson, 2014). This legislation has provoked a wide-ranging response from Islamic banking players and from a variety of consumers within the Islamic banking sector. It is unclear whether such responses amount to a comprehensive policy or merely a series of key statements. Furthermore, there appears to be a growing gap between the views held within the banking industry and the need to promote awareness of Islamic banking services to both Muslim and non-Muslim consumers.

According to Hassan (2008), non-Muslim consumers have gradually become the major users of Islamic banking in Malaysia. In terms of promoting awareness, the wrong perception of Islamic banking instruments and services has caused millions of potential assets from non-Muslim consumers to be channelled into the conventional banking sector. Furthermore, current promotion tools have failed to convince existing and new consumers, especially non-Muslims, to subscribe to Islamic banking.

The right promotional tools will help to improve awareness and promote the growth of the Islamic banking industry. The tools that can be used to create awareness among consumers include brand name, advertising, word of mouth and public relations (Berry, 2000). When that function is not well executed, and consumers are denied access to a real understanding of Islamic banking products and instruments, those consumers will participate less in the industry, which will lead to slower growth of the Islamic banking sector. In 2013, Islamic banking assets in Malaysia accounted for only 25% of the Malaysian banking system's assets (Bank Negara Malaysia, 2014). If the awareness and perception of Islamic banking increase, at least half of the MYR 1.6 trillion in assets of conventional banks in Malaysia is expected to shift to the Islamic banking sector.

The Arabic terms and terminology used to label Islamic banking products and services are often considered one reason for the non-Arabic-speaking population to comprehend only weakly the products offered in Islamic banking and to believe that Islamic banking is only for Muslims (Bley and Kuehn, 2004). Move towards more universal and friendly product names that all customers can understand is required.

As market dynamics are changing, Malaysia is recognising the need for Islamic banks to improve awareness and understanding of their best practices among banking consumers in general and non-Muslims in particular. Service quality, for one, will be a key issue, with competition among conventional banks becoming tighter moving forward. Service quality may lead to improved word of mouth and public relations apart from the brand name and advertising promotional tools (Amin and Isa, 2008). Another idea is to drive the education system to incorporate Islamic finance awareness as part of the required syllabus, thereby providing a correct understanding of the Islamic banking industry and promoting awareness of Islamic finance services for Muslims and non-Muslims alike (Hamid and Nordin, 2001).

Case questions for discussion

1   On what promotional tool(s) should the Islamic banking sector in Malaysia focus? How do you think the proposed promotional tool(s) is(are) suitable for the dual banking system practiced in Malaysia?
2   Discuss the major challenges the Islamic banking industry faces in creating awareness among non-Muslim consumers.
3   What would you recommend to the Islamic banking industry to improve its perception among consumers in general and non-Muslims in particular?

References

Abdullah, A. A., Sidek, R. and Adnan, A. A. (2012), "Perception of Non-Muslim Customers Towards Islamic Banks in Malaysia", *International Journal of Business and Social Science*, Vol. 3, No. 11, pp. 151–163.

Abdul Hamid, A. H. and Norizaton Azmin Mohd, N. (2001), "A Study on Islamic Banking Education and Strategy for the New Millennium-Malaysian Experience", *International Journal of Islamic Financial Services*, Vol. 2, No. 4, pp. 3–11.

Ahmad, N. and Haron, S. (2002), "Perceptions of Malaysian Corporate Customers Towards Islamic Banking Products and Services", *International Journal of Islamic Financial Services*, Vol. 3, No. 1, pp. 13–29.

Ainley, M. (1997), "Under a Veil of Regulation", *The Banker* (October), pp. 73–74.

Amin, M. and Zaidi, I. (2008), "An Examination of the Relationship Between Perception of Service Quality and Customer Satisfaction: A SEM Approach Towards Malaysian Islamic Banks", *International Journal of Islamic Middle Eastern Finance and Management*, Vol. 1, No. 3, pp. 191–209.

Anderson, E. W. (1998), "Customer Satisfaction and Word of Mouth", *Journal of Service Research*, Vol. 1, pp. 128–137.

Arora, R. and Stoner, C. (1996), "The Effect of Perceived Service Quality and Name Familiarity on the Service Selection Decision", *Journal of Services Marketing*, Vol. 10, No. 1, pp. 22–34.

Ayanwale, A. B., Alimi, T. and Ayanbimipe, M. A. (2005), "The Influence of Advertising on Consumer Brand Preference", *Journal of Social Science*, Vol. 10, No. 1, pp. 9–16.

Bank Negara Malaysia. (2013), Bank Negara Malaysia Legislation, 30 June. http://www.bnm.gov.my/index.php?ch=en_legislation

Bank Negara Malaysia. (2014), *Bank Negara Malaysia Statistic 2014*. www.bnm.gov.my

Berry, L. L. (2000), "Cultivating Service Brand Equity", Journal of the Academy of Marketing Science, Vol. 28, No. 1, pp. 128-137.

Bley, J. and Kuehn, K. (2004), "Conventional Versus Islamic Finance: Student Knowledge and Perception in the United Arab Emirates", *International Journal of Islamic Financial Services*, Vol. 5, No. 4, pp. 17–30.

Bovens, M., Paul't, H. and Peters, B. G. (2001), *Success and Failure in Public Governance: A Comparative Analysis*, Cheltenham: Edward Elgar.

Bristow, D. N., Kenneth, C. S. and Schuler, D. K. (2002), "The Brand Dependence Scale: Measuring Consumers' Use of Brand Name to Differentiate Among Product Alternatives", *Journal of Product and Brand Management*, Vol. 11, pp. 343–356.

Coakes, S. J., Steed, L., and Ong, C. (2010), *SPSS: Analysis Without Anguish: Version 17 for Windows*, Australia: John Wiley and Sons.

de Chernatony, L. (2010), *From Brand Vision to Brand Evaluation, the Strategic Process of Growing and Strengthening Brands*, 3rd ed. Heinemann: Elsevier Butterworth.

Ernst and Young (2016), "World Islamic Banking Competitiveness Report 2016: New realities, New opportunities", EY Publication, 31 December. http://www.ey.com/Publication/vwLUAssets/ey-world-islamic-banking-competitiveness-report-2016/

Gait, A. and Andrew, W. (2008), "An Empirical Survey of Individual Consumer, Business Firms and Financial Institutions Attitudes Towards Islamic Methods of Finance", *International Journal of Social Economics*, Vol. 35, No. 11, pp. 783–808.

Gerrard, P. and Cunningham, J. (1997), "Islamic Banking: A Study in Singapore", *International Journal of Bank Marketing*, Vol. 15, No. 6, pp. 204–216.

Grace, D. and O'Cass, A. (2005), "Examining the Effects of Service Brand Communications on Brand Evaluation. Journal of Product and Brand Management, Vol. 14, No. 2, pp. 106-116.

Hair, J., Black, W. C., Babin, B. J. and Anderson, R. E. (2010), *Multivariate Data Analysis*, 7th ed. Upper Saddle River, NJ: Pearson Education International.

Hamid, A. and Nordin, N. (2001), "A Study on Islamic Banking Education and Strategy for the New Millennium-Malaysian Experience", *International Journal of Islamic Financial Services*, Vol. 2, No. 4, pp. 3–11.

Haron, S., Ahmad, N. and Planisek, S. (1994), "Bank Patronage Factors of Muslim and Non-Muslim Customers", *International Journal of Bank Marketing*, Vol. 12, No. 1, pp. 32–40.

Hassan, A. (2008), *Shariah Compliance or Shariah Driven Approach? Towards Full Appreciation of the Philosophical Roots of Islamic Finance, proceedings of ISRA (Islamic Research Academy Malaysia)*, Islamic Finance Seminar, November 2008.

Husin, A. S. (2008). *Crossing Over: Islamic Banking Needs to Reach Out to New Customers*. www.gtnews.com (accessed 15 January 2012).

Islamic Financial Services Act 2013.

Jenkins, P. and Halls, C. (2012), "HSBC's Islamic Closures Highlight Dilemma", *The Financial Times*, 7 October.

KFH-Research. (2013), www.zawya.com/story/KFHResearch_USD_13_trillion_assets_of_Islamic_banks_by_end_of_2012-ZAWYA20130314140832/

Keller, K. L. (1993), "Conceptualizing, Measuring and Managing Customer-Based Brand Equity", *Journal of Marketing*, Vol. 57, pp. 1–22.

Keller, K. L. (2007), *Strategic Brand Management: Building, Measuring and Managing Brand Equity*, 3rd ed., New York: Prentice Hall.

Kent, R. J. and Allen, C. T. (1994), "Competitive Interference Effects in Consumer Memory for Advertising: The Role of Brand Familiarity," *Journal of Marketing*, Vol. 58, July, pp. 97–105.

Loo, M. (2010), "Attitudes and Perceptions Towards Islamic Banking Among Muslims and Non-Muslims in Malaysia: Implications for Marketing to Baby Boomers and X-Generation", *International Journal of Arts and Sciences*, Vol. 3, No. 13, pp. 453–485.

Mahamad, M. and Tahir, I. M. (2011). "Perception of Non-Muslims Towards Islamic Banking: A Pilot Study", *Journal of Humanitarian*, Vol. 16, pp. 1–8.

Malaysia International Islamic Financial Centre. (2014), "Islamic Finance Industry Outperforms in 2013", *MIFC New Insight*, 15 January. www.mifc.com

Marimuthu, M., Jing, C.W., Gie, L. P., Mun, L. P. and Ping, T.Y. (2010), "Islamic Banking: Selection Criteria and Implication", *Global Journal of Human Social Science*, Vol. 10, No. 4, pp. 52–62.

Naser, K., Jamal, A. and Al-Khatib, K. (1999), "Islamic Banking: A Study of Customer Satisfaction and Preference in Jordan", *International Journal of Bank Marketing*, Vol. 17, No. 3, pp. 135–150.

Nelson, E. F. (2014), Bank Islam Malaysia: A Global Leader in Islamic Finance. International Banker Bulletin 2014, December 2014, pp. 92–97.

Ngui, C.Y.K. (2004), Malaysian Business, May 16, p. 40.

Nienhaus, Volker (2010), Capacity Building in the Financial Sector: Strategies for Strengthening Financial Institutions, paper presented at the Inaugural Islamic Financial Stability Forum, Khartoum, Sudan – 6 April 2010

O'Cass, A. and Grace, D. (2004), "Exploring Consumer Experiences With a Service Brand", *Journal of Product and Brand Management*, Vol. 13, No. 4, pp. 257–268.

Oppenheim, A.N. (2004), The quantification of questionnaire data. In C. Seale (ed.), Social Research Method, London: Routledge, pp.141-148.

Pallant, J. (2010), *SPSS Survival Manual: A Step by Step Guide to Data Analysis Using SPSS*, 4th ed. Australia: Allen & Unwin.

Pew Research Centre (2011), The Future of the Global Muslim Population, www.pewforum.org/2011/01/27/the-future-of-the-global-muslim-population/

PricewaterhouseCoopers (2008), Malaysia, Asia's Islamic Finance Hub.

Rating Agency Malaysia (2014), Islamic Banking Bulletin, April 2014.

Sweeney, J. C., Soutar, G. N. and Mazzarol, T. (2012), "Word of Mouth: Measuring the Power of Individual Messages", *European Journal of Marketing*, Vol. 46, No. 1/2, pp. 237–257.

6 Brand values and the Islamic market

Ali Al-Makrami and Dorothy Yen

Learning outcomes

At the end of this chapter, readers should be able to:

1 Understand how religious teachings in Islam delineate consumption values and moderate consumers' perceptions of the brand value
2 Explain why brand managers ought to consider relevant restrictions while designing brand communications for Muslim consumers
3 Introduce a value-maximisation approach to build and empower brand equity in Islamic markets
4 Discuss the managerial implications of brand value construction in global and local Islamic contexts

Key points

1 Muslim consumers represent an affluent segment that is becoming increasingly important in international marketing.
2 Trading is a general permissible (Mubah) practice in Islam and Muslims are required to be fair and honest about doing business.
3 Muslim consumers follow the teachings of Islam, which dictate what they eat, how they spend their money and what they like to see.
4 Islamic rules are obvious about what is permissible (halal) and forbidden (haram) in terms of consumption.
5 Relationship between Islam and marketing and branding is complex and in need of thorough understanding by marketers and brand managers.
6 Islamic laws should be considered in marketing communications and brand positioning strategies should a brand supersede in Islamic markets.
7 Islamic marketing framework has the potential to work out in Christian and Jewish markets due to the profound similarities between Abrahamic religions.

Introduction

Religion represents the most basic element of its followers' cognitive and spiritual world and thus religious values can be meaningfully related to important lifestyles. These lifestyles are composed of a set of consumption patterns and beliefs that affect behaviour (Delener, 1990). Because marketplace behaviours are directed at facilitating those activities that define one's culture, marketing strategists must be aware of the extent to which value systems impact the information and maintenance of specific subcultures such as religion. A major challenge that constantly faces marketers is to identify consumer values that tend to be stable over time and that can serve as a basis for segmentation, targeting and positioning (Usunier and Lee, 2005). Furthermore, the ever-increasing role of multinational companies (MNCs) in the contemporary global economy makes it incumbent upon marketers to appreciate the dynamics of the Islamic perspective in order to gain a better understanding of the mindset of Muslim consumers. This chapter discusses the capabilities and strengths of the Islamic branding framework in creating and sustaining strong brands through a deliberate process of designing and delivering a superior value to target Muslim customers.

Islamic branding: an overview

The Islamic religious perspective warrants considerable importance in the field of brand management for four reasons. Firstly, Islam provides a framework that shapes the consumption behaviour of a growing number of Muslim populations around the globe. These consumers constitute about one quarter of the total world population and represent a majority in more than 50 countries. Secondly, an increasing number of Muslim countries represent some of the most affluent consumers in the world. The global halal market, for example, is worth $2.1 trillion today and Islamic financial assets grow at 15–20% a year (The-Guardian, 2014). Thirdly, there has been an increasing level of global brand penetration into Muslim countries over recent years (Alserhan, 2010). And finally, the current political mood indicates that there appears to be a definitive push towards greater Islamisation of countries where Muslims are in the majority (e.g. Egypt, Morocco, Indonesia, Malaysia, to name but a few) in the form of a return to the application of the Islamic law (*Shariah*) to all facets of life and thought.

The religion of Islam is the profound source of their consumption culture and its holy teachings determine what is right (i.e. permissible or *halal*) and what is wrong (i.e. forbidden or *haram*). Because the undertaking of each and every transaction represents a task that must be executed in accordance with Islamic law and teachings, it is not surprising to learn that market behaviours merit special attention in Islam and constitute a separate discipline underpinned by the two sources of Islamic teachings: the *Quran* (Islam's holy book) and *Hadith* (documented practices of the Prophet Mohammed (pbh).[1] A number of chapters in these documentations are dedicated to the subject of commercial transactions which offer a practical trading system for acceptable business decision making. Likewise, transactions that include permissible and forbidden consumption decisions are given special attention in Islam, whilst laying down a strict spiritual code of conduct for classifying and evaluating business and marketing offerings (Saeed et al., 2001).

With respect to the theory of customer-based brand equity (Keller, 1993), its widespread model emphasises the role of individual consumer and his/her consumption culture in understanding brand strengths and weaknesses. Brand managers should then design informed branding communications based on Islamic determinants, especially when targeting Muslim consumers. The ignorance in studying these determinants could pose a negative response and threaten the brand existence. For example, after claims raised by Muslim observers that they intentionally produced shoes with the word of God (Allah) and the Prophet (Mohammed) printed on the bottom of the product, Nike still suffers from a contaminated image in Muslim markets. Such perceptions could be enduring

(Nike's controversy happened in 1995!). Islam does not recognise any division between the temporal and the spiritual dimensions, since an individual's quest to propitiate God and follow His commands permeates through all aspects of the individual's daily activities (Saeed et al., 2001). That is, in essence, whatever the brand provides in terms of attraction or delighting its customers, it will not succeed with Muslim consumers unless found in line with Islamic rules of consumption.

According to Alserhan (2010), Islamic branding can be defined in three different ways, in all of which the descriptor 'Islamic' is used: Islamic brands by compliance, by origin or by customer. He also identified that, in general, the halal market can be divided into three interlinked categories; food, lifestyles and services. Since Islamic teachings span all attitudinal and behavioural actions, including response to marketing stimuli, marketing and brand strategists working in, or selling to, Muslim markets should understand the trading laws (*Ahkam*) in Islam. A thorough understanding of these *Ahkam* will help in preventing businesses from being in direct conflict with Muslim consumers by strategising permissible (*halal*) product design and communications.

The paradoxical relationship between Islam and branding

The principles of modern marketing and branding seem at first glance to be paradoxical to Islamic codes of business conduct. Branding, in essence, stems its foundations from the principal concept of marketing communications which are defined by Kotler, the pioneer of modern marketing, as the ability for *deception* (Kotler, 2003). According to Kotler, intelligence in marketing can be viewed in the seller's capability to convince the buyers by using *any* means to do so including using tricks and deception. However, there is no room in Islam to justify any cover up of deception or promotional behaviour. The Holy Quran condemns all forms and shapes of false assertions (*Kadhb*), unfounded accusations, concoctions and false testimonies (Quran 43:19; 33:19; 58:17–19; 102:8; 100:8; 3:14).

Even with Keller's branding model (Keller, 1993), whereby the value of brands is driven from intensive marketing communications, it is unethical for the company to overpraise its products and attribute to them qualities which they do not possess (see also Saeed et al., 2001). The latter has been categorised as fraudulent and hence not permissible by Islamic law. The Prophet (pbh) narrated specific examples to illustrate *Kadhb* (lying) and said once "If both the parties spoke the truth and describe the defects and qualities (of the goods), then they would be blessed in their transaction, and if they told lies or hide something, then the blessing of their transactions will be lost." The Prophet (pbh) added further, "The swearing by the seller may persuade the buyer to purchase the goods but that will be deprived of God's blessing" (Sahih-al-Bukhari, 3:296). He also said, "... One who sells his (inferior) wares with false oaths" (Shih-al-Bukhari, 3:301), for such behaviours there has been ear-marked a painful punishment. These sayings by the Prophet Mohammed (pbh) state clearly that deception is a forbidden practice by Muslims.

Therefore, general branding practices to exploit ambiguity, conceal facts by suppressing information that is unflattering to their products, exaggerate by making claims unsupported by evidence and employ psychological appeal to persuade consumers by appealing to their emotional needs and not to reason are against the spirit of religion in terms of clarity and frankness (Saeed et al., 2001). The Quran warns in this venue "Those who purchase the small gain at the cost of Allah's covenant and their oaths (they have no portion in the hereafter)" (Quran 3:77). According to Islamic principles, traders are required to "disclose all faults in (their) goods, whether obvious or hidden; to do otherwise is to act ...

fraudulently" (Ibn Al–Ukhuwa, 1983, p. 42). It is obligatory for the salesperson to reveal all available and known information regarding defects to the purchaser which cannot be seen "on the surface" and cannot be found out by a "cursory glance" (Niazi, 1996, p. 196). In addition, it is dictated that "[a] sale, without any stipulation, makes it necessary that the thing sold should be free from defect" (Tyser et al., 1967 in Saeed et al., 2001). Marketing disclosure is manifested either by assurance which will be given through word of mouth or in writing, or in some cases silence will mean assurance (Niazi, 1996, p. 197).

Likewise, the promotional techniques must not use sexual appeal, emotional appeal, fear appeal, false testimonies and a pseudo–research appeal or contribute to the dullness of mind and/or encourage extravagance (Saeed et al., 2001). Within the Islamic framework, these methods are forbidden since they are utilised purely to exploit the basic instinct of consumers with a view to gain profits and greater market share. Furthermore, Islamic rules strictly prohibit the stereotyping of women in advertising, excessive use of fantasy, the use of suggestive language and behaviour and the use of women as objects to lure and attract customers. These Islamic principles of promotional behaviour are not only mere ideals, but practicable everyday actions as in Saudi advertising guidelines and sales training (Abdul-Cader, 2015) and as shown by the Prophet (pbh) and his disciples. For example, a famous disciple, Jarir, always pointed out to customers the flaws in his goods. When told that his business was bound to collapse he replied, "We promised the Prophet (pbh) to deal honestly (in our marketing activities)" (Ibn Al–Ukhuwa, 1983, p. 42).

A final aspect of brand communications and yet questionable by Islamic systems is the use of celebrity branding. Giving a false impression of any kind to promote or sell a product is strictly prohibited within the Islamic framework of marketing. In this spirit, "To hire a salesman to make (unfair) speeches which shall facilitate the sale of goods is forbidden and anything received by the salesman on account of rank and dignity and the (consequent) respect paid to his work when selling products is forbidden" (Ibn Al–Ukhuwa, 1983, p. 24). The underlying rationale for this prohibition is to stop all means which will lead to fraud and deception in the case of using famous characters in the society. Sometimes there is no other way of revealing the hidden qualities of the products, but that should not be taken as an excuse for being involved in the area of deception. Furthermore, there is "no harm in parsing qualities present in the products if the purchaser could not otherwise be aware of them" (Ibn Al–Ukhuwa, 1983, p. 24). This means that using celebrities to recommend brands for true features is not forbidden in Islam. From the Islamic perspective, a marketer who feels accountable to God will be honest and fair in his marketing activities and only true features which reveal accurate specifications in terms of quality, contents, etc. will exchange hands. To practise otherwise constitutes "disgraceful", "dishonourable" and "shameful gain" through pandering, deceit, treachery, theft or injustice (Ibn Miskawayh, 1968, pp. 99–100).

In principle, an essential concern by Islamic law is the predominant profit–maximisation strategies which are considered as a lawful motive in classical business arenas, and the teachings of Islam which usually question the real beneficial outcomes of commercial transactions (Saeed et al., 2001). Does this mean that branding is totally unlawful (*haram*) in Islam? The answer to this question is quite problematic. Although it sounds paradoxical, this research paper intends to identify the salient features of the Islamic framework of brand communication in terms of process and contents. In particular, it highlights the capabilities and strengths of this framework in creating and sustaining a strong brand value to survive and nurture in Islamic contexts. To provide fruitful recommendations to brand managers, selected key brand management issues related to brand value creation and development are examined from an Islamic perspective. The developed framework can, it is argued, help to create a value-loaded Islamic branding framework for Islamic marketing in general, and establish harmony and meaningful cooperation between global brands and target Muslim markets in particular.

Consumption values and brand equity in Islam

Marketing is a discipline that aims at lasting and interactive relationships between the seller and the buyer through providing *value* to customers. This concept is emphasised in the latest definition of marketing as declared by the American Marketing Association (AMA, 2004): "Marketing is an organizational function and a set of processes for creating, communicating, and delivering **value** to customers and for managing customer relationships in ways that benefit the organization and its stakeholders" (emphasis added). For instance, several studies have demonstrated the key role of understanding, creating, delivering and maintaining a superior value in building sustainable businesses (Gallarza et al., 2011). Value plays a crucial role for both firms and customers. From a firm's perspective, creating market offerings that deliver superior value to customers is of the utmost importance because higher levels of retention are most likely to occur (Koller et al., 2011). On the customer side, value perceptions are omnipresent throughout the whole consumption process. Value drives customer satisfaction and overall convenience with shopping experiences (Carpenter, 2008). More recently, in a report revealed by the renowned *Forbes*, 'value is the deal' was on the top list of branding matters in the 2011–2020 decade (Forbes, 2011). Considering the unprecedented race between global brands to build a profound, loyal customer base, **value** is proven as a substantial source of competitive advantage.

Brands thus compete on this scale to provide a distinguished experience to customers by providing them with the value thy need in their products and services. Classical theories in consumer behaviour suggested that quality and value for money are amongst key features sought after in brands by customers (Zeithaml, 1988). However, brands are found in latter periods of research as objects that are able to create happiness and build lasting relationships with customers (Fournier, 1998) and thus research embracing other psychological and sociological factors has come to the forefront in customer value research (Kainth and Verma, 2011). Customers in turn are used to evaluate the 'value' of each brand they have the intention to, or already buy. They usually follow semi-systematic procedures to evaluate the brand in question. The more the brand shows of realistic and fictional 'added on' value, the better the brand is evaluated on the value scale (Sweeney and Soutar, 2001). In short, brand value is a marketing construct that summarises the benefits given by a brand to the customer compared to brands in the same product category.

Although the value of the brand can be evaluated from financial perspectives, which evaluates the brand in terms of dollar-based measures, the present study considers an indirect, albeit more comprehensive, conceptualisation of brand value. This approach assesses brands from a behavioural perspective, which takes into account the brand's resonance and preference in customers' minds and hearts (O'Reilly, 2005; Berthon et al., 2007). Customers' evaluations of the 'given' value are measured in a multifaceted scale (has both functional and psychological items). Relevant research provides evidence that responding to customers' wants and needs through creating suitable value leads to advanced levels of brand likeability and loyalty (Sweeney and Soutar, 2001; Tsai, 2005;

Pihlström and Brush, 2008; Koller et al., 2011). As the customer is the party who decides how to store and classify information about received values, sociological and other profound triggers of customer culture can also impact value perceptions to a large extent (Usunier and Lee, 2005).

A sound theory that presents customer value in an ample framework has been developed by Sheth, Newman and Gross (1991a, 1991b). The theory suggests that consumption values should be deconstructed from five dimensions, including functional, social, emotional, epistemic and conditional value. Functional value is defined as the "perceived utility acquired from an alternative's capacity for functional, utilitarian, or physical performance" (Sheth et al., 1991b, p. 160). Social value refers to the "perceived utility acquired from an alternative's association with stereotyped socioeconomic or cultural-ethnic groups" (p. 161). Emotional or affective value is the "perceived utility acquired from an alternative's capacity to arouse feelings or affective states" (p. 161). Epistemic value refers to the "perceived utility acquired from an alternative's capacity to arouse curiosity, provide novelty, and/or satisfy a desire for knowledge" (p. 162). Finally, conditional value is defined as the "perceived utility acquired by an alternative as the result of the specific situation or set of circumstances facing the choice maker" (p. 163). The theoretical framework implies that each dimension can contribute distinctly and collectively to a particular buying decision process. Relevant strands of research on consumer value, nonetheless, have found that conditional value is impractical at brand level (Sweeney and Soutar, 2001; Al-Makrami, 2013). In contrast, economic value is a *salient attribute* that can advance research on brand communication level (Sheth et al., 1991a, p. 34). Figure 6.1 portrays the major dimensions of consumer value.

In Islam, any commercial activity is governed by principles set out in Quran and Hadith, including how to assess the value received by customers and/or communicated by marketers. For the sake of enhancing brand-building strategies in the Islamic markets, it is imperative to first evaluate the impact of Islamic teachings on consumer value, as these teachings are capable of influencing the Muslim customers' response to branding from within. This understanding is vital in order to design and convey effective brand messages in majority-Muslim markets or whenever targeting Muslim consumers, the new affluent segment for global brands. Taking into account the principles of consumption values theory and its relations to brand consumption, various dimensions of brand value including functional, economic, social, affective and epistemic value are discussed within the Islamic branding framework.

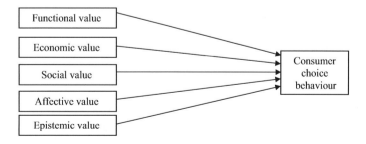

Figure 6.1 Theory of consumption values

Adapted from Sheth et al. (1991b), Sweeney and Soutar (2001) and Al-Makrami (2013)

Value-maximisation approach as a platform for branding in Islam

It has been noted previously that value plays a crucial role for customers' satisfaction and brand loyalty. However, value is a relative, subjective and perceptual concept and its orientations are mainly driven by a customer's personal perceptions (Zeithaml, 1988; Koller et al., 2011). Value has also been conceptualised with reference to consumers' subjective evaluations of what benefits are gained from the purchasing process (Sanchez-Fernandez and Iniesta-Bonillo, 2007). This entails marketers to study in more detail the factors that trigger attitudes and perceptions about marketplace offerings and marketing communications. While religion is an enduring factor that mediates believers' decisions about consumption choices and affects the formation of mainstream consumer culture (Jafari and Süerdem, 2012), it is not surprising to find that Islamic rules provide practical guidance for Muslims on how to appraise the value of brands.

In Islam, brands cannot be Shariah compliant and thus valued positively until they fulfil many conditions related to ingredients, logistics, impacts and intentions. Such fulfilment results in what is Islamically called *halal* or wholesome products. In this regard, religion plays an active role in transforming businesses into ethical entities whose goals rise above sales and revenues. Hence, according to Alserhan (2010), firms enduring the agony of changing their production processes and marketing practices to become Shariah compliant have earned the right to use the words 'halal and Islamic' to support their marketing efforts. However, it is not an easy task, although not impossible, to build up marketing and branding strategies that lie within the Islamic framework.

A key principle that can be applied to brand management in a pragmatic, systemised manner is the principle of value-maximisation (Saeed et al., 2001). Within the Islamic value-maximisation framework, the main aim of trading should be to create value and uplift the standard of living by providing satisfactory goods and services based on equity and justice (constituting just dealing and fair play) for the wider welfare of the society. The principle of value-maximisation is based on the concept of *justice*. Numerous Islamic scholars have analysed the application of *justice* in marketing by categorising it into 'fair play' and 'just dealing'. Ibn Miskawayh (1968), for example, defines fair play as to give and take in business according to the interest of all concerned, while just dealing is defined as a virtue which causes one to be fair to oneself and others by refraining from giving of more of the 'useful' to himself and less to others, and more of the 'harmful' to others and less to himself (Ibn Miskawayh, 1968). The Prophet (pbh) said: "You are not a believer of Allah, unless you like for your brother what you like for yourself." This emphasises the crucial sense of community and selflessness among members, organisations and society as a whole, for the achievement equity, equality and social integration. According to Ibn Miskawayh (1968), if the business orientation is shifted towards value-maximisation instead of profit-maximisation motives, and if justice becomes an inherent part of general marketing interactions and interdependence, a harmonious and collaborative business atmosphere will be created, whilst in no way jeopardising the competitive advantage of an organisation.

The consumption values theory described earlier has emphasised its foundations in that maximising value leads to enhanced seller-buyer relationships (Sheth et al., 1991a). Brand managers thus have the opportunity to harmonise principles of lawful marketing actions and value-maximisation to strategise the position of their brands in the marketplace and justify the preferable choices at consumers' mindset. Successful brands will exploit the fact that as Islam limits buying behaviour through market prohibitions, it allows followers to use brands within considerably wide permissions (*Ibaha*). When it comes to consumption

Table 6.1 Definitions of brand value constructs

Dimension	Definition
Brand value	*A marketing construct summarises the subjective evaluations of a brand capacity to provide multiple utilities to the individual consumer.*
Functional value	*Brand capacity to provide high quality products.*
Economic value	*Brand capacity to provide value-for-money products.*
Social value	*Brand capacity to enhance self-image in social environments.*
Affective value	*Brand capacity to connect with consumers on a relational basis.*
Epistemic value	*Brand capacity to provide knowledge and novelty.*

Adapted from Sheth et al. (1991b) and Al-Makrami (2013)

conditions (*Ahkam*) in Islam, the Islamic perspective has its foundation firmly rooted in the principle of *Ibaha*, which dictates that every object and action is considered permissible unless there is a prohibition of it in the Islamic scriptures (Quran 5:1; 7:157; 6:119). In the Quran: "... and whoever honours the sacred ordinances of Allah – it is best for him in the sight of his Lord. And permitted to you are the grazing livestock, **except** what is recited to you" (Quran 22:30, emphasis added). Applying the *Ibaha* principle and thus finding creative ways to enact branding without breaking the Islamic law could be a suitable exodus for brand managers. This section analyses the five dimensions of the brand value construct (i.e. functional, economic, social, affective and epistemic) within the context of brand building and communication contents as determined by these Islamic principles (see Table 6.1).

Functional value of brands

Functional value is a prime dimension in almost all consumer perceived value models because it refers to a basic need of the consumer, i.e. high quality products. This type of value is easily understood as instrumental, utilitarian and cognitive (Chandon et al., 2000), which relates to consumers' preference for higher standards of quality and reliable performance (Broyles et al., 2009). Thus, the conceptualisation of this dimension has been influenced by theory and research in economics, psychology, political science and market-ing and consumer behaviour (Sheth et al., 1991a). Perceived quality, brand effectiveness, efficiency, reliability, durability and performance are similar concepts used in pertinent literature to reflect upon brand functionality (Sweeney and Soutar, 2001; Keller, 2012). To project the consumer value of a brand, this type of value, as with other dimensions, can be measured on a developed scale to add to or subtract from the *overall* value of the brand (Keller, 2006).

From a religious Islamic sanction perspective, the quality of the production process and the final product is of paramount concern. The Quran declares that pursuance of safe and high quality ideals is one aspect of actualising safe and reliable products and services for the customers (Quran 2:168,172; 7:160; 20:81; 5:88; 8:69; 16:114; 23:51; 5:4; 7:157). In some of these Qur'anic verses the phrase "Eat pure things" precedes "do righteous deeds." Put simply, these phrases are meant to impress and emphasise the principle that righteous deeds are meaningless without purity in matters pertaining to production, consumption and marketing of pure and lawful products and services.

The production process in Islam is visualised quite differently compared to Western thinking. The Islamic perspective incorporates moral and transcendental elements within the production decision-making process and is guided by the principles of lawfulness,

purity, existence, deliverability and precise determination (Al-Misri, 1991). These principles dictate that firstly, the product should be lawful and not cause dullness of mind in
any form (Ibn Al-Ukhuwa, 1983, pp. 11, 20) or lead to public nuisance or immorality.
Secondly, the article for sale must specify exactly its quantity and quality, and the seller
must be able to point to the actual commodity where quality is determined by inspection while description cannot take the place of visual inspection (Ibn Al-Ukhuwa, 1983,
p. 20). Thirdly, the object should not be unclean. Ibn Al-Ukhuwa has categorised 'unclean'
things into four kinds; those unclean in essence (e.g. dogs and swine), those made unclean
by association (contamination), those made unclean by contamination but whose usefulness is not entirely destroyed (e.g. unclean garment) and things unclean by contamination
which entirely destroys their usefulness (e.g. contaminated olive oil). In other words, the
production process should be permissible (*halal*) and pure (*twayyib*) i.e. it should ensure
that ingredients have been taken/extracted/obtained from lawful sources, to the extent
that it is free from any harmful consequences. Islamic principles dictate that the production operations must be innocent and pure from beginning to end (Al-Faruqi, 1992,
p. 177).

A similar concept of quality that is reinforced by the Islamic guidance of production
to ensure optimal performance is *Itqan* (a quality-related term used by the Prophet (pbh)
to denote continually improving performance by the parties in any task, activity or function). Basically, the Islamic system was based on individual self-actualisation, which means
allowing individuals to reach the peak – *Itqan* – in the performance of their duties. For
instance, controlling brokers in markets to prevent any deception by emphasising honesty
and transparency in the production of goods and commodities is amongst issues discussed
by Muslim scholars as emanated from the two holy resources, The Quran and Hadith.

For instance, Allah asks us to achieve *Itqan*, as indicated in Sura Al-Namel (The Ant):
"It is the nature of Allah to perfect everything" (Quran 27:38). The Quran condemns all
deception in daily dealings as well as, and especially, in all matters of religion and daily
life. In Sura Al-Mutaffiffeen (The Defrauders), Allah says: "Woe to those that deal in fraud,
those who, where they have to receive by measure from men, exact full measure, but when
they have to give by measure or weight to men, give less than due. Do they not think that
they will be raised up on a Mighty Day" (Quran 83:1–5). Moreover, the Prophet (pbh)
asked his followers to act responsibly in performing their jobs and duties. In the famous
saying "Allah will be pleased with those who try to do their work in a perfect way," he
explains that Muslims should produce the best of quality at the workplace. Therefore,
through what they provide to the market, firms should be honest, transparent and just, and
maintaining the following approaches:

1   To draw from the perfection of Allah's work: "And be good, as God has been good to you.
    And do not seek corruption on earth, for God does not love the corrupt" (Quran 28:77).
2   To follow the best standards: "And follow the best of what has been revealed to you
    from your God" (Quran 39:55).
3   To have excellence. The Prophet (pbh) said: "Do the best as if you see Allah, if not,
    Allah sees you."
4   To ensure integration in any task and behaviour.
5   To be free from fraud or under-standardised commodities with defects.

Under the Islamic approach, the production process has to be guided by the criteria of
the value and the impact of the product upon the whole society. This is due to the highest

importance given to the actualisation of the optimum welfare of a human being and the society at large. To be engaged in the production process is a part of worship (*Ibadah*) to God (Al-Faruqi, 1992, p. 175). Ibn Al-Ukhuwa (1983), who discusses all aspects of a production process, for example, elaborating on the responsibilities of millers, states "(They) must clean the grain of earth before they grind it . . . the sieves must be renewed periodically . . . the official inspector must examine the flour to prevent admixture with flour of chick-pea, etc., and must prevent milling on the work particles of the miss stone, which causes harm to men" (Ibn Al-Ukhuwa, 1983, pp. 11–20). Regarding baker and bread-makers he states, "for kneading, men may not use their feet, knees and elbows as doing so implies a lack of respect for the food; also drops of sweat may fall into it . . . smocks with tight sleeves must be worn at the task and the face should be veiled . . . during the day time a man with a fly whisk should drive away the flies" (Ibn Al-Ukhuwa, 1983, p. 19).

Finally, Islamic values, using the so-called *Hisba* system (quality control), have stated clearly the importance of quality in Islam. The philosophy of *Hisba* as a quality control system has its roots in the Holy Quran. Many Islamic verses urge people to be righteous and to lead by example in order to perpetuate a culture of righteousness. For instance, Allah says: "Do you order people to be pious while forgetting yourselves, even though you read the book? Do you not understand?" (Quran 2:44). The purpose of *Hisba* is to prevent any deviation (Islamic standards being the reference point) from a required standard, adding value and hindering corruption so as to safeguard individuals and society as a whole from tort or any obstacles that might challenge the ultimate goal of improving the quality of life for everyone. The *Hisba* philosophy is basically a faith-based mission. It was developed mainly as a management control system to control institutions and businesses in the Islamic state. The primary goal of the *Hisba* system is the prevention of corruption, deviation and any other illicit behaviour in institutions.

Marketing strategists and brand managers should then forge the design of brands and the relevant functional value given by showing the high quality of their offerings including the evidence of purity and Shariah-compliant processes in between. There is no doubt that high quality products will be appreciated by consumers in general and should work as a very effective promotion strategy in Muslim markets in particular. The reason behind the potential success of emphasising 'top' quality and reliable performance of the brand is twofold. First, the concept of 'quality' is a preferred motive that Islamic principles tolerate in a steady manner, as proven in earlier discussion. Second, this notion is in line with previous research which found that consumers with more tendency to follow religious teachings usually prefer products which are classified as reliable and trustworthy (Delener, 1990; Mokhlis, 2006).

On the contrary, brands showing a lack of confidence about their market offerings might receive severe feedback by Muslim consumers. Those brands will not be judged only from a market perspective, but also will be considered as cheaters or 'defrauders' who must be punished for their violation to Islamic codes of acceptable business. Such perception can be enduring and could dilute the entire value of the brand. The Prophet (pbh) expressively condemned all manipulative behaviour stating that, "*One who cheats (Ghassh) is not one of us.*" Brand managers should be careful from offering low quality products under any cause of breaking down competitiveness or accelerating sale motion. Moreover, considering the theoretical level, the dimension of 'supply chain' seems of utmost importance to Muslim consumers. While most functional value scales in existing research have been conceptualised around the final product (e.g. Sweeney and Soutar, 2001; Vazquez et al., 2002; Tsai, 2005), the construct should be extended to embrace items related to production and supply chain management.

Economic value of brands

Value-as-price is a traditional school of thought drawn from economic pricing theories (Monroe, 1973). It indicates that the product price not only mediates the consumer perception at the part of the merchant, but also can moderate consumer perceptions about other attributes of the product such as perceived quality (Zeithaml, 1988) and emotional assessment (Hill, 2003). Price sensitivity, price elasticity, competitive prices and promotional prices are amongst terms used in brand value research to segment consumers' willingness to pay premium price for branded products (Mulhem et al., 1998). Within secular approaches, pricing strategies are rooted in the principle of profit maximisation whereby cost leadership strategies drive the main thrust behind some decision making on the part of business persons to produce sub–optimal prod- ucts. It is worth noting that such approaches have been dominant in shaping business teaching ideologies and therefore the attitudes and perceptions of international mar- keting executives over the years (Saeed et al., 2001). Not surprisingly, the practice of these teachings (rooted in secular ideologies) render marketing executives incapable of constructing or following any form of psychic mechanism or conscience that may act as a brake on feeding their drive towards maximising their earnings (Al-Faruqi, 1992).

In contrast, the Islamic perspective encourages a societal and welfare approach rather than decisions based on profit maximisation strategies. Therefore, the customer should feel and experience products which are worth the payoff in order to legalise the mer- chant from an Islamic perspective, although higher prices would not necessarily dilute the perceived value of the brands. Instead, the Muslim consumer could assess the worthiness of the brand – e.g. to what extent is the brand considered economical? With value-max- imisation approaches, economic utility theory emphasises the intervening role of price perceptions on ultimate evaluations of perceived utility, taking the implicit values of the buyer as an important indicator of price acceptance.

In classical pricing policies, market prices are formulated to exploit and manipulate human psychology, as witnessed by common practice whereby a recommended retail price which is printed on the product is often substantially higher than what the retailers actually charge (Saeed et al., 2001). The aim of such policies is to give buyers the false impression that they are in fact getting a bargain. Such practices are banned under Islamic law. Islam prohibits getting something too easily without hard labour (*Maisir*), or receiving a profit without working for it (*Tatfif*); increasing the price without altering the quality and/or quantity of the product; and cheating the easy-going customer for illicit gain. This doctrine prohibits marketers from practising price discrimination between bargain- ers (*Mumakis*) and non-bargainers (*Mustarsil*) by selling the same merchandise to them for different prices (see also Saeed et al., 2001). The Prophet (pbh) proclaimed, "*Do not urge someone to return what he has already bought* (i.e. in optional sale) *from another seller so as to sell him your own goods.*" Islam also prohibits false propaganda on the part of the marketer regarding the position of demand and supply through the media to affect price acceptance levels in consumers' minds.

Likewise, hoarding (*Ihtikar*) of any product is also banned in Islam. However, the system offers flexibility if compelling marketers to sell at one price amounts to coercion and distortion of the free market or if it means very high product prices. Under these cir- cumstances, and in view of safeguarding public interest, Islam officials can bring together market leaders representing a particular region or particular commodity, in the presence of others with a view to reaching a consensus on price level that would not be unjust to the consumer and at the same time reap reasonable profits to the marketers. The key impetus to intervene on such an ad hoc basis is to prevent "black-marketing" and "concealment of essential foodstuffs" (Saeed et al., 2001).

Moreover, Ibn Al-Ukhuwa (1983) emphasised the role of a public welfare official to ensure that prices remain fair and just by curbing any ethical lapses in price setting. He observes that "the public welfare official must see that a broker receives his commission only from the seller and must not cause the price to be abated in collusion with the buyer" (Ibn Al-Ukhuwa, 1983, p. 4). All unethical lapses in pricing are tantamount to injustice (*Dhulm*) and are sin. Hence, all profits earned through such unjustified prices are not only unethical, but also they infringe upon the unique status of man/woman and his/her role and responsibilities as viewed under the Islamic framework. The Prophet (pbh) remarked, "Do not raise prices in competition." In order to eliminate this type of 'injustice', the marketers must acknowledge that they have higher moral responsibilities on earth rather than to be preoccupied with profit maximisation alone. Furthermore, an Islamic business scholar defined a basic criterion of the perfect market in Islam as one that reflects equitable and fair prices (Al-Ghazali, 1971). This concept is consistent with similar proposals found in Western literature such as 'price fairness' (Oh, 2003; Na et al., 2007) and 'value as worth what paid for' (Brodie et al., 2009). These characteristics might manifest themselves in the way consumers making their perceptions about received value, i.e. greater self-restrain from buying on the spur of the moment and more concern about how much they spend or getting best buys (Mokhlis, 2006). In Quran, amongst the signs of Believers: "when they spend, do so not excessively or sparingly but are ever, between that, [justly] moderate" (Quran 25:76).

The Islamic perspective on price fairness would thus affect overrated branded products, i.e. luxury brands. Marketing managers believe that brands should be classified into price tiers according to consumers' willingness to pay premium prices (Pura, 2005; Pihlström and Brush, 2008). However, this market behaviour can be seen as conflicted with Islamic teachings for just prices. The charged price should be justifiable and add only reasonable profit margins to the trader. According to Miskawayh (1968), justice in Islam dictates one not to be greedy in lawful earning. Furthermore, an honest and just businessperson should have recourse to God, to His promise, and to His covenant at the utterance of every word, at every glance of the eye. A businessperson is not worthy of the rank of a 'just person' if s/he has an excessive love for money, for this eagerness of acquiring money prevents her/him from being kind, observing what is right and giving what s/he should. Pursuit of money alone will lead a businessperson towards the path of treason, lying, fabrication, false testimony, standing in the way of duty and assiduous search and the pursuit of valueless earnings (Saeed et al., 2001).

For brands still forgoing high price tags, brand managers should always explicate the reason behind marketed prices. They can communicate, for instance, a value-for-money market motive. This strategy can be legalised in Islam and accepted by Muslim consumers because *Isla* does not prohibit price controls and manipulations to meet the needs of the market e.g. charging higher prices as a result of natural scarcity of supply of a given commodity or setting price ceilings to curb opportunistic tendencies among merchants. In the Islamic value system, self-operating mechanisms of price adjustments and healthy competition (*Munafasah*) are in fact encouraged (Quran 83:26). Providing testimonies in brand ads about the worthiness of price paid compared to low-profile rivals' quality, durability and/or added value could justify the charged amounts. It is noted in practice that luxury brands, for instance, evade the price justification in their ads and just focus on imagery values. Such vague imagery process could be contradictory to the advised 'down to earth, clear' behaviour emphasised by several Islamic verses (Quran 25:63; 17:37; 31:18; 15:88; 26:215). Therefore, the essential conditions for the successful operation of pricing mechanisms in Islam dictate that there should be no corner market, no hoarding, no restriction on trade and no (unjustified) price manipulation.

Social value of brands

Social value is based on the premise that brands hold symbolic benefits for users which are appreciated by other members in the society. When a brand is capable of delivering additional value to an individual user in her or his social circles, the social value of the brand is discussed (de Chernatony and Riley, 1998a; Vazquez et al., 2002). Related theoretical fields pertaining to the social domain of value are social psychology, sociology, communications and anthropology. Furthermore, social class, symbolic value, reference groups, opinion leadership, conspicuous consumption and normative attitude are all relevant areas of research (Sheth et al., 1991a). Within the realm of brand management, advocating the brand as a social stimulus is widely acknowledged in brand value literature, a perspective that considers brands as lively objects that interact with consumer communities (Holt, 2002; O'Reilly, 2005; Cayla and Arnould, 2008).

In effect, there is a long tradition of studying the effects of religion's social authority on market activities. For instance, Mittelstaedt (2002) described the impact of religion as a socio-cultural force on the structure and organisation of local markets. Through *social authority*, religion controls the cultural beliefs and expectations of market participants and defines the boundaries of socially acceptable behaviour in the marketplace. Social authority is moral in nature, rather than legal or institutional. Here, religious teachings and institutions shape cultural views and social expectations and thus direct buying and selling behaviour in the market (Mittelstaedt, 2002). Whereas in most Muslim societies one can observe a strong religious socialisation, much stronger than Western, secularised contexts (Wilson and Liu, 2010), a thorough understanding of the interrelationships between religion, society and brand value sounds imperative to design direct marketing communication and empower social value of brands in relevant markets.

In this spirit, previous research has classified social motives into two domains: intrapersonal (mainly cognitive) and interpersonal (mainly behavioural) (Mokhlis, 2006). With intrapersonal levels of analysis, a person aims at satisfying personal needs that help enhancing his or her self through raising standards of one's own life. Sociologists suggest that materialistic objects such as luxury brands are amongst objects used by people to express themselves (Tifferet and Herstein, 2010) and pursue self-identity projects (Holt, 2002). Referring to faith-based connotations, intrapersonal religiosity is a construct that describes how an individual develops private relationships with God by enhancing spiritual and personal worship. The intrapersonal social motive and intrapersonal religiosity are relevant in that beliefs are mainly constructed 'within' oneself, regardless of the interface 'between' members of the same community. For instance, when a person performs a private worship or buys materials without considering the interaction with others, s/he aims to assure self-enhancement projects to satisfy God or self-image, respectively.

On the other hand, an interpersonal level of analysis mandates interaction with other members of one's social group such as family, friends, class or workmates. Individuals might acquire specific brands to attract people's attention in order to enhance self-image in the society. In the main, brands that are appreciated by the community are usually used to express oneself in a better manner (McCracken, 1988). For instance, when a person buys a luxury car (e.g. BMW), people's perceptions about his or her social status could significantly change if s/he used to drive a lower profile car. Another facet of interpersonal perspective is concerned with self-identification within certain groups through usage of certain products. Sheth et al. (1991b) discuss the social value as a value that is co-created at macro levels of people and refer to certain reference groups based on demographics, socioeconomics culture and ethnicity. In an Islamic context, the member of the insider society could also use commonly approved brands as legal or *halal* to construct parts of their identities (Elliott and Wattanasuwan, 1998). For instance, during the Muslims' boycott of American brands in the 1990s, drinking Coca Cola could negatively impact the image of the good Muslim in his or her society. Similarity, wearing a GAP t-shirt in public would be criticised due to a widespread concept stating that GAP stands for 'Gay And Proud'. Homosexuality is extremely banned behaviour in Islam.

Brand managers, though, can deal with these concepts carefully, in order to leverage the social utility of their brands. However, the meaning of social value is particularly challenging in Islamic marketing. Within the Islamic framework, not all social motives are considered righteous or *halal*. The concept of ego is particularly problematic as far as the Islamic value system is concerned. God guides followers to act in a more selfless manner for the sake of the welfare of the whole society. High involvement with materialistic objects would deviate believers from the supreme reason behind living; worship to God. In Quran, "And I (Allah) created not the jinn and humans except they should worship Me (Alone)" (Quran 51:56). Instead of being selfish and living just for the existing life and over consuming objects, worship to God includes being a good member of the society and avoiding selfish behaviours. The story of the two companions whereby one of them said, "I am greater than you in wealth and mightier in [numbers of] men" and the other replied, "Although you see me less than you in wealth and children" (Quran 18:34–39) provides an example of the sinned behaviour of those who see themselves as better than others for materialistic order only.

Likewise, the show-off behaviour (interpersonal motive) is also a prohibited (*haram*) conduct in Islam. People must be down to earth, moderate and never forget that all they own is given by God. In the Holy Quran:

> So he [the super rich man: Garoon] came out before his people in his adornment. Those who desired the worldly life said, "Oh, would that we had like what was given to Garoon. Indeed, he is one of great fortune." But those who had been given knowledge said, "Woe to you! The reward of Allah is better for he who believes and does righteousness. And none are granted it except the patient." And We caused the earth to swallow him and his home. And there was for him no company to aid him other than Allah, nor was he of those who [could] defend themselves.
>
> (28:79–80)

These Qur'anic verses, amongst many others, warn followers away from a banned behaviour in Islam; i.e. arrogance. Islamic teachings demand people to be modest in all walks of life, including what they eat, drink and how they dress. In principle, brands that compete on rarity and uniqueness, such as luxury brands, could be in direct conflict with similar Islamic teachings, since they build their value around differentiation and egotism in the society. However, Islam still encourages followers to look good and consider their appearance carefully. "But seek, through that which Allah has given you, the home of the Hereafter; and [yet], do not forget your share of the world" (Quran 28:77). Also, "O children of Adam, take your adornment at every masjid [mosque], and eat and drink, but be not excessive. Indeed, He likes not those who commit excess" (7:31). Here, Muslims are asked to be self-effacing in using worldly objects, but still having the right to look good in public, especially at religious occasions such like Juma'h (Friday) prayers, Eid (annual religious occasion), wedding parties, and so forth.

With respect to interpersonal orientations, the opportunity to brand managers to enhance the perceived social value of their brands seems to be more achievable than ego and self-image construction. Muslims, as with other religious communities, are known to be inherently of collectivist cultures (Hofstede, 1991). Collectivist cultures state that people living within similar landscapes act in harmonious, less confrontational ways. This behaviour refers to the strong desire for members of these societies to be identified with closely unified groups. Such behaviour would mean that when people from a religious society are convinced with a certain product or service, they will disseminate their experience to others and thus benefit businesses from their word-of-mouth communications. Therefore, the brand value will be augmented in individuals' minds due to the tendency for social identification through acquiring the membership of a desired group. According to Mittelstaedt (2002), social identification is a general characteristic of markets driven by religious values. For instance, religious individuals would prefer *halal* brands (e.g. Islamic banks) because they are helping them to identify with the Muslim community.

Finally, marketing managers can also augment the social value of their brands in an indirect way via Corporate Social Responsibility strategies. CSR is actually having similar drivers of social integration as the other Islamic principle, *Takaful*, calls for. Islam believes in a natural inclination to *higher ideals*. The Quran describes the clue of *Takaful* in numerous verses; ". . . for the scum disappears like froth cast out; while that which is for the good of mankind remains on the earth . . ." (Quran 13:17). The Islamic perspective, which prevailed within the ambit of Shariah, is concerned with social responsibility which regard to ethics and *Takaful* as enduring principles. It offers an integral, spiritual view based on the teachings of the Quran and Hadith providing a philosophical framework for man's interaction with nature as well as his fellowmen (Ahmad, 2002). Further, central to the understanding of Shariah is *Taqwa*, which means wariness of God, or God-consciousness. It guarantees the social fabric because people then become voluntarily committed to achieving the central goals of human welfare or *Falah*. Thus, understanding the applications of CSR as a profound Islamic motive could help to enhance the social value of brands in Islamic markets. This is very much in line with the increased involvement of multinationals in the promotion of social welfare, in developing countries in particular, through the facilitation of partnerships and co-operation with the public and non-profit sectors of the state in which they operate.

In short, individuals who are committed to their religious groups hold a strong social value and are thus more susceptible to normative influences as a result of their regular interaction with others affiliated with the same religious organisation. While these influences, it is argued, have created greater awareness in brand acquisition (Mokhlis, 2006), brand managers need to find the more blurred division between what is permitted and what is forbidden from the Islamic religious lens. The dangers come also from refusing the brand for anti-religious causes, which mean that brand-building endeavours in Islamic societies could collapse in such collectivist, ultra-conservative contexts. When the brand loses its face and thus its social value, the overall brand value could be severely diminished. On the contrary, focusing on representing the brand within Islamic communities as one which connects members of the society and participates in social occasions in harmonious manners will lead to a greater brand resonance in relevant markets. Muslim consumers will not face issues as a result of using Islamic-friendly brands in public, or even in the private case. The inclusion of CSR to the social value of brand is an advancement to the domain of this dimension of consumption by joining variant concepts in marketing into one unified construct.

Affective value of brands

This dimension reflects on how brands can provide value through provoking feelings and affective states. Consumption in general poses positive (or negative) emotions (Holbrook and Hirschman, 1982), and brands are keen to supply end users with emotional benefits. Consumers search for products to respond to a normative desire for convenience, joyfulness, happiness and other hedonic motives (Chaudhuri and Holbrook, 2002; Danes et al., 2012), and Muslim consumers are not an exception (Mokhlis, 2006). To theorise the affective dimension of customer value, Sheth et al. (1991a) referred in their theory to several models in psychology, including clinical, environmental and experimental psychology, together with research developed in the field such as motivation research, personality, promotions and nonverbal processing.

Brands inspire passion, and other affective aspects can augment consumer value at this dimension. A growing body of research has recognised that feelings and emotions are essential factors in brand experience (Babin et al., 1994; Thompson et al., 2006). Das et al. (2009), for instance, presented the mechanism of emotions as a salient component of the 'soul' of brands which represent the way consumers feel when they are geared up by excitement, enjoyment and well-being. Thus, the notion of 'emotional branding' became a substantial topic concerned with differentiation by forging enduring emotive bonds between consumers and brands (Roberts, 2004). In effect, emotional response is an integral part of the overall perceived value, and brands work deliberately to communicate its value as emotional partners to consumers.

However, according to Islamic teachings, the use of emotional appeal as a means of marketing is forbidden, because it has elements of coercion and exploitation of people's psycho needs (Saeed et al., 2001). As a result, psychological literature suggests that religious-oriented individuals tend to behave in a relatively more mature, disciplined and responsible manner (Delener, 1990). However, researchers of religious consumer behaviours found that Muslims can be in the mode of spending more time and money for hedonic bases (Essoo and Dibb, 2004; Mokhlis, 2006). This can be interpreted in the shade of *Ibaha*, an Islamic principle which dictates that shopping, in the main, is effectively allowed in Islam. Again, brand managers need to play the game carefully and gain deep understanding of how to endow their brands with acceptable, i.e. halal, emotional value.

The research of emotion and consumption relationships is extended to cover a wide spectrum of topics and has mainly found that emotional value is a salient trigger of customer evaluations (Sweeney and Soutar, 2001; Tsai, 2005; Al-Makrami et al., 2013). However, among these findings, an important aspect that can be utilised by brand managers in Islamic marketing, and related to emotional value, is the concept of relational value. In Islam, the relation between individuals and nature is of central importance. Therefore, values such as gratitude, friendship, trust, respect, kindness and loyalty are amongst principles supported by the religion of Islam. For instance, according to Islamic teachings, the commitment (*A'ahd*) is a value that compares in importance to the fear of God, "But yes, whoever fulfils his commitment and fears Allah – then indeed, Allah loves those who fear Him" (Quran 3:76) and "do not break oaths after their confirmation" (Quran 16:91).

These values also lie with what considered as common practice of modern marketing and relational marketing, including CRM. Customer Relationship Management as a marketing tool necessitates that marketing communications should be designed by considering what customers love and hate about the brand experience. According to Fournier (1998), sustaining relationships with customers based on trust and respect are amongst key indicators of brand success. Also, Duman and Mattila (2005) as well as Sánchez-Franco and Roldán (2005) provided evidence of how brands are valued more positively due to their sense of goodwill and sympathy. Therefore, maintaining good relationships with Muslim consumers could be invaluable and augment the relational, affective value of the brand.

The other factor related to consumers' emotions and might affect the perceived affective value of the brand is *uncertainty avoidance*. Hofstede (1991) explained in his theory of cultural differences that uncertainty avoidance is an enduring behaviour that is significantly associated with religious societies. People who follow religions tend to be suspicious about ambiguity and adventure, two preferable branding tools used by brand designers. Customers in these markets seek clarity and honesty to feel more comfortable about their merchandise before and after buying decisions. Examples of ambiguous branding tools are numerous; however, puzzles about brand names (e.g. FCUK), slogans and sales as well as marketing campaigns in other international markets could affect the brand positioning in local markets. For instance, American Budweiser tried to market a *halal* beverage in the Muslim markets under the same brand name, but due to its previous image in Muslim consumers' minds as a leading alcoholic beer in the world, their penetration into local markets has failed. In contrast, the rival Heineken has achieved much success through the acquisition of an Egyptian brand (Fayrous) which already has the image of *halal* as a Muslim brand. Muslim consumers had no doubt about the acquired brand and thus have kept the positive relationships irrespective of the change in ownership.

These certain emotion-driven facets – relational value and uncertainty avoidance – should also shed light on controversial practices within this domain of affective value. Brand ambassadors should not overuse religious signs to attract a positive reaction by Muslim consumers. It has been noted in the literature that this behaviour could be regarded as an "exploitive and inappropriate use of religious verses" (Taylor et al., 2010, p. 79) and thus raise proselytising concerns about the brand's intentions. If that is the case wherein both brands and consumers have the same religious references, it might be worse if a Western brand communicates to Muslim (usually sensible) consumers. An Australian meat brand which indicates they produce 'halal pork' was just an example of the wrong communication conflict which caused the brand to back-fire within Muslim communities around the globe.

While Carroll and Ahuvia (2006) introduced the concept of 'brand love' to reflect on emotional benefits and attachment characteristics of the customer–brand relationship, these sub-values, though, extend the existing theory on the emotional value of brands. Sources of love can be numerous, and intelligent marketing should convey their message to touch on the feelings of customers without hurting them. The current literature discusses emotional value as a concept of 'this brand makes me happy', 'this brand is enjoyable to me', 'puts me in a good mood' (Sweeney and Soutar, 2001; Tsai, 2005), whereas little attention is paid to the relational aspect of the customer–brand interaction. This dimension is indeed time sensitive. Relationships between customers and brands can extend and take various types of connections (Fournier, 1998). The strength of this relationship can also vary based on what consumers believe about brands. For instance, during Muslims' boycott of Danish brands, Sun Top juice brand withstood the sentiment in Saudi Arabia owing to its lasting, warm relationship with customers in the local market.

Epistemic value of brands

The last dimension of brand value and applicable at brand level is the epistemic value. This type of value relates to new, different features experienced by the customer as a result of using a product (Sheth et al., 1991a). Relevant areas of research, including personality and educational and environmental psychology, led to the theorisation of distinctive response in consumer behaviour, including innovation utility (de Chernatony, 1993; Ambler, 1997), novelty utility (Long and Schiffman, 2000) and product creativity (Rubera et al., 2011). As brands, by definition, represent novelty and innovation, consumers usually associate the meanings of the brand with creativity and expect added value through the novel features found in the branded products (Holt, 2002). Global brands are gradually expected to initiate and launch state-of-the-art technology (Aaker, 1996) and thus "branding works as an innovation engine, to drive significant new domains of customer value" (Heding et al., 2009, p. 236). Variety, novelty, curiosity arousal, aspirations and complexity are amongst sought-after benefits of consumptions (Sheth et al., 1991b) whereby consumers seek to improve their lifestyles and learn new things (Rindova and Petkova, 2007). Therefore, Aaker and Jacobson (2001) proposed that consumers will become, in an era of rapid innovation, more inclined towards brands that help them to integrate themselves to a more sophisticated lifestyle.

Compared to other facets of value, epistemic value has little or no restrictions in Islam. On the contrary, Islamic teachings are always on the side of education and self-learning. The first verse in Quran was "*Iqra*" which means "*Read!*" and this verse is frequently referred to by Muslim scholars as evidence of the priority of science and education in Islam. It also shows the necessity of adopting an open-sources lifestyle as long as these resources are lawful and *halal*. At the least, applications of epistemic value such as novelty, creativity, innovation, knowledge seeking, trying new products or coping with latest technologies can be seen as a direct implementation of Islamic principle of *Ibaha* (i.e. the rule states that, in essence, everything is permissible). As a testimony of this argument, penetration of high-tech brands into Islamic markets has no difficulty compared to brands in more controversial sectors. For instance, three out of the top five brands in the Middle East in 2014 were companies working in telecommunication businesses; namely STC, Etisalat and Mobily (Brand-Finance, 2014).

The relationship between consumption and innovations in religious contexts has been also discussed in the 'diffusion of innovation' theory in the 1980s (Arnould, 1989). In these waves of research, several models of how consumers respond to innovation are presented, and prove that innovation is a trigger of consumption choices at various levels of involvement. The progression of technologies has helped in the production of innovative products to cater to ever-changing consumption patterns. However, in markets that are governed by collectivist cultures and religious institutions, people would be even more prone to adapt new products and transfer the novel experience to other members of the group (Mokhlis, 2006). From a pure Islamic perspective, advice (*Nasiha*) is a recommended act by Muslims who should transfer any good or bad experience to other *brothers* in the society. This argument supports the speculation that this curiosity-satisfying dimension of value has the ability to influence Muslim consumers' opinions about the brand.

Consequently, two implementations to enhance epistemic value utility for brands can be proposed in Islamic marketing. Firstly, brand positioning in relevant markets must include a part of innovation and superiority claims. Muslim consumers will have no issues with such positioning at their cognitive and behavioural levels of involvement, compared to over socialised or emotional messages. For brands entering the market for the first time, marketing managers should attract customers to the differentiation and newness provided by the brand. In an ideal Islamic society, people would have a strong desire to try new things under *Ibaha* philosophy. Once a perception is accumulated about a brand, it will be more likely to last for a long time. However, brands argue that their ability to satisfy hunger for curiosity or to provide an unusual experience should be at their 'promise'. Otherwise, users will disseminate bad word of mouth about brand capabilities and it will be hard to fix infected images in these markets.

Secondly, the value at this level of utility should be spelled out in brand communications and not left for market speculations. Customers should be informed about the specifications of the 'new' thing along with clear instructions on how to use the new technologies. Convincing conservative consumers to try new products or brands will necessitate more than imaginative advertising. As the competition rises between leading high-tech brands (e.g. Apple vs. Samsung) and the trial of second-tier brands to pose a reasonable market share (e.g. HTC, Sony LG, etc.), targeting underdeveloped markets with explicit communications and direct-to-the-point brand messages could help these brands to gain larger market share in the long term.

While epistemic value on its own could reflect entertainment as well as knowledge-seeking motives (Sheth et al., 1991a), caution should be taken when targeting Muslim consumers. In Islam, Muslims are asked to spend time in useful actions that benefit oneself in the current life and, ultimately, at the day of Judgement. Although the concept of *halal* entertainment i.e. halal travel, halal media, halal games, is a common practice by Islamic businesses, the doctrine of spending huge amounts of time on leisure lifestyles and useless actions is a sin in Islam, "Man's feet will not move on the Day of Resurrection before he is asked about his life, how did he consume it, his knowledge, what did he do with it . . ." as the Prophet (pbh) said. Therefore, Muslims have been alerted in many verses in Quran about amusement and diversion and the effect of that on a believer's status (Quran 6:32, 29:64, 47:36), and thus Allah says "What is with Allah is better than diversion and than a transaction, and Allah is the best of providers" (Quran 62:11). The brand managers should be careful in advertising their products as time-wasting or 'full of diversion' and it is better to position them as providers of knowledge and learning useful things in life.

Conclusions

As religion is sacred and its value system is accepted unquestioningly by believers, marketers cannot forgo the analysis of religion in their decision making and market analyses (Delener, 1990). This view prevails more in Muslim countries wherein Islamic teachings are applied to all walks of life, compared to Western and capitalist markets, which build their social systems on the premise of the separation of Church and State (Epstein, 2002). Furthermore, as Muslim consumers adapt more Shariah conscious lifestyles, the need for customised marketing strategies will be more apparent to ensure the access of global brands into Muslims' hearts and minds. Such customised strategies can be translated into business opportunities that seek to provide Islamic versions of mainstream Western products and services such as fast food, gyms and luxury hotels, to mention only a few. Islam, therefore, should be viewed as a stable variable having a great influence on marketing and consumption.

Within Islamic contexts, international knowledge can by no means substitute Islamic knowledge simply because the Islamic market is fundamentally different in terms of motivations, structure and behaviour. Religion plays a central role in the decision-making process of Muslim consumers, and efforts to neutralise its effects on customers' decisions will backfire. Although acquiring such knowledge might seem lengthy and expensive, it is the only path to success with the increasingly observant Muslim consumer. While the implementation of Islamic-affirmed marketing programmes seems worth the cost paid in terms of time, money and even the amendment of brand values, the process can be performed effectively based on a thorough understanding of the Muslim consumer, the Shariah principles, and the implications of the concept of halal on various organisational marketing aspects. The Islamic doctrine of consumption should not be seen to threaten global brands, instead it must be seen as a customer need requirement that should be dealt with using professional, less ideological marketing systems.

Therefore, brands should carefully examine their cultural understanding when entering Islamic markets. Relying on classical, culture-free, branding expertise while overlooking the interlinking between cultural values and consumption values could greatly hamper branding efforts, whether domestic or international in scope. A hasty entry without thorough appreciation of the religious and cultural motivations and reasons underlying the Muslim consumer behaviour could hinder or even completely impede a brand's existence in relevant markets. Global brands, especially those based in the West, should be welcomed in the Muslim world provided that they can adapt their operations so that their Muslim clients are comfortable with their market practices. In other words, brand managers should embrace Islamism and not simply transmit and impose the dominant culture or values of the brand on which they are based. These businesses are allowing Muslims to express their religious principles through helping them to buy Islamic products, connecting to their Islamic roots by what they eat, wear and play.

Nevertheless, the concept of Islamic marketing is still in its infancy and thus has created a lively debate in recent years (Alserhan, 2010). Even though relevant trends portend a growing market for global brands, there is as yet no clear consensus on how best to advocate enduring value for Muslim consumers through the understanding of Islamic value systems. The brand, despite enjoying a worldwide clientele, that fails to look after its offerings as Shariah compliant will endure financial and penetration difficulties. Therefore, the current work is designed to help global brands to overcome the barriers that can prevail in its introduction and operation in Islamic markets or when building relationships with Muslim consumers. The Islamic concept of value maximisation has been introduced as a means that may provide a solution to this puzzle of building a shining image for a non-Islamic brand in the Muslim markets. Whenever the Muslim consumer feels and finds that brand values do not conflict with Islamic value systems, or even enhance them at individual and communal levels, the brand will be valued more positively and its market share will be more likely to grow.

Within the brand management realm, Gobe (2001, p. xxi) writes: "consumers . . . expect the brand to play a positive, proactive role in their lives." In a similar point of view, Keller (2012) points out that brand managers should not only depend on brands' intangibles; they have to help consumers to achieve their desired goals by responding to their personal and social or cultural needs. Specifically, in advertising, endorsement, direct sale and other elements of branding, brand strategists are called for to scrutinise contents and avoid confrontations with even the spirit of religion, let alone the basic principles. The peril of penetration into Islamic markets is the potential dilution of brand equity, should a penetration fail. Therefore, a careful assessment of religious value orientations will surface new brand opportunities and advocate a platform for repositioning attempts of existing brands trying to mitigate any negative effects from inadequate brand messages in the past. It also challenges prevailing beliefs about the importance of a unified global image and the role of brand communications, and expands the definition of 'best value' to the customer.

Managerial implications

The payoff for investing in Islamic markets can be great, but so can the risks. Marketers should keep an eye open whilst designing the contents and process for brands targeting Muslim consumers. Specifically, communicating the value of the brand should be in line with Islamic teachings by knowing the permissible i.e. *halal*, and the forbidden i.e. *haram* practices. The following discussion attempts to provide 'food for thought' for marketers developing Islamic brands as well as other international brands, by deploying the principle of value maximisation in brand value communication and thus capitalise on the brand equity in target markets.

First and foremost, brands should speak more to reason than passion while venturing and operating in Islamic markets. Islamic teachings oblige followers to be more responsible, less materialistic and appreciate objects as if they are presents from God. Spending many resources on worthless articles, or using them for a mere social show-off boasting are unacceptable behaviours in Islam. Of equal importance, marketers are ordered by Islamic codes of ethics to be honest about product quality and less aggressive when retailing products and to never use emotional appeals in their marketing activities. Marketing and brand managers should not step outside of the restraints of Islamic roles in this matter. Instead, focusing on permissible, yet preferable, aspects of the multiple dimensions of value provided by the brand and using the right track of communications would lead at the end of the day to equal financial outputs and avoid cultural clashes or anti-brand sentiments rising based on ideological motives. Marketing strategists might benefit from considering relevant principles of value maximisation as a predictor of Muslim consumer behaviour rather than simply as correlates of item purchasing.

From a functional value perspective, the product quality is of prime importance in Islam. *Itqan* is a term used by Islamic scholars, and producers are highly expected to provide reliable products to the market, otherwise the marketer or the brand would be considered as *"not one of us"* and thus could be out of Muslims' consideration set. Not surprisingly, brands that are associated with superior quality are always preferred by customers, and for Muslims they are correlated in mind with positive associations. Whereas the majority of MNCs tend to transcend a fictional image of their brands, it will be wise to include the notion of quality in brand communication in Islamic markets. For instance, Apple's advertising rarely provides testimony of its products' quality while in the meantime focusing on intangible features. If Apple uses more directive ways to instruct consumers about its superior quality compared to its rivals, for instance, the brand might even draw out more customers and increase its market share in the Islamic markets. Similarly, the economic value of the brand is linked to its perceived quality in the marketplace. While overrated prices are vulnerable to criticism according to Islamic teachings, brands can justify the high-priced tags by explaining their products' worthiness and sources of the excellence. For instance, as McDonalds charges more for its cheeseburger, almost double the price of street shops or even next door rivals such as KFC, they could inform customers about the eminence of their burger's ingredients in comparison to others.

For social and emotional value, the situation with added value is more controversial for the Muslim observant. As intimated previously, social value as understood by a classical school of consumption experience transfers personal values such as ego and individualistic meanings, concepts that are not honoured in Islam. Brand managers should instead focus on the social value as a motive of togetherness that helps individuals to define themselves within preferred groups in their social contexts. What other renowned brands such as Mango and Dior offer to the market as pure Islamic products (*Ihram* dress – for *Haj* [pilgrims to Mecca] and *hijab* [scarves], respectively) are two cases in point. Such creative marketing solutions prove what brands can do to help Muslim consumers identify themselves as Muslims, yet wearing well-received brands. With emotional value, brands can prove themselves as participatory partners of values that are accepted by the doctrine of Islam, including CSR and societal issues. To ensure an affective relationship with – usually sensible – Muslim consumers, brands should communicate a hassle-free image that provides clarity and honesty to end users.

Finally, MNCs should promote their image as a leading brand that advances technology and innovation in the market by providing high-end products. There is no sensitivity in Islam towards the epistemic value of consumption, and thus brands can show their best in this dimension of contemporary lifestyle. Brand communications, i.e. TV ads, should be informative about the brand's abilities and superiority. For instance, if LG or HTC would like to hit dominant brands in the mobile phone market (Samsung and Apple), they should demonstrate what their products can do that others can't. This can be done via long informative TV ads or by using YouTube services which should show in detail the superior epistemic value of the brand.

Issues for further discussion

1   What are the implications of the classical term "brand equity" and its components in comparison to the concept of "brand value" that has been discussed in this chapter and its dimensions: functional, economic, social, emotional and epistemic? Any conflict/harmony between the two terms with respect to the Islamic value-maximisation principle?

2   What most integral dimension of value do different global brands accommodate to reach out to the majority of Muslims? To what extent would singular-perspective of brand value have an impact on Muslim consumers versus multiple-perspective marketing communications?

3   What is the likeability for global brands to design a unified message for both Islamic and global audience? What is the empirical contributions for "glocal" marketing strategies?

4   How can appropriate processes be established to ensure a rigorous, systematic approach to recruiting and managing a Halal Committee that can assess the multiplicity of global brand value(s)?

Case study

Nestlé: the role model

Nestlé S.A. is a diversified global food company, established in 1905 in Switzerland. It is by now the world's largest food and beverage company and employs over a quarter of a million workers. The company started with condensed milk and infant formula. Now Nestlé sells baby food, bottled water, cereal, chocolate and other confections, frozen food, dairy, drinks, food service, health and sports nutrition, pet care and weight management products. With respect to its global business, Nestlé invests in countries where raw materials are produced and at the same time strives to be as decentralised as possible so that local decisions are made locally. Some of the basic Nestlé values and principles are to:

- show respect for diverse cultures and ensure operations integrate with them.
- encourage all employees, led by senior management, to follow these principles by integrating them into Nestlé's business processes.

Through smart strategic management decisions focused on enhancing their Shariah-friendly credentials, Nestlé succeeded and became a leading multinational company when it comes to developing marketing strategies for Muslim consumers. Nestlé produces over 100 brands, including many well known household names in Islamic markets such as Nescafé, Kitkat and Nesquik. Nestlé was a pioneer in identifying Muslim shoppers as an important demographic who should represent 50% of the potential audience in the so-called "next 11" emerging economies. The multinational shows a commitment in everything it does, from product design through to communications. Therefore, according to their compliance with Shariah, Nestlé's brands topped the Ogilvy Noor Brand Index table as brands most appealing to Muslims.

Nestle is one of the largest halal food manufacturers with halal sales of more than $5 billion, and has a strong presence in several nations where the majority of the population is Muslim, including Malaysia and Indonesia. Nestlé Malaysia produces about 300 halal products in its food and beverage range which are exported to more than 50 countries worldwide. Nowadays, a total of 85 out of Nestlé's 456 factories worldwide are halal certified. A halal inspection authority, such as the Halal Food Council of Europe, inspects the company's factories with a Nestlé Halal Committee member to ensure products comply with Islamic law before halal certification is awarded. But how does Nestlé excel in providing value to Muslim consumers, in line with the Islamic philosophy of value maximisation?

Functional value

Nestlé has built a solid reputation on the quality and purity of its products. Its slogan: Good Food Good Life, conveys a strong message about their organisational objectives of producing nutrition, health and wellness. To assure Muslims in a such controversial product category, the world's biggest food group has adopted a wider Shariah-friendly approach by publishing nutritional details about items on its product line. For instance, Nestlé Malaysia's Halal Policy outlines information on ingredients, sourcing, production, packaging and transportation of Nestlé halal products. While Islam mandates the principle of *Itqan* (quality assurance), Nestlé's factories apply advanced systems with high standards to track trends in quality data to make more accurate and timely decisions about process improvements. Therefore, halal certified products are sourced, manufactured, imported and distributed in accordance with Islamic law to meet the needs of Muslim consumers. A Halal Committee which includes senior executives from various areas in the company was established in the 1980s. It has become part of the policy to ensure it addresses matters in relation to halal certification in all factories of Nestlé worldwide. In Islamic terms, what such committees perform imitates the duties of *Hisba* system in Islam, both aims at the confirmation of product's quality and appropriation.

Economic value

Customers recognise that Nestlé charges reasonable prices for their products. Prices are affordable to almost all types of consumers and for different economy classes. For instance, Nestlé Water is sold at the same price as that of other local or low quality products in Saudi Arabia, while maintaining its quality. Compared to the French Evian and the Scottish Highland Spring, which are sold at much higher prices, Nestlé is more attractive to the Muslim consumer according to Islamic value system. Customers have become smarter and more investigatory, they respect Nestlé for its balanced pricing strategy over developed and developing markets whereby the price tags are almost similar across its geographical markets and product lines. When Muslim consumers travel abroad and compare its products' prices at local and international markets, they will appreciate the frankness of the company and feel the good deal of buying a global brand with high quality and low prices. They appreciate that the world's leading food company strives to maintain a good value-for-money motive irrespective of volatile currency values and raw material prices. When it intends to up the prices, the food manufacturer announces its update in a statement like "sharp upward movements and increased volatility in the commodity markets in the past year *forced* us to advance price increases for finished goods so as to partially absorb the higher input costs." Such clarification is consistent with Islam's permissibility of lifting prices when the marketer ought to, providing the honesty and clarity. The well-received economic value of Nestlé and its Shariah-compliant written principle of "prefer long term development over short term profit" protects its position during inflationary pressures and political instability in many Islamic regions.

Social value

Nestlé supports togetherness by investing in out-of-home consumption where people can gather and spend time together. It also creates social value by adding micronutrients to foods to improve health in impoverished regions, where many suffer from emerging markets. Over time the company has become a natural part of society, nourishing generations of Muslim families who appreciate the social value of the brand of Nestlé's brands and extend that to its diversified product lines. Nestlé also tries to be a genuine partner in sustainable development by increasing sustainable farming techniques in developing countries. Sustainable development is defined by Nestlé as "the process of increasing the world's access to higher quality food, while contributing to long-term social and economic development, and preserving the environment for future generations." This strengthens the connection to Nestlé's commitment to 'green' movement and developing new policies and initiatives on eco-efficiency and responsible business practice. Nestlé balances this against the need for growth whilst these practices can encompass ethical sourcing policies, an emphasis on nutrition and fair trade, which overlap with other aspects of CSR. While the efforts performed by Nestlé, an obvious connection to its brand portfolio must be clear to Muslim consumers to capitalise on the accumulated positive brand image. This is essential given the fact that some well-known brands of Nestlé are marketed individually and some consumers might not have realised that these brands were Nestlé products.

Affective value

Nestlé feels that it has a real role to show a genuine empathy and understanding with its business partners, suppliers and customers around the world. Responsible business practices don't just make moral sense; they make good business sense. The company has therefore developed policies and principles to help it meet its general aims of fairness, honesty and concern for people. Therefore, Nestlé has initiatives in building long-term relationships with its customers. For example, in Pakistan sales of milk per farmer have doubled in the last three years as a result of the support from Nestlé Agricultural Services provided to more than 115,000 farmers. As posted in the MNC's website: "Nestlé, through its activities wherever it operates, has to bring meaningful value to society at large by creating both direct and indirect jobs, working with farming communities, training and developing people, as well as bringing products to the market adapted to the taste and nutritional needs of local consumers. This is part of Nestlé's DNA and the long-term approach we take to everything we do." There is no doubt that such an emotional, responsible brand message has positioned Nestlé to be a leading brand in Islamic markets for a long time. This is because being engaged at individual and communal level is an important factor that humanises a firm, as opposed to seeing that firm as a purely commercial entity with selfish bottom line interests; it is like giving an MNC a local passport and accepting it as a member of the community instead of stamping it as a villain. The relational aspect also appears in one of the basic Nestlé values and principles: *to develop long term commitments and relationships with suppliers and customers*. The other preferred facet of emotional value associated with uncertainty avoidance is spelled out in another principle: *to recognise that consumers deserve information about the products they buy and the company behind the brand*. Muslim consumers are youthful, forward-looking consumers who are keen to engage with brands that can prove they are driven by the ethical principles behind Shariah law, and Nestlé has been responding to these principles in a transparent manner.

Epistemic value

Nestlé has been able to increase its competitive advantage by continuing to innovate or renovate products, gaining global market share and brand recognition, investing in innovation and market predictions. It has a large R&D division which affirms its commitment to creativity and innovation. This is coupled with innovative advertising which Nestlé can afford when its competitors might not be able to, at the same level. For instance, Nestlé sets a goal of 4% new organic internal growth in order to gain a global market share of the newly developed category of organic food. However, when targeting Islamic markets, Nestlé can be more creative by responding to local dietary systems and might help people around the globe to exchange the culture of food. There are several local meals that are not in the global menu and Muslim consumers cannot find easily when going abroad. For instance, while the Italian pasta (Buitoni) is popular in the Muslim market, can the Saudi Kabsa (rice and chicken cooked in high pressure pot) or the Egyptian Falafel (fried minced vegetarian) be marketed in Italy and other European countries?

Case questions for discussion

1 In which dimension of consumption values does Nestlé excel in terms of applying value maximisation implications to enhance its Islamic-friendly image? Explain how by giving real life examples.
2 How does Nestlé respond to Muslim consumers' culture of uncertainty avoidance?
3 When Nestlé applies CSR initiatives, does the religious factor appear clearly? Why or why not?
4 What could be the items of a developed value scale embracing the five dimensions of brand value?

Note

1 Peace be Upon Him.

References

Aaker, D. A. (1996), "Measuring Brand Equity Across Products and Markets", *California Management Review*, Vol. 38, No. 3, pp. 102–120.

Aaker, D. A. and Jacobson, R. (2001), "The Value Relevance of Brand Attitude in High-Technology Markets", *Journal of Marketing Research*, Vol. 38, No. 4, pp. 485–493.

Abdul-Cader, A. (2015), "Islamic Challenges to Advertising: A Saudi Arabian Perspective", *Journal of Islamic Marketing*, Vol. 6, No. 2, pp. 166–187.

Ahmad, K. (2002), "Islamic Ethics in a Changing Environment for Managers", in Sadeq, A. M. (Ed.), *Business and Management: Islamic and Mainstream Approaches*, London: Asean Academic Press.

Al-Faruqi, I. R. (1992), *AL TAWHID: Its Implications for Thought and Life*, Kuala Lumpur: IIIT.

Al-Ghazali. (1971), *Shifa al-Ghalil*, Baghdad: Al-Irshad Press.

Al-Makrami, A. H. (2013), *An Investigation Into Brand Value Dimensionality and Its Effects on Loyalty: Evidence From the High-Tech Brandscape in Saudi Arabia.* A doctoral thesis. London: Brunel University.

Al-Makrami, A. H., Yen, D. Y. and Melewar, T. C. (2013). *Brand Perceived Value: The Development of a Multidimensional Scale*, in Proceedings of the 42nd European Marketing Academy Conference. 4–7 June 2013, Istanbul, Turkey.

Al-Misri, A. N. (1991), *The Reminiscences of the Traveler: A Classical Manual of Islamic Sacred Law.* Trans. by Noah Ha Mim Keller. Abu Dhabi: Modern Printing Press.

Alserhan, B. A. (2010), "Islamic Branding: A Conceptualization of Related Terms", *Journal of Brand Management*, Vol. 18, No. 1, pp. 34–49.

AMA. (2004). [Online] www.marketingpower.com/mg-dictionary.php

Ambler, T. (1997), "How Much of Brand Equity Is Explained by Trust?" *Management Decision*, Vol. 35, No. 4, pp. 283–292.

Arnould, E. J. (1989), "Toward a Broadened Theory of Preference Formation and the Diffusion of Innovations: Cases From Zinder Province, Niger Republic", *Journal of Consumer Research*, Vol. 16, September, pp. 239–267.

Babin, B. J., Darden, W. R. and Griffin, M. (1994), "Work and/or Fun: Measuring Hedonic and Utilitarian Shopping Value", *Journal of Consumer Research*, Vol. 20, No. 1, pp. 644–656.

Berthon, P., Holbrook, M. B., Hulbert, J. M. and Pitt, L. F. (2007), "Viewing Brands in Multiple Dimensions", *MIT Sloan Management Review*, Vol. 48, No. 2, pp. 37–45.

Brand Finance. (2014). [Online] http://brandirectory.com/league_tables/table/middle-east-2014

Brodie, R. J., Whittome, J. R. M. and Brush, G. J. (2009), :Investigating the Service Brand: A Customer Value Perspective", *Journal of Business Research*, Vol. 62, No. 3, pp. 345–355.

Broyles, S. A., Schumann, D. W. and Leingpibul, T. (2009), "Examining Brand Equity Antecedent/Consequence Relationships", *Journal of Marketing Theory and Practice*, Vol. 17, No. 2, pp. 145–161.

Carpenter, J. M. (2008), "Consumer Shopping Value, Satisfaction and Loyalty in Discount Retailing", *Journal of Retailing and Consumer Services*, Vol. 15, pp. 358–363.

Carroll, B. A. and Ahuvia, A. C. (2006), "Some Antecedents and Outcomes of Brand Love", *Marketing Letters*, Vol. 17, No. 2, pp. 79–89.

Cayla, J. and Arnould, E. J. (2008), "A Cultural Approach to Branding in the Global Marketplace", *Journal of International Marketing*, Vol. 16, No. 4, pp. 86–112.

Chandon, P., Wansink, B. and Laurent, G. (2000). "A Benefit Congruency Framework of Sales Promotion Effectiveness", *Journal of Marketing*, Vol. 64, October, pp. 65–81.

Chaudhuri, A. and Holbrook, M. B. (2002), "Product-Class Effects on Brand Commitment and Brand Outcomes: The Role of Brand Trust and Brand Affect", *Jouranl of Brand Management*, Vol. 10, No. 1, pp. 33–58.

Danes, J. E., Hess, J. S., Story, J. W. and Vorst, K. (2012), "On the Validity of Measuring Brand Images by Rating Concepts and Free Associations", *Journal of Brand Management*, Vol. 19, No. 4, pp. 289–303.

Das, S., Stenger, C. and Ellis, C. H. (2009), "Managing Tomorrow's Brands: Moving From Measurement Towards an Integrated System of Brand Equity", *Journal of Brand Management*, Vol. 17, No. 1, pp. 26–38.

de Chernatony, L. (1993), "Categorizing Brands: Evolutionary Processes Underpinned by Two Key Dimensions", *Journal of Marketing Management*, Vol. 9, No. 2, pp. 173–188.

de Chernatony, L. and Riley, F. D. (1998a), "Defining a 'Brand': Beyond the Literature With Experts' Interpretations", *Journal of Marketing Management*, Vol. 14, pp. 417–443.

Delener, N. (1990), "The Effects of Religious Factors on Perceived Risk in Durable Goods Purchase Decisions", *Journal of Consumer Marketing*, Vol. 7, No. 3, pp. 27–38.

Duman, T. and Mattila, A. S. (2005), "The Role of Affective Factors on Perceived Cruise Vacation Value", *Tourism Management*, Vol. 26, pp. 311–323.

Elliott, R. and Wattanasuwan, K. (1998), "Brands as Symbolic Resources for the Construction of Identity", *International Journal of Advertising*, Vol. 17, No. 2, pp. 131–144.

Epstein, E. M. (2002), "Religion and Business – the Critical Role of Religious Traditions in Management Education", *Journal of Business Ethics*, Vol. 38, pp. 91–96.

Essoo, N. and Dibb, S. (2004), "Religious Influences on Shopping Behaviour: An Exploratory Study", *Journal of Marketing Management*, Vol. 20, No. 7/8, pp. 683–712.

Forbes. (2011), *The Brand Keys 12 for 12: Brand and Marketing Trends for 2012.* [Online] www.forbes.com/sites/marketshare/2011/12/13/the-brand-keys-12-for-12-brand-and-marketing-trends-for-2012-part-1/ (accessed 13 December 2011).

Fournier, S. (1998), "Consumers and Their Brands: Developing Relationship Theory in Consumer Research", *Journal of Consumer Research*, Vol. 24, No. 1, pp. 343–373.

Gallarza, M. G., Saura, I. G. and Holbrook, M. B. (2011), "The Value of Value: Further Excursions on the Meaning and Role of Customer Value", *Journal of Consumer Behaviour*, Vol. 10, pp. 179–191.

Gobe, M. (2001), *Emotional Branding: The New Paradigm for Connecting Brands to People*, New York: Allworth Press.

Heding, T., Knudtzen, C. F. and Bjerre, M. (2009), *Brand Management: Research, Theory and Practice*, London: Routledge.

Hill, D. (2003), "Why They Buy: What Really Goes on in the Mind of the Consumer", *Across the Board*, Vol. 40, No. 6, p. 27.

Hofstede, G. (1991), *Cultures and Organizations: Software of the Mind*, London: McGraw-Hill.

Holbrook, M. B. and Hirschman, E. C. (1982), "The Experiential Aspects of Consumption: Consumer Fantasies, Feelings, and Fun", *Journal of Consumer Research*, Vol. 9, September, pp. 132–140.

Holt, D. B. (2002), "Why Do Brands Cause Trouble? A Dialectical Theory of Consumer Culture and Branding", *Journal of Consumer Research*, Vol. 29, No. 1, pp. 70–90.

Ibn Al-Ukhuwa, D.-D. M. (1983), *Ma'alim al-Qurba fi Ahkam al-Hisbah*. London: Luzak.

Ibn Miskawayh, A. M. (1968), *The Refinement of Character*. Trans. by Constantine K. Zurayk. Beirut: The American University of Beirut.

Jafari, A. and Süerdem, A. (2012), "An Analysis of Material Consumption Culture in the Muslim World", *Marketing Theory*, Vol. 12, No. 1, pp. 61–79.

Kainth, J. S. and Verma, H. V. (2011), "Consumer Perceived Value: Construct Apprehension and Its Evolution", *Journal of Advanced Social Research*, Vol. 1, pp. 20–57.

Keller, K. L. (1993), "Conceptualizing, Measuring, and Managing Customer-Based Brand Equity", *Journal of Marketing*, Vol. 57, January, pp. 1–22.

Keller, K. L. (2006), "Measuring Brand Equity", in *The Handbook of Marketing Research: Uses, Misuses, and Future Advances*, pp. 546–568.

Keller, K. L. (2012), "Understanding the Richness of Brand Relationships: Research Dialogue on Brands as Intentional Agents", *Journal of Consumer Psychology*, Vol. 22, No. 2, pp. 186–190.

Koller, M., Floh, A. and Zauner, A. (2011), "Further Insights Into Perceived Value and Consumer Loyalty: A 'Green' Perspective", *Psychology and Marketing*, Vol. 28, No. 12, pp. 1154–1176.

146 *Ali Al-Makrami and Dorothy Yen*

Kotler, P. (2003), *Marketing Management*, 11th ed. Upper Saddle River, NJ: Pearson Prentice Hall.

Long, M. and Schiffman, L. (2000), "Consumption Values and Relationships: Segmenting the Market for Frequency Programs", *Journal of Consumer Marketing*, Vol. 17, No. 3, pp. 214–232.

McCracken, G. (1988), *Culture and Consumption: New Approaches to the Symbolic Character of Consumer Goods and Activities*, Bloomington: Indiana University Press.

Mittelstaedt, J. D. (2002), "A Framework for Understanding the Relationships Between Religions and Markets", *Journal of Macromarketing*, Vol. 22, No. 1, pp. 6–18.

Mokhlis, S. (2006), "The Effect of Religiosity on Shopping Orientation, an Exploratory Study From Malaysia", *Journal of American Academy of Business*, Vol. 9, No. 1, pp. 64–74.

Monroe, K. B. (1973), "Buyers' Subjective Perceptions of Price", *Journal of Marketing Research*, Vol. 10, No. 1, pp. 70–80.

Mulhem, F. J., Williams, J. D. and Leone, R. P. (1998), "Variability of Brand Price Elasticities Across Retail Stores: Ethnic, Income, and Brand Determinants", *Journal of Retailing*, Vol. 74, No. 3, pp. 427–446.

Na, W., Son, Y. and Marshall, R. (2007), "Why Buy Second-Best? The Behavioral Dynamics of Market Leadership", *Journal of Product and Brand Management*, Vol. 16, No. 1, pp. 16–22.

Niazi, L. A. K. (1996), *Islamic Law of Contract*, Lahore: Research Cell.

Oh, H. (2003), "Price Fairness and Its Asymmetric Effects on Overall Price, Quality, and Value Judgments: The Case of a Upscale Hotel", *Tourism Management*, Vol. 24, pp. 241–249.

O'Reilly, D. (2005), "Cultural Brands/ Branding Cultures", *Journal of Marketing Management*, Vol. 21, pp. 573–588.

Pihlström, M. and Brush, G. J. (2008), "Comparing the Perceived Value of Information and Entertainment Mobile Services", *Psychology and Marketing*, Vol. 25, pp. 732–755.

Pura, M. (2005), "Linking Perceived Value and Loyalty in Location-Based Mobile Services", *Managing Service Quality*, Vol. 15, No. 6, pp. 509–538.

Rindova, V. P. and Petkova, A. P. (2007), "When Is a New Thing a Good Thing? Technological Change, Product Form Design, and Perceptions of Value for Product Innovations", *Organization Sceince*, Vol. 18, No. 2, pp. 217–232.

Roberts, K. (2004), *Lovemarks: The Future Beyond Brands*, New York: Powerhouse Books.

Rubera, G., Ordanini, A. and Griffith, D. A. (2011), "Incorporating Cultural Values for Understanding the Influence of Perceived Product Creativity on Intention to Buy: An Examination in Italy and the US", *Journal of International Business Studies*, Vol. 42, pp. 459–476.

Saeed, M., Ahmed, Z. U. and Mukhtar, S.-M. (2001), "International Marketing Ethics From an Islamic Perspective: A Value-Maximization Approach", *Journal of Business Ethics*, Vol. 32, pp. 127–142.

Sanchez-Fernandez, R. and Iniesta-Bonillo, M. A. (2007), "The Concept of Perceived Value: A Systematic Review of the Research", *Marketing Theroy*, Vol. 7, No. 4, pp. 427–451.

Sánchez-Franco, M. J. and Roldán, J. L. (2005). "Web Acceptance and Usage Model: A Comparison Between Goal-Directed and Experiential Web Users", *Internet Research*, Vol. 15, pp. 21–48.

Sheth, J. N., Newman, B. I. and Gross, B. L. (1991a), *Consumption Values and Market Choices, Theory and Applications*, Cincinnati, Ohio: South-Western Publishing Co.

Sheth, J. N., Newman, B. I. and Gross, B. L. (1991b), "Why We Buy What We Buy: A Theory of Consumption Values", *Journal of Business Research*, Vol. 22, pp. 159–170.

Sweeney, J. C. and Soutar, G. N. (2001), "Consumer Perceived Value: The Development of a Multiple Item Scale", *Journal of Retailing*, Vol. 77, No. 2, pp. 203–220.

Taylor, V. A., Halstead, D. and Haynes, P. J. (2010), "Consumer Responses to Christian Religious Symbols in Advertising", *Journal of Advertising*, Vol. 39, No. 2, pp. 79–92.

The Guardian. (2014). [Online] www.theguardian.com/media-network/media-network-blog/2014/feb/18/islamic-economy-marketing-branding

Thomson, C. J., Rindfleisch, A. and Arsel, Z. (2006), "Emotional Branding and the Strategic Value of the Doppelgänger Brand Image", *Journal of Marketing*, Vol. 70, No. 1, pp. 50–64.

Tifferet, S. and Herstein, R. (2010), "The Effect of Indvidualism on Privae Brand Perception: A Cross-Cultural Investigation", *Journal of Consumer Marketing*, Vol. 27, No. 4, pp. 313–323.

Tsai, S.-P. (2005), "Utility, Cultural Symbolism and Emotion: A Comprehensive Model of Brand Purchase Value", *International Journal of Research in Marketing*, Vol. 22, No. 3, pp. 277–291.

Usunier, J. C. and Lee, J. A. (2005), *Marketing Across Cultures*, 4th ed. New York: Prentice Hall.

Vazquez, R., Rio, A. B. D. and Iglesias, V. (2002), "Consumer-Based Brand Equity: Development and Validation of a Measurement Instrument", *Journal of Marketing Management*, Vol. 18, No. 1/2, pp. 27–48.

Wilson, J. and Liu, J. (2010), "Shaping the Halal Into a Brand", *Journal of Islamic Marketing*, Vol. 1, No. 2, pp. 107–123.

Zeithaml, V. A. (1988), "Consumer Perceptions of Price, Quality, and Value: A Means-End Model and Synthesis of Evidence", *Journal of Marketing*, Vol. 52, pp. 2–22.

7 Islamic tourism products

Innovation in the tourism industry

Rusnah Muhamad

Learning outcomes

At the end of this chapter, readers should be able to:

1   Recognise that Muslims are now becoming an important consumer market for the entire world and forming an increasingly important segment for businesses across all sectors
2   Acknowledge the emergence of Islamic tourism as an increasingly popular sub-sector within the travel and holiday industry
3   Understand the product benefits at various stages for Islamic tourism products and services
4   Develop potential Islamic tourism products and services

Key points

1   The increasing Muslim populations in several emerging markets offer great opportunities for businesses; including for the tourism industry.
2   The growth of the new Islamic middle classes (young, educated and with a larger disposable income) has precipitated an increased propensity to travel, thereby indicating that travel and hospitality, and their various sub-sectors, now constitute one of the biggest markets within the Muslim consumer segment.
3   It is important to understand how Islamic values and norms affect Muslim travellers' needs and requirements while travelling in the offering of Islamic tourism products and services.
4   In order to be able to develop the potential Islamic tourism products and services that meet the requirements and needs of Muslim consumers in their quest for living proper Islamic lives, producers/managers need to understand the product benefits of Islamic tourism products and services at various stages.

Introduction

This chapter discusses the opportunities for developing innovative tourism products that target the Muslim tourist market segment. The innovation of products for this market segment needs to consider the specific needs of Muslim tourists while travelling. The two basic needs for Muslim tourists are the availability of halal food and facilities to perform the daily routine religious duties (particularly the daily prayers and fasting in the month of Ramadan). This chapter highlights and discusses the issues to be considered by marketers in the tourism industry in developing related tourism products for Muslim tourists/travellers. Henderson (2012) asserts that the Muslim market segment has become a powerful commercial force, and, hence, represents a major market opportunity and is becoming an increasingly important segment in the travel, tourism and hospitality industry. It has been reported that Muslim travellers spent US$142 billion on outbound expenditure in 2014 (representing 11 per cent of the global expenditure), and the amount is expected to grow to US$233 billion (representing 13 per cent of the global expenditure) by 2020.

The Muslim population is growing rapidly with Muslims residing in 200 countries. This represents more than 1.6 billion of the world's population, and is expected to increase at a rate of 35 per cent, rising to 2.2 billion by 2030, or 26.4 per cent of the world's total projected population of 8.3 billion (Akyol and Kilinç, 2014; MasterCard and CrescentRating, 2015). It has been forecast that by 2030, 79 countries are expected to have a million or more Muslim inhabitants (currently, only 72 countries) (Temporal, 2011). The majority of the world's Muslims (over 60 per cent) reside in the Asia-Pacific region, while about 20 per cent are located in the Middle East and North Africa. Although Muslims are expected to remain in relatively small minorities in Europe and the Americas, it is anticipated that they will constitute a growing share of the total population in these regions. Muslims are now becoming an important consumer market for the entire world and forming an increasingly important segment for businesses across all sectors. Faith is increasingly influencing the purchasing decisions of Muslim consumers, as has been demonstrated in the accelerated growth of the halal food, Islamic banking and lifestyle sectors over the last decade. MasterCard and CrescentRating (2015) report that, typically, Muslim consumers are young, educated and with a larger disposable income, which has precipitated an increased propensity to travel, thereby indicating that travel and hospitality, and their various sub-sectors, now constitute one of the biggest markets within the Muslim consumer segment. It has been predicted that Muslim travel will continue to be one of the fastest growing travel sectors in the world. Therefore, there is huge potential for producers in the tourism industry to innovate products and services that take into account the faith-based needs of Muslim travellers.

The travel and tourism industry is one of the world's largest industries with a global economic contribution (direct, indirect and induced) of almost USD 8 trillion in 2014, and 973.8 million international tourist arrivals worldwide. By 2030, international tourist arrivals are expected to exceed 1.8 billion. Although Europe has been the region that receives the largest number of visitors each year, more recently the Asia-Pacific region has grown to become the second largest destination for travellers. The direct economic impact of the industry, including accommodation services, food and beverage services, retail trade, transportation services and cultural, sports and recreational services contributed approximately US$2.6 trillion in 2014. DinarStandard and CrescentRating (2012) estimated that the global Muslim tourism market in 2011 was US$126.1 billion in outbound expenditure, covering leisure, business, and other tourism segments, which constituted 12.3 per cent of the total global outbound tourism expenditure in 2011. This expenditure excludes the core religious travel expenditure of *hajj* and *umrah* and is expected to grow by another 4.8 per cent through 2020, which is higher than the global average of 3.8 per cent (DinarStandard and CrescentRating, 2012). The tourist spending of Muslims is expected to grow to US$233 billion by 2020, representing 13 per cent of the global expenditure. The global increase in the number of well-educated and high earning committed Muslims (Akyol and Kilinç, 2014) provides a potentially lucrative market for airlines, tourism destinations and hotels/resorts that cater to the unique needs of Muslim travellers.

Table 7.1 Tourist arrivals in Malaysia for 2010–2014

Panel A: Non-OIC countries arrivals

Destination	2010	2011	2012	2013	2014	Growth (%)
Singapore	13,042,004	13,372,647	13,014,268	13,178,774	13,932,967	6.39
Thailand	1,458,678	1,442,048	1,263,024	1,156,452	1,299,298	−12.27
India	690,849	699,056	691,271	650,989	770,108	10.29
Australia	580,695	558,411	507,948	526,342	571,328	−1.64
UK	429,965	403,940	402,207	413,472	445,789	3.55
Germany	130,896	124,670	132,626	136,749	158,453	17.39
South Africa	26,395	31,441	23,635	22,473	22,667	−16.45

Panel B: OIC countries arrivals

Destination	2010	2011	2012	2013	2014	Growth (%)
Indonesia	2,506,509	2,134,381	2,395,448	2,548,021	2,827,533	11.35
Brunei	1,124,406	1,239,404	1,258,070	1,238,871	1,213,110	7.31
Saudi Arabia	86,771	87,693	102,365	94,986	113,921	23.83
UAE	25,645	24,212	14,365	18,253	19,772	−29.70
Turkey	9,149	8,577	9,909	12,109	10,448	12.43
Pakistan	–	–	79,989	81,397	97,144	17.66
Oman	–	–	22,166	27,869	34,534	35.81
Iraq	–	–	21,812	25,849	26,222	16.82
Egypt	–	–	15,463	20,352	25,605	39.61
Kuwait	–	–	12,224	12,775	16,493	25.88
Qatar	–	–	1,908	2,527	2,407	20.73

Source: Tourism Malaysia

Malaysia is a multicultural country located in the heart of Southeast Asia. It is renowned for its beaches, rainforests and diversity in culture, thus making Malaysia an attractive tourist destination. The data on tourist arrivals in Malaysia for five years (2010 to 2014) show that most of the tourists from the non–Organisation of Islamic Cooperation (OIC) countries are from Singapore and Thailand, followed by India, Australia and the UK (Table 7.1; Panel A). The tourist arrivals from the OIC countries (where the majority of the population are Muslim) are shown in Panel 2 of Table 7.1. The top three countries are Indonesia, Brunei and Saudi Arabia. Overall, the number of tourists from the OIC countries has increased, indicating the potential market for the Islamic tourism industry in Malaysia. In addition, Malaysia has been ranked number 1 in the top 10 halal-friendly holiday destinations for the OIC countries since it was first introduced in 2011 by the CrescentRating (DinarStandard and CrescentRating, 2012). In 2013, Kuala Lumpur was ranked number one in the top 10 halal friendly airports and second in the top 10 halal-friendly shopping destinations for the OIC countries. Therefore, there are opportunities for the tourism industry players in Malaysia to develop innovative tourism products for Muslim travellers.

Tourism and the economic contribution

Services are the highest sector contributing to the Malaysian gross domestic product (GDP), with a contribution of 55.4 per cent. The service sector contributes 3.1 per cent of the total of 5.5 per cent of the country's economic growth and has continuously contributed the highest share to Malaysia's economic growth for the past three years, from 2012 to 2014. Tourism is becoming the top foreign exchange earner next to manufacturing (Salleh et al., 2014), and is an important source of foreign exchange earnings in the service sector (RM72 billion in 2014, an increase of 27.4 per cent from RM56.5 billion in 2010). Malaysia is one of the world's leading tourist destinations. Furthermore, Muslim countries, including Malaysia, are becoming increasingly popular destinations for Muslim tourists following the tragedy that took place on 11 September 2000 (Syuriye and Daud, 2014; Al-Hamarneh, 2012; Salleh et al., 2010; Henderson, 2003). Tourist arrivals have increased from 24.6 million in 2010 to 27.4 million in 2014. The tourism industry provided 2.2 million jobs or 16.8 per cent of the total employment in 2013.

Malaysia is also acknowledged to be the world leader in the halal industry, providing an excellent ecosystem for innovative tourism products and services for Muslims. The halal certification process in Malaysia is under the jurisdiction of a government agency under the Prime Minister's Office, and, therefore, is considered credible and trustworthy. Malaysia released the first halal standard in 2000 and became the first country to have a documented and systematic halal assurance system. The Department of Islamic Development Malaysia (JAKIM) extended its halal section into a halal hub in 2005. JAKIM was the world's first halal certification body responsible for monitoring the halal industry. In 2011, the Trade Descriptions Act was amended giving JAKIM a stronger mandate to regulate the halal industry. Its programme for international halal bodies is the most stringent and sought-after bilateral halal system recognition programme in the world. To date, more than 50 international bodies have registered with the JAKIM halal programme. The Halal Industry Development Corporation (HDC) was later formed under the Ministry of International Trade and Industry (MITI) in 2008 to develop Malaysia's industrial capacity and bring foreign direct investment (FDI) into the country. Malaysia hosts two of the most important annual events in the halal industry, namely, the Malaysia International Halal Showcase (MIHAS) and the World Halal Forum (WHF). Currently, Malaysia is the leader in the global halal hub, exporting halal products worth RM35.4 billion annually and contributing approximately 5.1 per cent of the total exports of the country. The halal portfolio has also expanded beyond food and beverages, venturing into various other sectors, such as cosmetics, logistics, pharmaceuticals and, most recently, tourism. The halal industry and tourism are highlighted in the Eleventh Malaysia Plan as having the potential to generate high-income employment opportunities.

The concept of Islamic tourism

Although Islamic tourism has recently become an increasingly popular sub-sector within the travel and holiday industry, it is often neglected and underestimated. It is a new concept and is a fast growing market segment (Chookaew et al., 2015; Chanin et al., 2015). Various similar terms are used, such as halal tourism, Muslim friendly tourism or shariah compliant tourism. According to El-Gohary (2016), Islamic tourism is considered to be a sub-category of religious tourism. Al-Hamarneh (2012) explains that the term "Islamic" tourism consists of three main concepts – economic, cultural and religious conservative. The economic concept is an extension and expansion oriented concept that focuses on the importance of intra-Muslim and intra-Arab tourism in terms of the inclusion of new tourist markets and tourist destinations, particularly after the September 11 tragedy. Under this concept, Muslim countries are considered to be among the emerging tourist markets of the future with huge potential in terms of the economy, demographics and destination. The cultural concept for Islamic tourism includes the vision and idea that outline the inclusion of Islamic religious–cultural sites in tourism programmes. The religious–conservative concept of Islamic tourism considers the conservative interpretation and understanding of Islam in respect of the tourism products and services. Al-Hamarneh (2012) describes this concept as "community tourism" and mentions that the concept includes Islamic accommodation, Islamic destinations, and Islamic programmes and entertainment.

Recently, an increasing proportion of Muslims worldwide have been becoming more affluent and travelling with their families and friends, thus providing huge opportunities for the tourism industry to develop innovative Islamic tourism products and services to cater for the needs of this largely untapped but lucrative niche market. Islam is not simply a religion, but a way of life, and many Muslims strictly observe the religious requirements every single moment of their life and would not compromise their commitment just for the sake of relaxation/leisure. Therefore, it is crucial for producers of Islamic tourism products to fully understand the religious requirements of Muslim tourists to tap this segment of consumers.

Rahman (2014) defines tourists as people who visit and stay in places outside their usual location for more than a day and not more than one year for business, leisure or other purposes. Thus, tourism comprises the activities of persons travelling to and from, and staying in places outside their usual environment for leisure, business or other purposes (Chookaew et al., 2015). Islamic tourism is defined as the activities of Muslims travelling to and staying in places outside their usual environment for not more than one consecutive year for participation in activities that originate from an Islamic motivation, which are not related to the exercise of any activity remunerated from within the place visited (Akyol and Kilinç, 2014; Duman, 2011). Said (2015) defines Islamic tourism as any activity, event or experience undertaken in a state of travel that is in accordance with Islam. Similarly, Mohsin et al. (2015) describe halal tourism as the provision of a tourism product or service that meets the needs of Muslim travellers to facilitate worship or dietary requirements that conforms to Islamic teachings. Halal tourism is, therefore, a type of tourism that adheres to the values of Islam. In essence, Islamic tourism integrates the requirements of the religion of Islam in its products and services. These products and services may include tour packages and destinations, hotels and accommodation, restaurants and eating outlets, transportation, shopping and recreational activities.

Traditionally, Islamic tourism is generally related to religious activities, such as *hajj* and *umrah* (Fahim and Dooty, 2014). Henderson (2003) asserts that many Muslims also appear to share a common enthusiasm for leisure travel, as domestic and outbound tourism are increasing with their growing affluence. Similarly, Akyol and Kilinç (2014) argue that the increasing level of education and income of the Muslim population has changed the spending habits of this social group, and, hence, more Muslims are travelling for leisure and business purposes. According to Saad et al. (2014), there is an increasing number of Muslim travellers globally with the average spending being 10 to 50 per cent higher than that of the average leisure or business traveller. More importantly, Akyol and Kilinç (2014) stress that Muslim travellers want to remain loyal to their religious requirements. Hence, product offerings in the tourism industry must consider the specific requirements of Muslim travellers. Among the important considerations are the provision of halal meals, and facilities to perform daily prayers and activities that totally exclude gambling, drinking and all other party-related activities. The itineraries of the tour packages could include visits to mosques and other Islamic related sites as well as allocating appropriate time for prayers throughout the tour.

Characteristics of Islamic tourism products and services

Kotler and Armstrong (2014) define a product as anything that can be offered to a market for attention, acquisition, use or consumption that might satisfy a want or need. According to them, services are also considered as products. Consumers see products as complex bundles of benefits that satisfy their needs and wants (Kotler and Armstrong, 2014). These benefits can be categorised into three different levels – core consumer value/product, actual product and augmented product. Therefore, product developers need to understand the products and services to be developed based on these three distinct levels. This strategy is generally known as the total product concept or augmented product, or three levels of product or onion theory of marketing. The three different levels of products and services for the Islamic tourism products are illustrated in Figure 7.1.

The first level is the core consumer value/product. It is considered to be the most basic level and simply considers what consumers want to buy and what benefits producers would like their product to offer to consumers. The core consumer values/products for the Islamic tourism products are those elements that are considered the basic needs (core values) for Muslim travellers. As Muslim travellers need to eat and perform their daily prayers, the provision of halal meals or information concerning the accessibility of halal food and the availability of facilities for the daily prayers are treated as the core consumer values that should be included at the first level for service providers who plan to offer Islamic tourism products and services. Take for example, a tourist agency that wants to offer Islamic tour packages: it should include the provision of halal meals and set times with appropriate places (for example a mosque or a restaurant that provides a prayer room) for the daily prayers in the tour itinerary.

The second level is known as the actual product, which is concerned with translating the list of core product benefits into a product that consumers want to buy. There may be competitor products offering the same benefits in the market so the main aim is to design a product that will be preferred by consumers as compared to other available competing products. The second level involves deciding on the level of quality, product and service features, styling, branding and packaging. For the Islamic tourism products and services, the second level may include providing added facilities, which may enhance the satisfaction for Muslim travellers. For example, accommodation providers can provide a prayer

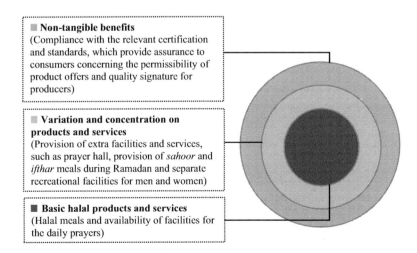

Figure 7.1 Onion theory of marketing for the Islamic tourism products and services

hall, special arrangements for *sahoor* and *ifthar* buffets in the month of Ramadan and separate recreational facilities (such as spas, pools and gyms) for men and women.

Finally, the producers of products should build an augmented product around the core benefit and actual product through the offering of additional consumer services and benefits; more often in the form of non-tangible benefits. Non-tangible benefits offer consumers peace of mind and demonstrate that the producer has faith in the quality of its product. For the Islamic tourism products and services, this level represents the compliance with the various certifications and standards of the industry players. In Malaysia, various certifications and standards are introduced to give assurance concerning the permissibility (halal) of a product, and as a quality signature from producers. A restaurant that possesses halal certification from JAKIM, for example, provides assurance and peace of mind to consumers of the food served as well as signifies that the restaurant operator has faith that the food served in the restaurant is genuinely halal.

Standards and rating tools in Islamic tourism

Shuriye and Daud (2014) emphasise that Islamic hospitality is driven by wisdom and courtesy, as prescribed in shariah law. Shariah law has precise rules concerning the process and procedure relating to matters, such as halal meals, accommodation, salutations and conversations, to ensure that guests feel safe and comfortable. The increasing awareness among Muslims for the need to lead their lives in accordance with the requirements of shariah affects the needs and requirements of Muslim travellers while travelling in terms of, among others, consuming halal meals, accommodation and entertainment, as well as recreational activities.

The Development of Standards Malaysia is the national standards and accreditation body that governs the issuance of all standards in Malaysia, including the halal standards (Halim and Salleh, 2012). The halal standards in Malaysia are developed through consensus by established committees that comprise a balanced representation of producers, users, consumers and other relevant stakeholders. Generally, Malaysian standards are adopted from or aligned to the greatest extent possible with the international standards (Halim and Salleh, 2012). Halal standards that are relevant to the Islamic tourism industry are *MS1500:2009 Halal Food – Production, Preparation, Handling and Storage – General Guidelines (Second Revision); MS1900:2005 Quality Management Systems – Requirements from Islamic Perspectives and MS2610:2015 Muslim Friendly Hospitality Services.* These standards are briefly discussed in the following section.

MS1900:2005 Quality Management Systems – Requirements from Islamic Perspectives

This standard was initiated based on the *ISO 9001:2000 Quality Management System* (QMS) standard, which is recognized worldwide, but with additional elements concerning quality management from the Islamic perspective. These elements include the aspect of the production process of halal products, delivery of services, and application of ethics and Islamic practical virtues in the workplace, such as fairness, honesty, sincerity, punctuality, discipline, dedication and systematic work.

MS1500:2009 Halal Food – Production, Preparation, Handling and Storage – General Guidelines (Second Revision)

This standard provides practical guidance for the food industry concerning the preparation and handling of halal food, and serves as a basic requirement for halal food products and food trade/businesses in Malaysia. However, this standard does not cover all the requirements needed for halal certification approval, which is under JAKIM's jurisdiction.

Hygiene, sanitation and food safety are prerequisites in the preparation of halal food. This includes the various aspects of personal hygiene, clothing, devices, utensils, machines and processing aids and the premises for the processing, manufacturing and storage of food. Halal food means food and drink and/or ingredients permitted under shariah law, which fulfil the following conditions:

a   does not contain any part or product of animals that is not permitted under shariah law or any part or product of animals that is not slaughtered according to shariah law;
b   does not contain najs (نجس) (unclean, impure, defiled, sinful and untouchable) according to shariah law;
c   safe for consumption, non-poisonous, non-intoxicating or non-hazardous to health;
d   not prepared, processed or manufactured using equipment contaminated with najs (نجس) (unclean, impure, defiled, sinful and untouchable) according to shariah law;
e   does not contain any human part or its derivatives that is not permitted by shariah law;
f   during its preparation, processing, handling, packaging, storage and distribution, the food is physically separated from any other food that does not meet the requirements as stated in items (a) to (e), or any other thing that is deemed to be *najs* (نجس) (unclean, impure, defiled, sinful, and untouchable) by shariah law.

MS2610:2015 Muslim Friendly Hospitality Services

The standard on Muslim friendly hospitality services comprises shariah guided requirements for the tourism industry players in setting up an assurance system to preserve the integrity of the products and services provided for Muslim travellers. The standard is developed with the aim of ensuring that the products and services provided for Muslim travellers are in accordance with shariah principles. The main objectives of this standard are:

a   to enhance the ability of an organisation/individual to produce and/or manage Muslim friendly tourism products and services that comply with shariah principles;
b   to preserve and protect the integrity of Muslim friendly tourism products and services through the effective application of the standard; and,
c   to enhance consumer satisfaction by fulfilling consumer requirements.

Analysing from the perspective of the onion theory of marketing, the certification and accreditation obtained under these standards are the non-tangible value added to the Islamic tourism products and services. The accreditation obtained manifests a signature of product warranty, which provides consumers with peace of mind and demonstrates that producers have faith in the quality of their products. CrescentRating is a well-recognised international and independent rating body for Islamic tourism (the term "halal" travel is used on its website). The following section discusses the role of CrescentRating as a rating system for Islamic tourism.

The CrescentRating: a rating system for Islamic tourism

CrescentRating is a Singapore-based Muslim travel consultancy firm. It was established in 2008 as the first world rating system for travel and hospitality services and facilities for

Muslim travellers. It developed the world's first rating system to rate travel and hospitality services and facilities for halal friendliness. These include the availability of halal food or information on halal food, prayer facilities and information relating to prayers and other related information that relates to the needs of Muslim travellers.

CrescentRating has developed a rating service that combines detailed analysis, assessment and benchmarking, and is now established as the premier halal standard for the tourism industry. The CrescentRating rating service is used by every tier of the tourism industry globally, from government bodies and tourism agencies to hospitality service providers. The CrescentRating rating system enables the producers of products and services in the tourism industry to design and develop products and services that meet and serve the needs of Muslim travellers. Currently, more than 200 hotels and restaurants are utilising the CrescentRating rating system to rate and certify their products and services. Services offered by CrescentRating include rating and accreditation, research and consultancy, workshops and training, ranking and indices, event support/partnerships and content provision.

CrescentRating first established the ranking for the top 10 halal friendly holiday destinations in 2011. The ranking criteria include the level of safety in a country, the ease of access to halal food and prayer facilities and whether hotels cater to the needs of Muslim guests. In 2011, the first year that the ranking was used, Malaysia was ranked number one, followed by Turkey, Egypt, Morocco and Indonesia. Others include Thailand, Sri Lanka, Singapore, South Africa and Australia (Gold Coast). CrescentRating also established the ranking for the top Muslim friendly shopping destinations. Dubai (United Arab Emirates) and Kuala Lumpur (Malaysia) were the two top Muslim friendly shopping destinations for 2011. These two destinations offer a great shopping experience for Muslim shoppers as well as ease of access to halal food and prayer facilities in the shopping malls.

The top 10 halal friendly holiday destinations were divided into two main categories in 2012, whereby the ranking was made separately for the OIC and non-OIC countries. Malaysia continues to lead the list for the OIC countries, followed by Egypt, Turkey, Indonesia and the United Arab Emirates. The other five countries are Morocco, Tunisia, Jordan, Brunei and Qatar. Bosnia and Herzegovina was ranked the top destination for the top 10 halal friendly holiday destinations among the non-OIC Countries. Others included Singapore, South Africa, Sri Lanka, Gold Coast (Australia), Delhi (India), London (UK), Bangkok (Thailand), Munich (Germany) and Vienna (Austria). Other rankings made by the CrescentRating in 2012 were for the top 10 halal friendly airports for both OIC (Kuala Lumpur International Airport, in Malaysia was ranked the top) and non-OIC countries (Suvarnabhumi International Airport in Bangkok was ranked the top), top 10 halal friendly shopping destinations (Dubai and Kuala Lumpur continue to lead the list), top 10 halal restaurants, top 10 halal food blogs/sites, and top 5 Islamic art museums.

CrescentRating began to publish the scores obtained by all countries surveyed for the top halal friendly holiday destinations in 2013. Table 7.2 presents scores for the CrescentRating Halal Friendly Travel (CRaHFT) for the top 10 halal travel holiday destinations. Malaysia heads the list for the OIC countries with a score of 8.3, and Singapore is top of the list for the non-OIC countries, with 6.3 points.

The top 10 halal friendly shopping destinations are presented in Table 7.3. Dubai is top of the list for the OIC countries, while Singapore still leads the list in this category for the non-OIC countries.

Table 7.4 presents the scores for the countries listed as the top 10 halal friendly airports. Kuala Lumpur International Airport (KLIA) in Malaysia leads the list for the OIC countries, while Suvarnabhumi International Airport in Thailand ranks first in the list for the non-OIC countries.

Table 7.2 CRaHFT – Top halal friendly holiday destinations for 2013

Ranking	OIC Countries	CRaHFT Score	Non-OIC Countries	CRaHFT Score
1	Malaysia	8.3	Singapore	6.3
2	Egypt	6.7	Bosnia & Herzegovina	5.9
3	UAE	6.6	Thailand	5.9
4	Turkey	6.6	South Africa	5.8
5	Saudi Arabia	6.4	India	5.6
6	Indonesia	6.1	United Kingdom	5.3
7	Morocco	6.1	Sri Lanka	5.2
8	Jordan	6.1	Australia	4.7
9	Brunei	6.0	Germany	4.5
10	Qatar	6.0	Hong Kong	4.5

Source: www.crescentrating.com

Table 7.3 CRaHFT – Top 10 halal friendly shopping destinations for 2013

Ranking	OIC Countries	Non-OIC Countries
1	Dubai	Singapore
2	Kuala Lumpur	Delhi
3	Istanbul	London
4	Jeddah	Bangkok
5	Cairo	Mumbai
6	Abu Dhabi	Johannesburg
7	Doha	Hong Kong
8	Jakarta	New York City
9	Amman	Melbourne
10	Bali	Barcelona

Source: www.crescentrating.com

Table 7.4 CRaHFT – Top 10 halal friendly airports for 2013

Ranking	OIC Countries	Non-OIC Countries
1	Kuala Lumpur International Airport (Kuala Lumpur)	Suvarnabhumi International Airport (Bangkok)
2	Dubai International Airport (Dubai)	Changi International Airport (Singapore)
3	Abu Dhabi International Airport (Abu Dhabi)	Manchester Airport (Manchester)
4	Ataturk International Airport (Istanbul)	Hong Kong International Airport (Hong Kong)
5	King Khalid International Airport (Riyadh)	Tambo International (Johannesburg)
6	Soekarna-Hatta International Airport (Jakarta)	Munich Franz Joseph Strauss Airport (Munich)
7	Doha International Airport (Doha)	London Heathrow (London)
8	Cairo International Airport (Cairo)	Bandaranaike International Airport (Colombo)
9	Queen Alia International (Amman)	John F Kennedy Airport (New York)
10	King Abdul Azeez International (Jeddah)	Melbourne Airport (Melbourne)

Source: www.crescentrating.com

CrescentRating has also established three other rankings, namely, the top 10 halal food Facebook pages, top 10 halal food websites/blogs, and top 10 destinations for newlyweds. Table 7.5 presents the list for the top 10 halal food Facebook pages and top 10 halal food websites/blogs.

The MasterCard-CrescentRating Muslim Travel Shopping Index (MTSI) is a jointly established index created by CrescentRating and MasterCard. This index was introduced in 2015. The MTSI comprises nine rating indicators; namely, shopping, safe travel, Muslim visitor shopping, dining options, prayer space area, airport services, accommodation, communication and visa requirements. The summaries of the top 10 halal friendly holiday destinations from 2011 to 2014, and the MasterCard-CrescentRating MTSI for 2015 for both categories of country are presented in Tables 7.6 and 7.7, respectively. Details of the

Table 7.5 CRaHFT – Top 10 halal food Facebook pages and top 10 halal food blogs for 2014

Ranking	Top 10 Halal Food Facebook Pages	Top 10 Halal Food blogs
1	Fauzia's Kitchen Fun	Fauzia's Kitchen Fun
2	"Its Yummy!! Yummy!! to my Tummy!!"	AinyCooks
3	AinyCooks	Laiji's Creative Corner
4	The Zayka Lounge	My Halal Kitchen
5	Delicious yummy recipes Dubai Halaal tried and tested	Yummy Food
6	Chaska House	Halaal Recipes
7	Home Food Cook – Bahrain	Cape Malay Cooking
8	Suzi and Shaz bite	Chocolate & Chillies
9	My Halal Kitchen	Halal Girl About Town
10	Cape Malay Cooking	Cooking with Thas

Source: www.crescentrating.com

Table 7.6 CrescentRating for the top 10 halal holiday destinations for 2011 to 2015 (OIC countries)

Rank	CrescentRating Halal Friendly Travel Ranking						Global Muslim Travel Index	
	2011	2012	2013	Scores	2014	Scores	2015	Scores
1	Malaysia	Malaysia	Malaysia	8.3	Malaysia	8.4	Malaysia	83.8
2	Turkey	Egypt	Egypt	6.7	United Arab Emirates	7.0	Turkey	73.8
3	Egypt	Turkey	United Arab Emirates	6.6	Turkey	6.7	United Arab Emirates	72.1
4	Morocco	Indonesia	Turkey	6.6	Indonesia	6.5	Saudi Arabia	71.3
5	Indonesia	United Arab Emirates	Saudi Arabia	6.4	Saudi Arabia	6.5	Qatar	68.2
6	–	Morocco	Indonesia	6.1	Morocco	6.4	Indonesia	67.5
7	–	Tunisia	Morocco	6.1	Jordan	6.3	Oman	66.7
8	–	Jordan	Jordan	6.1	Qatar	6.3	Jordan	66.4
9	–	Brunei	Brunei	6.0	Tunisia	6.2	Morocco	64.4
10	–	Qatar	Qatar	6.0	Egypt	6.2	Brunei	64.3

Source: www.crescentrating.com

Notes: CrescentRating halal friendly travel ranking started in 2011, but the scoring-ten was used in 2013. The ranking title was changed to the Global Muslim Travel Index in 2015, and scoring-hundred was used.

Table 7.7 CrescentRating ranking for the top 10 halal holiday destinations for 2011 to 2015 (non-OIC countries)

Rank	CrescentRating Halal Friendly Travel Ranking						Global Muslim Travel Index	
	2011	2012	2013	Score	2014	Score	2015	Score
1	–	Bosnia & Herzegovina	Singapore	6.3	Singapore	6.4	Singapore	65.2
2	–	Singapore	Bosnia & Herzegovina	5.9	South Africa	5.8	Thailand	59.4
3	–	South Africa	Thailand	5.9	Thailand	5.5	United Kingdom	55
4	–	Sri Lanka	South Africa	5.8	United Kingdom	5.5	South Africa	51.1
5	–	Australia	India	5.6	Bosnia & Herzegovina	5.5	France	48.2
6	Thailand	India	United Kingdom	5.3	India	5.4	Belgium	47.5
7	Sri Lanka	United Kingdom	Sri Lanka	5.2	Hong Kong	4.8	Hong Kong	47.5
8	Singapore	Thailand	Australia	4.7	Germany	4.8	United States	47.3
9	South Africa	Germany	Germany	4.5	Australia	4.8	Spain	46.5
10	Australia	Austria	Hong Kong	4.5	Tanzania	4.8	Taiwan	46.2

Source: www.crescentrating.com

Notes: CrescentRating halal friendly travel ranking started in 2011, but the scoring-ten was used in 2013. The ranking title was changed to the Global Muslim Travel Index and the scoring-hundred was used.

scoring for both the OIC countries and non-OIC countries for the nine rating indicators in 2015 are given in Tables 7.8 and 7.9, respectively.

The information in Table 7.6 shows that Malaysia was the top halal friendly holiday destination for the OIC countries from 2011 to 2014, as well as for the Global Muslim Travel Index when it was first introduced in 2015. The information in Table 7.7 exhibits the ranking for the non-OIC countries, in which Thailand headed the list in 2011, Bosnia and Herzegovina was ranked top in 2012, and Singapore topped the list for the non-OIC countries for the period from 2013 to 2015.

The detailed scores presented in Table 7.8 indicate that three cities in Malaysia – Kuala Lumpur, Penang and Malacca – have been rated in second, ninth and thirteenth place, respectively, among the top holiday cities for the OIC countries. Malaysia scored 100 points for the indicators – safe travel, prayer space area and airport services. As for the other indicators, those three cities obtained scores of more than 60 points. However, for the shopping destination, only Kuala Lumpur attained more than 50 points and was ranked in second place after Dubai, while Penang and Malacca achieved less than 10 points each. All OIC countries achieved 100 points for the prayer space area except for Bali, which only obtained 90 points. These countries also scored higher points for the dining options, safe travel and airport services. Malaysia leads on the indicators, such as accommodation, communication and visa requirements.

The scoring presented in Table 7.9 shows that Singapore, London, Paris, Bangkok and New York ranked as the top 5 for the non-OIC countries in 2015. Based on the established

Table 7.8 MasterCard-CrescentRating MTSI for the OIC countries in 2015

Rank	Destination	MTSI Score	Shopping	Safe Travel	Muslim Visitor Shopping	Dining Options	Prayer Space Area	Airport Services	Accommodation	Communication	Visa Requirements
1	Dubai	79.5	52.8	100.0	88.1	80.0	100.0	86.7	60.0	73.0	67.0
2	Kuala Lumper	73.3	53.7	100.0	37.4	90.0	100.0	100.0	65.0	71.8	94.0
3	Istanbul	64.2	41.3	83.2	48.6	75.0	100.0	86.7	48.0	40.0	58.0
4	Antalya	61.2	41.9	83.2	34.5	75.0	100.0	86.7	48.3	33.5	58.0
5	Doha	59.6	12.4	100.0	17.6	90.0	100.0	100.0	55.0	73.0	73.0
6	Manama	59.5	5.1	86.0	54.5	70.0	100.0	86.7	41.7	74.0	67.0
7	Riyadh	59.3	6.1	86.0	31.4	95.0	100.0	100.0	60.0	54.5	64.0
8	Bali	58.2	47.0	89.5	14.8	75.0	90.0	60.0	48.6	54.5	79.0
9	Penang	56.9	9.5	100.0	8.7	80.0	100.0	100.0	60.0	71.8	94.0
10	Sharjah	55.3	3.5	100.0	8.8	90.0	100.0	86.7	60.0	73.0	67.0
11	Abu Dhabi	54.8	5.1	100.0	12.3	80.0	100.0	86.7	60.0	73.0	67.0
12	Jakarta	54.3	11.4	89.5	9.6	80.0	100.0	100.0	48.6	54.5	79.0
13	Malacca	52.8	7.9	100.0	14.5	80.0	100.0	0.0	60.0	71.8	94.0
14	Amman	52.4	0.0	89.5	12.5	80.0	100.0	85.0	40.1	77.0	76.0
15	Marrakech	48.7	7.0	73.0	10.2	75.0	100.0	50.0	42.2	65.0	76.0

Source: www.crescentrating.com

Table 7.9 MasterCard-CrescentRating MTSI for the non-OIC countries in 2015

Rank	Destination	MTSI Score	Shopping	Safe Travel	Muslim Visitor Shopping	Dining Options	Prayer Space Area	Airport Services	Accommodation	Communication	Visa Requirements
1	Singapore	71.6	74.1	100.0	55.1	80.0	70.0	66.7	44.0	78.2	76.0
2	London	64.7	100.0	88.0	30.5	60.0	70.0	46.7	35.0	78.9	46.0
3	Paris	52.7	84.6	79.0	25.8	40.0	50.0	50.0	37.0	44.3	52.0
4	Bangkok	51.1	53.7	73.0	16.3	55.0	55.0	86.7	50.0	49.9	79.0
5	New York	49.9	84.5	85.0	18.8	45.0	30.0	41.7	30.0	77.5	40.0
6	Barcelona	46.6	71.3	94.0	25.6	40.0	25.0	41.7	27.0	16.0	76.0
7	Seoul	43.5	72.8	100.0	10.1	40.0	15.0	38.3	45.0	37.8	52.0
8	Phuket	41.8	29.0	73.0	10.6	50.0	50.0	53.3	50.0	49.9	79.0
9	Cape Town	39.4	4.3	82.5	13.1	55.0	65.0	63.3	21.2	56.1	52.0
10	Hong Kong	39.0	32.7	87.0	12.1	50.0	30.0	50.0	32.0	52.5	52.0
11	Johannesburg	38.5	8.1	82.5	0.0	60.0	65.0	50.0	21.3	56.1	52.0
12	Tokyo	37.4	43.0	100.0	7.9	35.0	30.0	56.7	28.7	24.2	40.0
13	Shenzhen	36.5	55.5	87.0	10.3	35.0	25.0	20.0	31.8	21.0	40.0
14	Berlin	35.6	20.3	91.0	0.0	40.0	35.0	70.0	33.0	51.7	52.0
15	Sydney	35.2	29.2	85.0	8.7	40.0	25.0	43.3	28.1	76.4	40.0
16	Amsterdam	34.5	15.2	85.0	0.0	45.0	45.0	38.3	25.0	51.7	55.0
17	Mumbai	33.5	10.8	68.5	0.0	50.0	50.0	50.0	32.1	43.0	40.0
18	Pattaya	32.5	8.1	73.0	0.0	40.0	45.0	20.0	50.0	49.9	79.0
19	Nairobi	31.9	15.4	62.0	9.7	45.0	40.0	56.7	21.1	34.6	46.0
20	Beijing	31.8	20.8	87.0	7.3	40.0	30.0	46.7	31.8	21.0	40.0
21	Shanghai	29.5	23.3	87.0	7.3	35.0	25.0	20.0	31.8	21.0	40.0
22	Milan	29.3	21.9	85.0	0.0	30.0	15.0	41.7	42.3	34.6	52.0
23	Rome	29.1	23.5	85.0	0.0	30.0	15.0	38.3	42.3	34.6	52.0
24	Moscow	26.6	4.0	78.0	10.7	30.0	25.0	43.3	26.0	37.5	46.0
25	Guangzhou	24.4	4.2	87.0	0.0	35.0	25.0	10.0	31.8	21.0	40.0

Source: www.crescentrating.com

indicators by CrescentRating, London leads for the shopping destination followed by Paris, New York and Singapore (the scores obtained are 100, 84.6, 84.5 and 74.1, respectively). However, for the Muslim visitor shopping indicator, only Singapore achieved more than an average score, with 55.1 points, while London ranked in second place with a score of 30.5 points. Three countries obtained 100 points for the safe travel indicator; namely, Singapore, Seoul and Tokyo. Other countries in the list achieved more than 50 points for this indicator. Singapore, Bangkok, Barcelona, Phuket and Pattaya earned more than 76 points for the visa requirements indicator. Singapore leads the list for the dining options (with a score of 80 points). London and Johannesburg both obtained the same score of 60 points and were ranked joint second. However, the majority of the countries in the list scored very low in terms of prayer space area and accommodation.

On the whole, the OIC countries need to improve in terms of three specific indicators – shopping, accommodation and communication – while the non-OIC countries ought to consider improving the indicators related to the dining options, prayer space area and accommodation.

Islamic tourism products and services – innovation opportunities

With the increasing Muslim population around the world, Muslims are now becoming an important segment for businesses across all sectors, including the tourism industry. There are great opportunities for the tourism industry players to innovate and offer tourism products that are able to meet the religious requirements of Muslim travellers. Among the potential products and services are *Muslim friendly accommodation, Muslim friendly airlines, Muslim friendly airports, Muslim friendly tour agencies, Muslim friendly shopping malls* and *Muslim friendly restaurants*. As previously discussed in Section 4 on the characteristics of Islamic tourism products, the fundamental criteria to be considered in developing Islamic tourism products are the availability of halal meals and facilities for Muslim travellers to perform their daily prayers. Therefore, the tourism industry players should at least consider including these two fundamental characteristics in their product offerings and specifically develop them for Muslim travellers. The following section presents a brief discussion on these products.

Muslim friendly accommodation

The review of the extant literature establishes that various definitions are used to describe the Islamic related accommodation concept (see for example, Saad et al., 2014; Ozdemir and Met, 2012; Zulkharnain and Jamal, 2012; Okasha, 2010; Weidenfeld, 2005; Henderson, 2003). Generally, these definitions can be broadly categorized into three main groups:

1   Dry accommodation/hotel – denotes that the accommodation/hotel does not serve alcohol on their premises.
2   Partially shariah compliant accommodation/hotel or also known as Muslim friendly accommodation/hotel – refers to accommodation/hotel that provides additional services for Muslims, such as halal food or information concerning the accessibility of halal food, prayer rooms, and provides a copy of the Quran and a prayer mat in each room, and separate facilities/separate time schedules for men and women.
3   Fully shariah compliant accommodation/hotel – describes accommodation/hotel that is fully governed by shariah law in all aspects of its operations including the facilities provided, design, interior and financial matters.

The extant literature on Muslim friendly hotels and related literature mentioned that the most fundamental services that are required by Muslim travellers are the availability of halal meals and facilities to perform the daily prayers, which includes a sign for Qiblah (the direction of Mecca), provision of prayer mat (readily available in the room or upon request from guests) and the availability of appropriate facilities for Muslim guests to perform ablutions (وضوء) and other related cleansing activities (قطهار) (see for example, Din, 1982; Stephenson et al., 2010; Razalli et al., 2012; Muhamad-Yunus et al., 2014).

Currently, no specific rating system for Muslim friendly hotels is available in Malaysia, as the hotels are simply rated according to the star rating system established by the Ministry of Tourism and Culture (MOTAC). The system assigns points from 1 to 10 for six different criteria to determine the star rating of a hotel. The six specific criteria used for the evaluation in granting the points are the appearance and cleanliness of the hotel common areas; availability and quality of hotel facilities; quality and ambiance of bedroom; quality and variety of services provided by hotel; safety and hygiene of hotel; and professionalism of hotel staff. The 5-star rated hotels are those hotels that have scored a minimum of 9 out of 10 points. Hotels with a minimum score of 7 points, 5 points, 3 points and 1 point are rated as a 4-star, 3-star, 2-star and 1-star hotel, respectively. The star rating system for hotels in Malaysia is given in Table 7.10.

As no specific rating on Muslim friendly hotels exists at present, hotels in Malaysia may use the CrescentRating guideline as a benchmark to guide them in providing specific services to fulfil the requirements of Muslim travellers if they are interested in tapping into the Muslim tourist market segment. The CrescentRating system is briefly explained in the following section.

The CrescentRating standard for hotels rates the overall halal friendliness of hotels on a scale of 1 to 7. A score of 1 represents the lowest rating and 7 stands for the highest standard. Table 7.11 explains in detail the indicators for the evaluation of the overall ratings.

The rating 1–3 denotes that hotels are considered as "helpful" to Muslim travellers and the information is made available for hotel guests upon request. Unless otherwise specifically stated in the hotel listing on CrescentRating.com or HalalTrip.com, these hotels do not provide halal food on their premises. A rating of 4 denotes that the hotels are considered as "accommodating" in terms of Muslim travellers. The hotels under this category are able to provide information regarding the prayer times and prayer direction as well as information concerning nearby halal food and mosques. These hotels may have some level of halal food services in their hotels, either halal breakfast and/or room service. The rating 5 is also considered as "accommodating" in terms of Muslim travellers. The hotels under this category are able to provide information regarding prayer times and prayer direction as well as information on nearby halal food and mosques. In addition, this category of hotel also has a halal certified kitchen or restaurant (except in the Middle East,

Table 7.10 The star rating system for hotels in Malaysia

Points Scored	Star Rating Granted
9–10	5
7–8	4
5–6	3
3–4	2
1–2	1

Table 7.11 CrescentRating indicators

Rating	1–3	4	5	6–7
Indicators	• Able to provide information on prayer times and prayer direction or nearby mosques. • Able to provide information on nearby halal food.	• Able to provide information on prayer times and prayer direction and nearby halal food and mosques. • Have some level of halal food services; either halal breakfast and/or room service.	• Able to provide information on prayer times and prayer direction and nearby halal food and mosques. • Have a halal certified kitchen or restaurant (except in the Middle East).	• Most of the needs of a halal conscious traveller in their services and facilities. • Serving only halal food and beverages apart from having other family friendly facilities.

Source: www.crescentrating.com

Table 7.12 CrescentRating criteria

Items Evaluated	Halal Food Facilities	Salaath (Prayer) Facilities	Services during Ramadan	Level of Non-halal Activities in the Hotel
1	Availability of list of halal restaurants in the vicinity.	Availability of list of mosques in the vicinity.	Availability of basic necessities for breakfast, e.g. dates and water.	Availability of any nightclub or casino.
2	Halal meals and menus.	Answers to queries concerning prayer time and direction.	*Ifthar* during Ramadan.	Any adult channel or non-halal friendly activity.
3	Halal items in the mini bar.	Quran, prayer mat and prayer timetable.	*Sahoor* and *ifthar* buffets.	Separate spa and pool times for men and women.
4	Halal certified kitchens.	*Qiblah* marked in the rooms.	Halal room services or halal restaurant in the area.	Completely separate spas, pools and gyms for women.
5	Halal certified restaurants.	All required facilities for a Muslim guest to perform their daily prayers.	Meals for *sahoor* and *ifthar* and transportation to local mosques.	
6	Only halal food and beverages on the entire premises.			

Source: www.crescentrating.com

where the majority of the population are Muslim, and, therefore, formal certification is not necessary). The rating 6–7 signifies that most of the needs of halal–conscious Muslim travellers are provided by the hotel. These hotels only serve halal food and beverages and also provide other family friendly facilities. These hotels are categorised as "specialised" hotels catering to Muslim travellers' requirements.

Table 7.12 shows the specific criteria that are evaluated to produce the overall ratings. There are four criteria altogether, which include the availability of halal food (six items are evaluated), Salaath (prayer) facilities (are evaluated based on five items), services provided during the month of Ramadan (are evaluated based on five items) and the level of non-halal activities that are available in the hotel (four items are evaluated). Therefore, hoteliers and accommodation providers who are interested in tapping into the Muslim guests market segment may want to consider the criteria discussed in this section as guidance for the products offerings relating to the provision of Muslim friendly hotel/accommodation.

Muslim friendly airlines

Air transport is the fastest growing sector in the transportation industry globally in recent years. It is one of the major sectors of the global economy, which generates annually about 413 billion dollars in revenue (Olipra, 2012). Bieger and Wittmer (2006) noted that air transport is the main form of transport to many tourist destinations, and, in some cases, constitutes up to 100 per cent of the international tourism arrivals. According to Olipra (2012), the air transport market has experienced significant and major changes globally. He mentions that one of the major changes is the emergence and rapid development of low-cost airlines, which makes air travel increasingly affordable to more people. The availability of cheap air transport is considered to be one of the main driving forces in the growth of international tourism (Bieger and Wittmer, 2006). Olipra (2012) further stresses that low-cost airlines can positively influence the less famous destinations and can help these destinations to promote and increase the number of tourist arrivals. The recent development in the Muslim tourist market segment, which has seen a high propensity for religious/business/leisure travel spending, provides opportunities for airline companies to innovate services that meet the needs and requirements of Muslim travellers.

The discussion in Section 4 highlights that the basic criteria in the product offerings for Muslim friendly tourism products are the availability of halal food and facilities/assistance to perform the daily prayers (such as the direction of *Qiblah* and information concerning prayer times). Additionally, airline companies can provide halal food for *sahoor* and *ifthar* in the month of Ramadan. Flight attendants can provide assistance and information concerning the prayer, *sahoor* and *ifthar* times for Muslim travellers or upon their request. Halal certification from an established religious authority can further enhance the product offerings giving Muslim travellers peace of mind and confidence in consuming the food served as well as in terms of the quality signature for these companies.

Some examples of the services provided by Muslim friendly/halal airlines, as found on the MuslimBreak website (www.muslimbreak.com/halal-friendly-airlines/), are illustrated in Table 7.13. The main focus of these airlines is providing fully certified halal food or serving certified halal food when a request has been made in advance by the traveller. Only Etihad Airways provides the direction of Qiblah and Islamic entertainment materials.

The discussion above provides clear guidelines concerning the consideration and necessary action to be taken by airline companies that are interested in tapping into the Muslim travellers' market segment.

Muslim friendly airports

Bieger and Wittmer (2006) highlighted that air transport was the main form of transport used by tourists to reach most tourist destinations. There is a global opportunity for airports to offer Muslim friendly airport services with the increasing number of Muslims travelling for business and leisure worldwide. Therefore, it is important for the airport management that are intent on offering Muslim friendly airport services to understand the basic religious requirements of Muslim travellers.

Table 7.13 Examples of Muslim friendly airlines

Airlines	Description of Services
Qatar Airways	The state-owned carrier operates in more than 140 destinations across all continents and has more than 150 aircraft. Among several dietary options (vegetation, vegan, diabetic, etc.) it offers a fully halal menu, completely free from haram products. Qatar Airways is a member of the Oneworld alliance, and was the first Gulf airline to sign with one of the three airline alliances. Definitely one of the most popular Muslim halal friendly airlines.
Etihad Airways	With its headquarters in Abu Dhabi, Etihad is the second largest government owned Emirati carrier and the third largest in the Middle East. Clearly Islamic-orientated, besides offering a fully halal menu, passengers can consume Islamic media content, such as audio prayers or relevant video material. One of the highlights is that the entertainment screens regularly show the distance from Mecca as well as the distance from the final destination!
British Airways	Although Muslim meals may not be available on all flights, British Airways generally follows a halal friendly policy, as they have many Muslim consumers. Muslim meals on Comair operated flights should be requested at least 48 hours before the flight departs.
Qantas Airways	Recently crowned as the safest airline in the world, Australian Qantas knows how to keep their consumers happy. It is the flag carrier airline of Australia and due to its multicultural character, it offers, among others, a fully halal meal on request.
Virgin Atlantic	The second most important British carrier, Virgin offers halal meals on all flights, regardless of the destination. The airline's Muslim-friendly menu does not contain pork or alcohol or derivatives of these products. The meat used is 100 per cent halal.

Based on the discussion on the basic considerations to be taken into account by marketers in offering Islamic tourism products in Section 4, the main criteria for Muslim friendly airport services would be the availability of halal food (that is, the availability of halal certified eating outlets/restaurants) and facilities to perform the daily prayers (that is, the availability of a decent prayer room situated in an appropriate location with facilities for ablutions). An increasing number of international airports in non–Muslim majority countries have taken the initiative to brand their airports as Muslim friendly. Among these are Thailand, Japan and the United Kingdom. However, Muslim friendly airports are more common in Muslim majority countries, such as Malaysia and most Middle Eastern countries, as halal food can easily be found and prayer rooms are available in most airports in these countries.

Examples of Muslim friendly airports in selected non–Muslim majority countries, namely, Thailand and Japan, are briefly discussed. In Thailand, examples of Muslim friendly airports are Suvarnabhumi Airport, Don Mueang International Airport, Phuket International Airport, Chiang Mai International Airport and Hat Yai International Airport (www.halaltrip.com/other/blog/thailands-best-airports-for-muslim-travelers/). Prayer rooms and halal restaurants can be found in these airports to cater to Muslim travellers. In Japan, Kansai International Airport, Narita International Airport, Haneda Airport, Fukuoka Airport and the New Chitose Airport are listed by HalalTrip as Muslim friendly airports (www.halaltrip.com/other/blog/facilities-for-muslims-at-japans-busiest-airports/). At Kansai International Airport and Narita International Airport, prayer rooms and facilities as well as halal restaurants are available to cater to Muslim travellers. However, at Haneda Airport and Fukuoka Airport, although prayer rooms and facilities are available, there are no known halal restaurants in these airports. Furthermore, in New Chitose Airport a multi-faith prayer room is provided but there are no known halal restaurants at this airport.

In conclusion, airport management may want to consider the basic requirements for Muslim travellers, as discussed in the preceding section, if they want to claim or brand their airports as Muslim friendly airports.

Muslim friendly tour agencies

The Tourism Industry Act 1992 defines a *travel agency business* as "any business that provides all or any of the services of selling, arranging or making available for commission, tickets entitling a person to travel on any conveyance either by land, sea or air." MS 2610 (2015) Muslim friendly hospitality services defines *travel agent* as "a company carrying on travel agency business under licence granted under the Tourism Industry Act 1992 (Act 482), and promotes, arranges and sells land, sea or air transportation, hotel accommodation and travel related services in Malaysia or outside of Malaysia for commission." According to Ayob et al. (2016), the role of a travel agency is to provide travel information, arrange the booking of appropriate transportation mode, prepare a travel itinerary, design a tour package, prepare the necessary travel documents and protection, and conduct tours.

The basic consideration for a travel agency in the offering of Muslim friendly tour packages is to ensure the availability of halal food and facilities to perform the daily prayers, as described in Section 4. Some examples of the possible considerations that may need to be included in the Muslim friendly tour package are listed in Table 7.14 (adapted from Ayob et al., 2016). The main aspects include accommodation, ground transfers, selection of tourism products, itinerary, facilities and travel protection.

Table 7.14 Basic considerations in a Muslim friendly tour package

Accommodation	Arrange accommodation that is compliant with shariah requirements, for example, the availability of the direction of *Qiblah* in the room, sufficient space in the room to perform the daily prayers, proper facilities for ablutions, hand bidet in washroom for cleansing, halal certified kitchen.
Ground transfer	Should comply with the applicable safety and regulatory requirements. The package should, upon request, be able to provide exclusive transportation for women guests.
Selection of tourism products	Tourism products included in the package should reflect the Islamic values experience, for example mosques, Islamic museums or Islamic related historical sites.
	Should not include in the itinerary visits to sites that manufacture non-halal or related products and activities that are not permissible by shariah, for example, liquor and pork, places of worship of other religions.
Itinerary	Should include allocated time in the schedule to cater to the need of Muslim tourists, such as time for the daily prayers and *sahoor* and *ifthar* during Ramadan.
Facilities	Should ensure that the selected tourism products have the appropriate facilities (such as prayer room with ablution facilities and washroom with hand bidet for cleansing purposes) for Muslim tourists and to ensure that these facilities are in good condition and clean.
Food & beverages	Should be certified halal by competent authority, and, if the package does not include meals, they should provide guests with a list of halal certified restaurants within the vicinity.
Travel protection plan	Provide shariah compliant protection scheme, i.e. *takaful*.

In summary, the above discussion provides guidance for the management of travel agencies that are interested in offering Muslim friendly tour packages about the basic criteria to be considered relating to the religious requirements for Muslim travellers.

Muslim friendly shopping malls

Mr. Taleb Rifai, the Secretary-General of the World Tourism Organization (UNWTO), states in the foreword of the Global Report on Shopping Tourism for 2014 that shopping is becoming an increasingly relevant component of the tourism value chain (UNWTO, 2014). He highlights that shopping is a significant determinant factor affecting destination choice, an important component of the overall travel experience, and, in some cases, the prime travel motivation. Therefore, tourism authorities have an immense opportunity to leverage on this new market trend by developing an authentic and unique shopping experience. More importantly, according to him, shopping is one of the major categories of tourist expenditure, representing a significant source of income for national economies both directly and through the many linkages to other sectors in the economy.

Shopping complexes/malls that aspire to attract Muslim shoppers need to at least consider making available the two basic religious requirements of Muslims, namely, halal food and facilities for prayers. These are the two core components of Islamic tourism products, as discussed in Section 4. Malaysia has become a major destination for shopping tourism in Southeast Asia. Three of the 10 largest shopping malls in the world can be found in Kuala Lumpur, namely,[1],[2] Utama (465,000 square metres), Mid Valley Megamall (420,000 square metres) and Sunway Pyramid (396,000 square metres). The Ministry of Tourism of Malaysia has created the Malaysian Mega Sales Carnival to promote shopping tourism in Malaysia. Generally, halal food and prayer rooms are easily available in most shopping complexes in Malaysia, which can be a major attraction for shopping destinations for Muslim tourists. Table 7.15 presents the top 10 biggest malls in the world (which include three from Malaysia), as listed on the Richest website (www.therichest.com/rich-list/nation/the-top-10-biggest-malls-in-the-world/).

Table 7.15 The top 10 biggest malls in the world

Rank	Malls	Brief Description
1	New South China Mall, Dongguan, China – 659,612 square metres.	Opened in 2005 and is located in Dongguan, China. It has space for 2,350 stores.
2	Golden Resources Mall, Beijing, China – 557,419 square metres.	Opened in 2004. It has more than 1,000 shops.
3	SM City North EDSA, Quezon City, Philippines – 482,878 square metres.	Opened in 1985 and has more than 1,100 shops and 400 dining establishments.
4	Isfahan City Centre, Isfahan, Iran – 470,000 square metres.	Opened in November 2012 and features more than 750 stores. It is the largest shopping mall in Iran and the Middle East.
5	1 Utama, Selangor, Malaysia – 465,000 square metres.	Opened in 1995, with a newer wing being inaugurated in 2003. The two wings feature more than 700 stores.
6	Persian Gulf Complex, Shiraz, Iran – 450,000 square metres.	Opened in September 2011 and has space for 2,500 stores. It is located in the city of Shiraz, the cultural capital of Iran.

Rank	Malls	Brief Description
7	Central World, Bangkok, Thailand – 429,500 square metres.	Opened in 1990 as the World Trade Centre. It was renamed to Central World Plaza in 2002 and to Central World in 2005. It features 495 shops and services.
8	Mid Valley Megamall, Kuala Lumpur, Malaysia – 420,000 square metres.	Opened in 1999 and features 430 stores and services.
9	Cehavir Mall, Istanbul, Turkey – 420,000 square metres.	Opened in 2005 and is the largest shopping mall in the European continent. It features 343 shops, 48 restaurants, 12 movie houses, a show stage, a bowling hall and a roller coaster ride.
10	Sunway Pyramid, Subang Jaya, Malaysia – 396,000 square metres.	Opened in 1997 with some redevelopment done in 2007. It has more than 800 shops and services available.

Muslim friendly restaurants

Food catering forms an important sector for the tourism industry as it is directly related to the satisfaction of tourists concerning their travelling experience. According to Scott and Jafari (2010), the food selection of tourists also has a religious aspect and plays a crucial role in shaping a tourist's destination selection criteria. According to them, the religious aspect of food selection criteria is very visible for Muslim tourists. Muslims can only consume halal food. Therefore, it is crucial for restaurants or any eating outlet that is planning to tap the Muslim consumers segment to ensure that they are selling halal certified food on their eating premises. Authorised halal certification will be even more crucial if the operators of the restaurant/eating outlet are not Muslims.

It is important for the operators of the restaurants/eating outlets to understand what halal actually means to Muslims so that they can fully abide by all the requirements of Islamic law regarding the preparation of halal food. Often, the concept of halal is still misconstrued by some restaurants/eating outlets operators as simply being "pork free" or the non-inclusion of pork related ingredients/alcohol in the preparation of the food served. The two main considerations that need to be taken into account by restaurants that aspire to be a Muslim friendly restaurant are that the food served on their premises has to be halal and the availability of proper facilities to perform daily prayers. Possessing halal certification from a well-established authorization body provides assurance to Muslim consumers that the food served is halal and is also a signature of quality on the part of the eating outlet operators as cleanliness is one of the critical aspect of halal.

Muslim travellers can search for halal restaurants in most parts of the world on the HalalTrip website. HalalTrip.com is a sister travel platform for CrescentRating.com. CrescentRating has migrated some of the content that was initially on the CrescentRating.com website to HalalTrip.com. HalalTrip is an online travel specialist catering specifically to the needs of Muslim travellers.

Conclusion

The goal of this chapter is to highlight the emergence of Islamic tourism as an increasingly popular new sub-sector within the travel and holiday industry. Recently, more Muslims worldwide are becoming more affluent and travelling with their families and friends, thus presenting huge opportunities for the tourism industry players to develop innovative Islamic tourism products and services to cater to the needs of this largely untapped but lucrative niche market. Understanding the needs and religious requirements of Muslim travellers is crucial for producers of Islamic tourism products and services to successfully compete in this consumer market segment. Adopting the onion theory of marketing, the most fundamental criteria to be considered in developing Islamic tourism products and services are the availability of halal food and facilities for Muslim travellers to perform daily prayers. Hence, interested marketers should include these two core consumer values in designing and developing the related Islamic tourism products and services.

Issues for further discussion

1   Is the Muslim tourist segment represented in the niche market that should be considered for product innovation in the tourism industry?
2   What are the available opportunities for the tourism industry players that wish to target the Muslim tourist segment?
3   Do you think that a global halal certification is necessary to boost the confidence among Muslim tourist on Islamic tourism products and services?
4   How should Islamic tourism products and services be branded and positioned in the global market?

Case study

The rating of halal-friendly hotels

Sonesta Hotel El Olivar is a luxury five-star family friendly hotel located across from the famous Olive Grove Park, in the heart of the San Isidro district of Lima, the vibrant capital of Peru. The Lima International Airport is 11 miles north of the hotel. The hotel was opened to the public in 1998. The hotel offers 134 luxury accommodation options for guests as well as a wealth of facilities including 12 meeting rooms, on-site gift shops, sports and fitness facilities and wireless Internet access. Sonesta Hotel El Olivar is a property owned by the Sonesta International Hotels Corporation. Sonesta Hotels own over 55 properties located in several countries around the globe – USA, Chile, Colombia, Ecuador, Egypt, Panama, Peru and the Caribbean. Sonesta Hotels boast over 75 years of experience in the hospitality industry and strives to offer guests a unique travel experience that reflects the culture of the destination.

The management of Sonesta Hotel El Olivar has recently decided to obtain accreditation as a Muslim friendly hotel from CrescentRating, a Singapore-based Muslim travel consultancy firm that specialises in the rating for travel and hospitality services and facilities for Muslim travellers. Mr. Carlos Reyes, the Corporate Director of Sonesta Hotel El Olivar, said, "We wanted to know more about Muslim travellers, their needs and what they expect from the hotels they visit. We then reached out to CrescentRating for their rating because we wanted the Muslim world to know that Peru could now boast Latin America's first five-Star hotel with a halal-friendly rating."

The management of Sonesta Hotel El Olivar has taken various actions to transform the hotel into a Muslim friendly hotel following that decision. With a commitment to cater to its Muslim guests, Sonesta Hotel El Olivar offers a wide range of facilities and services. For prayer facilities, guests are offered dedicated prayer areas as well as prayer mats and prayer timetables. Hotel rooms are marked with the direction for prayer for guests who prefer to pray in the privacy of their rooms. A list of the mosques located in close proximity to the hotel can be obtained on request should guests wish to visit a nearby mosque.

Muslim guests will find a number of halal dining options at Sonesta Hotel El Olivar, including a wide range of authentic Peruvian cuisine, which is halal certified by "Halal Peru". Room service menus also offer halal options. If required, the hotel is also capable of arranging halal banquets for guests – which is ideal for group reservations. *Ifthar* and *sahoor* facilities are available for Muslim guests who travel during Ramadan.

Other facilities for Muslim guests include a swimming pool with separate times for males and females. Sonesta Hotel El Olivar also offers a fully equipped fitness centre, on-site gift and souvenir shops and extensive meeting facilities that are capable of accommodating as many as 300 people.

Sonesta Hotel El Olivar is located across from Lima's historic Olive Grove Park and is just minutes away from several prominent sites in the city. The district of San Isidro is famed for its upscale residences, businesses, shopping complexes and parks, making it an excellent destination for leisure travellers and business travellers alike.

Case questions for discussion

1   What is the rating that will be awarded to Sonesta Hotel El Olivar based on the CrescentRating standard for the halal friendliness of hotels with the new wide range of facilities and services offered to cater to its Muslim guests?
2   Describe the product benefits that have been considered by the management of Sonesta Hotel El Olivar from the perspective of the onion theory of marketing in the offerings of its newly established services.
3   What is your advice to the management of Sonesta Hotel El Olivar to possibly improve the rating?

Notes

1 The case is based on information available on the Sonesta Hotel El Olivar and CrescentRating websites.
2 We would like to acknowledge the financial support provided by University of Malaya under the Equitable Society Research Cluster (ESRC) research grant RP007C-13SBC.

Bibliography

Akyol, M. and Kilinç, Ö. (2014), "Internet and Halal Tourism Marketing", *International Periodical for the Languages, Literature and History of Turkish or Turkic,*Vol. 9, No. 8, pp. 171–186.

Al-Hamarneh, A. (2012). *Islamic Tourism: A Long Term Strategy of Tourist Industries in the Arab World after 9/11?* www.staff.uni-mainz.de/alhamarn/Islamic%20Tourism%20-%20paper%20for%20BRISMES%20 2004.htm

Ayob, H., Amin, N. and Ramli, N. (2016), "Consumer Protection in Muslim Friendly Travel Agencies Services". Paper presented at the *International Language and Tourism Conference 2016* (ILTC 2016).

Bieger, T. and Wittmer, A. (2006), "Air Transport and Tourism-Perspectives and Challenges for Destinations, Airlines and Governments", *Journal of Air Transport Management,*Vol. 12, No. 1, pp. 40–46.

Chanin, O., Sriprasert, P., Abd-Rahman, H. and Don, M. S. (2015), "Guidelines on Halal Tourism Management in the Andaman Sea Coast of Thailand", *Journal of Economics, Business and Management,*Vol. 3, No. 8, pp. 791–794.

Chookaew, S., Chanin, O., Charatarawat, J., Sriprasert, P. and Nimpaya, S. (2015), "Increasing Halal Tourism Potential at Andaman Gulf in Thailand for Muslim Country", *Journal of Economics, Business and Management,*Vol. 3, No. 7, pp. 739–741.

CrescentRating. (2015), *CrescentRating's Halal Friendly Travel (CRaHFT)*. www.crescentrating.com/cres centrating-rankings.html (accessed December 2015).

Department of Standards Malaysia. (2005), *MS900:2005 Quality Management Systems- Requirements from Islamic Perspectives.*

Department of Standards Malaysia. (2009), *MS1500:2009 Halal Food.*

Department of Standards Malaysia. (2014), *MS2610:2014 Muslims Friendly Hospitality Services.*

Din, H. K. (1982), "Tourism in Malaysia: Competing Needs in the Plural Society", *Annals of Tourism Research,*Vol. 9, pp. 453–480.

DinarStandard and CrescentRating. (2012), *Global Muslim Lifestyle Travel Market: Landscape and Consumer Needs.* www.dinarstandard.com/travel-study/ (accessed December 2015).

Duman, T. and Tanrisevdi, A. (2011), "Profiling of English Tourists Visiting Turkey Based on Attitudes Toward Internet Use in Vacation Decision Making", *Journal of Hospitality Marketing and Management,*Vol. 20, No. 5, pp. 525–550.

El-Gohary, H. (2016). "Halal tourism, is it really Halal?" *Tourism Management Perspectives*, Vol. 19, pp. 124–130.

Fahim, S.T. and Dooty, E. N. (2014), "Islamic Tourism: In the Perspective of Bangladesh", *Global Journal of Management and Business Research: F Real Estate Event and Tourism Management,*Vol. 14, No. 1, pp. 21–26.

Halim, M.A.A. and Salleh, M. M. (2012), "The Possibility of Uniformity on Halal Standards in Organization of Islamic Countries (OIC) Country", *World Applied Sciences Journal,*Vol. 17, No. 17, 6–10.

Henderson, J. C. (2003), "Managing Tourism and Islam in Peninsular Malaysia", *Tourism Management,*Vol. 24, No. 4, pp. 447–456.

Henderson, J. C. (2012), "Conserving Heritage in South East Asia: Cases From Malaysia, Singapore and the Philippines", *Tourism Recreation Research,*Vol. 37, No. 1, pp. 47–55.

Kotler, P. and Armstrong, G. (2014). *Principles of Marketing* (14th Edition). New Jersey: Pearson Educations, Inc.

MasterCard and CrescentRating. (2015), *MasterCard-CrescentRating Global Muslim Travel Index 2015 (GMTI 2015)*. http://skift.com/wp-content/uploads/2015/03/MasterCard-Muslim-Index.pdf (accessed 22 March 2016).

Mohsin, A., Ramli, N. and Alkhulayfi, B. A. (2015). "Halal Tourism: Emerging Opportunities", *Tourism Management Perspectives.* Online first, http://dx.doi.org/10.1016/j.tmp.2015.12.010

Muhamad-Yunus, N. S. N., Abd-Razak, N., & Ghani, N. M. A. (2014). "Consumer purchase intention towards Sharia Compliant Hotel (SCH)". In S.M. Radzi, M.F.S. Bakhtiar, Z. Mohi, M.S.M. Zahari, N, Sumarjan, C.T. Chik, and F.I. Anuar, (Eds.), *Theory and Practice in Hospitality and Tourism Research* (pp.155–160). London: Taylor & Francis Group.

Okasha, Q. (2010). *Sharia Compliance Hotel a Framework for Destination Selection Applied on Kuwait and UK.* Unpublished thesis. Netherlands: Maastricht School of Management.

Olipra, L. (2012), "The Impact of Low-Cost Carriers on Tourism Development in Less Famous Destinations", *Cittaslow 2012*.

Ozdemir, I. and Met, O. (2012). "The Expectations of Muslim Religious Customers in the Lodging Industry: The Case of Turkey", In A. Zainal, S.M. Radzi, R. Hashim, C.T. Chik and R. Abu (Eds.), *Current Issues in Hospitality and Tourism Research and Innovation* (pp. 323–328). London: Taylor & Francis Group.

Rahman, M. K. (2014), "Motivating Factors of Islamic Tourist's Destination Loyalty: An Empirical Investigation in Malaysia", *Journal of Tourism and Hospitality Management*, Vol. 2, No. 1, pp. 63–77.

Razalli, M. R., Abdullah, S. and Hassan, M. G. (2012). *Developing a Model for Islamic Hotels: Evaluating Opportunities and Challenges*.

Saad, H., Ali, B. and Abdel-Ati, A. (2014), "Sharia-Compliant Hotels in Egypt: Concept and Challenges", *Advances in Hospitality and Tourism Research*, Vol. 2, No. 1, pp. 1–13.

Said, Z.M. (2015). Islamic Tourism: Sharing Malaysia's best practices on being the top Muslim Friendly holiday destination. Retrieved on 12 December 2015 from http://cf.cdn.unwto.org/sites/all/files/pdf/best_practice_islamic_tourism_centre.pdf

Salleh, N. H. M., Osman, R., Noor, A. H. S. M. and Hasim, M. S. (2010), "Malaysian Tourism Demand From the Middle East Market: A Preliminary Analysis", *Journal Antarabangsa Kajian Asia Barat*, Vol. 2, No. 1, pp. 37–52.

Salleh, N. Z. M., Hamid, A. B. A., Hashim, N. H., & Omain, S. Z. (2014). "The practice of Shariah-compliant hotel in Malaysia", *International Journal of Trade, Economics and Finance*, Vol. 5, No. 1, p. 26.

Scott, N., and Jafari, J. (Eds.) (2010). *Tourism in the Muslim World Bridging Tourism Theory and Practice, Vol. 2*. Bedfordshire: Emerald Group Publishing.

Shuriye, A. O. and Che-Daud, M. R. (2014), "Hospitality and Leisure Between Religious Maxims and Modern Facilities", *Mediterranean Journal of Social Sciences*, Vol. 5, No. 27, pp. 1127–1135.

Stephenson, M. L., Russel, K. A. and Edgar, D. (2010), "Islamic Hospitality in the UAE: Indigenization of Products and Human Capital", *Journal of Islamic Marketing*, Vol. 1, No. 1, pp. 9–24.

Temporal, D. (2011), "Islamic Branding and Marketing: Opportunities and Challenges", *European Financial Review June 2011*. www.europeanfinancialreview.com/?p=2829 (accessed December 2015).

Tourism Malaysia. *Resources, Facts and Figures*. www.tourism.gov.my (accessed December 2015).

UNWTO (2014), Global Report on Shopping Tourism, Affiliate Members Global Report, Volume 8. Retrieved on 22 March 2016 from http://www.e-unwto.org/doi/pdf/10.18111/9789284416172

Weidenfeld, A. (2005), "Religious Needs in the Hospitality Industry", *Tourism and Hospitality Research*, Vol. 6, No. 2, pp. 143–159.

Zulkharnain, A. and Jamal, S. A. (2012). "Muslim Guest Perception of Value Towards Syariah Concept Hotel", In A. Zainal, S.M. Radzi, R. Hashim, C.T. Chik and R. Abu (Eds.), *Current Issues in Hospitality and Tourism Research and Innovation* (pp. 337–340). London: Taylor & Francis Group.

Part III

Strategic global orientation

8   Global marketing and Islamic countries

Cedomir Nestorovic

Learning outcomes

At the end of this chapter, the reader should be able to:

1   Understand why economic environment is the decisive part of the environmental analysis for marketing
2   Understand why global marketing concepts such as the EPRG scheme or BoP (Bottom of the Pyramid) need to be adapted to Islamic countries
3   Understand the huge diversity in the Islamic world in terms of economic performance, expressed either in GDP growth or Gini index
4   Have an in-depth knowledge about how to analyse the economic environment of Islamic countries

Key points

1   Islamic countries represent an interesting opportunity for marketers because of the combined increase of population and purchasing power.
2   The analysis of the available GDP and GDP per capita figures does not reflect fully the potential Islamic countries because of hidden and non-reported incomes.
3   Clustering of Islamic countries as targets for marketers can be done according to geography, but also according to incomes and marketing convergence.
4   There is no natural centre for the Islamic world but some places, like Saudi Arabia, Malaysia, Bahrain and Dubai, vie for the leadership of the Islamic world as far as business opportunities and influence are concerned.

Introduction

Islam has a definite influence on Muslim consumer behaviour because this religion affects public life, private life and family life. From a marketing standpoint this is essential because Islam will define what is prescribed, what is forbidden or what is permissible, so the offer has to be in tune with the tenets of Islam. The Muslim behaviour is expected to be the same one for all Muslims worldwide and there should be just one offer for all Muslims. The Muslim world is however diverse and the differences are based on interpretations of Islam on one side and economic realities on the other side. For these reasons, it is difficult to have one unique homogenized Islamic market.

In this chapter we will focus specifically on the economic dimensions of the Islamic world and see how the differences between countries will influence a differentiated marketing approach.

Economic indicators and assessment of Islamic countries' potential market

Looking for relevant information and knowledge about the economic environment is not easy in general and in Islamic countries in particular (Nestorovic, 2016). The very fact that a large number of Islamic countries are relatively poor means that the quantity and quality of relevant information for marketers is reduced because the infrastructure for collecting and disseminating knowledge is not developed. Companies need to answer basic questions such as what to sell, why to develop a certain offer, where to establish operations and make products available and when to start operations and offer products and services (Fletcher, Harris and Richey, 2013). All this will be determined by economic factors. The usual definition of a market potential combines purchasing power of the potential consumers on one side and the number of potential customers on the other side (Sissors, 1966). The company needs a critical number of potential consumers and a minimal purchasing power. If for instance, Brunei has a high GDP per capita (US$77,900 per head) but a small population (440,000 inhabitants in 2015), it would be difficult for a company such as Coca-Cola to have a bottling unit for the Bruneian market alone. Coca-Cola would prefer to ship cans and bottles from Indonesia, Malaysia or Singapore where the market is bigger rather than the opposite.

Islamic countries, members of the Organization of Islamic Cooperation (OIC), have a very diverse situation when it comes to economic performance (see Table 8.1). Two basic indicators are usually taken into account when it comes to measuring economic performance: overall GDP and GDP per capita. The overall GDP is given at the current exchange rate but the problem is that very often currencies in the Islamic countries either are non-convertible or have their values fixed by the state and not the market. This is why the expression of the GDP at PPP (purchasing power parity) is much more useful because it tends to circumvent problems with inflation and exchange rates.

Table 8.1 Total GDP and GDP per capita at purchasing power parity in 2015 in OIC countries

Country	GDP at PPP in US$ billion	GDP per capita at PPP in US$
Indonesia	2,842	11,100
Saudi Arabia	1,683	53,600
Turkey	1,589	20,400
Iran	1,371	17,300
Nigeria	1,092	6,100
Egypt	1,048	11,800
Pakistan	931	5,000
Malaysia	815	26,300
United Arab Emirates	647	67,600
Algeria	578	14,500
Bangladesh	577	3,600
Iraq	544	15,500
Kazakhstan	429	24,300
Qatar	319	132,000
Kuwait	288	70,200

Country	GDP at PPP in US$ billion	GDP per capita at PPP in US$
Morocco	273	8,200
Uzbekistan	187	6,100
Oman	171	44,600
Azerbaijan	169	18,000
Sudan	167	4,300
Tunisia	127	11,400
Libya	92	14,600
Turkmenistan	88	16,400
Lebanon	83	18,200
Jordan	82	12,100
Uganda	79	2,000
Cote d'Ivoire	78	3,300
Yemen	75	2,700
Cameroon	72	3,100
Bahrain	64	50,100
Afghanistan	62	1,900
Syria	55	5,100
Senegal	36	2,500
Mali	35	2,200
Gabon	34	18,600
Brunei	33	79,700
Mozambique	33	1,200
Albania	32	11,900
Burkina Faso	30	1,700
Chad	30	2,600
Tadjikistan	23	2,700
Benin	22	2,100
Kyrgystan	20	3,400
Niger	19	1,100
Mauritania	16	4,400
Guinea	14	1,200
Sierra Leone	10	1,600
Togo	10	1,500
Suriname	9	16,300
Guyana	5	7,500
Maldives	5	14,900
Somalia	4	400
Gambia	3	1,600
Djibouti	3	3,200
Guinea Bissau	2	1,500
Comoros	1	1,500

Source: CIA World Fact Book and Statistical, Economic and Social Research and Training Centre for Islamic Coun-tries (SESRIC), a subsidiary organ of the OIC producing socio-economic information about the member countries. It can be reached at www.sesric.org

Islamic countries clusters according to total GDP

According to the table above, the disparity between the highest and the lowest GDP in the Islamic world is tremendous because the multiplier is 2,842 between Indonesia (2,842 bil-lion of dollars) and Comoros (1 billion) but we can also identify a certain number of clus-ters. The clusters will help marketers identify countries with similar level of development as expressed by the GDP, even if they are not geographically close to each other. The first cluster puts together six countries ranging from US$2,842 billion to US$1,000 billion.

These countries are Indonesia, Turkey, Saudi Arabia, Iran, Nigeria and Egypt. This group of countries might be joined by two other countries which are close to US$1,000 billion (Pakistan and Malaysia) provided there is no high political and/or economic instability in these two countries. Within this top group the ranking for Saudi Arabia can change according to the price of oil, which is the main export commodity of the Kingdom, and petroleum contributes 55 percent of the Saudi GDP. It is therefore extremely dependent on oil prices and the total GDP of Saudi Arabia can shrink drastically if the price of oil passes from US$140 per barrel to only US$40 per barrel as it happened between 2008 and 2009. In order to reduce its dependence on oil, Saudi Arabia launched an ambitious *Vision 2030* plan to increase non-oil revenues and stabilize the economy, but it remains to be seen how the plan is going to be implemented (*The Economist*, 2016). The position of Iran is interesting because it is at the fourth place even if the country is under embargo of a series of Western countries, including the United States. There is certainly a potential for growth for Iran, and if it happens that the economic embargo disappears totally, as the thawing of relations between the United States and Iran suggests (*The Financial Times*, 2016), there are serious chances that it could challenge Saudi Arabia in becoming the second most important Islamic country in terms of overall GDP (Indonesia is out of reach for the moment). A newcomer on the list is Egypt, which is slowly recovering from the revolution in 2011, so there are two African countries in the Top 6 for the first time.

The second group is also represented by six countries: Pakistan, Malaysia, the United Arab Emirates, Algeria, Bangladesh and Iraq. They are in the range of US$500–1,000 billion. They also represent different geographies because they span from Algeria to Bangladesh but the common element to practically all of them is the volatility. For a majority of countries in this group, volatility is linked to the price of oil (this is directly the case for Iraq, Algeria and United Arab Emirates but also to Malaysia to a certain extent), while in Pakistan, the political situation could impede its economic performance. However, with a total GDP at US$931 billion, Pakistan can very soon join the first group. On the other side of the Indian subcontinent, Bangladesh performs surprisingly well, but everything depends on the political stability, which used to be great in the past but deteriorated recently. Its economy, however, does not depend on oil and its price fluctuations, so its economic resilience is higher than for the UAE or Iraq.

The third group is larger, composed of nine countries in the range of US$100–500 billion per year. The countries are Kazakhstan, Qatar, Kuwait, Morocco, Uzbekistan, Oman, Azerbaijan, Sudan and Tunisia. Contrary to the first two groups of countries, where we have large populations (Indonesia, Nigeria, Pakistan and Bangladesh), in the third group on the contrary there are rather small populations, ranging from 38 million in Sudan to 2.5 million in Qatar (foreign workers included). Because the population is smaller, the GDP per capita could be higher than in the first two groups of countries seen above. Three more countries (Syria, Libya and Yemen) used to be part of this group but due to the open-war situation, Syria practically halved its GDP from US$107 billion in 2014 to US$77 billion in 2015 and Yemen and Libya also experienced a significant drop in their GDP from 2014 to 2015, making marketing efforts useless.

At the bottom of this list, countries such as Somalia, Guyana, Gambia, Maldives, Djibouti, Guinea Bissau and Comoros are in the range US$1–5 billion per year. This will present a serious challenge for marketers and raise some ethical problems linked to the sales to the poor and making profit out of selling to the poor. Even if many companies do their best to address the Bottom of the Pyramid (a concept we will look at later on), questions of ethical responsibility in addressing vulnerable population still exist (Brenkert, 1988; Palmer and Hedberg, 2013).

Islamic country clusters according to GDP per capita

The Organization of Islamic Cooperation groups countries where the majority of the population is Muslim or if the government decided to be part of the Organization even if Muslims do not represent the majority, such as Gabon, Guyana and Cameroon. Muslims live in Western countries as well and the market potential they represent can be quite big. If we take a conservative estimate about the Muslim population living in France for instance at about 6 million people and the average GDP per capita in France at US$41,200, the combined 'Muslim GDP' in France is worth US$247 billion. It is certain that all Muslims in France do not enjoy the average GDP per capita but it is the only indicator available for comparison with other countries. The result of this simple computation is that the Muslim market in France is bigger than that of Morocco, Tunisia or Jordan and is very close to the size of GDP in Kuwait. Marketers prefer to use the GDP per capita because it divides the overall GDP by the number of inhabitants in the country. It does not mean that this is the amount of money people dispose of in the country but it is useful for comparison purpose.

The multiplier between the first and last country on the list is 330 (Qatar with a GDP per capita at US$132,000 compared to Somalia at US$400). It is lower than the multiplier we have for the overall GDP when the multiplier is 2,842 between Indonesia and Comoros. The multiplier of 330 is, however, enormous because we cannot find this kind of discrepancy in any group in the world, be it the EU, NAFTA, ASEAN, or even the Organization of African Unity. The two extremes are in fact the biggest extremes in the world because Qatar has the highest GDP per capita in the world and Somalia has the lowest in the world. It means that from the GDP per capita point of view there is not one Muslim market but many of them. The first cluster is represented by Qatar alone. It is like playing in a league of its own because the second highest GDP per capita in the world is to be found in Luxembourg at US$99,000, which is much lower than in Qatar. In present circumstances there is no chance that any country from the list could approach Qatar in the near future. So Qatar is and will remain the single most important country from the GDP per capita point of view.

The second cluster is composed of six countries and it is in the range of US$40,000–79,700 per capita. This is not far away from the situation that exists in a series of developed Western countries such as Norway (US$68,400), Switzerland (US$58,600), Germany (US$46,900) and the United States (US$55,800). The six countries are Brunei, Kuwait, United Arab Emirates, Saudi Arabia, Bahrain and Oman, all oil and gas exporting countries and, with the exception of Brunei, all coming from the Gulf Cooperation Council (GCC). The GCC as a group outperforms the Arab non-GCC countries on a number of variables, and countries in the GCC tend to vary less among themselves than do the non-GCC countries. This is why this group is usually targeted first, because it represents a rather homogenized market in terms of language and consumer behaviour (Nissan and Niroomand, 2015). If the American or the German markets are interesting for companies from the GDP per capita point of view, the Saudi or the Bahraini markets should be interesting as well because figures are comparable. Of course, the number of people and their consumer behaviour is not the same, but the GDP per capita is.

The third group is composed of 18 countries in the range of US$10,000 to US$40,000 per head, including Malaysia, Turkey, Iran, Kazakhstan and Indonesia. This is in tune with some developed countries such as Japan and Italy, or some emerging European countries such as Slovakia and Russia. These 18 countries do not represent the most populous countries in the Muslim world like Bangladesh, Pakistan and Nigeria, which fall in the group of US$3,000–6,000 per capita but some of them are still populous, like Indonesia, Turkey and Iran. At first sight this group of countries with a GDP per capita lower than US$10,000 does not represent an attractive target unless we address the Bottom of the Pyramid on one side and the luxury segment on the other side. On the other hand, countries like Ukraine, the Philippines and Vietnam are also under US$10,000 per head and per year and all companies nevertheless want to access these countries. There is no reason that something which is valid for Vietnam at US$6,000 will not be valid for Uzbekistan and Nigeria (both of them at US$6,100).

The combination of overall GDP and GDP per capita singles out Indonesia, Iran, Turkey and Saudi Arabia as the countries with the highest overall GDP and interesting GDP per capita at the same time. All other countries either lack a high overall GDP, like in the case of Qatar, or a high GDP per capita for Bangladesh and Nigeria. According to these two criteria, these four countries make up the most attractive targets in the Islamic world for marketers.

Gini coefficient and Islamic countries

GDP per capita is an average figure dividing the total GDP by the number of inhabitants in the country, while the Gini coefficient or Gini index measures income inequality in a given country. A Gini coefficient of zero expresses perfect equality, for example, where everyone has the same income. A Gini coefficient of 1 (or 100 percent) expresses maximal inequality, for example, where only one person has all the income or consumption, and all others have none. From the marketing point of view, this coefficient is giving valuable information because if a car company targets three segments of the population (the affluent class, the middle class and low-income class) with different models of cars, the company will know immediately which type of cars it will put emphasis on in terms of communication. There is no point advertising on middle-class segment cars if there is a high Gini coefficient, because the population is made up of only super-rich and super-poor people. As far as OIC countries are concerned, their Gini coefficient is somewhere between 29 and 46, which is close to Western countries (see Table 8.2). All things being equal, it means that what is valid in terms of marketing approach in a country such as Norway, with a Gini coefficient of 33, would be similar to Bangladesh, with a Gini coefficient of 32. Things are, however, not equal between Norway and Bangladesh, especially when we consider the GDP figures. Therefore the Gini coefficient cannot be used alone. It must be used as an element among others in assessing the marketing potential of a given country.

For many countries in the OIC, there are no figures about the Gini coefficient, either because the country is at war, like in Afghanistan or Libya, or because the country does not want to publish results. The main reason why countries do not want to publish results is that they fear what would be the reaction of the population if the Gini coefficient is too high. The official statistics in China put the Gini coefficient at 46.9 in 2014, while many economists believe that the Gini coefficient in this country is much higher today. It is worth mentioning that no GCC country publishes data about the Gini coefficient. It cannot be because the population is too big. On the contrary it is quite small, so if a country like Nigeria with a much bigger population publishes its Gini coefficient, it can be done in the GCC as well. The bulk of incomes in the GCC come from the public sector, so there is a fair assumption that the government knows about incomes distributed to the population and computing a Gini coefficient should not be a problem.

Table 8.2 Gini coefficient in OIC countries (selected countries)

Country	Gini Index	Year
Albania	30	2008
Algeria	16.6	2005
Bangladesh	32	2010
Benin	43.4	2011
Egypt	30.8	2008
Gabon	42.2	2005
Guyana	44.6	1998
Indonesia	38	2011
Iran	37.4	2013
Iraq	29.5	2012
Kazakhstan	26.4	2013
Malaysia	46.3	2009
Morocco	40.7	2007
Pakistan	29.6	2010
Suriname	57.6	1999
Turkey	40	2012
Turkmenistan	40.8	1998
Uganda	42.4	2012

Source: Gini coefficient (World Bank estimate) at http://data.worldbank.org/indicator/SI.POV.GINI

Another pitfall for the Gini coefficient is the year of reference. In some cases like Uganda, Albania and Benin we have very recent figures (year 2013 in the first case and 2012 for the other two countries), but in the case of Turkmenistan and Guyana, the latest data go back to 1998 (Algeria posts results from 2005 only), which is more than 15 years ago, and information is not pertinent anymore. Many of the OIC countries have an important informal sector (which is not accounted for in the Gini coefficient), permitting people to consume even if official statistics show otherwise. This is particularly the case in rural areas where agricultural income is not declared, so we can have only assessments. This is why marketers have to take into account informal and non-declared incomes when they assess the purchasing power of populations in the OIC.

Diaspora and remittances

Since the majority of OIC countries fall in the Low Income Group or Low Middle Income Group of countries as defined by the World Bank, members of families living and working in developed countries contribute to the standard of living of people who stay at home. The remittances (money transfers from one country to another) represent a huge source of income for poor countries (see Table 8.3). For countries such as Pakistan, Egypt, Bangladesh, Nigeria and Indonesia, remittances are an important part of GDP and international institutions such as the World Bank and the International Monetary Fund scrutinize money transfers closely because remittances are considered to be an annual gift nationals working in developed countries send back home. To some extent the World Bank and the IMF would question why a country like Egypt is asking for a loan from multilateral organizations when at the same time the country receives US$10 billion each year free of charge from its nationals working in the Middle East. In case of war, and many of the OIC countries have a very unstable security environment, it is understandable that

Table 8.3 Remittances in 2015 expressed in US$ (selected countries)

Country	Receiving 2015	Outward flows 2015
Bahrain	0	2,364,000,000
Bangladesh	15,771,000,000	0
Cote d'Ivoire	385,000,000	736,000,000
Egypt	20,391,000,000	0
Indonesia	10,487,000,000	4,119,000,000
Iraq	277,000,000	548,000,000
Jordan	3,776,000,000	3,558,000,000
Kazakhstan	182,000,000	3,558,000,000
Kuwait	4,000,000	18,129,000,000
Lebanon	7,456,000,000	5,604,000,000
Malaysia	1,678,000,000	8,074,000,000
Morocco	6,679,000,000	0
Nigeria	20,771,000,000	0
Oman	39,000,000	10,301,000,000
Pakistan	19,609,000,000	0
Qatar	503,000,000	11,230,000,000
Saudi Arabia	274,000,000	36,924,000,000
Tunisia	2,347,000,000	0
Turkey	1,085,000,000	918,000,000
United Arab Emirates	0	19,280,000,000

Source: The World Bank, *Migration and Remittances Factbook 2016*

diaspora will actively participate in sustaining families living at home, much more than countries where this kind of problem does not exist (Carling, Erdal and Horst, 2012).

According to the World Bank, the three countries benefitting most from remittances are Nigeria, Egypt and Pakistan (in the range of US$20 billion per year), while the countries where money comes from are Saudi Arabia, Kuwait and the United Arab Emirates.

Evidence from Senegal shows that Senegalese migrant remittances help to cover the day-to-day expenses, especially in terms of food and basic-needs products, but they rarely help to buy durable products and real estate. It means that marketers can capitalize on this money for fast-moving consumer goods, telecommunication expenses and other services while this money will not be available or sufficient enough for big-ticket products such as durable products or real estate purchases (Lessault, Beauchemin, Sakho and Dutreuilh, 2011).

Bottom of the Pyramid marketing in Islamic countries

According to the Social Research and Training Centre for Islamic Countries (SESRIC), the combined GDP of OIC countries represented 11.2 percent of world GDP in 2013. More important than the absolute figure, the growth rate is significant because the OIC countries posted a growth of 3.9 percent in 2013, higher than in many developed countries. Even if the growth in oil and gas exporting countries is slowing down, it is compensated by higher growths in Asia and Africa. This kind of growth means that many consumers now have enough purchasing power and disposable income to buy branded products and climb the ladder on the Maslow pyramid, moving from physiological needs to safety and other needs. For marketers, the time has come to address seriously markets which have not been served before, and the time pressure is getting stronger and stronger.

Since many Islamic countries are on the bottom of the GDP per capita ranking, it is evident that these countries would be among the first to be concerned by Bottom of the Pyramid (BOP) marketing. The biggest multinational companies such as Nestlé, Danone, Orange and Procter and Gamble invest heavily in Egypt or in sub-Saharan Africa targeting the poor (Payaud, 2014). Some case studies are famous now about companies addressing the poor. Danone, for instance, uses its joint venture with Grameen Bank in Bangladesh and addresses two issues: quality, healthy products at an affordable price on one side and delivery of fresh products in rural Bangladesh with the involvement of local community on the other side (Rodrigues and Baker, 2012). One low-income country can be used as a test market for another low-income country, so the market will not be limited from the geographical point of view. Similar levels of development can be addressed with similar offers and these products can also find their way to more mature markets as well (Prahalad, 2004). This kind of reverse innovation worked well for companies such as Nokia, Tata and Godrej (Sinha, 2013).

Targeting the poor is everything but easy because multinational companies do not have a significant track record in this domain. Large multinational companies are at ease dealing with more mature markets because information is available. In low-income countries where information is not as available, failures can happen, as has been demonstrated by Unilever a few years ago. Its motto 'Doing well by doing good' did not correspond to reality, because the company announced that it serves the poor market with a quality product through its subsidiary Hindustan Lever in India, while at the same time it deliberately targeted the middle and high class rather than the bottom of the pyramid (Karnani, 2007).

Grouping OIC countries in clusters

Marketers can choose to target just one country at a time or try to access several countries simultaneously. The reasons for targeting one country at a time can be diverse. They may have few resources so they cannot have a 'sprinkler' approach because they lack funds for communication and distribution. Or they can decide to use one market as a test market and launch products and services on other markets only if they have succeeded in the test market. As far as Islamic countries are considered, the company can decide that all Islamic countries are different, so it should approach them separately. Conversely, launching an offer on several markets at the same time also has significant benefits – the first being economies of scale and the second preventing fake products or copies to be spread before the original products come on the market. If the product is a Shariah-based or Shariah-compliant product, it is expected that it should be accepted by Muslims worldwide, so there is no need to use one country as a test country. Finally, an established cooperative group of countries usually permits free trade between country members so the company can benefit from these incentives. The need for a simultaneous approach is fuelled also by the fact that volatility produced by political instability is so great in Islamic countries that it is worthless to adapt products and services because the circumstances change so often that adaptation is not going to be pertinent anymore from one year to the other.

Economic analysis shows that discrepancies are so huge among Islamic countries that it is difficult to apprehend all of them simultaneously. So far, integrative initiatives or organizations such as a hypothetical Islamic Common Market or Islamic Economic Union do not exist. It is therefore hard to talk about an Islamic economy, be it on a global stage serving the whole *Umma* (Muslim community worldwide) or on a regional level.

The only attempt at grouping exclusively Islamic countries is the GCC. The GCC is pursuing political and economic goals, contrary to the Arab League, which is a political initiative and not an economic one. The GCC puts together six states with various sizes, demographics and/or economic strengths, such as the Kingdom of Saudi Arabia on one side and Bahrain on the other side, the other countries being the United Arab Emirates, Kuwait, Oman and Qatar. The advantage of this group is that countries are close to each other and it has set up ambitious goals when it was established in 1981, such as establishing a monetary union with a single currency before 2010. Because of the rivalry between member states, the economic union is still far away and the monetary union has not been developed either. If the Gulf Cooperation Council did not succeed in building an economic or a monetary union when the six countries share so much in terms of culture and mindset, it is hard to imagine that other regional groups can succeed either. From the marketing point of view, it could be interesting to consider the GCC as a single entity but even this cannot be done because of strong differences between countries such as Saudi Arabia and Bahrain. There is a causeway between the two countries and Saudis routinely come to enjoy weekends in Bahrain, but rules about allowed products, distribution channels and networks and especially communication strategies are completely different. It means that marketers have to develop country-per-country approach and cannot capitalize on and pool resources in addressing several countries at the same time in the GCC. Even within one country, namely the United Arab Emirates, there are huge differences between Dubai, which is often viewed as progressive, cosmopolitan and open to other ideas and products, and another emirate such as Sharjah, which is much more conservative. The marketing plans will definitely be different within the same country.

So far there is no institutional push on a world level to build a common Muslim market. As a consequence, companies which operate in the Middle East and Asia at the same time such as Nestlé and McDonald's will not set up a so-called 'Muslim' division within their companies. They will use a geographical pattern instead of a religious one when it comes to organizational structure.

Conclusion

Global marketing means that a company can have a global offer for a global consumer. Islam being a universal religion present all over the world, the Muslim consumer is by definition a global consumer and a company can target him/her with a global offer. The problem is that this global Muslim consumer lives in very different conditions, making it difficult to target him/her with a unique offer and strategy. There is no economic unity of the Islamic world (no economic union, no common currency and no incentive to foster trade between Islamic countries), so we cannot talk about a unified and unique Muslim world. At the same time, there are no economic indicators specific to these countries, so companies will use a standardized approach that is used elsewhere when it comes to screening and choosing countries to establish a presence. In that sense the usual indicators will be GDP, the Gini index and/or the Corruption Perceptions Index. Apart from these individual indicators, synthetic indicators have been developed such as the Market Potential Index (MPI) proposed by GlobelEdge, a unit of Michigan State University, and the Global Retailer Development Index (GRDI) proposed by McKinsey, among other synthetic indicators. All these indicators are used routinely in global marketing, so marketers are used to them and know how to take the best from them.

However, the consumer is not only *homo economicus*, making decisions on rational grounds only. His decisions take into account also non-economic parameters, among them the spiritual ones. This is where religion is entering the equation, and marketers must also study the influence of religion on consumer behaviour. Since Islam has a very strong effect on consumer behaviour, it is necessary for the marketer to complement economic analysis with a socio-cultural one in order to have a comprehensive view of the potential of Muslim countries.

Issues for further discussion

1   Speculate about the possibility to have a common Muslim market in the future. Will the initiative come from the governments, consumers or the corporate world?
2   Are the economic indicators commonly used on the global scene adequate to assess the economic performance of Islamic countries?
3   Will the economic attractiveness of the Islamic countries push companies to adapt their marketing policies to serve these markets better?

Case study

How the EPRG scheme as a global marketing concept is adapted to Islamic countries

When companies go abroad, they will have to choose among four basic possibilities, which are ethnocentrism, polycentrism, regiocentrism and geocentrism (Perlmutter, 1969). Religion was not part of the equation but in this case study we will adapt the concept to Islamic countries. The four basic possibilities are the following:

* **E for Ethnocentrism** puts emphasis on a home country management orientation while overseas operations are secondary. The company considers that the home market is big enough, so it does not need to go abroad. Going abroad brings unnecessary complexity with dubious outcomes, so the company prefers to stay at home. The company can also assume that the products and practices are very successful in the home country, so due to their demonstrated superiority, these products and services will be successful anywhere, so it does not need to invest time and money in exploring other markets. These markets will come to them spontaneously.
    The concept launched in 1969 was definitely referring to Western countries, the United States as a focal point. All products coming from the United States were considered to be superior to the others so there was no need for adaptation. The question is to know if there is today a country of reference for the Muslim world. If such a country exists, all products and services coming

from this country would enjoy the same comparative advantage as American companies used to enjoy in the past. From this perspective point of view, the Kingdom of Saudi Arabia could be a natural candidate. It is the home of Mecca and Medina, the Prophet Muhammad was from Mecca and this is where the revelation has descended to mankind. The Kingdom would be tempted to consider that it is the center of Islam and other Islamic countries and Muslims worldwide have to adopt rules and customs practiced in Saudi Arabia. The assumption is that success in Saudi Arabia would guarantee success in all other Muslim countries. This is far from being true because there is no evidence that Saudi products sell better than products coming from Malaysia or Iran. However, the symbolic value is tremendous, especially when the pilgrims come back from the annual pilgrimage in Mecca. They usually buy huge quantities of products only because they originate from Mecca.

- **P for Polycentrism** describes management's often unconscious belief or assumption that each country in which a company does business is unique. The fact that the country's environment is unique pushes companies not only to adapt the product strategy but also other elements of the marketing mix as well as organizational procedures and production methods (Lee and Chen, 2003). Contrary to the ethnocentric approach, which favours standardization, polycentrism gives precedence to adaptation. If McDonald's sells beer (as part of a menu) in France, it will not propose it in Muslim countries. If Coca-Cola sells halal-certified beverages in Singapore, it will not sell halal-certified beverages in Saudi Arabia because all food and beverages are assumed to be halal in Saudi Arabia, so there is no need to certify them. The polycentric approach puts the consumer at the center of its discussion and the company does not hesitate to adapt its offer if necessary. If the consumer in Oman does not want Islamic Finance products, the bank operating in this country will not propose them, since there is no legal obligation to propose Islamic Finance there. So the same bank (for instance Standard Chartered) will not offer Islamic Finance in Lebanon while it will offer Islamic Finance products in Malaysia through its branch Standard Chartered Saadiq. This is a typical example of the adaptation theory for a multinational company as opposed to the globalization theory. Adaptation can go even further, based on the size and diversity of a given country. A case in point is Indonesia, with more than 17,000 islands and unique cultures and ethnic groups. The company can have an offer for Borneo and a completely different one for Timor.
- **R for Regiocentrism** is a valuable strategy when a firm is focused on a particular region, the European Union, or part of European Union known under the name Visegrad Group (Poland, Czech Republic, Slovakia and Hungary). As seen above, Muslim countries have not developed trade blocs yet and we

can find Islamic countries on all continents, so there is no homogenous group of Muslim countries. Because stereotypes play a huge role, some companies might be tempted to view South Asia as a homogenous group of countries, where Pakistani, Indian and Bangladeshi Muslims are put in one basket and companies may believe that they can have a standardized offer for all of them. Because all these areas have been part of British India, the assumption is that their behaviour will be similar. Other clusters may also be attractive for companies such as the North Africa group, the francophone Africa group or the Arab group of countries. Differences and rivalries are great between countries which may be part of one of these groups, so it is difficult to target all of them with the same offer even if the language is the same, like the use of common Bahasa for Indonesia, Malaysia and Brunei.

- **G for Geocentrism** considers the whole world as its home market. Contrary to the ethnocentric approach, where the company exports a product or a service designed for a home country, in the geocentric approach there is no home market. The company designs a global product which might not even be sold in the home country of the company. The company either becomes global gradually because of the demand coming from outside and evolves from ethnocentrism, regiocentrism or polycentrism to geocentrism, or it is from the start a 'born-global' company (Chetty and Campbell-Hunt, 2004). Apple sells more iPhones in China than in the US, so the company from Cupertino, California does not necessarily take the American market as a basis for launching the global product (an iPhone 6s for instance). Taking the world as a whole can be a pro-active strategy adopted by the company or it may be the consumer defining the whole world as his home (Cleveland, Laroche and Papadopoulos, 2009). Because Islam is a universal religion and Muslims consider that they are part of one *Ummah*, it is possible to use this kind of approach. It fits perfectly with the emergence of the Internet Global websites catering to the Muslim community worldwide and proposing services such as the explanation of Qur'an and the Hadiths, apparel or dating websites. An example is the company 'Awakening' dealing with Muslim lifestyle and entertainment, very present on the Internet. They are famous for the launching of global Muslim singers such as Sami Yusuf (7.7 million likes on Facebook) and Maher Zain (26 million likes on Facebook). These are Muslim superstars and any company sponsoring them will have access to a world base of potential clients.

Case questions for discussion

1   Would Nestlé use Saudi Arabia as a country of reference for its halal products worldwide?
2   Will BNPParibas use a different product policy depending on the ethnicity of its customers in Malaysia?

3   Will it be beneficial for companies to use stereotyped messages about 'Arabs' and 'Asians' in its advertising campaigns?
4   Propose a unique selling proposition for an 'Islamic car' targeting Western countries.

Bibliography

Alserhan, B. A. (2011), *The Principles of Islamic Marketing*, Gower.

Brenkert, G. (1988), "Marketing and the Vulnerable", *Business Ethics Quarterly*, Special Issue, Ruffin Series: New Approaches to Business Ethics, pp. 7–20.

Carling, J., Erdal, M. B. and Horst, C. (2012), "How Does Conflict in Migrants' Country of Origin Affect Remittance-Sending? Financial Priorities and Transnational Obligations Among Somalis and Pakistanis in Norway", *International Migration Review*, Vol. 46, No. 2, Summer, pp. 283–309.

Chetty, S. and Campbell-Hunt, C. (2004), "A Strategic Approach to Internationalization: A Traditional Versus a 'Born-Global' Approach", *Journal of International Marketing*, Vol. 12, No. 1, pp. 57–81.

Cleveland, M., Laroche, M. and Papadopoulos, N. (2009), "Cosmopolitanism, Consumer Ethnocentrism and Materialism: An Eight-Country Study of Antecedents and Outcomes", *Journal of International Marketing*, Vol. 17, No. 1, pp. 116–146.

"Saudi Arabia's Post-Oil Future", *The Economist*, 30 April.

"Iranian Sanctions Lifted" (2016), *The Financial Times*, 16 January.

Fletcher, M., Harris, S. and Richey, R. G. Jr. (2013), "Internationalization Knowledge: What, Why, Where, and When?" *Journal of International Marketing*, Vol. 21, No. 3, pp. 47–71.

Karnani, A. (2007), "Doing Well by Doing Good – Case Study: 'Fair and Lovely' Whitening Cream", *Strategic Management Journal*, Vol. 28, No. 13, pp. 1351–1357.

Kuran, T. (2005), *Islam and Mammon, the Economic Predicaments of Islamism*, Princeton: Princeton University Press.

Lee, J-R. and Chen, J-S. (2003), "Internationalization, Local Adaptation, and Subsidiary's Entrepreneurship: An Exploratory Study on Taiwanese Manufacturing Firms in Indonesia and Malaysia", *Asia Pacific Journal of Management*, Vol. 20 N° 1, March, pp. 51–72.

Lessault, D., Beauchemin, C., Sakho, P. and Dutreuilh, C. (2011), "International Migration and Housing Conditions of Households in Dakar", *Population*, Vol. 66, No. 1, January–March, pp. 195–225.

Nestorovic, C. (2016), *Islamic Marketing, Understanding the Socio-Economic, Cultural and Politico-Legal Environment*, New York: Springer.

Nissan, E. and Niroomand, F. (2015), "Economic, Welfare, Demographic and Gender Inequalities Among Selected Arab Countries", *Journal of Economics and Finance*, Vol. 39, No. 2, April, pp. 396–411.

Palmer, D. and Hedberg, T. (2013), "The Ethics of Marketing to Vulnerable Populations", *Journal of Business Ethics*, Vol. 116, No. 2, August, pp. 403–414.

Payaud, M. (2014), "Marketing Strategies at the Bottom of the Pyramid: Examples From Nestlé, Danone and Procter and Gamble", *Global Business and Organizational Excellence*, Vol. 33, No. 2, January–February, pp. 51–63.

Perlmutter, H.V. (1969), "The Tortuous Evolution of the Multinational Corporation", *Columbia Journal of World Business*, Vol. IV, January–February, pp. 9–18.

Prahalad, C. K. (2004), "Why Selling to the Poor Makes Good Business", *Fortune International*, 15 November.

Rodrigues, J. and Baker, G.A. (2012), "Grameen Danone Foods Limited", *International Foods and Agrobusiness Management Review*, Vol. 15, No. 1, pp. 127–158.

Sandikci, Ö. and Rice, G. (eds.) (2013), Handbook of Islamic Marketing, Cheltenham, UK: Edward Elgar Publishing.

Sinha, R. (2013), "Reverse Innovation: A Gift From Developing Economy to Developed Economy," *Business Perspectives and Research*, Vol. 2, No. 1, July–December, pp. 69–78.

Sissors, J. Z. (1966), "What Is a Market", *Journal of Marketing*, Vol. 30, No. 3, July, pp. 17–21.

9 Brands and communication strategy

Sarah Turnbull

Learning outcomes

At the end of this chapter, the reader should be able to:

1 Understand the importance of Islamic ethics and Muslim culture when developing brand communications for Islamic brands
2 Appreciate the types of brand communication appeals and messages that are appropriate for Muslim consumers
3 Understand the importance for brand communication to be fair and truthful and to show respect for elders and women
4 Recognise why some Islamic brands draw on Islamic culture and heritage in their brand communications

Key points

1 A sound understanding of Islamic ethics and Muslim culture is required by brands if they are to develop successful communication strategies.
2 It is critical for brands to avoid promoting *Haram* (forbidden) products and to be aware of the types of appeals and messages that may be offensive to Muslim consumers.
3 Brands must ensure that all their communications are fair and truthful and avoid misleading potential consumers, particularly vulnerable groups.
4 Communication must show respect for elders and women. Brands should also demonstrate an appreciation of women's role in society.
5 Brands should show respect for Islamic culture and faith and show an appreciation for Islamic heritage.

Introduction

This chapter explores communication strategies employed by Islamic brands and brands targeting Muslim consumers. This is an emerging area of academic and practitioner study and the chapter considers current theoretical perspectives as well as contemporary practice from the marketing communications industry.

The role of brand communications

Communication plays a central role in the development and maintenance of successful brands. In particular, marketing communications allows brands to position their product or service clearly in the mind of the consumer and create an emotional bond that is difficult for competitors to replicate. This can provide a sustainable competitive advantage for brands and generate long-term brand loyalty. De Chernatony and Dall'Olmo (1998) suggest that marketing communications is seen to support brands in a number of ways, including:

- Transferring brand reputation (particularly in the case of brand extensions)
- Projecting the brand heritage
- Facilitating consumer brand choice through differentiation
- Creating a brand personality
- Reinforcing consumer perceptions of the brand and by association the consumer's own self-perception.

Marketing communications is therefore seen to have a variety of roles that enable brands to clearly position themselves in the mind of the consumer. Keller (2009) argues that marketing communications is a valuable tool that can contribute towards the development of brand resonance, allowing the consumer to feel 'in sync' with the brand. He argues that brand resonance is made up of four key dimensions: behavioral loyalty, attitudinal attachment, active engagement and sense of community. Developing a sense of kinship or affiliation with other consumers is seen to be an important factor in the development of brand resonance, and he stresses that brand resonance is more likely to occur when brands generate feelings that appeal to both the head and the heart (Keller, 2009). This is of particular significance to Islamic brands that seek to align themselves with the values of Muslim consumers.

Since Islamic branding is a relatively new area of interest for academics and practitioners, it is important to understand the nature of differences that exist between brands. Alserhan (2011) differentiates between types of Islamic brands and has classified them according to whether they are Halal (Shariah-compliant), originate from an Islamic country and target Muslim consumers. His classification of Islamic brands provides us with four distinct categories:

- True Islamic brands – Halal, from an Islamic country and targeting Muslim consumers
- Traditional Islamic brands – Halal assumed, from an Islamic country and targeting Muslim consumers
- Inbound Islamic brands – Halal, targeting Muslim consumers, but do not originate from an Islamic country
- Outbound Islamic brands – Halal, from an Islamic country, but do not target only Muslim consumers

(Alserhan, 2011, p. 163)

Such classification of Islamic brands is helpful, since it recognises that some brands have been trading in Islamic countries long before the notion of Islamic branding and Islamic marketing. Therefore developing strategies and implementing brand communications for Muslim consumers is not a new phenomenon. The concept of Islamic marketing is, however, an emerging paradigm and with relatively few academic studies in the area, our theoretical knowledge is limited. Hence we draw heavily on our knowledge of 'True Islamic brands' in order to further encourage debate and identify new areas for future research.

The 'True' and 'Traditional' Islamic brands that originate from Islamic states have a good understanding of Muslim culture and the communication style and appeals that resonate with Muslim consumers. As well as the knowledge gained from Islamic brands we are also able to draw on the experience of global brand marketing in Islamic states. Many global brands have had considerable experience and expertise developing and implementing marketing communications campaigns for Muslim consumers. They are well versed in Muslim culture and attitudes. They recognise the importance of understanding Muslim values and developing communication strategy that reflect these values. A study of multinational organisations' advertising strategies in the Middle East by Melewar, Turnbull and Balabanis (2000) identified that global brands are aware of the importance of local culture and taste and adapt their advertising strategy in many markets to reflect this.

Academic and practitioner insights are used in this chapter to examine what we know about developing marketing communications strategy for Muslim consumers.

Brand communications to Muslim consumers: key features

The concept of Islamic marketing is a recent phenomenon. Recognition of an increasingly profitable global Muslim consumer has attracted significant attention from both academics and brand owners (Wilson et al., 2013). Global brands are keen to ensure they gain a share of newly emerging product categories, and new Islamic brands are being launched to meet the needs of this new global consumer group. New categories such as *Halal* travel and tourism, *Halal* logistics and media opportunities have emerged in recent years. In addition, a number of advertising and branding agencies have been established to service the marketing communications needs of these new Islamic brands.

While we should be careful not to assume that Muslim consumers are a homogenous group with identical attitudes and needs, they do share common values. Understanding these values and how they influence and impact consumers' lives is important. It is particularly important for brand owners to understand the influence of Islamic ethical values. Islam embraces all aspects of Muslim life as Yusuf (2010, p. 220) argues, "the social life of a Muslim is Islam; the economic life of the Muslim is Islam; the political life of the Muslim is Islam." Any aspect of business practice therefore needs to consider the importance of Islamic ethics. In particular there are six dominant principles: Unity (*Tawheed*), Faith (*Iman*), Trusteeship (*Khilafah*), Justice (*Adl*), Balance and Free will (Alserhan, 2011). Each of these ethical values has important implications for the development and implementation of brand strategy to Muslim consumers. For Islamic brands these values should be embedded within the brand promise and be an intrinsic aspect of everything the brand does. For brands targeting Muslim consumers it is important for brand owners to understand these ethical principles if they are to develop long-term relationships with consumers.

These values have important implications for brand communications. In 2002, Rice and Al-Mossawi suggested that these values could be organised into four cultural dimensions: relationships with people, time orientation, human nature orientation and activity orientation. They outline the practical implications of each category for advertising:

- Relationships with people: communication style should be polite and honest. Advertising should appreciate diversity, the role of women and be fair and just.
- Time orientation: Advertising luxury products is acceptable. Communication should also show appreciation for education and science.
- Human nature orientation: Modesty of dress and approach in advertising is important.
- Activity orientation: Emphasise *Halal*. Advertising should also stress cleanliness, good health and environmental friendliness.

(Rice and Al-Mossawi, 2002)

The authors argue that as advertising should attempt to reflect the values of a society and its value systems, an understanding of these value dimensions is important for brands targeting Muslim consumers (Rice and Al-Mossawi, 2002). Hence a prerequisite for developing marketing communications strategy is knowledge of what these values are and how they can be applied. Some of the key considerations should include:

- Avoid promoting *Haram* products and services.
- Communication should be fair and truthful.
- Communication should show appreciation and respect for women.
- Messages need to show respect for elders and avoid misleading vulnerable groups.
- Communication should reflect Islamic culture and respect the faith.
- Communication should reflect an appreciation of heritage.

Avoid promoting *Haram* products and services

Some products and services are not allowed and are considered *Haram*. In many Islamic states there will be restrictions on the promotion of such brands. Luqmani, Yavas and Quraeshi (1989) provide some examples of such products and communication styles/inferences that should be avoided in the Saudi Arabian market:

- Alcohol
- Gambling
- Cheating
- Idol worship
- Usury
- Adultery
- Immodest exposure

In countries where brand communication for such products is permitted, brand owners need to consider how communication choices and appeal styles could affect their relationship with Muslim consumers. Brands need to be aware of the sensitivity of such products and services and to ensure they are respectful to these consumer groups.

Some communication styles may also be viewed as inappropriate by some Muslim consumers. Rice and Al-Mossawi (2002) suggest that the communication style used in advertising should be polite and that brands need to consider how messages are framed to avoid offence. One style of message that may be contentious is price-led promotions. Some authors argue that price-led promotional messages are seen to be too direct and rude for some Middle East consumers and should be avoided (Haque, Ahmed and Jahan, 2010). While price-led advertising is used in many Islamic states, brands would be advised to consider consumers' attitudes to this approach in more sensitive categories.

Other contentious elements in advertising that have been identified are pop music and songs which may be seen as inappropriate by some Muslim consumers (Michell and Al-Mossawi, 1999). As music is used by many brands in Islamic states in their advertising, this element does not appear to be universally contentious amongst Muslim consumers, but brands need to be aware of the different sensitivities that exist. Other authors suggest that slogans and jingles should be treated with caution in some Middle East Islamic states, as they may also be seen to be inappropriate (Luqmani, Yavas and Quraeshi, 1989).

While promoting non-Islamic festivals and celebrations may be considered inappropriate, acknowledging Islamic holidays such as Eid al-Fitr and Eid al-Adha is common. Many brands in the Middle East, for example, will celebrate by placing advertising in the local newspapers and magazines. It is also common for some brands to time their promotional activity around these holidays. Emirates Holidays, based in the United Arab Emirates (UAE), for example, will promote a range of Eid holidays for those consumers wishing to take the opportunity to have a short break (Emirates Holidays, 2013).

Fair and truthful messages

Truth and fairness are important aspects of communication with Muslim consumers. While the need for such integrity should be seen as imperative in marketing communications to all consumer groups, it is particularly important that communication strategy should be based on truth and fairness when targeting Muslim consumers. Justice (*Adl*) is an important ethical consideration for Muslim consumers, and brands need to ensure that they respect these values if they wish to gain their consumers' trust. Those brands that do not respect this risk offending Muslim consumers and are unlikely to develop long-term relationships with them.

Brands need to avoid over-promising consumers in their brand communications. Arham (2010) argues that brands should avoid any promotional campaign that over-promises, as this may lead to consumers feeling deceived. This is an important consideration in communication strategy, and brand messages need to ensure that claims are carefully considered. While in many countries advertising regulations act to prevent such over-claiming, less developed countries may still lack guidelines, and hence it is important for brands to self-regulate advertising messages.

The Code of Advertising Practice in Malaysia is influenced by Islamic values (De Run et al., 2010) and therefore provides guidance on what style of message is appropriate within an Islamic culture. The Code of Practice states, "Advertisements should not contain any statements or visual presentation which directly or by implication, omission, ambiguity, or exaggerated claim, is likely to mislead the consumer about the product advertised, the advertiser, or about any other product or advertiser" (Malaysian Code of Advertising Practice, 2008, p. 7). We can also draw on codes from Middle East Islamic states for guidance on this aspect. The Gulf Media International W.L.L. Bahrain Code of Acceptance, for example, identifies that any advertising materials will be rejected if they "contain illustrations or copy which are distorted or exaggerated in such a way as to convey false impressions, are calculated to deceive the public, or contain statements of a knocking or extravagant nature" (Al-Mohamed, 1997 cited in Rice and Al-Mossawi, 2002, p. 11).

Honesty of communication is essential. While Rice and Al-Mossawi (2002) warn against using messages that exaggerate and deceive, they do however suggest that advertising which makes the exaggeration very obvious would be acceptable. While such creative routes have been popular in the West in the last decade, brand owners need to be careful that such creative routes would be judged by the consumer and the advertising regulators to be seen as exaggeration.

Another aspect of fairness is the manner in which brands treat their competitors. Brands need to treat competitive products fairly and should avoid using comparative advertising as this too could be interpreted as being unfair. A number of studies have been undertaken in Middle East Islamic states that recommend avoiding the use of comparative advertising, and in particular suggest advertising should not make any reference to competitive brands (Rice and Al-Mossawi, 2002). Instead Al-Olayan and Karande (2000) argue that brands with advantages over competitive brands should use terms such as:

- "the best"
- "number one"
- "better than any other product"

Ensuring that brand communications are fair and truthful is therefore seen to be an important aspect for Islamic brands and brands that target Muslim consumers. Developing strategies that avoid direct comparison with other brands and communications that are seen to be honest are more likely to build trust with consumers.

Respect for women

An important aspect for any brand to consider is how it portrays women in its brand communications. While there is a universal need to show respect for women in advertising or any other form of brand communications in any culture, for brands that seek to position themselves for Muslim consumers this is especially significant. Showing respect for women demonstrates an understanding of and respect for the important Islamic ethical value of Trusteeship (*Khilafah*).

There are a number of academic studies that provide insight into how this ethical value could be observed in practice. Luqmani, Yavas and Quraeshi (1989), in their study of advertising content and regulation in Saudi Arabia, emphasise the importance of covering a woman's body and showing conservative dress. They provide the example of cosmetic brands in the country that avoid using 'sensuous' female models and choose women that are wearing a robe and headdress, showing only their face. They also recommend that 'sexually sensitive' ads substitute cartoon characters for women. More recent examples of brand communications show that some advertising avoids using women in their ads altogether. An example of this is a 2014 TV commercial for "du", a telecoms provider in the UAE. The ad tells the story of a well-known local celebrity, Hussain Al Jassmi, who is able to keep his mobile telephone number when he changes his phone. The ad is shot in a number of locations, including the park and his home. The creative execution has cleverly avoided using any women in the commercials and has used cartoon characters to depict the celebrity's numbers (Campaign ME, 2014). This avoids offending Islamic values and means the ad is less likely to violate any country's advertising codes.

Other brands have similarly developed cartoon characters specifically for the Middle East market. Lay's potato chips, for example, developed a female character called Liza Lay for their 'Do Us a Flavour' campaign (Impact BBDO, 2012). The character ran in a wide range of integrated communication material including TV ads and allowed the brand the freedom of using a female character shown searching for their perfect partners, without concern for causing offence in any of the countries.

Modesty of dress is an important aspect of this as Rice and Al-Mossawi (2002) highlight. They suggest that brand owners need to carefully consider the modesty of dress in advertising. They identify that there are likely to be different levels of acceptability dependent on the level of conservatism of the country; however, they suggest using a more modest approach than in non-Islamic countries. Some practical guidance of what is appropriate dress for Muslim women is given by Huda (2014):

- Covered body: the body should be covered except for face and hands. This is inter-preted by most Muslims as requiring head coverings for women. Some Muslim women cover their entire body (including face and hands).
- Loose clothing: no tight or body-hugging clothes.
- Thick material: material should not reveal skin or body shape.
- Modest and dignified appearance.
- Should not imitate others.
- Decent but not flashy.

While these guidelines offer some good practical advice for brands wishing to include women in their communication material, it should also be noted that, for some Muslims, showing women in ads is only seen to be appropriate if the product is related. Some authors suggest that women appearing in advertising could be considered contrary to Islamic values (Al-Makaty et al., 1996); hence, brands need to be cautious about using women in their marketing communications material and ensure that no offence will be caused.

Showing respect for women goes beyond conservative dress, however, and a brand's communication strategy needs to recognise the important role of women. Rice and Al-Mossawi (2002), for example, suggest that women are recognised within advertising for their positive contribution to society. This means that they should not be shown just within their family role, but also in their career or in making other contributions to society.

This is reflected in the Malaysian Code of Advertising Practice (2008, p. 3) which states, "Advertisements must not identify or type-cast each particular racial group or sex with vocations, traditional values and backgrounds."

One company that has developed a brand communication strategy that demonstrates respect for womens' role in society is Mubadala, an investment and development com-pany based in the UAE. The company website hosts a powerful short video of how they develop their Emirati female future leaders which shows the respect and value they have for their female employees (Mubadala, 2014). The company has also run a press advertis-ing campaign which features a photograph of an Emirati female career woman in her profession, hence recognising the value of women to society (Mubadala, 2012). The cam-paign clearly positions the brand as one that respects women and values the contribution women make to society.

While there appear to be differences between countries and cultures regarding regula-tions and attitudes towards women in advertising, it is important to ensure that women are shown respect. Consideration of how women are portrayed needs to be embedded within the overall brand communication strategy.

Respect for elders and avoid misleading vulnerable groups

Respecting elders and protecting vulnerable members of society are important aspects of Muslim culture and society. Brand communications of any form should respect elders and must avoid misleading the more vulnerable members of society. In particular there is a responsibility to protect children and young people, and this needs to be observed in advertising and promotions of any kind. This is important as it demonstrates respect for Trusteeship (*Khilafah*).

Some authors, such as Kalliny and Gentry (2007), argue that in the Middle East, Arab culture would not permit derogatory statements to be made about deceased members of the family and that loyalty and respect must be shown towards parents and elders; hence, brands need to be careful to avoid offending Muslim consumers in their marketing appeals.

The Malaysian Code of Advertising Practice (2008) provides clear guidance on advertising to children and young people, "Advertisements addressed to children and young people or likely to be seen by them, should not contain anything which might result in harming them physically, mentally or morally or which might exploit their credulity, lack of experience or natural sense of loyalty" (Malaysian Code of Advertising Practice, 2008, p. 22).

Islamic culture and faith

All forms of communication are seen to be embedded within the culture in which they are developed. Advertising in particular is seen to reflect the cultural norms and values of society. In Islamic states or for Islamic brands, advertising often draws heavily on aspects of heritage and culture.

The choice of imagery used in communication material is an important consideration. Symbols can be particularly contentious and need to be carefully considered before use. In addition, some imagery such as dogs and statues, for example, would be seen as inappropriate and should be avoided where they are likely to cause offence (Melewar et al., 2000). In contrast, some images are seen to be more appropriate for Muslim consumers and the use of indigenous animals and birds are very popular. In Middle East countries, Luqmani, Yavas and Quraeshi (1989) suggest that horses, camels and falcons are suitable for marketing communication material. These images are often seen in advertising and other forms of communication material for brands in the Middle East markets and are seen to show respect for Arabic culture.

In particular the use of falcons is a popular choice in advertising in the Middle East Islamic states. Gulf Air, the Bahrain national airline, for example, use the image of a falcon in their logo and have named a number of their products and services after the falcon. The airline's frequent flyer programme is called Falconflyer and their cargo division is Falconcargo. The falcon is used throughout their communications and demonstrates how birds are used in brand imagery.

Islamic architecture and Arabic calligraphy are other types of imagery used in Middle East Islamic states. While architecture is seen to be an important component of any brand's visual identity (Melewar and Jenkins, 2002), for Islamic brands and in Islamic markets the use of architecture is particularly relevant as it represents Islamic heritage. The Museum of Islamic Art in Qatar, for example, has recently developed a new visual identity to reflect Islamic art and culture (Museum of Islamic Art, 2014). The new identity uses symbolic imagery that is based on Islamic geometry and was inspired by the architecture of the museum building itself. The logo uses six different colours and six different scripts which are seen to represent the diversity of Islamic civilisations: Kufi, Thuluth, Naskh, Taaliq, Diwani and Ruqaa (Museum of Islamic Art, 2014). Using such symbolic imagery provides the brand with a strong identity and clearly positions the museum as a centre for Islamic art and culture. This demonstrates the importance of Islamic heritage for Islamic brands and provides an example of how this can be embedded within brand imagery and communication.

Brands need to avoid excessiveness in their communication activity. Moderation in living is encouraged and hence brands need to be careful to avoid offending Muslim consumers by using costly or excessive advertising (Haque et al., 2010). While there is a need to further understand what is seen to be excessive in brand communication terms, avoiding overtly excessive strategies in either media or messages is advisable.

Appreciation of heritage

Heritage is highly valued by Muslims, especially in the Middle East. Demonstrating respect for and an appreciation of local heritage is important for brands in Islamic states. Many brands choose to embed traditional themes within their marketing communications in order to reflect their Islamic heritage. Some of the best examples of heritage appreciation are in the marketing communications campaigns for destination brands in the Middle East.

Destination brands such as Oman Tourism draw on national heritage to build their brand identity. In particular their 'Beauty Has an Address' campaign draws heavily upon Oman's rich heritage to promote the country as a destination (Oman Tourism, 2012). As well as a series of press ads, the campaign includes a 10-minute video which takes viewers on a tour of the country's heritage. The video shows many of the country's World Heritage Sites, as well as traditional sailing boats (*dhows*), local markets (*souks*), frankincense production and distinctive local architecture to position Oman as a world class heritage destination.

Other brand destinations in the Middle East similarly draw on aspects of their heritage and use traditional themes and imagery in their advertising campaigns. A recent campaign by Abu Dhabi Tourism, for example, showcases a number of traditional aspects of Arabic hospitality and heritage (Abu Dhabi Tourism, 2011). In a series of TV commercials, the campaign showcases a number of indigenous animals such as camels and Arabian Oryx and includes a traditional *dhow* that reminds consumers of the country's trading heritage. The TV ad, entitled "And You Think You've Seen It All?", provides an impressive tour of the Emirate's Islamic architecture and historical sites and provides a strong link with the country's heritage.

Family heritage is important in Muslim culture and studies undertaken in the Middle East support this. Kalliny (2010, p. 99) argues the importance of tradition in Arab society and highlights the extent to which old customs and convention affect culture today, "[P]eople are proud of the founding fathers and what they have done to build their country." This pride is evident in advertising messages seen in the Middle East as many brands choose to draw on their family history in their brand communications. An example of this is Ahmed Seddiqi & Sons, a UAE-based retailer that was established in the Emirate over 60 years ago. Their 2011 press advertising campaign depicts the original business by reconstructing Ahmed Qasim Seddiqi (the late founder's) desk in the original store in Bur Dubai as it was in the 1940s. Using nostalgic imagery and a black and white photograph of the male family members, the press ad demonstrates the value the company places on heritage, as well as its respect for elders (Gulf business, 2011).

The use of Arabic language is also seen to respect culture and heritage, especially in the Middle East. Arabic proverbs and phrases are often used in advertising. Luqmani, Yavas and Quraeshi (1989) recommend that advertisers show respect by introducing their messages with Quranic words to demonstrate that brands are in accordance with Islamic values and beliefs. They suggest words and phrases such as:

- "In the Name of Allah, the Most Gracious, the Most Merciful"
- "By the Grace of God"
- "God is Great (Allah–o–Akbar)"

Brands must be careful when including Islamic phraseology in their communications to ensure that it is considered to be appropriate by the consumer. This relates back to the need to be fair and truthful in communications. It would not be appropriate to infer a brand is compliant with Islamic values when it is not.

Showing an appreciation for education and science in brand communications is also recommended. Rice and Al-Mossawi (2002), for example, suggest using scientific appeals in communications and in particular recommend making reference to the Muslims' scientific heritage from the Medieval Ages. Such approaches show respect for cultural values and an appreciation of the past, which are important for Muslim consumers.

Conclusion

This chapter has explored the communication strategies employed by Islamic brands and brands targeting Muslim consumers. It highlights the need for brand owners to have a sound understanding of Islamic ethics and Muslim culture and to ensure that the message and appeal style used is appropriate. In particular it demonstrates the need for brand communications to be fair and truthful, to demonstrate an appreciation for women's role in society and to respect elders. The chapter also highlights the importance of showing respect for Islamic culture and faith and demonstrates how some brands reflect their Islamic heritage in their brand communications.

Issues for further discussion

1   Discuss ways in which marketing communications for Islamic brands are likely to differ from non-Islamic brands.
2   Explain why, when targeting Muslim consumers, it is important to respect their ethical values.
3   Discuss the main issues that need to be taken into account when developing marketing communications for Muslim consumers.
4   Suggest ways in which Islamic brands can demonstrate that they are compliant with Islamic values.

Case study

Developing a brand communication strategy for HalalBooking.com

HalalBooking® is seen as a pioneer of Halal tourism. Started in London 2009 by a group of Muslim businessmen, the company's website www.HalalBooking.com

offers online booking service for Halal holidays. The company identified a gap in the market for holidays with an 'Islamic ethos' and set about filling this niche. Selecting resorts and hotels that are aligned to Muslim beliefs, customs and life-style, they provide the Muslim tourist with the opportunity to travel and enjoy holi-days without compromising their values.

Hospitality is seen to be an important aspect in Muslim culture and HalalBook-ing® have embedded Islamic hospitality within their brand. Understanding what the Muslim consumer expects as part of this hospitality has been the key to their success.

The company offers a number of different types of Halal holidays that range from Beach Resorts, offering full sun and beach leisure holiday experience, to City Break Hotels, which serve halal food and provide an opportunity to visit sites of Islamic and other cultural heritage. The range of holidays they offer includes:

- Beach holidays – beach resort and spas
- City breaks – hotels and guided heritage tours
- Health holidays – thermal resorts and spas
- Villa holidays – villa with private swimming pools

Such holidays differ from other holiday packages on offer in that the facilities and food offered by the resorts and hotels are Muslim friendly. This means that Muslim tourists are able to relax or explore new destinations with the knowledge that the accommodation they are staying in will enable them to maintain their customs and uphold their values. Only hotels and resorts that are aligned to this ethos are included on HalalBooking.com website. More specifically the resorts and hotels selected offer the following:

- Halal food
- Beach resorts and hotels do not serve alcohol
- Separate pool and spa facilities for men and women
- Family orientated facilities
- Women only beaches, proving complete privacy
- Family-friendly beaches with a modest swimming dress code
- Prayer facilities on site
- Qibla direction and prayer mats in all rooms
- Guided heritage tours to sites of Islamic and other cultural interest

While there appears to be no strict definition of what makes a holiday a Halal holiday, there seems to be some consensus in the industry that Halal food, fam-ily-friendly resorts, women only leisure facilities and prayer areas are essential components. These provide Muslim tourists with the opportunity to maintain their Muslim customs and practices while they are on holiday.

Hospitality has always been seen as an important part of Muslim culture and tradition and many of the resorts and hotels offering such holidays are in Turkey and the Middle East. In addition to the Halal accommodation on offer, the region is served by a number of national airlines and airports that meet specific needs of Muslim passengers. For a holiday to be considered halal, it is important that the holidaymaker's customs and values are considered at every stage of the holiday.

One of the many hotels offered on HalalBooking.com is Tamani Hotel Marina in Dubai in the United Arab Emirates. As well as guarantees that only Halal food is served in the hotel and there is no alcohol served, the hotel offers female guests an exclusive ladies floor served by female butlers. Hotel rooms are decorated with Islamic art, which is another important consideration as this is sensitive to Muslim culture. All rooms have a Prayer mat and Holy Quran. Providing such facilities is respectful to Muslim guests.

Many Halal holidays provide a range of cultural and heritage activities for their Muslim clients. For clients visiting Istanbul, for example, HalalBooking.com recommends seeing the Topkapi Palace, Blue (Sultanahmet) Mosque, Hagia Sophia Museum, Basilica Cistern and Grand Bazaar. In other cities, such as Dubai, activities on offer may be more leisure and shopping orientated, but still appealing to their Muslim clients.

Since HalalBooking started their business, there has been considerable growth in the Halal tourism market. A recent study published by DinarStandard and CrescentRating estimated that the value of the global Muslim tourism market in 2011 was $126.1 billion. More significantly the study estimates Muslim tourism will increase at a much faster rate than international tourism and that by 2020 the Muslim tourism market will be worth US$192 billion. Although a number of Halal holiday providers have now emerged, HalalBooking have earned considerable media coverage in both mainstream press and specialist Muslim magazines as a result of being one of the first in the market.

HalalBooking have a website and all resorts and hotels are displayed online. Their current marketing communications activity consists of online banner ads on numerous sites, textual ads on Google and Yandex.ru search websites and advanced use of Search Engine Optimisation (SEO) tools, targeting Muslim consumers searching online for Halal holidays. The company also uses email marketing and social networks like Facebook to engage with Muslim consumers, although they are careful not to be intrusive in their direct marketing. The website is in six languages and the company has separate marketing teams for six market segments – English, Arabic, Turkish, French, German and Russian. Each team adjusts their marketing approaches to fit the cultural and linguistic specifics of its market segment. The company has call-centres for 20 countries with staff answering calls in the above-mentioned languages.

The company pride themselves on the good relationships they have developed with their customer base. All the resorts and hotels have been tried and tested by a member of the HalalBooking team and much of their business comes from repeat customers. Since it was launched in 2009 the company has been seen as a global leader of Halal holidays. The company believes the key to their success has been the genuine alignment of their brand with Muslim values and world-class family-friendly online booking system.

Case questions for discussion

1 When developing a new advertising campaign for HalalBooking, what issues do you think the company need to consider? In particular what will be the main influences on the creative strategy?
2 What criteria do you think HalalBooking need to consider when choosing media for an advertising campaign?
3 When choosing an advertising agency to develop their campaign, what factors do you think HalalBooking would consider important?

Sources

HalalBooking® website available at: www.HalalBooking.com

Global Muslim Lifestyle Travel Market 2012: Landscape and Consumer Needs Study, by DinarStandard and CrescentRating. Available at: file:///C:/Users/Sarah/Downloads/CR_TravelReport_ExecSummary02.pdf

References

Abu Dhabi Tourism. (2011). www.youtube.com/watch?v=XwzjrU1LLfQ&list=PLB33A1AC05E0C F1A4

Al-Makaty, S. S., Van Tubergen, G. N., Whitlow, S. S. and Boyd, D. A. (1996), "Attitudes Toward Advertising in Islam", *Journal of Advertising Research*, Vol. 36, pp. 16–26.

Al-Olayan, F. S. and Karande, K. (2000), "A Content Analysis of Magazine Advertisements from the United States and the Arab World", *Journal of Advertising*, Vol. 20, pp. 69–83.

Alserhan, B. A. (2011), *The Principles of Islamic Marketing*, Farnham: Gower.

Arham, M. (2010), "Islamic Perspectives on Marketing", *Journal of Islamic Marketing*, Vol. 1, No. 2, pp. 149–164.

Campaign ME. (2014), *du TV Commercial Accessed From Campaign Middle East Website*. http://campaignme. com/2014/01/26/15331/du-hussain-al-jassmi/

de Chernatony, L. and Dall'Olmo Riley, F. (1998), "Defining a 'brand': Beyond the Literature With Experts' Interpretations", *Journal of Marketing Management*, Vol. 14, pp. 417–443.

Cyril De Run, E., Mohsin Butt, M., Fam, K. S., & Yin Jong, H. (2010). "Attitudes towards offensive advertising: Malaysian Muslims' views". *Journal of Islamic Marketing*, Vol. 1, No. 1, pp. 25–36.

Emirates Holidays. (2013), www.emirates.com/english/about/news/news_detail.aspx?article=1297987

Gulf Business. (2011). "Ahmed Seddiqi & Sons Advertisement", Vol. 15, No. 11.

Haque, A., Ahmed, K. and Jahan, S. I. (2010), "Shariah Observation: Advertising Practices of Bank Muamalat in Malaysia", *Journal of Islamic Marketing*, Vol. 1, No. 1, pp. 70–77.

Huda. (2014), *Islamic Clothing Requirements*. http://islam.about.com/od/dress/p/clothing_reqs.htm

Impact BBDO. (2012), http://impactbbdo.com/#!&pageid=0&subsection=5&itemid=3

Kalliny, M. (2010), "Are They Really That Different From Us: A Comparison of Arab and American Newspaper Advertising", *Journal of Current Issues and Research in Advertising*, Vol. 32, No. 1, pp. 95–108.

Kalliny, M. and Gentry, L. (2007), "Cultural Values Reflected in Arab and American Television Advertising", *Journal of Current Issues and Research in Advertising*, Vol. 29, No. 1, pp. 15–32.

Keller, K. L. (2009), "Building Strong Brands in a Modern Marketing Communications Environment", *Journal of Marketing Communications*, Vol. 15, pp. 139–155.

Luqmani, M., Yavas, U. and Quraeshi, Z. (1989), "Advertising in Saudi Arabia: Content and Regulation", *International Marketing Review*, Vol. 6, No. 1, pp. 59–72.

Malaysian Code of Advertising Practice, (2008), www.asa.org.my/code.php

Melewar, T. C. and Jenkins, E. (2002), "Defining the Corporate Identity Construct", *Corporate Reputation Review*, Vol. 5, No. 1, pp. 76–90.

Melewar, T. C., Turnbull, S. and Balabanis, G. (2000), "International Advertising Strategies of Multinational Enterprises in the Middle East", *International Journal of Advertising*, Vol. 19, pp. 529–547.

Mubadala. (2012), "Mubadala Press Advertisement", *Arabian Business Magazine*, Vol. 13, No. 37.

Mubadala. (2014), www.mubadala.com/en/why-we-do-it/investing-in-abu-dhabi

Museum of Islamic Art. (2014), *Our New Branding*. www.mia.org.qa/en/about/the-new-museum-branding

Michell, P., and Al-Mossawi, M. (1999), "Religious Commitment Related to Message Contentiousness", *International Journal of Advertising*, Vol. 18, pp. 427–444.

Oman Tourism. (2012), *Beauty Has an Address*. www.youtube.com/watch?v=Z8523uL7_YE

Rice, G. and Al-Mossawi, M. (2002), "The Implications of Islam for Advertising Messages: The Middle Eastern Context", *Journal of Euromarketing*, Vol. 11, No. 3, pp. 1–16.

Wilson, J. A., Belk, R. W., Bamossy, G. J., Sandikci, Ö., Kartajaya, H., Sobh, R. and Scott, L. (2013), "Crescent Marketing, Muslim Geographies and Brand Islam: Reflections From the *JIMA* Senior Advisory Board", *Journal of Islamic Marketing*, Vol. 4, No. 1, pp. 22–50.

Yusuf, J. B. (2010), "Ethical Implications of Sales Promotion in Ghana: Islamic Perspective", *Journal of Islamic Marketing*, Vol. 1, pp. 220–230.

10 Marketing strategy in the emerging Muslim–majority markets

Özlem Sandıkcı

Learning outcomes

At the end of this chapter, the reader should be able to:

1   Recognize the great diversity characterizing emerging Muslim-majority markets and evaluate the significance of these markets for marketing strategy and practice
2   Critically assess the implications of the new Muslim middle classes and Muslim entrepreneurs and business networks on consumption, competition, and global marketing management
3   Acknowledge that successful marketing strategy in these markets require a situated and non-essentialist understanding of Muslim consumers and marketers
4   Critically evaluate socio-cultural and economic factors that contribute to the success or failure of products and services targeting Muslim consumers

Key points

1   Several of the emerging markets have large Muslim populations and offer great opportunities for businesses; yet, a great diversity characterizes the Muslim market.
2   Although there are universal Islamic values and norms, how these are interpreted, negotiated and experienced in the daily lives of Muslim consumers are far from uniform and fixed.
3   The growth of the new Muslim middle classes coincides with the increasingly significant role Islamic business networks and Muslim entrepreneurs play in the global markets.
4   In order to be able to devise successful marketing strategies, managers need to go beyond stereotypical and static understandings and a preoccupation with difference and develop a critical, situated, and dynamic engagement with Muslim consumers and marketers.
5   Marketing emphasis should be on providing solutions to Muslim consumers in their quest for living proper Islamic lives while enjoying the benefits of the material world.

Introduction

This chapter discusses the marketing strategy implications of the emerging Muslim-majority markets and provides an analysis of their key dynamics. It emphasizes the great diversity characterizing these environments and argues that in order to be successful, marketers need to refrain from essentialist and celebratory conceptualizations of Muslim consumers and marketers. Managers need to develop a situated market understanding which is attentive to the sociohistorical, political, moral, and competitive specificities and devise strategies that take into account commonalities as well as differences.

Emerging markets

The so-called emerging markets (EMs) have become highly important for marketing theory and strategy in the last decade (e.g., Burgess and Steenkamp, 2006; Sheth, 2011). The term was introduced in the 1980s by then World Bank economist Antoine van Agt-mael to account for countries considered to be in a transitional phase between developing and developed status (van Agtmael, 2007). EM standing is generally understood to indicate rapid economic development, institutional transformations, adoption of free-market economic policies, and intermediate income level (Vladimir, 2009). EMs vary significantly in terms of their socio-cultural and political composition and cover a wide spectrum of geographical areas, ranging from Eastern Europe to Asia, Africa, and Latin America. Among the biggest EMs are the BRIC countries: Brazil, Russia, India, and China. Indonesia, Malaysia, Mexico, Colombia, Poland, Turkey, Kenya, Nigeria, and Bangladesh constitute other major emerging economies (Goldman Sachs, 2007; Khanna and Palepu, 2013). According to the International Monetary Fund, in 2013, for the first time in history, EMs accounted for more than half of the world GDP on the basis of purchasing power (IMF, 2014). Indeed, for many analysts, EMs are the "lands of opportunities" where future growth lies (Mahajan and Banga, 2005).

EMs present both opportunities and challenges for marketing. Many of the EMs share histories of closed economies characterized by marketplace scarcity and poor quality products. With the opening up of economies and liberalization of trade, global brands flood the marketspaces of the EMs, contributing to the development of a Western-style consumption culture (Askegaard, 2006; Ger and Belk, 1996). Studies show that global brands are received generally favorably in the EMs. Most EM consumers associate global brands with high perceived quality (Holt, Quelch, and Taylor, 2004; Ozsomer and Altaras, 2008) and regard them as vehicles for participation in an aspired-to global consumer culture (e.g., Holt et al., 2004; Strizhakova, Coulter, and Price, 2008).

For developed-country multinational companies, EMs constitute new and attractive markets for their products and services. Indeed, the demographic composition of the EMs renders them as key growth markets for the global brands. In contrast to the decreasing and aging populations that characterize much of the advanced world, most EMs have high birth rates and a young population. According to forecasts, by 2030, some 1.2 billion of the world's 1.3 billion new citizens will be born in emerging countries and 40 percent of the population in EMs will be under 25 years old, compared to 25 percent in developed countries (Berger, 2013). Equally importantly, it is estimated that, by 2030, approximately 80 percent of the middle class will live outside Europe and the United States (ibid.). Referred to as the new middle classes, this consumer segment has received considerable research attention in recent years (e.g., Cavusgil and Kardes, 2013; Kravets and Sandıkcı, 2014). The growth of the new middle classes and their increasing purchasing power are regarded as among the megatrends shaping marketing and international business today.

EMs also bring new challenges to marketing strategy. As Sheth (2011) summarizes, EMs differ from developed markets on five critical dimensions. EMs exhibit high heterogeneity on key market statistics and suffer from unequal income distribution. This results in wide disparities in consumption between haves and have-nots. The marketspaces of the EMs are also characterized by unbranded competition, poor infrastructure, and chronic shortage of resources in production, exchange, and consumption. Finally, institutional structures such as religion, government, business groups, nongovernmental organizations, and local community tend to play a more prominent role in the EMs and influence market dynamics and governance. Each of these dimensions requires that multinational companies rethink their marketing strategies and make adjustments accordingly. Furthermore, the recent decade has witnessed the emergence of the so-called emerging giants, multinational companies originating in the EMs and competing head-to-head with advanced-country firms (Khanna and Palepu, 2013). As EM companies become global contenders through acquisitions and organic growth, they profoundly impact the dynamics of global competition.

Overall, economic, socio-demographic, and political developments of the last decades have rendered EMs as key growth markets for global brands and changed the competitive dynamics in the world. Scholars and practitioners agree that the complexity and distinctive aspects of the EMs require reconsideration of marketing theory and strategy. The need for reassessment becomes particularly visible in the case of the emerging markets of the Muslim-majority countries. According to the Global Intelligence Alliance, 10 of the top 30 emerging markets have large Muslim populations. These include India, Indonesia, Turkey, Malaysia, Nigeria, Saudi Arabia, UAE, Egypt, Bangladesh, and Pakistan. Some analysts consider the Muslim segment as the next growth opportunity for Western multinationals and discuss the emergence of an 'Islamic' economy across the world (Ogilvy Noor, 2010; Thomson Reuters, 2014). The next section discusses in detail the growth of the 'Islamic' economy.

Emerging markets and the growth of the 'Islamic' economy

Muslims constitute around 20 percent of the world population and have been actively participating in the global economy as suppliers, manufacturers, bankers, investors, traders, and consumers for decades. Yet, it is in the last 10 years or so that Muslim consumers and marketers have begun to attract academic and managerial interest (for a critical review, see Jafari, 2012; Jafari and Sandıkcı, 2015; Sandıkcı, 2011). One can trace such interest in the increasing number of academic articles and books; the establishment of specialist journals, such as the *Journal of Islamic Marketing* and *International Journal of Islamic Marketing and Branding*; the organization of academic conferences and executive workshops; the production of high-profile consultancy reports; and the circulation of news stories about Muslim consumers and Islamic businesses in the global media.

Structurally, the growing attention on the Muslim market can be located within the new world political economy. Since the 1980s, neoliberal restructuring has characterized the development path of much of the emerging countries, including the Muslim-majority ones (Ong, 2006; Rudnyckyj, 2009). The ramifications of neoliberal development extend well beyond the economic realm to the political, social, and cultural domains (Harvey, 2005). Among many transformations associated with neoliberalism are religious revivalism and the resurgence of all kinds of faith movements. Many researchers link new forms of religio-ethno-economic practice to the logic of neoliberal capitalism (Gauthier, Martikainen, and Woodhead, 2013) and argue that while secularization theory predicted privatization of faith in the modern world, today religion has become even more prominent, public, and visible (Wilson and Steger, 2013). Indeed, with globalization and marketization of developing country economies, construction, enactment, and communication of religious identities, including Muslim identities, through consumption practices and marketplace resources become more evident and commonplace (e.g., Gokariksel and Secor, 2009; Jafari and Suerdem, 2012; Sandıkcı and Ger, 2010).

From this perspective, the growing interest on the emerging Muslim market can be related to various social, cultural, political, and economic developments: the emergence of a pious Muslim middle class interested in modern consumption; the growth of the *ummah*, a supranational community of Muslim believers, enabled by information technologies and connected through values and lifestyles; the expansion of a new class of pious Muslim entrepreneurs who successfully blend religious principles and capitalist aspirations; the increasing social, economic, and political power of the new Islamic social movements; and the post 9/11 forces shaping the global political economy and international relations (Sandıkcı, 2011). Each of these developments carries important implications for marketers operating or planning to enter the emerging Muslim-majority markets. Hence, it is not surprising that there has been an increase in the number of consultancy reports that seek to educate Western marketers on the Muslim market in the recent years. Among the most prominent of these are A.T. Kearney's *Addressing the Muslim Market* (2007), JWT's *Understanding the Islamic Consumer* (2009), Ogilvy Noor's *Brands, Islam and the New Muslim Consumer* (2010), and Thomson Reuters' *State of the Global Islamic Economy* (2014).

A closer look at these publications indicates that while providing many important insights, they often depict a rather limited and stereotyped image of the Muslim consumers. Similar to the cases of other non-mainstream consumer groups such as blacks, gays, and Hispanics in the US, the emphasis of the marketing research and consultancy companies seem to be mostly on the demographic size and purchasing power of Muslims. As a common approach, the reports start with numbers of Muslims categorized along key socio-economic variables, such as age, education, income level, and country of residence, to make a case for the financial relevance of the Muslim market. Once Muslims are identified as an untapped and viable segment, the analyses set out to convince the reader of the 'unique' and 'different' nature of Muslim consumers. Typically, the authors outline the five pillars of Islam and key Islamic values, such as modesty and gender relations, and discuss how they shape consumption practices of Muslims in particular ways. Unfortunately, although well-intentioned, these approaches tend to produce (and reproduce) an exceptionalist, essentialist, and normative view of Islam and the Muslim market (for criticism, see Jafari and Sandıkcı, 2015). The emphasis on the 'uniqueness' of Muslims and their lifestyles creates a view of Muslim consumers as fundamentally different from consumers in general. This exceptionalist view is further reinforced by a depiction of Muslims whose engagement with consumption and marketing practices are governed by a series of rigid normative Islamic principles. The result is an essentialist approach that reifies difference and positions Muslim identity as fixed, ahistorical, context independent, and universal. Even though the authors mention diversity of Muslim populations, the multiplicity of lived experiences of being a Muslim *and* a consumer/marketer and their implications for marketing strategy remain mostly overlooked.

I argue that in order to be able to devise successful marketing strategies, managers need to go beyond stereotypical and static understandings and a preoccupation with difference and demographics and develop a more critical, situated, and dynamic engagement with Muslim consumers and businesses. Such a move requires developing an understanding of how individuals construct themselves as Muslim consumers and Muslim marketers in particular socio-temporal contexts using religious as well as marketplace resources. Critically oriented research within and outside the marketing field provides important insights into these interactions.

Muslim consumers: multiplicity of identity and diversity of lived experiences

As it is the case with the EMs in general, the Muslim–majority emerging countries are not a homogeneous set. While adherence to Islamic principles and values is a common denominator, Muslim-majority EMs widely differ along political, cultural, economic, and social dimensions. However, a mere acceptance of diversity fails to provide an in-depth and layered understanding of Muslim consumer subjectivity. A situated analysis requires acknowledging that identity is always multiple and relational. In other words, one is never only a Muslim, Christian, Hindu or else but a female, poor, middle age, Turkish Muslim, for example. There are multiple aspects to identity and it is imperative to understand which of those aspects become more or less visible and dominant under what conditions, when, and with what implications.

A common tendency in the managerially oriented literature is to prioritize a normative view of religiosity as the basis of identity (Sandıkcı, 2011). In other words, there seems to be an assumption that adherence to Islamic principles culminates in a particular Muslim consumption practice that can be targeted at uniformly. However, while Muslim consumers share a universal set of values and norms, they are also marked by differences along gender, class, age, nationality, ethnicity, and so on. Allowing for multiple components of identity to work together in a co–constitutive manner enables identifying commonalities and variations among different Muslim communities as well as between different communities of faith. Consider for example Muslims in Germany, Turkish Muslims in Germany and Muslims in Turkey. Islam appears to be the common descriptor in these different. However, a closer look at the consumption practices of these three different groups reveals a much diversified picture.

The domain of fashion consumption is a case in point. Modesty constitutes a key principle in Islam, shaping both consumption behavior and male-female interaction. According to the interpretations of Muslim scholars, modesty encompasses all aspects of life and calls for decency, humility, and moderation in speech, attitude, dress, and total behavior. While the principle of modesty applies to all believers and covers all domains of life, it becomes particularly important in the case of female clothing. Because women are deemed to more easily arouse the sexual feeling of a man than the other way around, they are required to cover parts of their body that can attract the male gaze. However, while modesty is a universal principle of Islam, what constitutes modest dressing style is a complex matter. Studies conducted in different parts of the Muslim world show that Islamic clothing styles differ significantly from context to context (e.g., Brenner, 1996; Lewis, 2013; Sandıkcı and Ger, 2010). Moreover, the meanings and practices of veiling are not fixed and uniform even within one country and vary across time and different social classes.

For example, in their study of veiling practices in Turkey, Sandıkcı and Ger (2010) show the multiplicity and dynamism of modest clothing and trace the changes in its meaning and practice in the last few decades. The authors report that 'traditional' forms of veiling characterized by a loosely tied headscarf gave way to a combination of large headscarf covering the head, neck and shoulders and long loose overcoat in the 1980s. By the 2000s, Muslim women in smaller headscarves and tighter and shorter coats, skirts, pants, and jackets in brighter and trendy colors became more visible on the streets. The once dominant large headscarf and the long, loose overcoat came to be associated with the poor while a multitude of styles of clothing and ways of tying variously shaped and sized headscarves have developed as markers of taste and social position among the urban upper classes.

As much as Turkish Muslim women's modest dressing practices changed and diversified so did those of Turkish Muslim women living in Germany. Historically, there have always been social, cultural and economic ties between the two communities. With the rise of political Islam in Turkey, the visibility and impact of various Islamic organizations also increased in Germany. As more and more Turkish-descent Muslim women in Germany took on veiling, new practices of modest dressing emerged. Some Turkish Islamic clothing companies have branches in Germany and sell the styles and models designed in Turkey. However, these women, especially the second and third generations, have a plethora of other resources in shaping their modest clothing style. They live in a multi-cultural context together with Muslims from different countries who have different covering practices. They also interact with non-Muslims and are exposed to a variety of fashion practices. All of these interactions yield to a multiplicity of modest dressing practices and render 'Islamic fashion' a very complex, dynamic, and diverse concept.

Even this one single case illustrates that although there are universal Islamic values and norms, how these are interpreted, negotiated, and experienced in the daily lives of Muslim consumers are far from uniform and predictable. Furthermore, the case also shows that a situated understanding of Muslim consumers requires a focus on the lived experience. In other words, while Islamic norms create a perception of difference between Muslim and non-Muslim consumers, how such differences are played out in the daily lives of consumers requires critical attention. Such an approach calls for examining the religious, political, cultural, and economic resources, forces, and tensions that consumers experience and negotiate as they (re)construct and communicate their identities as Muslims and paying attention to the dynamics of particular contexts and temporalities that particular Muslims inhabit. Insights gathered from such studies can provide a deeper understanding of the current situation and offer a better guidance for future possibilities.

In this regard, it is important for marketing scholars and practitioner to locate the development of an Islamic consumption culture within a general increase in consumerism and commoditization of everyday life (Maqsood, 2014; Sandıkcı and Ger, 2007). In the late 1980s and early 1990s many Muslim countries, similar to other emerging markets, went through a process of neoliberal globalization that resulted in an influx of global brands, proliferation of advertising and marketing practices, and emergence of new spaces of shopping. These economic changes along with major socio-political transformations contributed to the development of a conservative but consumption-oriented segment. In countries such as Turkey, Egypt, Malaysia, and Indonesia, to name a few, accumulation of wealth concomitant with the increasing influence of Islamic movements has resulted in the creation of a new middle class "conservative in values but avant-garde in consumption practices" (Sandıkcı and Ger, 2002, p. 467; see also Nasr, 2009; Wong, 2007).

A growing market seeks to cater to the demands of new Muslim middle classes. A wide variety of 'Islamic' and 'halal' positioned products exist, ranging from clothing to holiday resorts, food, gated communities, hajj packages, decorative objects, pop music, toys, lifestyle magazines, and cosmetics. According to Nasr, the consumption demands of a global Islamic middle class represents an economic counterbalance to China's consumer power as "this upwardly mobile class consumes Islam as much as practicing it, demand[ing] the same sorts of life-enhancing goods and services as middle classes everywhere" (2009, p. 14). Nasr's accent on similarity resonates with the findings of a recent study on the new middle classes (Kravets and Sandıkcı, 2014). The authors find alignment with an imagined global middle class and assimilating to their consumption practices emerges as a key consumption motivation for the new middle classes in the EMs. Rather than seeking difference and demanding to be treated differently, these consumers want to engage in "ordinary" and "normal" consumption practices that align them with the global middles classes.

Overall, these studies suggest that Muslim consumer subjectivity is deeply embedded in the logic of consumerism and evolving towards a harmonization of similarity and difference. Indeed, the growing popularity of Islamic Barbies, Islamic videogames, and Islamic hotels to name a few, suggest adaptive Islamization of Western forms of consumption practices rather than creation of new 'unique' forms of Islamic consumption. As discussed in the next section, Muslim entrepreneurs seem to be the key actors driving this trend.

Muslim marketers: Islamic business networks and pious entrepreneurship

The growth of the new Islamic middle classes coincides with the increasingly significant role Islamic business networks and Muslim entrepreneurs play in the global markets. From Malaysia to Turkey, India, Syria, the UK, USA, and Australia, these pious businessmen design, manufacture, and market products that cater to the demands of modern Muslim consumer subjectivity. Some popular examples are Turkish *Tekbir*, an Islamic clothing company; Syrian Newboy Design Studio, producer of *Fulla* dolls; Australian Ahiida, marketer of modest swimsuit *Burqini*, a term derived from merging 'burqa' and 'bikini'; and the UK-based *emel*, a Muslim lifestyle magazine. In each case, an aspiration to achieve business success and enable Muslims to live properly Islamic yet modern lives underlines the entrepreneurial story.

Tekbir is one of the earliest and largest Islamic fashion companies in Turkey. The company is famous for initiating once much controversial Islamic fashion shows and successfully utilizes all tools of fashion marketing. The company's collections are distributed through a wide network and reaches to consumers in and outside Turkey. Tekbir's fashionable clothes aim to 'make covering beautiful' and inspire women to adopt the veil (Gokariksel and Secor, 2010; Sandıkcı and Ger, 2007). Syrian born NewBoy, now headquartered in Dubai, UAE, markets various toys, food, and stationery products in the Middle East and North Africa. The company is famous for its Fulla doll, a Barbie-like fashion doll targeting Muslim children. Fulla dolls, available in many Muslim-majority and minority countries, including the USA and China, act as role models for Muslim girls, offering an alternative to the flirtatious and hedonistic Barbie (Yaqin, 2007). The Lebanese Australian Aheda Zanetti is the inventor of burqini, a swimsuit designed to comply with the Islamic requirements of modesty. The Burqini is positioned as a "modernizing invention that brings Muslim women's fashion and leisure pursuits (nearly) up to speed with those of their non-Muslim female counterparts" (Fitzpatrick, 2009, p. 4). Launched in 2003, *emel* is a Muslim lifestyle magazine with subscribers from over 60 countries and mainstream distribution in the UK, USA, Middle East, and Southeast Asia. *Emel* provides lifestyle tips informed by Islamic principles and ethical consumerism to its readers (Lewis, 2010). Overall, these and many other examples indicate the vibrant entrepreneurial culture and the interest in hybridizing Islamic principles and values with capitalist business practices. As Bassens, Derudder, and Witlox point out, "these 'Islamic businesses' have made compliance to or respect for the sensitivities of Islamic faith a fundamental aspect of the products and/or services they offer and/or the rationale behind the firm's organization and functioning" (2012, p. 338).

Scholars relate the emergence of this new class of Muslim entrepreneurs, located both in Muslim-majority and minority societies, to the contemporary political economy (Adas, 2006; Osella and Osella, 2009; Sloane, 1999) and in particular to a new form of "pious neoliberalism" (Atia, 2011). According to Atia, pious neoliberalism refers to "the discursive combination of religion and economic rationale in a manner that encourages individuals to be proactive and entrepreneurial in the interest of furthering their relationship with God" (2011, p. 2). Drawing on a globalized religious discourse and combining it with entrepreneurship, pious neoliberalism cultivates subjects who are driven toward material success in the present life and spiritual success in the afterlife. The emphasis on prosperity in this and the other world encourages Muslims to pursue economic success and reframes a proactive and entrepreneurial engagement with the market as a religiously appropriate endeavor (Atia, 2011).

Some analysts liken Muslim entrepreneurs to Weber's portrayal of Calvinists (Adas, 2006; Ignatow, Johnson, and Madanipour, 2014). Similar to the Calvinist work ethic, Muslim entrepreneurs "sanctify hard work, economic success and pursuit of wealth as important religious obligations" and believe that "a good Muslim should be an entre-preneurial Muslim" (Adas, 2006, p. 129). As Osella and Osella (2009) also observe, these entrepreneurs "inscribe their specific business interests and practices into rhetorics of the 'common good'" (p. S 203) and see combining material success with moral connected-ness as the "exemplary contemporary way of being a modern, moral, Muslim" (p. S 204). Furthermore, many scholars interpret Islam's engagement with the neoliberal economic system as emergence of market-friendly forms of Islam (e.g., Haenni, 2005; Ignatow, John-son, and Madanipour, 2014; Rudnyckyj, 2009).

Research on market-friendly forms of Islam reveal that these formations have an ideo-logical character as well and are often connected to the new Islamic movements. The new Islamic movements seek to create networks of shared meaning through mobilization of various resources such as political parties, religious organizations, NGOs, schools, and social networks (Bayat, 2005; Wiktorowicz, 2004). Market and consumption play impor-tant roles in the growth and spread of these movements. As Yavuz (2004) argues, Islamic groups have benefited from the new 'opportunity spaces' created by economic liberaliza-tion in countries like Turkey and used these market-oriented venues, such as the media, financial institutions, and businesses to propagate the Islamic lifestyles and generate finan-cial resources. Similarly, Hosgor (2011) reports that religious orders and movements have played a significant role for Islamic business especially during the early phase of capital accumulation. These networks collect money from their members through various forms of charities and use the money for providing religious courses, building mosques, and establishing schools and dormitories. However, as Hosgor argues, beyond intracommunity support, these networks fulfill some important business functions. Members obtain loans from each other, undertake joint investments, and collectively purchase inputs to reduce transportation and transaction costs. Furthermore, religious networks help construct a religiously sensitive customer base and promote the purchase of the products of Muslim entrepreneurs as a 'religious duty' (also see Karatas and Sandıkcı, 2013). These various forms of support contribute to the growth of Islamic businesses and help them become not only big domestic players but large transnational companies.

Overall, research on Islamic business networks and Muslim entrepreneurs shows that neoliberal ideals are being articulated through an Islamic rhetoric, creating new forms of pious marketing as well as consumption practices. The new forms of the so-called market-friendly Islam appear to be relevant and observable in many different parts of the Muslim geography and especially in the emergent Muslim-majority countries, shaping competition and marketplace dynamics and creating opportunities as well as threats for the global brands. Next I discuss the implications of these developments for marketing strategy.

Implications for marketing strategy

The discovery of Muslims as consumers resembles the discovery of non-mainstream communities such as gays, Hispanics, immigrants, and blacks as viable market segments (Sandıkcı and Ger, 2010). Similar to these groups, a shift in meaning from 'marginalized' consumers to a lifestyle community embedded in the language of consumption is visible in the case of the Muslim market. The dramatic growth of the global halal industry indicates that Muslim consumers are increasingly seen as a segment with significant purchasing power. While it is not clear what an 'Islamic lifestyle' entails, products and services labeled halal or Islamic proliferate and take their places in the global retailscape. However, as mentioned in the beginning of the chapter, a deep understanding of the Muslim market requires going beyond the normative, essential, and stereotypical depictions of Muslim consumers and marketers to one that is situated, attentive to the socio-political and economic context and concerned with everyday practices. Research reviewed in the previous sections reveal the multiplicity of Muslim identity and diversity of the lived experiences of being a Muslim consumer. It also shows the role of religious movements and Islamic business networks in fostering new forms of pious entrepreneurship that blend Islamic principles and capitalist ambitions.

Overall, this multidisciplinary perspective on Muslim consumers and marketers suggests that marketing managers should refrain from regarding Muslims as a homogeneous segment. As much as there is no single and uniform gay, Hispanic, or black consumer market, there is no single and uniform Muslim market. At the very least social class, gender, and ethnicity in combination with religious sensitivities culminate in multiple, sometimes overlapping, sometimes conflicting, taste structures and practices. The starting point for any marketing strategy should be conducting marketing research in the emerging markets of the Muslim-majority countries to get a sound and actionable set of insights. In this regard in addition to quantitative assessments and surveys of Muslim consumers, ethnographic studies of the market are needed. As Cayla and Arnould (2013) show, ethnography facilitates market learning and ethnographic stories give managers unique means of understanding market realities. Such market research analyses can equip marketing managers with a perspective on the cultural realities of individuals rather than imposing preexisting categories to explain their behaviors. Furthermore, it urges practitioners to look beyond the lens of religious norms and values and pay attention to how Islamic norms and values are interpreted, negotiated, and experienced in the daily lives of Muslim consumers and marketers.

Marketing managers should also refrain from approaching the Muslim market as a segment already existing and bounded. Research on the emergence of blacks, Hispanics, gays, and other collectivities as consumer segments report that these 'segments' were not preexisting entities that marketers simply needed to appeal to but constructions (Davila, 2001; Sender, 2004). That is, it is through marketing practices such as segmentation, targeting, product development, and advertising that groups of consumers become analytical categories to act upon. In this regard, a closer examination of Islamic businesses and Muslim entrepreneurs can give valuable insights to global brands seeking to enter or already operating in the emerging Muslim-majority markets. Consider for example Mattel, the company behind the Barbie dolls. The company can learn much about the Muslim families and children as well as marketers from analyzing the motivations, claims, and practices of NewBoy, the firm behind the Fulla doll. Such contextualized understanding can help Western multinationals to devise better strategies both in marketing their products and competing with local alternatives.

Segmentation constitutes the basis of marketing strategy. However, as years of research and practice show, for devising a successful segmentation approach one needs to go beyond demographic descriptors. This simple yet important observation is particularly relevant for the Muslim market. The use of religion as a profiling variable leads to an overemphasis of faith at the expense of other aspects of identity. Furthermore, the discrepancy between belief and practice may result in misreading of the market potential. For example, in calculating the size of the halal market, consultants and market research analysts tend to look at the size of the Muslim population. Identification as a Muslim does not necessarily result in consumption of only halal products and brands. The high market shares of many Western-originated brands in many Muslim-majority countries suggest that multiple sensitivities are at play in consumption preferences and choices. Consider for example the case of modest fashion, a market often deemed as highly lucrative. As mentioned before, the meanings and practices of what constitutes proper Islamic dress vary significantly. Moreover, Muslim women blend different styles, products, and brands, be it local or global, Islamic or not, in crafting their fashionable looks. In countries like Turkey and Saudi Arabia, Western brands like Zara, H&M, and Mango dominate the market rather than Islamic fashion brands. Western and Islamic brands coexist and cater together to the demands of Muslim consumers. As our own research shows, rather than shopping only at Islamic clothing stores, Turkish covered women look for and buy outfits that they think help them achieve their desirable modest styles from a plethora of outlets, including local and global brand shops (Sandıkcı and Ger, 2010).

Hence, a more productive marketing approach might be segmenting around the job to be done rather than predefined consumer groups (Christensen, Cook and Hall, 2005). As Christensen et al. (2005) explain, when consumers need to get something done, they 'hire' products to do the job for them. For example, if they are looking for something that will ease their boring morning commute, they might hire a milk shake to do the job for them. As the authors point out, the marketers' task is "to understand what jobs periodically arise in customers'' lives for which they might hire products that the company could make" (2005, p. 76). When applied to the context of Muslim markets, this perspective calls for exploring the kind of jobs that Muslim consumers are trying to accomplish (for example, how to dress in a properly Islamic way and enjoy swimming) rather than merely profiling them along demographic, psychographic, and behavioral characteristics. Focusing on daily practices and problems Muslim consumers face in their everyday lives can provide insights to multinational companies in regard to new product development or adjustment of existing offerings. The emphasis on providing solutions to consumers in their quest for proper Islamic lives while enjoying the benefits of the material world and technological advancement rather than a rigid focus on halal certification appears to be a more grounded and holistic marketing approach.

Furthermore, traditional segmentation approaches tend to favor the most profitable and easily accessible consumer group. In this case they are the Islamic middle classes. Given the prevailing assumption of Muslims as an untapped consumer segment waiting to be served by international companies, much of the managerial focus is on the relatively wealthy, educated, and urban Muslim consumers and their consumption practices. While there are indeed extremely rich Muslim consumers, a significant portion of Muslims live under conditions of poverty, vulnerability, and social and economic inequality. Around 40 percent of the Muslim population languishes in abject poverty, with nearly 350 million living under US\$1.25 a day (COMCEC, 2014). More than half of the world's 57 Muslim countries are listed as low-income food deficit countries by the Food and Agriculture Organization of the United Nations (FAO, 2014) and almost half of them rank in the low category in the United Nations Development Program's Human Development Index (UNDP, 2014). Given these bleak statistics, Muslims constitute a significant portion of the bottom-of-the-pyramid segment. Despite the economic growth observed in the last decade in the emerging Muslim–majority markets, there too poor consumers represent significant numbers. A situated understanding of the needs and problems of the Muslim poor can provide new growth opportunities for multinational as well as local companies. The solutions companies can generate are also likely to contribute positively to the quality of life and bring some relief to the Muslim poor.

In devising marketing strategies, managers should also pay close attention to the nature and dynamics of competition and the motives, aspirations, and practices of Muslim entrepreneurs. While Islamic businesses have the advantage of a local understanding of Islam, multinational companies might be better positioned in drawing from a global pool of experiences and resources. The complexities and diversity characterizing the emerging Muslim–majority markets suggest that as much as competition, cooperation might be a valid strategy. Mergers and acquisitions can help multinationals to develop an understanding of the local Islamic culture relatively quickly and begin devising appropriate solutions for consumers. Overall, as any market, emerging Muslim–majority countries present many challenges and opportunities for marketers, and their dynamics suggest that one-size-fits-all Muslim products will be unlikely to deliver sustainable success.

Conclusion

The goal of this chapter has been to sensitize marketers on the multiplicities and complexities of the Muslim market. Understanding Muslim consumers and marketers requires doing away with essentialist approaches that exceptionalize Muslims and reify their difference. What the examples and discussions presented above indicate is the necessity of adopting a socio-culturally situated approach to the Islamic market. Instead of focusing on a narrow conceptualization of halal, marketing scholars and practitioners need to pay attention to how Islamic norms and principles play out in the daily lives of Muslims. In other words, we need to examine the religious, political, cultural, and economic resources, forces, and tensions that individuals experience and negotiate as they (re)construct and communicate their identities as Muslim consumers and marketers. Such an approach can help marketers to achieve a sustainable and profitable position in the emerging markets of Muslim–majority countries and can bring novel insights into the conceptualizations of religion–market interaction.

Issues for further discussion

1   Is the Muslim segment the next growth market for multinational companies?
2   What are the opportunities existing for companies that wish to target the poor consumers in the emerging markets of Muslim-majority countries?

3   Do you think that Muslim entrepreneurs will be able to challenge global brands out-
    side their local markets?
4   Given the heterogeneity of the Muslim market and the diversity of everyday practices
    of Muslim consumers, what does positioning a product as 'Islamic' really mean?

Case study

Marketing halal nail polish[1]

In 2009, Inglot launched a new line of nail polish, named O2M, which stands
for oxygen and moisture. Inglot is a Polish cosmetics company with over 500
stores in 70 countries, including the USA, Canada, the UAE, Saudi Arabia, Mexico,
France, the UK, Malaysia, and South Africa. The company claims that O2M is
a revolutionary breathable nail enamel which ensures oxygen and water vapor
permeability. According to the company website, O2M was created specifically
for health reasons and designed as a healthier alternative to standard nail polish.
Interestingly, although Inglot developed the product not with the Muslim market in
mind, O2M created a significant buzz on social media and became an unexpected
hit among Muslim consumers.

Wearing nail enamel is a contentious issue for pious Muslim women. The problem is not nail polish itself but its effect on performing ablution, a ritualized body
cleansing process that every Muslim should undertake before prayer. Nail polish
sets a permanent barrier between water and nail, preventing water from reaching
every part of the hand. Hence, when a Muslim woman needs to perform ablution,
she should first remove the nail polish. This severely limits the use of nail enamel
among practicing Muslim women. Many never wear nail polish; some wear it only
during their menstrual period, when they are exempt from praying. Others use the
product in between praying times, putting it on only to take it off in a couple of
hours.

O2M captured Muslim consumers' interest after Mustafa Umar, an Islamic
scholar and a director at the Islamic Institute of Orange County, California, USA,
published the results of a test conducted by one of his students on his blog on
November 2012:

> One of my students decided to perform a test to see whether or not water
> actually seeped through when using the Inglot O2M nail polish. As a test case,
> she applied standard pink nail polish and purple O2M on a coffee filter and
> allowed both to dry. She then placed another coffee filter below the painted one,
> squeezed two drops of water over the polish, and applied some pressure with
> her finger. After about ten seconds it was clear that the water was prevented
> from seeping through [even to the back side of the first filter] on the standard
> polish but clearly went through the O2M and even wet the second filter. This

is sufficient to show that the claims made by the manufacturer are correct and water does indeed permeate through to the nail. (http://mustafaumar.com/2012/11/is-breathable-nail-polish-sufficient-for-wu%E1%B8%8Du/)

The blog entry, which came to be known by many as "the nail polish fatwa", went viral. The news of Inglot's breathable nail polish spread quickly from woman to woman over the internet, leading to a sharp rise in interest in the product.

The buzz about 'halal' nail polish attracted more companies to the sector. In June 2014 the Dubai-based BCI Group launched the first halal certified nail polish in the UAE under the brand name 'H'. In order to get halal certification, nail polish should be free of alcohol and non-halal derivatives. H has increased the absorptive capability that allows water to pass through the nails, carries a guarantee that it is not tested on animals, and is certified by the Al Iman Islamic Society, Australia. H is distributed across the UAE.

Outside the Muslim-majority countries, two other companies, located in the USA and Canada, are involved in the halal nail market. Tuesday in Love is a Canadian company specialized in water permeable nail polish. The company claims to have a unique micro-pore technology that allows water molecules to penetrate through the semi-permeable color membrane. Tuesday in Love is also not tested on animals and does not contain any harsh chemicals and alcohol. The product is halal certified by Talim Ul Islam, Canada. Tuesday in Love did not have presence outside North America until 2012 when a Malaysian entrepreneur, Eliz Ramskay, became interested in the product. Observing the latent demand for halal nail polish, Ramskay became a distributor for Tuesday in Love nail polish in Malaysia. She decided to market the brand with the name 'Modern Inai' or modern henna, a substance traditionally used to color nails and hands in the Muslim geographies. Acquarella is based in Arizona, USA and specializes in water based nail products. The company prides itself on high-quality safe and healthy products that do not contain harsh petrochemicals and are not tested on animals. Acquarella products became known among Muslim consumers through Saaima Moola, a South African entrepreneur. Looking for nail polish that is appropriate for the use of Muslim consumers Mrs. Moola came across with the Acquarella brand. After conducting her own test, she became convinced for water permeability of the product and now works as the exclusive distributor of the company in South Africa. Acquarella is also approved by Mufti Omar Dawood of Islamic Lifestyle Solutions, a non-profit organization based in South Africa. While the company does not have a distribution network in the Muslim geographies, it accepts international online orders.

With the rise of a Muslim-oriented consumer culture and lifestyle marketing, the demand for 'halal' beauty and personal care products is thriving. Nail care is a significant and high potential segment of the cosmetics market. Currently the halal nail care market is characterized by local players and smaller companies and is relatively free of multinational companies. While Inglot is largely responsible for the increasing popularity of halal nail polish, it is not actively marketing O2M as a halal product. It seems that the market is still not much crowded and offers good opportunities for global brands.

Case questions for discussion

1   How should Inglot Cosmetics respond to the demand from the Muslim consumer segment? Should the company specifically target this segment and if so how? Should they introduce other Muslim-friendly products in related categories such as makeup and skin care?

2   Should big multinational companies such as L'Oréal and Procter and Gamble pursue the emerging 'halal' nail polish market? What are the risks and opportunities in entering this market?

3   Does 'halal' nail polish have potential outside the Muslim market? What are possible positioning strategies to market the product to both Muslim and non-Muslim consumers?

Note

1 The case is based on information available on company websites and various online sources.

References

Adas, E. B. (2006), "The Making of Entrepreneurial Islam and the Islamic Spirit of Capitalism", *Journal for Cultural Research*, Vol. 10, No. 2, pp. 113–137.

Askegaard, S. (2006), "Brands as a Global Ideoscape", in J. E. Schroeder and M. Salzer-Mrling (Eds.), *Brand Culture*, London: Routledge Press, pp. 91–101.

Atia, M. (2011), "'A Way to Paradise': Pious Neoliberalism, Islam, and Faith-Based Development", *Annals of the Association of American Geographers*, Vol. 102, No. 4, pp. 808–827.

Bassens, D., Derudder, B. and Witlox, F. (2012), "'Gatekeepers' of Islamic Financial Circuits: Analysing Urban Geographies of the Global Shari'a Elite", *Entrepreneurship and Regional Development*, Vol. 24, No. 5–6, pp. 337–355.

Bayat, A. (2005), "Islamism and Social Movement Theory", *Third World Quarterly*, Vol. 26, No. 6, pp. 891–908.

Berger, R. (2013), "8 Billion Consumers – How to Reach Emerging Market Consumers With New Strategies", *Think, Act, Study*, Vol. 3, January, pp. 1–29.

Brenner, S. (1996), "Reconstructing Self and Society: Javanese Muslim Women and 'the Veil'", *American Ethnologist*, Vol. 23, No. 4, pp. 673–697.

Burgess, S. M. and Steenkamp, J. B. E. (2006), "Marketing Renaissance: How Research in Emerging Markets Advances Marketing Science and Practice," *International Journal of Research in Marketing*, Vol. 23, No. 4, pp. 337–356.

Cavusgil, S. T. and Kardes, I. (2013), "Brazil: Rapid Development, Internationalization and Middle Class Formation", *Revista Elecronica de Negocios Internationais*, Vol. 8, No. 1, pp. 1–16.

Cayla, J. and Arnould, E. (2013), "Ethnographic Stories for Market Learning", *Journal of Marketing*, Vol. 77, No. 4, pp. 1–16.

Christensen, C. M., Cook, S. and Hall, T. (2005), "Marketing Malpractice", *Harvard Business Review*, Vol. 83, No. 12, pp. 74–83.

COMCEC. (2014), "Poverty Outlook 2014: Multidimensional Poverty", The Standing Committee for Economic and Commercial Cooperation of the Organization of the Islamic Cooperation. www.mod.gov. tr/Lists/RecentPublications/Attachments/66/COMCEC%20Poverty%20Outlook%202014%20- %20Revised%20Edition.pdf

Davila, A. (2001), *Latinos Inc.: The Marketing and Making of a People*, Berkeley, CA: University of California Press.

FAO. (2014), "Low-Income Food-Deficit Countries (LIFDC): List for 2014", *Food and Agriculture Organization of the United Nations*. www.fao.org/countryprofiles/lifdc/en/

Fitzpatrick, S. (2009), "Covering Muslim Women at the Beach: Media Representations of the Burkini", *Thinking Gender Papers*, UCLA Center for the Study of Women, UC Los Angeles. http://escholarship. org/uc/item/9d0860x7

Gauthier, F., Martikainen, T. and Woodhead, L. (2013), "Acknowledging a Global Shift: A Primer for Thinking About Religion in Consumer Societies", *Implicit Religion*, Vol. 16, No. 3, pp. 261–276.

Ger, G. and Belk, R. W. (1996), "I'd Like to Buy the World a Coke: Consumptionscapes of the Less Affluent World", *Journal of Consumer Policy*, Vol. 19, No. 3, pp. 271–304.

Gokarıksel, B. and Secor, A. (2010), "Islamic-ness in the Life of a Commodity: Veiling-Fashion in Turkey", *Transactions of the Institute of British Geographers*, Vol. 35, No. 3, pp. 313–333.

Gokarıksel, B. and Secor, A. J. (2009), "New Transnational Geographies of Islamism, Capitalism and Subjectivity: The Veiling-Fashion Industry in Turkey", *Area*, Vol. 41, No. 1, pp. 6–18.

Goldman Sachs. (2007), *Brics and Beyond*, Goldman Sachs International. www.goldmansachs.com/our-thinking/archive/archive-pdfs/brics-book/brics-full-book.pdf

Haenni, P. (2005), *L'Islam de marche': L'autre re'volution conservatrice*, Paris: Editions du Seuil et La Re'publique des Idees.

Harvey, D. (2005), *A Brief History of Neoliberalism*, Oxford: Oxford University Press.

Holt, D. B., Quelch, J. A. and Taylor, E. L. (2004), "How Global Brands Compete", *Harvard Business Review*, Vol. 82, No. 9, pp. 68–75.

Hosgor, E. (2011), "Islamic Capital/Anatolian Tigers: Past and Present", *Middle Eastern Studies*, Vol. 47, No. 2, pp. 343–360.

Ignatow, G., Johnson, L. and Madanipour, A. (2014), "Global System Theory and 'Market-friendly' Religion", *Globalizations*, Vol. 11, No. 6, pp. 827–841.

IMF. (2014), World Economic Outlook 2014. *International Monetary Fund*. www.imf.org/external/pubs/ ft/weo/2014/02/

Jafari, A. (2012), "Islamic Marketing: Insights From a Critical Perspective", *Journal of Islamic Marketing*, Vol. 3, pp. 22–34.

Jafari, A. and Sandıkcı, O. (2015), "'Islamic' Consumers, Markets, and Marketing: A Critique of El-Bassiouny's (2014) 'The one billion-plus marginalization'", *Journal of Business Research*. http://dx.doi. org/10.1016/j.jbusres.2015.04.003

Jafari, A. and Suerdem, A. (2012), "An Analysis of Material Consumption Culture in the Muslim World", *Marketing Theory*, Vol. 12, No. 1, pp. 61–79.

Karatas, M. and Sandıkcı, O. (2013), "Religious Communities and the Marketplace: Learning and Performing Consumption in an Islamic Network", *Marketing Theory*, Vol. 13, pp. 465–484.

Khanna, T. and Palepu, K. (2013). *Winning in Emerging Markets: A Road Map for Strategy and Execution*, Boston, MA: Harvard Business Press.

Kravets, O. and Sandıkcı, O. (2014), "Competently Ordinary: New Middle Class Consumers in the Emerging Markets", *Journal of Marketing*, Vol. 78, July, pp. 125–140.

Lewis, R. (Ed.). (2013). *Modest Fashion: Styling Bodies, Mediating Faith*, London: IB Tauris.

Lewis, R. (2010), "Marketing Muslim Lifestyle: A New Media Genre", *Journal of Middle East Women's Studies*, Vol. 6, No. 3, pp. 58–90.

Mahajan, V. and Banga, K. (2005), *The 86 Percent Solution: How to Succeed in the Biggest Market Opportunity of the Next 50 Years*, Upper Saddle River, NJ: FT Press.

Maqsood, A. (2014), "'Buying Modern' Muslim Subjectivity, the West and Patterns of Islamic Consumption in Lahore, Pakistan", *Cultural Studies*, Vol. 28, No. 1, pp. 84–107.

Nasr, V. (2009), *Forces of Fortune: The Rise of the New Muslim Middle Class and What It Will Mean for Our World*, New York: Free Press.

Ogilvy, N. (2010), *Brands, Islam and the Muslim Consumers*. www.ogilvynoor.com/index.php/ publications

Ong, A. (2006), *Neoliberalism as Exception: Mutations in Citizenship and Sovereignty*, Durham: Duke University Press.

Osella, F. and Osella, C. (2009), "Muslim Entrepreneurs in Public Life Between India and the Gulf: Making Good and Going Good," *Journal of the Royal Anthropological Institute*, pp. S202–221.

Ozsomer, A. and Altaras, S. (2008), "Global Brand Purchase Likelihood: A Critical Synthesis and an Integrated Conceptual Framework", *Journal of International Marketing*, Vol. 16, No. 4, pp. 1–28.

Rudnyckyj, D. (2009), "Market Islam in Indonesia", *Journal of the Royal Anthropological Institute*, Vol. 15, No. s1, pp. S183–S201.

Rudnyckyj, D. (2009), "Spiritual Economies: Islam and Neoliberalism in Contemporary Indonesia", *Cultural Anthropology*, Vol. 24, No. 1, pp. 104–141.

Sandıkcı, O. (2011), "Researching Islamic Marketing: Past and Future Perspectives", *Journal of Islamic Marketing*, Vol. 2, pp. 246–258.

Sandıkcı, O. and Ger, G. (2010), "Veiling in Style: How Does a Stigmatized Practice Become Fashionable?" *Journal of Consumer Research*, Vol. 37, No. 1, pp. 15–36.

Sandıkcı, O. and Ger, G. (2007), "Constructing and Representing the Islamic Consumer in Turkey", *Fashion Theory*, Vol. 11, No. 2–3, pp. 189–210.

Sandıkcı, O. and Ger, G. (2002), "In-Between Modernities and Postmodernities: Investigating Turkish Consumptionscape", *Advances in Consumer Research*, Vol. 29, pp. 465–470.

Sender, K. (2004), *Business, Not Politics: The Making of the Gay Market*, New York: Columbia University Press.

Sheth, J. N. (2011), "Impact of Emerging Markets on Marketing: Rethinking Existing Perspectives and Practices," *Journal of Marketing*, Vol. 75, No. 4, pp. 166–182.

Sloane, P. (1999), *Islam, Modernity, and Entrepreneurship Among the Malays*. Hampshire, UK: St. Martin's Press.

Strizhakova, Y., Coulter, R. A. and Price, L. L. (2008), "Branded Products as a Passport to Global Citizenship: Perspectives From Developed and Developing Countries," *Journal of International Marketing*, Vol. 16, No. 4, pp. 57–85.

Thomson Reuters. (2014), *State of the Global Islamic Economy*.

UNDP. (2014), "Human Development Report 2014", *United Nations Development Program*. http://hdr.undp.org/sites/default/files/hdr14-report-en-1.pdf.

van Agtmael, A. (2007). *The Emerging Markets Century: How a New Breed of World-Class Companies Is Overtaking the World*, New York: Simon and Schuster.

Vladimir, K. (2009), *The Global Emerging Market: Strategic Management and Economics*, New York, London: Routledge.

Wiktorowicz, Q. (2004), *Islamic Activism: A Social Movement Theory Approach*, Bloomington, IN: Indiana University Press.

Wilson, E. K. and Steger, M. B. (2013), "Religious Globalisms in the Post-secular Age", *Globalizations*, Vol. 10, No. 3, 481–495.

Wong, L. (2007), "Market Cultures, the Middle Classes and Islam: Consuming the Market?"' *Consumption Markets and Culture*, Vol. 10, No. 4, pp. 451–480.

Yaqin, A. (2007), "Islamic Barbie: The Politics of Gender and Performativity," *Fashion Theory*, Vol. 11, No. 2, pp. 173–188.

Yavuz, H. (2004), 'Opportunity Spaces, Identity and Islamic Meaning in Turkey", in Wiktorowicz, Q. (Ed.), *Islamic Activism: A Social Movement Theory Approach*, Bloomington, IN: Indiana University Press, pp. 270–288.

11 Supply chain management within the Middle East business environment

Nesrine Eltawy and David Gallear

Learning outcomes

At the end of the chapter, the reader should be able to:

1 Recall the origin and definitions given to supply chain management in the previous literature
2 Appreciate the importance of supply chain and its management and the need for successful supply chain management to deal with dynamic and complex business environments
3 Appreciate the nature of the Middle East business environment and the challenges facing companies working within the Middle East region
4 Understand how multinational companies working within the Middle East region perceive the importance of supply chain management and are focusing on improving it through supply chain relationships and supply chain partnerships in particular

Key points

1 Although there is considerable research on supply chains and their management, further research is required to provide a clear definition and understanding of the concept.
2 The Middle East region is an attractive area for future research; such research will help the region's countries to compete with outside competition.
3 Middle East–based companies require a clear understanding of supply chain management in order to compete successfully within their business environments.
4 The importance of supply chain relationships and partnerships for the companies working within the Middle East business environments are recognised within this research as a means for improving their supply chain performance.

Introduction

Supply chain management, as a business and management concept, has received great attention from academics and practitioners (Cousins et al., 2006). This is evidenced by the increase in the number of published articles by both practitioners and academics, the increase in supply chain management conferences, the increase in development and training programmes for professionals and even in the supply chain management courses taught by universities (Burgess et al., 2006).

Supply chain management

The emphasis on the supply chain and its management has increased as a consequence of industrial practitioners and academics recognising that it is a key factor for companies not just to compete, but to survive and stay in the marketplace (Li et al., 2005). This is because nowadays companies consider supply chain management as a core vehicle for success inside the competitive business environment and as the factor that enables them to provide a sustainable image for their products or service offerings inside their marketplace (Jones, 1998; cited in Li et al., 2005).

Cousins et al. (2006) argue that companies within both the private and the public sectors recognise the importance of supply chain management and its role in achieving success. Christopher (1992) insists on this by arguing that *"competition in the future will not be between individual enterprises but between competing supply chains."* Van der Vorst (2004) suggests that business managers recognise the importance of the effective coordinating, integrating, and managing of core processes among all the supply chain members and consider it as the key factor for the success of their organisations. Similarly, Li et al. (2005) argue that most organisations realise the importance of their supply chains and are increasing their efforts to enhance them. They suggest that it is not enough for the companies simply to improve their internal organisational efficiencies, but they must also improve their supply chains in order to strive for or maintain a competitive position within their marketplace (Li et al., 2005). This argument was also proffered by Power et al. (2001), amongst many others, who argue that management attention on achieving effective supply chain management is necessary for achieving profitable gains.

As alluded to above, several factors have led to the perceived importance of supply chain management. Arguably one of the main factors is an increasingly competitive business environment, especially after the emergence of "global" competition (Jain and Banyouccef, 2008). The "new" competition affects how organisations deal with organising and operating their supply chains (Jain and Benyoucef, 2008). Li et al. (2005) highlight that competition, and especially global competition, is now an important challenge that faces organisations in providing their products and offering their services in the most suitable places, at the most suitable times, with the lowest possible cost.

Similarly, Kisperska-Moron and Swiercczek (2009) summarise the multitude of factors that have led to the importance of supply chain management into two main categories: the economic and the technological environmental changes. These changes have led to increasing globalisation and an "international economy", which have forced companies to enhance their ability to serve customers, have greater control over new business markets, to face great competitive pressure, to deal with growing informational and technological pressures, to deal with a burgeoning variety in customers' needs and wants, to face the growing trends in new management approaches to be able to lower operational costs, to deal with investment costs and to face new customers' expectations (Kisperska-Moron and Swiercczek, 2009).

Although the importance of supply chain management and its various elements is widely recognised, the success stories of effective management are far from widespread. For example, as far back as 1998, Boddy et al. (1998) noted that more than half of their survey respondents were not applying supply chain partnering successfully. It therefore appears that its management in an effective manner is still not widely implemented. Much more recently this has also been suggested by other researchers, such as Gunasekaran et al. (2004), who argue that although there are several techniques and frameworks of supply chain performance measures in the literature, there is still a gap concerning the empirical testing and analysis of such performance measures in real supply chains. It is reasonable to argue that this is as a result, partly at least, of the supply chain management complexity and the lack in research identifying the means and methods that can help organisations to implement supply chain management effectively (Li et al., 2005). Moreover, Cousins et al. (2006) state that although supply chain management has been studied through different disciplines and from different theoretical perspectives, which leads to richness in the field, this has also led to unclear literature as well as overlapping constructs and inconsistent results. Cousins et al. (2006) argue that this unclear state in the literature lies also in the complex and context specific domain of buyer–supplier relationships elements; they posit that there are many theories for supply chain management and buyer–supplier relationships. Based on the work of Chen and Paulraj (2004) it is also suggested that there is a lack in supply chain literature of clear construct definitions and conceptual models upon which research can be based, which leads to non-generalisability. Van der Vorst (2004) suggests that among the factors that make it difficult for companies to implement supply chain management successfully are: the lack of trust between the company and its partners, differing objectives, managerial philosophies and reward systems.

The literature cited above highlights the great attention given to supply chain management as a business concept and emphasises its importance in helping companies to stay competitive inside their marketplace. However, a gap still exists in the supply chain management literature regarding how companies can effectively implement supply chain management in a way that can enable them to respond as quickly and effectively as they can to changes in this highly dynamic and competitive business world.

Supply chain management: origin and definition

Supply chain management was first introduced in 1982 by logistics researchers to describe an inventory management approach with regard to the managing of raw materials supply (Oliver and Webber, 1982, cited in Van der Vorst, 2004). Until the early 1990s supply chain as a concept of linking value-added activities in a common chain had not been widely applied. However, since the mid-1990s supply chain and consequently its management have become important terms in the business environment at both the practical and academic levels (Presutti and Mawhinney, 2007). Presutti and Mawhinney (2007) argue that the emergence of the supply chain into the business and economic world may be considered as the most important development in the business environment management after US firms began using the JIT concept in the early 1980s. They propose an answer to the question concerning the reason behind the great importance and consequently the great attention to supply chain. They suggest that managers recognise the role played by the supply chain to provide their companies a unique and sustainable competitive advantage, in the pursuit of high profitability. They argue that effective management of the supply chain may lead to gaining competitive advantage in four performance dimensions: cost, quality, response time and flexibility.

Chen and Paulraj (2004) in their research on the origin of the concept argue that the concept of supply chain has been developed as a result of the focus and emphasis placed on other related fields. Among these areas are: the revolution of quality concept (Dale et al., 1994), and the management of material and logistics (Carter and Price, 1993; Forrester, 1961). They suggest that the concept of supply chain management was first introduced by researchers during the 1980s (Oliver and Webber, 1982. They also highlight that supply chain management has been used to describe the flow of materials and information and how well the company is able to plan and control such flow processes, not only inside its borders, but also between the company and other external parties (Cooper et al., 1997; Fisher, 1997). According to Chen and Paulraj (2004), in addition, the concept has been used to describe other related areas. They suggest that the focus of some academic researchers – in fields such as purchasing and supply management; logistical and transportation fields; production and operations management; marketing; organisational theory; information systems as management information systems; as well as strategic management areas – has led to the high growth in the supply chain management concept. However, they argue that this may lead to the concept being curtailed unless there is a clear conceptual base (New, 1996). They also show that there are several authors focusing on the need for reliable well-defined constructs for supply chain management, as well as a well-explained conceptual framework for it (Saunders, 1995; Cooper et al., 1997; Babbar and Prasad, 1998; Saunders, 1998).

The same meaning has been argued by Ryu et al. (2009), as they suggest that supply chain management has been studied from different extended subject areas. They suggest that supply chain management has been extended to cover issues outside the company's borders for the sake of the whole supply chain partners, with support and encouragement from the main companies to decrease operational costs and enhance customer service, which result in a comparative advantage for all the supply chain partners (Subramani, 2004; Wang et al., 2006, cited in Ryu et al., 2009).

Supply chain management has been defined by several researchers, and from a number of different perspectives. For example, it is defined by 'The Council Of Logistics Management' (2000) as "the systematic, strategic coordination of the traditional business functions and tactics across these businesses' functions within a particular organisation and across businesses within the supply chain, for the purpose of improving the long term performance of the individual organisations and the supply chain as a whole" (cited in Li et al., 2005, p. 618). A supply chain can be considered as a set of activities that are used by any company to provide value to its customers, either ultimately as a product, service or both (Lin and Shaw, 1998, cited in Samaranayke, 2005). Samaranayke (2005) defines a supply chain as a network of individual or partially linked business parties combined together upstream or downstream in cooperation to produce goods and/or services to their end users. Supply chain management, therefore, is a process of integrating materials and the flow of information between different parties as customers, manufacturers and suppliers (Samaranayke, 2005).

Despite the efforts undertaken and still in progress by academic researchers to define supply chain and its management, until now the literature is lacking a unified accepted definition. This is also observed by Naslund and Williamson (2010), who reach this conclusion after a critical and deep review of a large part of the literature on supply chain management. Therefore, the researchers can argue that there is no unified definition for supply chain management, and still more work is needed to provide a well unified agreed-upon definition for such an important concept in today's complex and dynamic business environment, and in the absence of which select the definition provided by the Council of Logistics Management (2000) as the definition for the research background. The selected definition involves all the coordination and cooperation that can take place across the organisational functional units and across the supply chain members, and can be considered as the main focus of the research as it emphasises the importance of the supply chain in the ability of the companies in managing their internal and external activities, and internal and external relationships for the purpose of improving their own performance as well as their supply chain performance. This definition is therefore very suitable for this research.

The need for supply chain management

Nowadays, the rapid changes in both economic conditions and business conditions have led to several consequences for firms operating in industrial and commercial markets. The changes in economic conditions have led to reduced attention for trends such as vertical integration including economies of scale, large amounts of capital and huge physical infrastructure investments, and have given greater attention to issues such as specialisation, speed, agility and high growth (Samaranayke, 2005). Together with business conditions such as deregulation, increases in globalisation and a business environment characterised by integration, cooperation, sharing in information and information technologies, such changes have led companies not to depend solely on their internal resources and experience, but to also depend on external parties in order to deliver high value to their customers (Samaranayke, 2005). Therefore, companies are now searching for a business philosophy that includes the importance of managing and integrating the activities undertaken by several parties either inside or outside the company's boundaries, and which has been termed as "supply chain management" (Archibald et al., 1999, cited in Samaranayke, 2005).

Ismail and Sharifi (2006) argue that the focus and the attention given to supply chains during the 1990s are due to two main drivers. The first is that many researchers, such as Bowerox et al. (1998) and Christopher (1998), now consider supply chains as a unit of competition. The reason for this emphasis on the importance of supply chains is the decreasing interest in using vertical integration with other organisations and the greater degree of competition and globalisation (Lummus and Vokurka, 1999, cited in Ismail and Sharifi, 2006). The second driver is to optimise the organisation by integrating with other supply chain organisations' goals and activities (Cooper et al., 1997; Lummus and Vokurka, 1999).

In 2010, Naslund and Williamson critically reviewed the literature on (supply chain) management, and summarise the benefits for companies for managing their supply chains as follows: improving the firm's returns on investment (ROI) and return on assets (ROA), reducing redundancy costs, reducing inventory levels, less lead time and less demand changing risk. Among other benefits are improvements in the product quality, customer service, market responsiveness level and access to the target markets as a result of improving the process performance. Performance improvement is also achieved with the effective managing of the firm's supply chain, where the effective use of both the internal and the external abilities can lead to a more integrated supply chain (Naslund and Williamson, 2010).

The Middle East business environment

The context of any research plays an important role in explaining differences in the organisational processes and outcomes (Child et al., 2010, cited in ElBanna, 2012). This can be clearly shown from the increase in the research studies that focus on non-US countries such as Japan, Germany and even developing countries such as China and Taiwan (Papadakis et al., 2010, cited in ElBanna, 2012). Therefore some information must now be provided about the regional setting that has been selected for this study.

The Middle East Arab countries have been always understudied settings, despite the global central geographical location, high valuable natural resources (such as oil and natural gas) and huge human resources – where this last factor can be of great importance for any business working there. Furthermore, the Middle East is an attractive huge market for investors. Demirbag et al. (2011), in a study regarding Japanese subsidiaries in the region, consider the Middle East and North Africa as an attractive region for foreign businesses, based on solid structured reforms that provide the opportunities for investors to invest their liquid assets into projects with a high level of growth. As mentioned above, the Arab Middle East region can be characterised by having a huge population, with Egypt as the most populous country in the region. The Middle East market can be considered as an emerging market for several multinational companies working in several types of industries.

From another perspective, doing business within this region is not easy. Although the huge population and high consumption rate may encourage the investor to invest within this region, this needs more efforts from the investors. In a study about the Arab Middle East, Zahra (2011) considers there are some missing institutions that are important for investments and doing business within this region of countries. Among them are: the laws concerning intellectual property and the effective legal systems for solving any commercial issues. Zahra (2011) also comments on the restrictions found in the emergence and dominance of the huge informal economics in the Arab Middle East countries, and the existence of bankruptcy laws that manage the exit and entry from and to such countries.

Zahra (2011) details six strategies for the Arab Middle East countries to join the world village and to be able to compete more effectively. These strategies include: enhancing and diversifying exports, enhancing and effective development of technological infrastructures, determining their specialisation within the global supply chain, enhancing innovation and knowledge creation strategies, developing new educational systems and research on ways of thinking and encouraging and learning from more foreign direct investments.

Methods

This research used a case study approach as its methodology. The case study approach is defined as "the development of detailed, intensive knowledge about a single 'case' or a small number of related 'cases'" (Robson, 1993, p. 40; cited in Saunders et al., 2000, p. 94). It is considered as a process of examining or evaluating a specific phenomenon inside a particular context and is considered as a research methodology under the phenomenological research paradigm (Collis and Hussey, 2003). It is also considered to be the best approach to the answer questions of 'why' and 'how' (Yin, 1989), as well as the 'what' questions (Robson, 1993; cited in Saunders et al., 2000).

One in-depth case study was used as the case study for the research. For confidentiality of the data, this multinational company will be referred to as ABC Company. ABC Company was selected to be the in-depth case study because it is considered one of the most important and famous brand names in the fast-moving consumer goods (FMCG) industry. Moreover, it has expanded its investment in the last several years in the Middle East region. In addition to this, it is known for its excellent management of its supply chains, both globally and locally in specific targeted regions. Therefore, it provided a good opportunity to learn from its experienced practitioners/managers, and hence to enrich the research on supply chain management from such a successful worldwide company.

Four different sites for ABC Company were visited by the researcher to collect data for this study for several reasons:

1   It is a multinational company working within the FMCGs industry, which is charac-
    terised as being a volatile and turbulent business sector.
2   It is one of the multinational companies that have focused on opening new markets
    especially in developing countries, and the Middle East is one of these attractive mar-
    kets for such companies.
3   The Middle East, and especially Egypt, is the home country of one of the researchers
    and this enabled access to the different location sites to be gained more easily.
4   This latter also enabled the researcher to be more aware of the surrounding environ-
    ment, including the different culture, customer requirements and preferences and
    logistics issues existing within the Middle East region.

Data collection and analysis

Collecting data for quantitative research is usually considered a relatively easy and rapid process; however, the problems encountered in data collection are usually more apparent during the collection of data for qualitative research (Collis and Hussey, 2003). Therefore, before explaining the means for collecting data for qualitative research, it is beneficial to determine and clarify the sequence or the procedures of the qualitative data collection process. Creswell argues that there are three main steps involved in the qualitative data collection process (2003, pp. 185–188). The first step is to determine the target site and the individuals for the proposed research study, to enable the researcher to better understand the research problems: in this research the case study company and its multiple sites have been selected carefully, as well as the participants. The managerial offices and the manu-facturing facilities in both Egypt and the United Arab Emirates (Dubai) were selected to be visited in this research. Egypt is considered the main location of ABC's business unit; Egypt can also be considered the oldest country in the Middle East, along with Saudi Arabia, to be entered by ABC Company. It also includes large manufacturing plants and facilities for all the products' categories and was identified as the only country among ABC Company's Middle East region countries that includes the production of the three main product categories. In addition, Jebel Ali, Dubai, United Arab Emirates was consid-ered to be an important location of data collection for the study, because it is considered the main place for managing the Gulf area. It is the home office for most of the managers who manage ABC Company in the Middle East region, as it is the home of the regional headquarters. It also includes a tea manufacturing plant that is considered one of the most important tea manufacturing plants for ABC Company in the Middle East, and the sec-ond largest among the ABC Company's global manufacturing plants.

The participants were selected carefully. All of the interviewees who participated in this research study hold senior managerial positions within ABC Company Middle East. It is these senior representatives who are likely to be the most knowledgeable about the importance, practices and features of supply chain management within ABC Company, as such they are best placed to be knowledgeable about the supply chain importance within the FMCG environment in the Middle East context. It is also important to mention here that most of the participants' managerial positions are closely related to the management of the supply chain and the relationships with supply companies, sources and purchasing departments.

The second step (Creswell, 2003) involves the core data collection means. The first data collection means used by the research is the "interview"; the primary data for the research was collected in two rounds of data collection. The researcher used the semi-structured interview as the technique for collecting the primary data. Face-to-face interviews were used throughout the first and the second data collection rounds. Data collection can also involve the collection/analysis of documents from newspapers, journals, diaries and e-mails, and handwritten work, which provides good evidence and can save money and time. This method was also used as the researchers gathered some data from the ABC Company's website and some documents were collected from the participants during the researcher visits and through e-mail; however, these items will not appear directly due to confidentiality purposes.

The third step of the data collection procedure, according to Creswell (2003), is data analysis and interpretation. The data analysis process starts by preparing the data for analysis and determining the different methods of analysis needed to provide the necessary depth of understanding.

Findings and analysis

On asking the interviewees their opinions on the suggestion argued by Christopher and Towill (2001) that individual companies can no longer compete on their own, but that instead competition now lies in the hands of the overall supply chains, almost all were in agreement. The Demand Planner (for UAE for all products) said "Very correct, definitely. I mean going back to the definitions of supply chain; it's a function that basically consists of all functions, so definitely I agree with this point that for a company to be competitive the supply chain will definitely have to be [working] with each other. Supply chain means to be able to produce goods in the cheapest way possible, most efficient way, environmentally friendly and with the quality of course. So as long as you improve quality, and supply and demand, definitely this will improve the competitiveness of your supply chain."

Similarly, the Technical Project Manager (ABC Company Gulf for all products) explained that the supply chain as a whole needs to be appreciated, where the customer is waiting at the end of the chain and therefore all the links have to work together to satisfy that customer: "We look at the supply chain from an end-to-end perspective because if my supplier will not supply me, my customer is also waiting on the other side. I cannot supply to my customer [alone]." This is supported by the Planning Manager of the tea factory plant (ABC Company Gulf), who agreed with the statement and hence on the importance of the supply chain, as today's companies are mostly doing the same internally, and what makes the difference is how a company can work with its supply chain members to achieve its aims: "Correct, I agree, because now actually as you see, all the companies speak the same language and so what happens is that you are trying for the same KPIs, we are driving for the same targets."

In a broader explanation, the National Supplier Development Manager noted that nowadays the competition is not just between the supply chains for different companies, but can also be between the supply chains within the same company: "Definitely, because the competition had to extend within the same company, for example, [ABC Company in] Egypt is competing with other [ABC Company's branches] working in other countries, for example Saudi Arabia or Morocco, or Dubai, the complete mass of supply chain, for ABC Company, whatever will provide the cheapest price within the same region, will force other branches to shut down, for instance, certain products are produced here in Egypt with lower cost and some are at a much cheaper cost than in Morocco and therefore this production line has been closed and we produce here in Egypt and export to that market."

Finally, from a more technical point of view, the tea factory manager in Egypt explained that he also agreed on the statement: "[I] agree, from my experience about 80 percent of lead time to react comes from supply chains. If you decrease the lead time by 1 percent in supply chains, this will affect positively the time to market and also supply chains are the competing units. If we consider innovations you may find the same innovation found in several companies, however the one who will reach market and customers first will have the initiative, and he will gain."

From the data collected it can be argued that ABC Company in the Middle East has shown that it has built and maintained strong partnerships with its main suppliers and customers as a means for improving and developing successful supply chain management. ABC Company in the Middle East emphasises the importance of the supply chain and its management. It considers the achievement of effective supply chain management as a key point for success and achieves successful supply chain management through its partnerships and collaborations with its supply chain partners. ABC Company in the Middle East focuses on developing and helping their suppliers with the aim of improving its overall supply chain performance level. This observation is supported by the tea factory manager in Egypt, who describes the importance of maintaining supplier partnerships for the sake of both his company and the main supplier within the same supply chain context: "You know supply chain is a chain, partnership is important for growth for both sides, not only for us."

The benefits from having partnerships with the core suppliers extend to long-term benefits, as suggested by the Planning Manager (for Personal Care for Kuwait and Qatar), who mentioned that working in a team with core suppliers can ensure for both parties the achievement of common goals and can lead, at the end, to long-term gains: "When you work like a partner you're working on the same side of the team and if you're working on the same side of the team you're going to work for the same goals, for the same benefit. So you're going to try and figure out how to support each other, so working like partners there's definitely the form of support, there's the ability to openly communicate. If there is a problem and you have open communication with your supplier you're able to resolve those problems together for the benefit of the company and the business. So I think the openness that comes as a partnership is very important and you're looking at long term goals, so it's not short term, it is not something that's going to come today and not have a long term benefit."

Some examples of the practices or the strategies undertaken by ABC Company in the Middle East for improving its supply chain partners' performance are, for example, a list of requirements for its suppliers for helping them improve and develop themselves. ABC Company has also published a program for determining the gaps and areas in its core suppliers' performance that need further improvements. All of these efforts are considered important by ABC Company in the Middle East for improving and enhancing its main suppliers' performance and increasing their overall supply chain performance. A further example of ABC Company in the Middle East focusing on improving its supply partner within the supply chain context is a programme which was conducted in October 2007 to assist suppliers to decrease their carbon effects.

The tea factory manager in Egypt also emphasised the importance of improving partnerships and working closely with other supply chain partners, explaining that "if we talk from a supplier side, the supplier is a factory including staff and employees, we begin to apply the TQM programme and TQM starts from people. We begin to see whether people as a team [have] common goals and aims, need special skills from each operation or business process. The people responsible for the supplier development programme can determine where the gap is and help them to overcome it by sending [them] for training in some factories. From the customer side or the other side if we talk about for example, Carrefour, there are people working in Carrefour selling our products, we are always giving them training courses, and can be considered as responsiveness for us at Carrefour in front of the final customer. They can reach the final consumer easily as they receive any problem or complaint and sometimes the final customer may send to us through our website some complaints about these people and so we can reach where is the gap and deal with it through giving or providing them with some type of training programmes suitable for the type of the problem."

Conclusion

This research is part of broader research undertaken in the Middle East on the importance of supply chain management, buyer–supplier partnerships and supply chain agility. The focus on the supply chain management literature showed that although there are several frameworks and empirical studies for achieving a high level of supply chain performance, due to several overlapping definitions, the models and practices have led to greater ambiguity and a non-unified understanding of the concept. Therefore, more research was required to satisfy this point and give more depth and coherence to practitioner managers' efforts to effectively administer their supply chains. This provided the basis for the research aim and objectives. The research aim and objectives were generated from identifying a gap in the extant literature. The research problem was therefore concerned with investigating the level of understanding for the concept by the multinational ABC Company including its locations in the Middle East. ABC Company in the Middle East emphasises improving its supply chain performance and working with its supply chain members as a whole in order to achieve its goals. This is due to the important role played as a supply chain as a whole. Working as one cohesive team within ABC Company's supply chain is clearly evidenced by the data collected and analysed during the research.

Investigating supply chain's importance in the Middle East region is considered an important contribution for this study. As mentioned above, the Middle East region is not well studied in the extant literature, and therefore should be focused on to a greater extent in any future research. This research took place within one case study working within the FMCG industry. Although this gave the researchers the opportunity to research in depth and understand the phenomenon deeply, it raised the issue of generalisability. Further research is needed in other types of companies to augment generalisability. The importance of supply chain management from a Middle East company's perspective has to be investigated in more than one company, and also in small and medium-sized enterprises, and in manufacturing and service organisations. From a practitioner perspective, this research is important for industry practitioners, especially for managers either in the local Middle East companies or managers in the multinationals working within the region. It is important for them to recognise the level of their understanding for the supply chain management concept and the approach they must employ in order to deal with the rapid changes and diverse alternatives they face within the regional and country-specific business environments.

Issues for further discussion

1   Does the meaning and importance of supply chain management differ from one context to another, or from one type of industry to another?

2   Is supply chain management as essential for small and medium enterprises as for large organisations?
3   Are supply chain relationships and partnerships beneficial for all types of industries?
4   Which supply chain member is most important for the company to build a strong relationship with?

Case study

Canon Middle East (www.canon-me.com)

Canon Middle East is considered a subsidiary of Canon Europe. It is based in Dubai, UAE, and manages Canon Middle East, North, West and East Africa. It has been in the region for about 40 years and has been successfully developing a strong customer base and an important market share throughout the whole region's countries (www.canon-me.com/about_us/).

Canon Middle East is working within a challenging business environment. The multinational company is aware of the challenges and is trying to deal with and respond to them. The people in Canon Middle East working within the MENA (Middle East North Africa) region recognise that although the whole Middle East region population share several similarities there remain differences that make each country unique: "The Mena markets are growth territories each with its own specific challenge: language; borders, unrest; customs; regulations, accessibility, etc. we at Canon understand and have the ability to support the uniqueness of each of these markets" (www.arabiansupplychain.com/article-7817-supply-chain-case-study-canon-middle-east/1/print/).

Canon Middle East believe that their success within the region is based primarily on a deep understanding in dealing with the different customer requirements and by the strong coordination between their business and their management of supply chain. Therefore they are moving now to be a demand-driven supply chain, as was commented on by Canon's Director of Supply Chain Management, Richie Cuthbert, who discussed it with the *Logistics Middle East* magazine in 2012, "the supply chain management function is an integral part of our business, supporting sales to regional partners from demand creation through to accurate fulfilment and on-time shipment to meet customer requirements. Our focus on continuous improvement of our supply chain demonstrates our commitment to the business initiatives that deliver a clear competitive advantage. We've recently introduced a new approach to demand management and fulfilment, as we move towards a truly demand-driven supply chain" (www.arabiansupplychain.com/article-7817-supply-chain-case-study-canon-middle-east/1/print/).

The people at Canon Middle East place great emphasis on the importance of supply chain management. On their website, they emphasise the importance of moving to a demand-driven supply chain in their operations: "the supply chain is generally viewed as a cost within any organisation, therefore it's important that its function is aligned closely to the business and marketing plans, and that the business is aware of its capabilities and the costs associated with serving customer requirements. The supply chain function is Canon's tool towards delivering a competitive edge to the business" (www.arabiansupplychain.com/article-7817-supply-chain-case-study-canon-middle-east/1/print). They explain the importance of applying a demand-driven supply chain, as it helps them to increase abilities such as their stability, predictability and delivery forecast reliability.

Canon Middle East is improving its relationships with the other supply chain members as a way of enhancing its overall supply chain performance within the region, and constantly seeks open opportunities for outsourcing. Therefore Canon Middle East strives to work with its partners to improve their sustainable long-term partnerships. They are well known for their emphasis on outsourcing, as their website shows: "we know that outsourcing helps organisations keep ahead of the game and gain competitive advantage over their closest rivals, but this support comes at a cost and needs to deliver value" (www.canon-me.com/about_us/press_centre/press_resources/white_papers_and_reports/businesses_need_to_look_beyond_simple_cost_savings_from_suppliers.aspx).

Canon Middle East as a subsidiary of Canon Europe has successfully recognised that this cost can be saved and effectively managed through the formulation of successful partnerships, as demonstrated by Phil Sargeant, Research Manager, "technological challenges have moved on from simply hardware and software. Just merging the two together doesn't always provide the best outcome. The partnership of two or more parties is an essential third element for customer growth and prosperity. It involves bringing their individual but complementary strengths together to deliver both a tailored solution and quality of service."

Case questions for discussion

1   What are the challenges facing Canon in the Middle East?
2   How can Canon deal with these challenges? What are the practices adapted by Canon to deal with them?
3   What are the important keys of success for Canon Middle East?
4   How does Canon perceive supply chain partnership as a key element for success?

Source

www.canon-me.com/about_us/press_centre/press_resources/white_papers_and_reports/businesses_need_to_look_beyond_simple_cost_savings_from_suppliers.aspx

References

Archibald, G., Karabakal, N. and Karlsson, P. (1999), "Supply Chain vs Supply Chain: Using Simulation Beyond the Four Walls", Proceedings of the 1999 Winter Simulation Conference, pp. 1207–1214.

Babbar, S. and Prasad, S. (1998), "International Purchasing, Inventory Management and Logistics Research: An Assessment and Agenda", *International Journal of Operations and Production Management*, Vol. 18, No. 1, pp. 6–36.

Boddy, D., Cahill, D., Charles, M., Fraser-Kraus, H. and Macbeth, D. (1998), "Success and Failure in Implementing Partnering". *European Journal of Purchasing and Supply Management*, Vol. 4, No. 2, 3, pp. 143–151.

Bowersox, D. J., Closs, D. J. and Hall, C. T. (1998), "Beyond ERP – the Storm Before the Calm", *Supply Chain Management Review*, Vol. 1, No. 4, pp. 28–37.

Burgess, K., Singh, P. J. and Koroglu, R. (2006), "Supply Chain Management: A Structured Literature Review and Implications for Future Research", *International Journal of Operations and Production Management*, Vol. 26, No.7, pp. 703–729.

Carter, J. R. and Price, P. M. (1993), *Integrated Materials Management*, London: Pitman.

Chen, I. J. and Paulraj, A. (2004), "Towards a Theory of Supply Chain Management: The Constructs and Measurements", *Journal of Operations Management*, Vol. 22, pp. 119–150.

Child, J., Elbanna, S. and Rodrigues, S. (2010), "The Political Aspects of Strategic Decision Making", in Nutt, P. and Wilson, D. (Eds.), *Handbook of Decision Making*, Chichester: Wiley, pp. 105–137.

Christopher, M. (1992), *Logistics and Supply Chain Management*, London, UK: Pitmans.

Christopher, M. (1998), *Logistics and Supply Chain Management*, London, UK: Pitmans.

Christopher, M. and Towill, D. (2001), "An Integrated Model for the Design of Agile Supply Chains", *International Journal of Physical Distribution and Logistics Management*, Vol. 31, No. 4, pp. 235–246.

Collis, J. and Hussey, R. (2003), *Business Research: A Practical Guide for Undergraduate and Postgraduate Students*, 2nd ed. London: Palgrave Macmillan.

Cooper, M. C., Ellram, L. M., Gardner, G. T. and Hanks, A. M. (1997), "Meshing Multiple Alliances," *Journal of Business Logistics*, Vol. 18, No. 1, pp. 67–89.

Council of Logistics Management (CLM). (2000), *What It's All About*. Oak Brook, IL: Council of Logistics Management.

Cousins, P. D., Lawson, B. and Squire, B. (2006), "Supply Chain Management: Theory and Practice-the Emergence of an Academic Discipline?" *International Journal of Operations and Production Management*, Vol. 26, No. 7, pp. 697–702.

Creswell, J. W. (2003), *Research Design: Qualitative, Quantitative and Mixed Methods Approaches*. Thousand Oaks, CA: Sage.

Dale, B., Lascelles, D. and Lloyd, A. (1994), "Supply Chain Management and Development" in Dale, B. G. (Ed.), *Managing Quality*, London: Prentice-Hall, pp. 292–315.

Demirbag, M., Apaydin, M. and Tatoglu, E. (2011), "Survival of Japanese Subsidiaries in the Middle East and North Africa", *Journal of World Business*, Vol. 46, pp. 411–425.

Elbanna, S. (2012), "Slack, Planning and Organizational Performance: Evidence From the Arab Middle East", *European Management Review*, Vol. 9, pp. 99–115.

Fisher, M. L. (1997), "What Is the Right Supply Chain for Your Product?", *Harvard Business Review*, Vol. 75, pp. 105–116.

Forrester, J. (1961), *Industrial Dynamics*, New York: Wiley.

Gunasekaran, A., Patelb, C. and McGaugheyc, E. (2004), "A Framework for Supply Chain Performance Measurement". *International Journal of Production Economics*, Vol. 87, No. 3, pp. 333–347.

Ismail, H. S. and Sharifi, H. (2006), "A Balanced Approach to Building Agile Supply Chains", *International Journal of Physical Distribution and Logistics Management*, Vol. 36, No. 6, pp. 431–444.

Jain, V. and Benyoucef, L. (2008), "Managing Long Supply Networks: Some Emerging Issues and Challenges", *Journal of manufacturing Technology Management*, Vol. 19, No. 4, pp. 469–496.

Jones, C. (1998), "Moving Beyond ERP: Making the Missing Link", *Logistics Focus*, Vol. 6, No. 7, pp. 2–7.

Kisperska- Moron, D. and Swiercczek, A. (2009), "The Agile Capabilities of Polish Companies in the Supply Chain 'an empirical study'", *International Journal of production Economics*, Vol. 118, pp. 217–224.

Lin, F. and Shaw, M. J. (1998), "Reengineering the Order Fulfilment Process in Supply Chain Networks", *The International of Flexible Manufacturing Systems*, Vol. 10, pp. 197–229.

Li, S., Rao, S. S., Ragu-Nathan, T. S. and Ragu-Nathen, B. (2005), "Development and Validation of a Measurement Instrument for Studying Supply Chain Management Practices", *Journal of Operations Management*, Vol. 23, No. 6, pp. 618–641.

Lummus, R. R. and Vokurka, R. J. (1999), "Defining Supply Chain Management: A Historical Perspective and Practical Guidelines", *Industrial Management and Data Systems*, Vol. 99, No. 1, pp. 11–17.

Naslund, D. and Williamson, S. (2010), "What Is Management in Supply Chain Management? – A Critical Review of Definitions, Frameworks and Terminology", *Journal of Management Policy and Practice*, Vol. 11, No. 4, pp. 11–28.

New, S. J. (1996), "A Framework for Analysing Supply Chain Improvement", *International Journal of Operations and Production Management*, Vol. 16, pp. 19–34.

Oliver, R. K. and Webber, M. D. (1982), "Supply Chain Management: Logistics Catches Up With Strategy", in Christopher, M. G. (Ed.), *Logistics: The Strategic Issue*, London: Chapman & Hall.

Papadakis, V., Thanos, I. C., and Barwise, P. (2010), "Research on Strategic Decisions: Taking Stock and Looking Ahead", in Nutt, P. and Wilson, D. (Eds.), *The Handbook of Decision Making*, Chichester: Wiley, pp. 31–69.

Power, D. J., Sohal, A. S. and Rahman, S. (2001), "Critical Success Factors in Agile Supply Chain Management", *International Journal of Physical Distribution and Logistics Management*, Vol. 31, No. 4, pp. 247–265.

Presutti, D. W., and Mawhinney, J. R. (2007), "The Supply Chain- Finance Link". *Supply Chain Management Review*, Vol. 11, No. 6, pp. 32–38.

Robson, C. (1993), *Real World Research: A Resource for Social Scientists and Practitioners-Researchers*, Oxford: Basil Blackwell.

Ryu, I., So, S. and Koo, C. (2009), "The Role of Partnership in Supply Chain Performance", *Industrial Management and Data Systems*, Vol. 109, No. 4, pp. 496–514.

Samaranayke, P. (2005), "A Conceptual Framework for Supply Chain Management: A Structural Integration", *Supply Chain Management: An International Journal*, Vol. 10, No. 1, pp. 47–59.

Saunders, M. J. (1995), *Chains, Pipelines, Networks and Value Stream: The Role, Nature and Value of Such Metaphors in Forming Perceptions of the Task of Purchasing and Supply Management*. First Worldwide Research Symposium on Purchasing and Supply Chain Management, Tempe, AZ, pp. 476–485.

Saunders, M. J. (1998), *The Comparative Analysis of Supply Chains and Implications for the Development of Strategies*. Seventh International IPSERA Conference, London, UK, pp. 469–477.

Saunders, M., Lewis, P. and Thornhill, A. (2000), *Research Methods for Business Students*. Gosport: Printed and bound in Great Britain by Ashford Colour Press Ltd.

Subramani, M. (2004), "How Do Suppliers Benefits From Information Technology Use in Supply Chain Relationships?", *MIS Quarterly*, Vol. 28, No. 1, pp. 45–73.

Van der Vorst, J. G. A. J. (2004), "Supply Chain Management: Theory and Practices", in T. Camps, P. Diederen, G. J. Hofstede, and B. Vos (Eds.), *The Emerging Science of Chains and Networks: Bridging Theory and Practice*, Reed Business Information, chapter 2.1, pp. 105–128.

Wang, E. T. G., Tai, J. C. F. and Wie, H. L. (2006), "A Virtual Integration Theory of Improved Supply Chain Performance", *Journal of Management Information Systems*, Vol. 23, No. 2, pp. 41–64.

Yin, R. K. (1989), *Case Study Research: Design and Methods*. London: Sage.

Zahra, S. (2011), "Doing Research in the (New) Middle East: Sailing With the Wind", *Academy of Management Perspectives*, Vol. 25, No. 4, pp. 6–21.

Conclusion

Islamic marketing: moving forward and challenges

Mazia Yassim

Learning outcomes

At the end of this chapter the reader should be able to:

1 Critically evaluate the concept of Islamic marketing and its progress to date
2 Explore the potential avenues for the discipline to develop into
3 Critically appraise the impact of Islamic marketing as a discipline

Key points

1 Research in Islamic marketing has grown considerably over the years and has made great strides in establishing Islamic marketing as a distinct discipline.
2 A variety of contexts have been researched in the field but widening this to include other critical and growth areas of mainstream marketing would help the discipline add depth and breadth of insight.
3 Similar to mainstream marketing, the growth of Islamic marketing has meant a debate and discourse on which approaches are more appropriate.
4 In order to gain holistic insights it is important that the alternative approaches are used to add insight and shape the discipline as it grows.
5 One of the greatest challenges facing researchers in the field is to sift through the complexities of culture and religion to provide both meaningful and practical implications to organisations as well as researchers.

Introduction

The various chapters in this book have explored and discussed how Islamic marketing has managed to grow and carve its place as a distinct discipline within the mainstream marketing framework since its conception in 2011. As Sandıkcı (2011) explained, the growth and establishment of Islamic marketing as a discipline can be attributed to the increasing visibility of Muslims and their purchasing power. This has encouraged organisations and academics to view Muslims as a yet fully unexplored worthwhile market segment. With the emergence of a multitude of research looking at Muslims as consumers and Muslim geographical areas, there has also been a steady call to explore different viewpoints and approaches in order to help move the discipline forward constructively (Wilson, 2012).

This chapter explores the challenges facing Islamic marketing and provides some insights into how it may move forward. In doing this, three areas are discussed: research contexts, research approaches, and research implications.

Research contexts

Tournois and Aoun (2012) identified that, from its initial exploration of business ethics frameworks, Islamic marketing has branched out to other areas such as: financial services, Islamic law and its principles, 'halal' and 'haram' practices and consumption as well as branding.

Testing and approving existing marketing theories into the context of Islamic marketing is one area of exploration that can be undertaken by Islamic marketing researchers (Wilson, 2012). However, the basic premise of 'halal' and 'haram' or even the traditional marketing principles of the 7 P's and branding provide a limited understanding of what Islamic marketing is about and its implications (Wilson and Grant, 2013). It can be argued that having provided some useful insights and understanding of some basic Islamic principles and its applications to organisations as well as consumption behaviour, it is high time that the discipline started to explore more complex contexts.

Not discounting the great research that has emerged within Islamic marketing over the past few years, much other research has focused on explaining the application of Islamic principles in organisational and consumption contexts. In a field that is relatively new and emerging, there is a great need for this nature of explanatory research. However, if the discipline is to move forward whilst making sustainable progress towards knowledge and understanding as well as establishing itself more firmly within the mainstream marketing framework, it is time that researchers within the field look towards more challenging and even controversial avenues to explore.

A critical look at the concept of Islamic consumers is a good starting point. Many authors have already argued for the need to understand what it means to be a Muslim consumer from a practical perspective rather than an ideological or theological perspective (e.g. Sandıkcı, 2011, Jafari, 2012). This will be further explored when discussing research approaches below. For the purpose of the discussion here, it needs to be highlighted that from a practical perspective, rather than trying to find this elusive idea of a 'Muslim consumer' researchers need to look at providing effective and measurable means to segment this complex market. A simplistic approach of looking at people's religious beliefs or cultural backgrounds does not translate into what it means to be a so-called Muslim consumer. Are we expecting these Muslim consumers to behave in the same way just because they have a certain belief system? Do we know if and to what degree consumption decisions are influenced by religious beliefs when considering various product classes and sectors? Do religious beliefs influence every aspect of a Muslim's consumption or is it more prevalent in specific consumptions? What are then the implications of these to organisations?

Going even beyond consumption of products and services, there are many critical areas emerging within the mainstream marketing framework that have not been fully explored within the context of Islamic marketing. Social marketing and the critical evaluation of marketing's benefit to society are concepts that have been steadily gaining relevance and importance. Islamic marketing scholars need to fully engage with this with a view to making a greater contribution to areas such as social marketing as well as establishing Islamic marketing as a context that can add value to not just food and finance but every aspect of marketing. It is not sufficient to say that as Islam as a religion is based on certain ethical values and principles, therefore almost by default, adoption of these principles can tackle issues such as social responsibility and marketing's role within it. It needs to be approached as a genuine alternative which demonstrates, from a practical point of view, how Islamic principles may have an impact on these disciplines, how these can be incorporated within the wider marketing framework from a critical and practical perspective.

There are critical societal issues such as community cohesion and even radicalisation that can benefit from the use of a combination of social marketing and Islamic principles. The use and implications of these issues have been largely unexplored by Islamic marketing researchers. Entering into these varied contexts and engaging with mainstream marketing researchers to achieve this will provide a sound base for widening the applications of Islamic marketing.

Research approaches

In a discourse on the role of Islamic marketing researchers, Wilson (2012) raised the question of whether Islamic marketing refers to religion or culture. As the discussion on contexts above mentioned, there has been many calls for the need to look at Islamic marketing as a concept and Muslims as consumers from a practical perspective rather than an ideological perspective.

El-Bassiouny (2014) argued that since Islam is a religious ideology which transcends every action in life, a Muslim will be impacted by the precepts of his or her faith in every action he or she takes, including consumption behaviour. This ideological assumption that every Muslim will interpret and follow their religious precepts in the same way, to the same degree of commitment, is highly questionable and only promotes stereotypical profiles of consumers with little or no practical relevance to organisations. This has been discussed widely and critically by Sandıkcı (2011), Jafari (2012), Wilson (2012), Koku and Jusoh (2014), Jafari and Sandıkcı (2015) and others. Despite these many calls for critical engagement between ideological precepts and practical interpretation reflected in behaviour combined with cultural influences, there is still very little research emerging which addresses these issues. As the discipline of Islamic marketing grows further, this is a crucial aspect which is needed to nourish its growth.

Attempting to untangle this complicated web of culture, religion, theological precepts, interpretation and translation of these precepts into behaviour is by no means a simple task and none of the authors who have called for this so far have claimed that this was a simple task. This complexity is probably the reason why a lot of researchers seem to prefer a reductionist approach to understanding Islam as a religion and how Muslims 'should be' thinking and behaving. However, this is similar to the discourse that also occurs in mainstream marketing when researching consumer behaviour: the so-called simplistic and easy to measure logical approaches and the call for inductive and other alternative approaches to help understand the holistic nature of consumption with all its inherent complexities. Hence, this discourse is not unique to Islamic marketing but rather a natural path that is inherent in any emerging discipline and part and parcel of the Kuhnian paradigmatic shift. The challenge facing Islamic marketing is the need for researchers to apply various approaches to explore and understand the complexities within their discipline.

Authors such as Jafari (2012) have called for more inductive approaches in Islamic marketing. Setting aside the debate on the merits of one or another approach, there have been calls from both mainstream marketing and Islamic marketing to understand a given phenomenon from differing perspectives. Koku and Jusoh (2014) felt that the approach appropriate to study Islamic marketing 'will emerge from a consensus of opinions' as researchers strive to build theories within this discipline. Is it even feasible to come to any consensus in a complex field such as Islam with its various interpretations, sects and followings? Would this need for consensus push us more towards reductionist approaches that critical scholars want us to avoid? As Foxall (1990, p. 172) argued, "the emergence of a unitary coherent theory of human behaviour is improbable and almost certainly undesirable." Therefore, in Islamic marketing, as with mainstream marketing, there is a need to explore our understanding through various lenses.

The lenses through which we aim to understand the concept of Islamic marketing and Muslim consumers could range from positivism, interpretivism, realism, constructivism to all other approaches that have also been used within mainstream marketing. In addition to this, there are other, less well explored theories that can come to our aid. One such theory is Kelly's (1970) personal construct psychology. Kelly believed in what he termed "constructive alternativism" where all knowledge and information are subject to alternative constructions. People themselves place their own construction or meaning on any event or situation that they experience in life (Kelly, 1970). It could be argued that, as various researchers have been arguing that the extent to which Islamic beliefs and values are understood, accepted and translated into behaviour varies from culture to culture and individual to individual, then constructive alternativism would help us understand these alternative views and sift through for significant similarities and differences and the reasons behind these similarities and differences.

Research implications

As has been argued above, Islamic marketing research to a large extent seems to be operating under the hypotheses that Muslims are different from the rest of the consumer groups and as such organisations need to make specific effort to appeal to this segment. However, as we have also discussed above, Muslims are not and are never likely to be a unitary segment. In order for the discipline to establish itself as providing genuine insights into Islamic marketing and Muslim consumers, future researchers should look hard at the implications of their research.

At the risk of generalising across the discipline, much research that is published fails to take the findings further and convert these into insights. What is needed is for researchers to undertake a critical evaluation of the similarities and differences of their research with that of mainstream marketing. Exploration of these similarities and differences would surely be a strong foundation with which to continue to build Islamic marketing as a discipline as well as provide a basis to break out of this exceptionalism (Jafari and Sandıkcı, 2015) that seems to guide Islamic marketing research.

Taking an ideological and even an ethnocentric standpoint sets up the claim that due to the inherent values and principles of Islam, all Muslims will follow these values when seeking consumption experiences, whether this be a bar of chocolate or a family holiday. Yet, mainstream marketing is still attempting to understand why someone's personal values and ethics may have an impact on consumption of one class of products and not others. This again highlights the complex nature of consumer behaviour across the board, including Islamic marketing. These complexities need to be reflected and their implications explored in research. This would be a much valuable insight than a mere statement of factors influencing Muslim consumer behaviour with little effort to provide a critical viewpoint. In this way implications for not just business practice but theoretical advancement of the discipline as a whole will have more impetus.

Conclusion

Islamic marketing has made great strides since its formal conception and has managed to establish itself as a distinct discipline. Many scholars have already provided critical discourse within the discipline, the nature of current research within the discipline and calls for how the discipline should evolve in the future. This chapter drew upon this discourse and highlighted the need for researchers to expand the contexts which they study, and called for variety in approaches as well as more insightful implications. The greatest challenge that we face as Islamic marketers is being critical of ourselves and asking why we are engaged in this discipline and whether we are prepared to fully immerse ourselves in the complex debate and commit ourselves to shaping the future of the discipline.

References

El-Bassiouny, N. (2014), "The One Billion Plus Marginalisation: Toward a Scholarly Understanding of Islamic Consumers", *Journal of Business Research*, Vol. 67, No. 2, 42–49.

Foxall, G. (1990), *Consumer Psychology in Behavioural Perspective*, London: Routledge.

Jafari, A. (2012), "Islamic Marketing: Insights From a Critical Perspective", *Journal of Islamic Marketing*, Vol. 3, No. 1, pp. 22–34.

Jafari, A. and Sandıkcı, Ö. (2015), "Islamic Consumers, Markets, and Marketing: A Critique of El-Bassiouny's (2014) The One-Billion-Plus Marginalisation,' *Journal of Business Research*, Vol. 68, pp. 2676–2682.

Kelly, G. A. (1970), "A Brief Introduction to Personal Construct Theory," in Bannister, D. (Ed.), *Perspectives in Personal Construct Theory*, London: Academic Press.

Koku, P. S. and Jusoh, O. (2014), "Where Do We Go From Here? Towards a Theory in Islamic Marketing", *Journal of Islamic Marketing*, Vol. 5, No. 3, pp. 366–378.

Sandıkcı, Ö. (2011), "Researching Islamic Marketing: Past and Future Perspectives", *Journal of Islamic Marketing*, Vol. 2, No. 3, pp. 246–258.

Tournois, L. and Aoun, I. (2012), "From Traditional to Islamic Marketing Strategies: Conceptual Issues and Implications for an Exploratory Study in Lebanon", *Journal of Islamic Marketing*, Vol. 5, No. 2, pp. 134–140.

Wilson, J. (2012), "The Role of Islamic Marketing Researchers: Scribes, Oracles, Trend Spotters – or Thought Leaders? Setting the Agenda", *Journal of Islamic Marketing*, Vol. 3, No. 2, pp. 104–107.

Wilson, J. and Grant, J. (2013), "Islamic Marketing – a Challenger to the Classical Marketing Canon?", *Journal of Islamic Marketing*, Vol. 4, No. 1, pp. 7–21.

Index

Note: Page numbers in *italic* indicate a figure and page numbers in **bold** indicate a table on the corresponding page.

Kahf, M. 70
Kalliny, M. 198, 199
Kamali, M. H. 39
Karande, K. 196
Kearney, A. T. 208
Keller, K. L. 16, 42, 120, 137, 192
Kelly, G. A. 238
Kent, R. J. 108
Kilinc, Ö. 152
Kirchgeorg, M. 18
Kisperska-Moron, D. 222
Knudtzen, C. F. 15
Koku, P. S. 237–238
Korschun, D. 18
Kosher products 13
Koshy, A. 43
Kotler, P. 120, 153
Kucukemiroglu, O. 41
Kuehn, K. 108

Lada, S. 38
Laldin, M. A. 72
Li, S. 222
lifestyle, Islamic 41, 213
Lindstrom, M. 16
Liu, J. 24, 29, 43
Loo, M. 108
Luqmani, M. 194, 196, 198, 199–200

Mahamad, M. 106
Mahmud, M. W. 73
Maisir 128
Majid, M. Z. A. 73
Malaysia: case study on Halal development in 96–98; Code of Advertising Practice in 195, 197, 198; consumers' awareness and perceptions of Islamic banking in 114–115; Islamic banking in 103–113; tourism in *see* tourism, Islamic
Malik (Imam) 21
Maltby, J. 14
Mandi, L. 62
Maqasid al-Shari'ah 72–74
Marimuthu, M. 106
marketing, global 186–187; bottom of the pyramid marketing 184–185; case study 187–190; diaspora and remittances to Islamic countries and 183–184; economic indicators and assessment of Islamic countries' potential market for 178, **178–179**; EPRG scheme 187–190; Gini coefficient and Islamic countries and 182–183; grouping OIC countries in clusters for 185–186; introduction to 177–178; Islamic countries clusters according to GDP per capita and 181–182; Islamic countries clusters according to total GDP and 179–180
marketing in Muslim-majority markets: emerging markets 206–209; Halal nail polish case study

216–218; introduction to 205–206; Islamic business networks and pious entrepreneurship in 211–213; multiplicity of identity and diversity of lived experiences and 209–211; strategy implications 213–215
markets, Islamic 57–58
Marsden, P. 18
Martikainen, T. 55
Mattila, A. S. 134
Mawhinney, J. R. 223
McDonald, M. 16
Mecca Bingo 25
Mecca Cola 59
Mecca USA 25
media and recreation, Islamic 88–89, **89–90**
Melewar, T. C. 193
MINT (Mexico, Indonesia, Nigeria, Turkey) nations 12
Mitchell, R. K. 17, 19
Mittelstaedt, J. D. 130
Muhamad, R. 78
Muhammad (Prophet) 20, 21, 126–129
Mukhtar, A. 71
Mumakis 128
Munafasah 129
Musa, R. 94
Muslim consumers 1, 28–29; assumptions about 'Islamic' business and markets and 56–61; brand communication to 193–194; changing consumption patterns of 27–28; emerging markets of 206–209; geographies and economic factors 12–13; growth in numbers of 36–37, 207; identity and consumption 37–38; Islamicness and *see* Islamicness; market segmentation 2, 76–80; multiplicity of identity and diversity of lived experiences of 209–211; principles of Shari'ah and 72; traditionalist and futurist 78–80
Muslim Council of Britain 37
Muslim identity 37–38; multiplicity of 209–211
Muslimlifestyle.co.uk 41
Mustarsil 128
MYPURE case study 62–64

nail polish, Halal 216–218
Naslund, D. 224
Nasr, V. 210
necessities 73
neoliberal capitalism 207, 212
neo-spiritualism 13–15
Nestlé case study 140–143
Newman, B. I. 123
non-Muslim customers and Islamic banking 106
Noortel 79

O'Cass, A. 108
Ogilvy Noor 12, 52, 58, 208; study of traditionalists and futurists 78–80